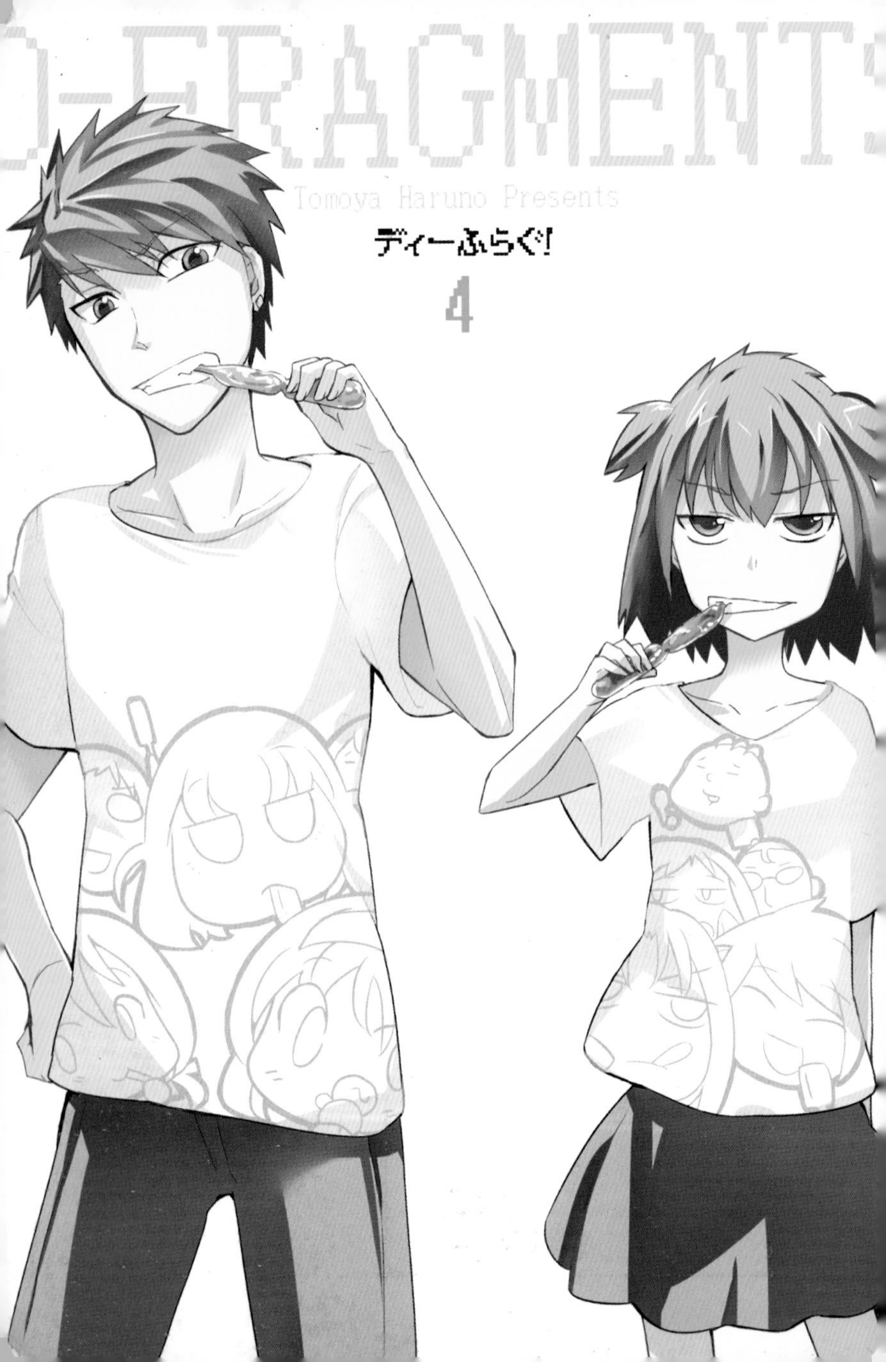
D-FRAGMENTS
Tomoya Haruno Presents
ディーふらぐ!
4

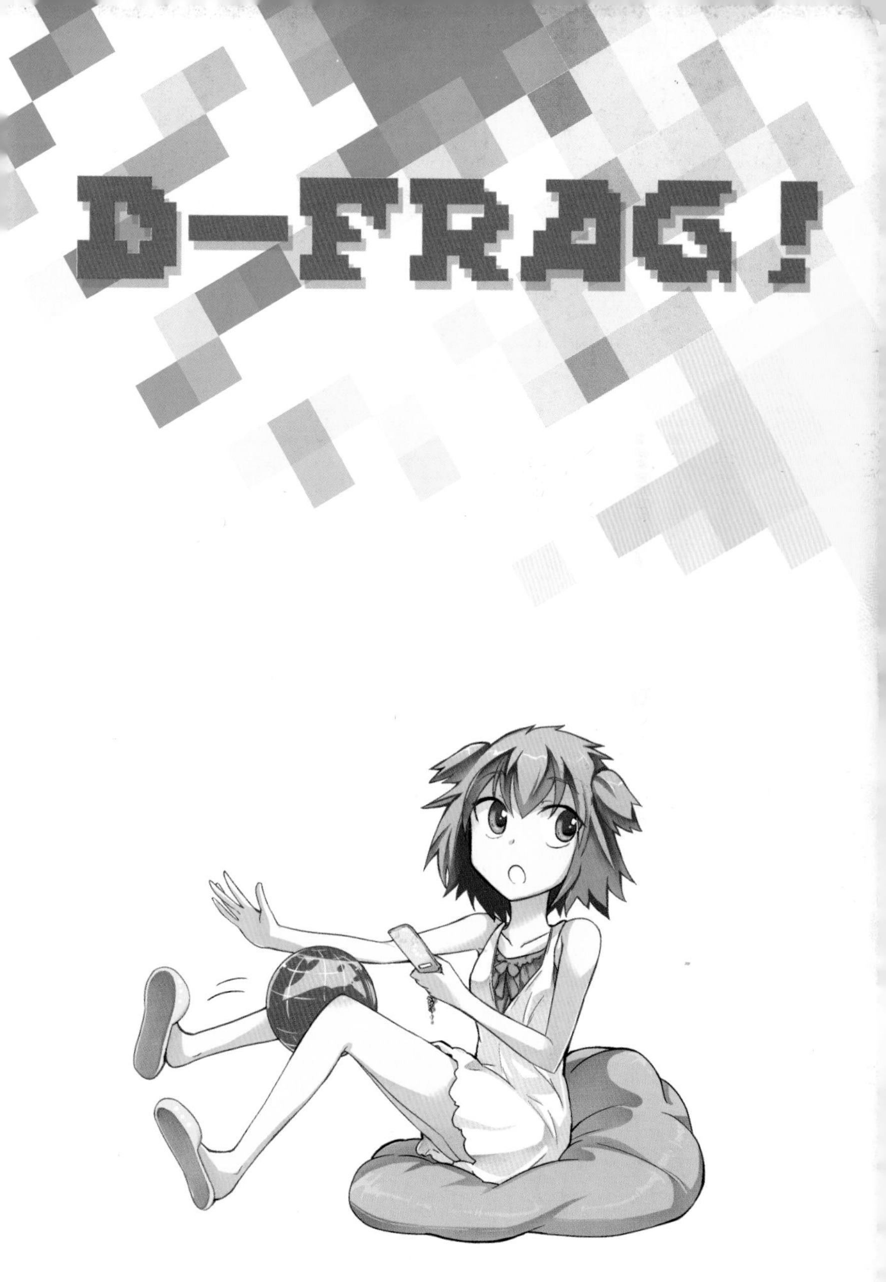
D-FRAG!

D-FRAG!

STORY SUMMARY

D-FRAG MENTS

One day, Kazama Kenji decided on a whim to go into the "Game Development Club" room. There, he met club captain Shibasaki Roka and her psychotic club members. Before he knew it, tough guy Kenji was beaten up by the girls' elemental-affinity attacks and "voluntarily" (a.k.a. forced) joined the club himself.

But then Kenji discovered the "Real" Game Dev. Club, led by Captain Takao. Takao challenged the "fake" club to a contest during the Culture Festival, with the winning club getting to be the "official" game dev. club! However, Kenji made unrepentant use of a fellow club-member's power and influence to easily win the challenge. It was only afterwards that they learned they've been an official club the whole time, called the "Game Development Club (Temp)"!

A little while later, Kenji met a member of the Game Dev. Club he never knew existed: Shio Hachi. Seeing Kenji as a rival, Hachi challenged Kenji to a duel with one of Roka's bags as the prize. But thanks to interference by Chitose, what started as a one-on-one match between Hachi and Kenji turned into a school-wide mega-tournament. Surviving through rounds of games like thumb-wrestling and musical chairs, Kenji and Roka met in the finals to settle things between them once and for all. Kenji ends up winning not only Roka's prized bag, but also her respect (maybe?).

And now, Kazama Kenji's adventures with the Game Dev. Club (Temp.) continue...

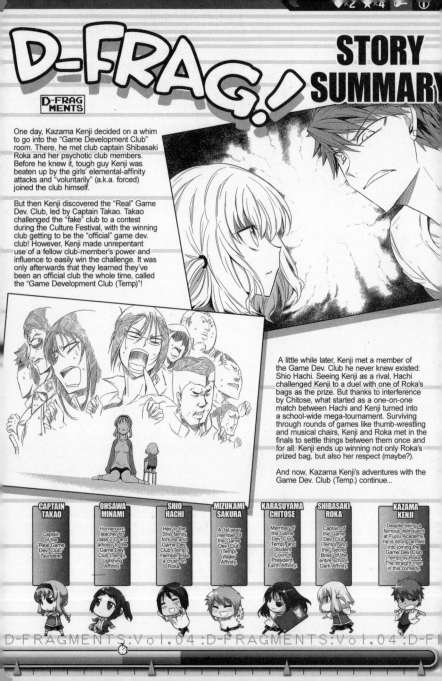

CAPTAIN TAKAO	OHSAWA MINAMI	SHIO HACHI	MIZUKAMI SAKURA	KARASUYAMA CHITOSE	SHIBASAKI ROKA	KAZAMA KENJI
Captain of the "Real" Game Dev. Club. *Tsundere*.	Homeroom teacher for class 2-D and advisor to the Game Dev. Club (Temp.). *Lightning Affinity*.	Heir to the Shio family fortune and Game Dev. Club (Temp.) member. Has a crush on Roka.	A 1st-year member of the Game Dev. Club (Temp.). *Water Affinity*.	Member of the Game Dev. Club (Temp.) and Student Council President. *Earth Affinity*.	Captain of the Game Dev. Club (Temp.) and the "Secret Boss" of the entire school. *Dark Affinity*.	Despite being a famous delinquent at Fujou Academy, he is strong-armed into joining the Game Dev. Club (Temp.) by Roka. The straight man in this comedy.

SEVEN SEAS ENTERTAINMENT PRESENTS

D-FRAG!

story and art by TOMOYA HARUNO

VOLUME 4

TRANSLATION
Adrienne Beck

ADAPTATION
Shannon Fay

LETTERING AND LAYOUT
Ma. Victoria Robado

LOGO DESIGN
Courtney Williams

COVER DESIGN
Nicky Lim

PROOFREADER
Lee Otter
Conner Crooks

MANAGING EDITOR
Adam Arnold

PUBLISHER
Jason DeAngelis

D-FRAG! VOL. 4

Edited by MEDIA FACTORY.
First published in Japan in 2011 by KADOKAWA CORPORATION, Tokyo.

ISBN: 978-1-626921-17-7

Printed in Canada

First Printing: March 2015

10 9 8 7 6 5 4 3 2 1

FOLLOW US ONLINE: ***www.gomanga.com***

READING DIRECTIONS

This book reads from ***right to left***, Japanese style. If this is your first time reading manga, you start reading from the top right panel on each page and take it from there. If you get lost, just follow the numbered diagram here. It may seem backwards at first, but you'll get the hang of it! Have fun!!

1
2
3
4
5
6
7
8
9

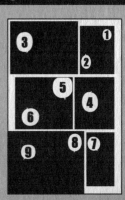

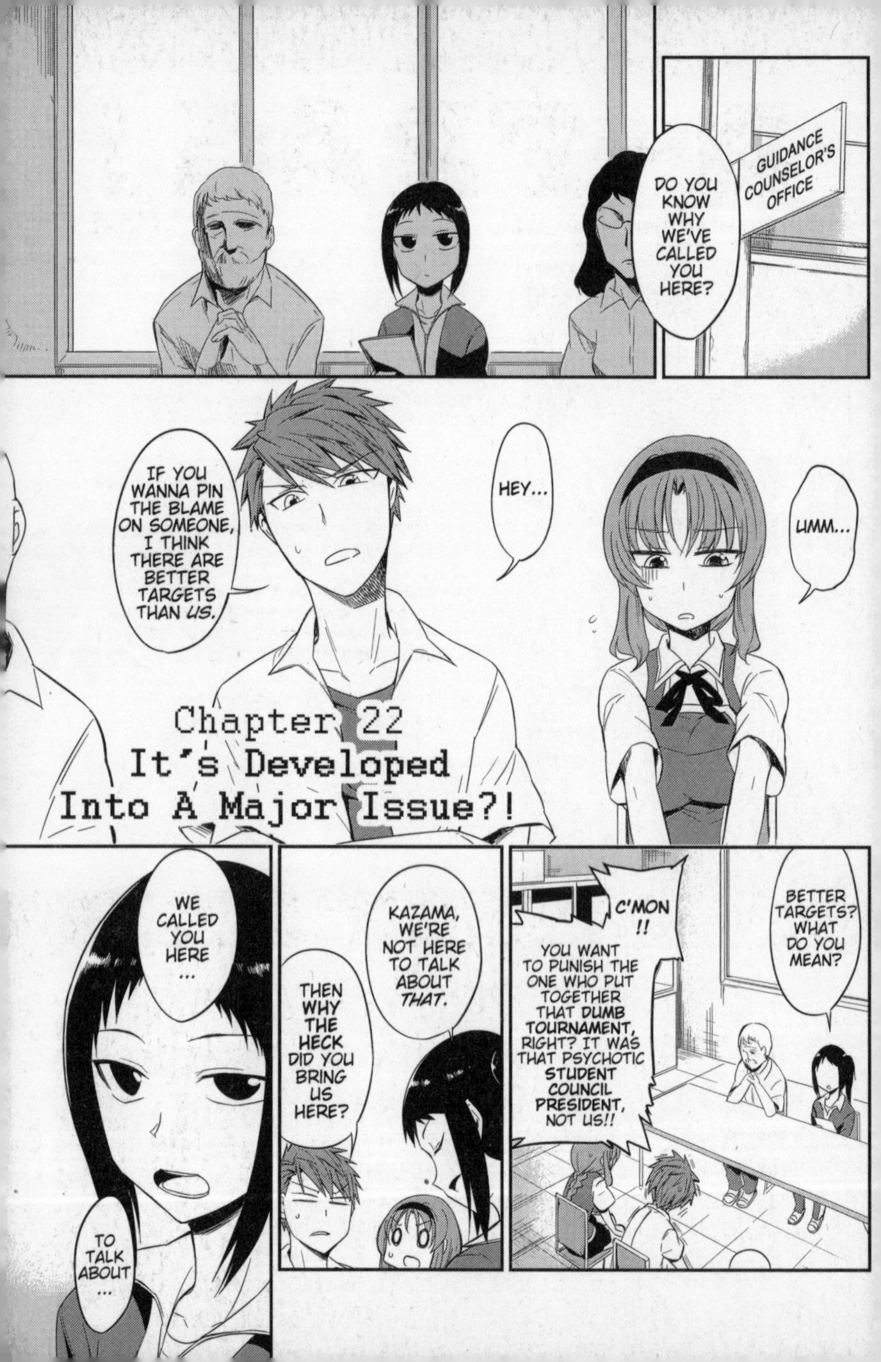
GUIDANCE COUNSELOR'S OFFICE
DO YOU KNOW WHY WE'VE CALLED YOU HERE?
UMM...
HEY...
IF YOU WANNA PIN THE BLAME ON SOMEONE, I THINK THERE ARE BETTER TARGETS THAN *US*.
Chapter 22 It's Developed Into A Major Issue?!
BETTER TARGETS? WHAT DO YOU MEAN?
C'MON !!
YOU WANT TO PUNISH THE ONE WHO PUT TOGETHER THAT DUMB TOURNAMENT, RIGHT? IT WAS THAT PSYCHOTIC STUDENT COUNCIL PRESIDENT, NOT US!!
KAZAMA, WE'RE NOT HERE TO TALK ABOUT *THAT*.
THEN WHY THE HECK DID YOU BRING US HERE?
WE CALLED YOU HERE ...
TO TALK ABOUT ...

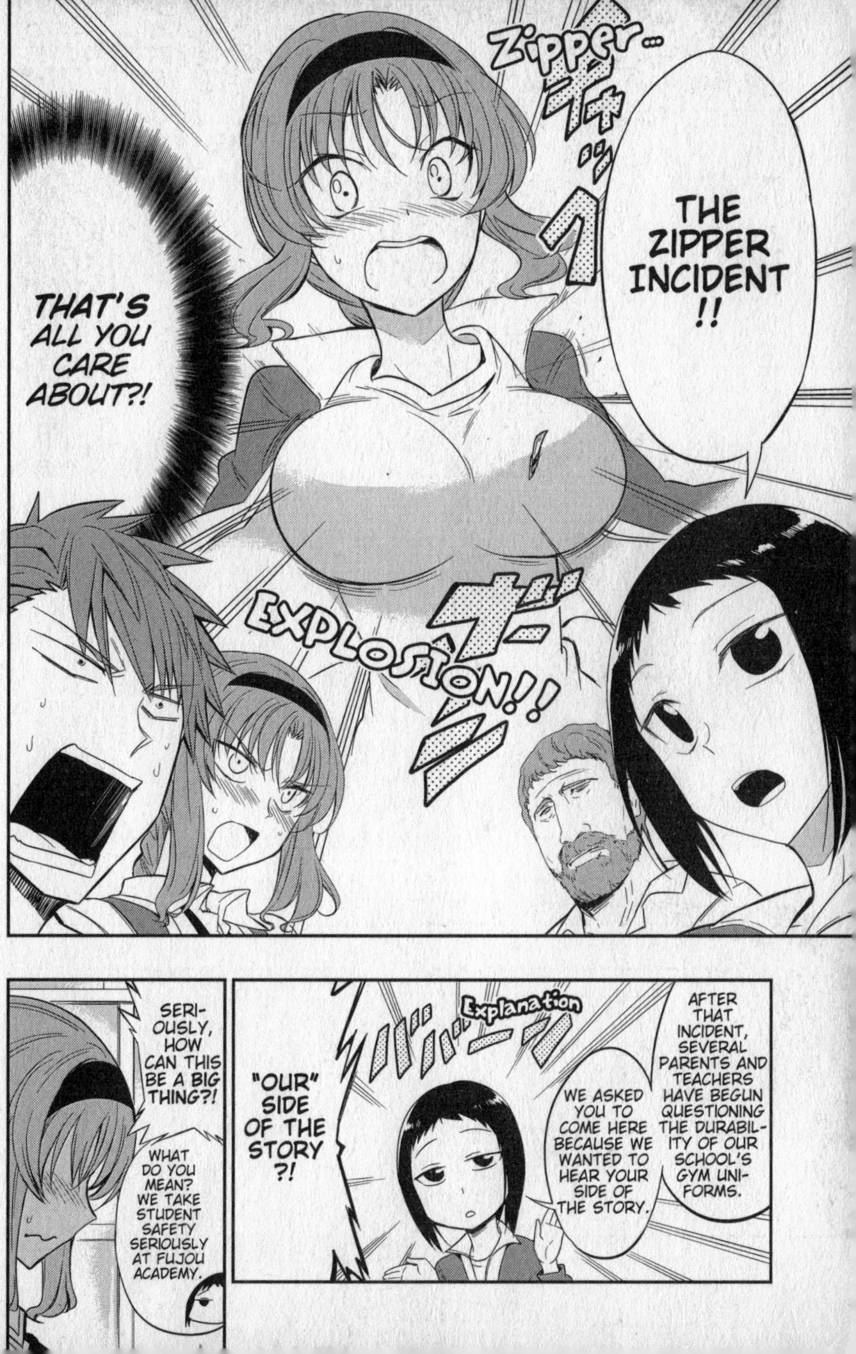
Zipper...
THE ZIPPER INCIDENT!!
THAT'S ALL YOU CARE ABOUT?!
EXPLOSION!!
Explanation
AFTER THAT INCIDENT, SEVERAL PARENTS AND TEACHERS HAVE BEGUN QUESTIONING THE DURABILITY OF OUR SCHOOL'S GYM UNIFORMS.
WE ASKED YOU TO COME HERE BECAUSE WE WANTED TO HEAR YOUR SIDE OF THE STORY.
"OUR" SIDE OF THE STORY?!
SERIOUSLY, HOW CAN THIS BE A BIG THING?!
WHAT DO YOU MEAN? WE TAKE STUDENT SAFETY SERIOUSLY AT FUJOU ACADEMY.

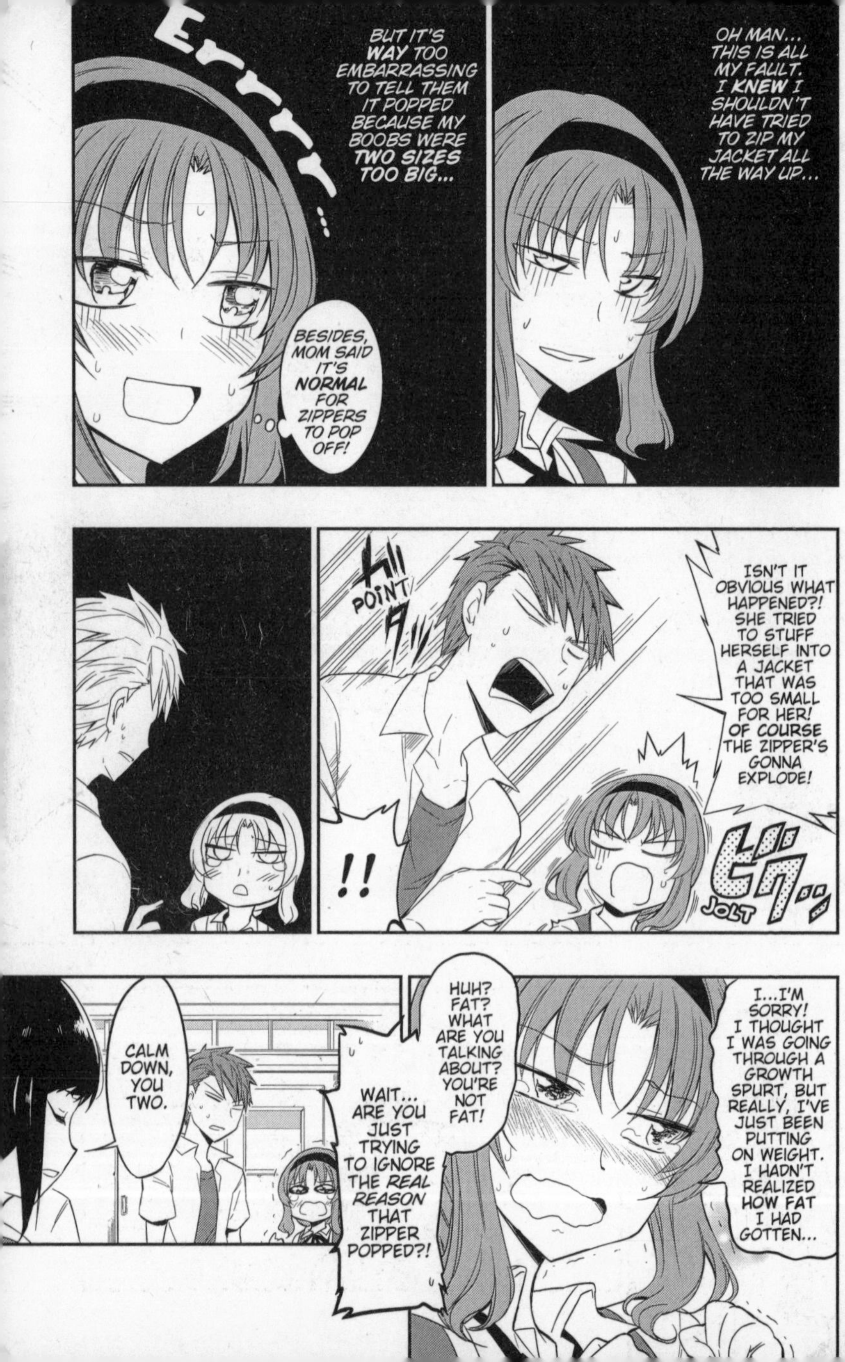
OH MAN... THIS IS ALL MY FAULT. I **KNEW** I SHOULDN'T HAVE TRIED TO ZIP MY JACKET ALL THE WAY UP...
BUT IT'S **WAY** TOO EMBARRASSING TO TELL THEM IT POPPED BECAUSE MY BOOBS WERE **TWO SIZES** TOO BIG...
Errrr...
BESIDES, MOM SAID IT'S **NORMAL** FOR ZIPPERS TO POP OFF!
ISN'T IT OBVIOUS WHAT HAPPENED?! SHE TRIED TO STUFF HERSELF INTO A JACKET THAT WAS TOO SMALL FOR HER! **OF COURSE** THE ZIPPER'S GONNA EXPLODE!
POINT
!!
JOLT
I...I'M SORRY! I THOUGHT I WAS GOING THROUGH A GROWTH SPURT, BUT REALLY, I'VE JUST BEEN PUTTING ON WEIGHT. I HADN'T REALIZED HOW FAT I HAD GOTTEN...
HUH? FAT? WHAT ARE YOU TALKING ABOUT? YOU'RE NOT FAT!
WAIT... ARE YOU JUST TRYING TO IGNORE THE *REAL* REASON THAT ZIPPER POPPED?!
CALM DOWN, YOU TWO.

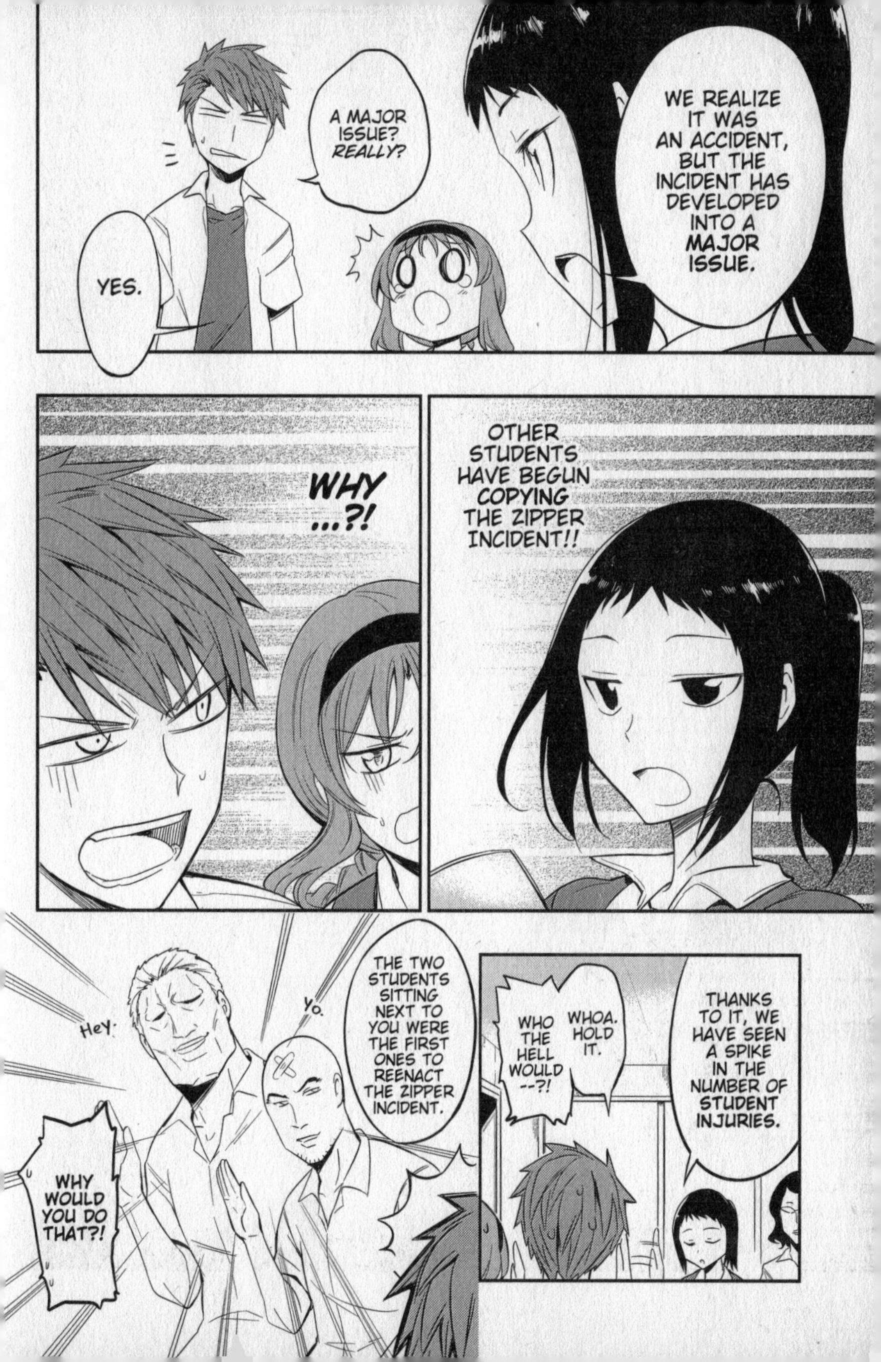
WE REALIZE IT WAS AN ACCIDENT, BUT THE INCIDENT HAS DEVELOPED INTO A MAJOR ISSUE.
A MAJOR ISSUE? *REALLY?*
YES.
OTHER STUDENTS HAVE BEGUN COPYING THE ZIPPER INCIDENT!!
WHY ...?!
THANKS TO IT, WE HAVE SEEN A SPIKE IN THE NUMBER OF STUDENT INJURIES.
WHOA. HOLD IT.
WHO THE HELL WOULD --?!
THE TWO STUDENTS SITTING NEXT TO YOU WERE THE FIRST ONES TO REENACT THE ZIPPER INCIDENT.
Yo.
Hey.
WHY WOULD YOU DO THAT?!

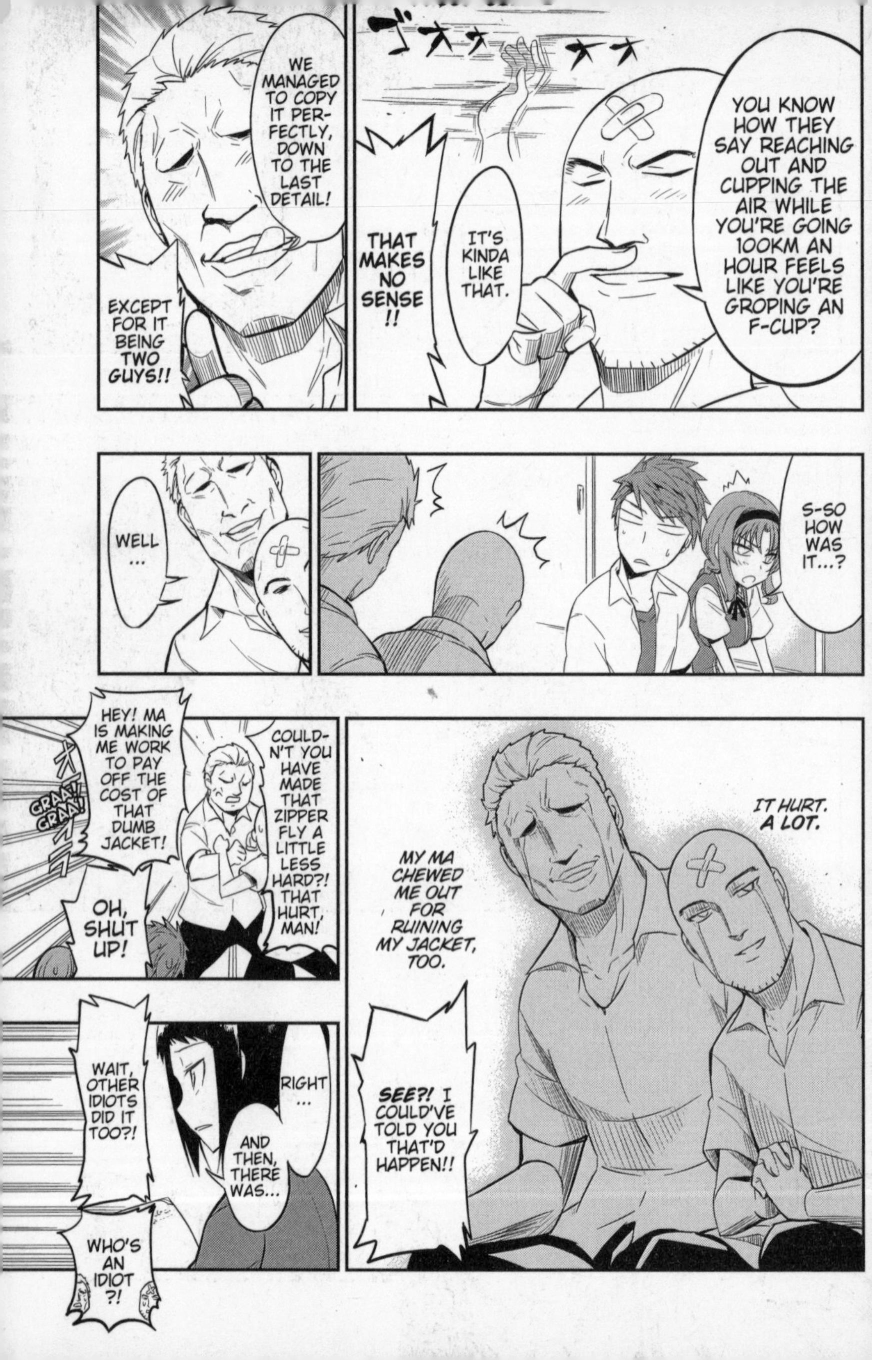
YOU KNOW HOW THEY SAY REACHING OUT AND CUPPING THE AIR WHILE YOU'RE GOING 100KM AN HOUR FEELS LIKE YOU'RE GROPING AN F-CUP?
IT'S KINDA LIKE THAT.
THAT MAKES NO SENSE!!
WE MANAGED TO COPY IT PERFECTLY, DOWN TO THE LAST DETAIL!
EXCEPT FOR IT BEING TWO GUYS!!
S-SO HOW WAS IT...?
WELL...
IT HURT. A LOT.
MY MA CHEWED ME OUT FOR RUINING MY JACKET, TOO.
SEE?! I COULD'VE TOLD YOU THAT'D HAPPEN!!
COULDN'T YOU HAVE MADE THAT ZIPPER FLY A LITTLE LESS HARD?! THAT HURT, MAN!
HEY! MA IS MAKING ME WORK TO PAY OFF THE COST OF THAT DUMB JACKET!
GRAA! GRAA!
OH, SHUT UP!
RIGHT...
AND THEN, THERE WAS...
WAIT, OTHER IDIOTS DID IT TOO?!
WHO'S AN IDIOT?!

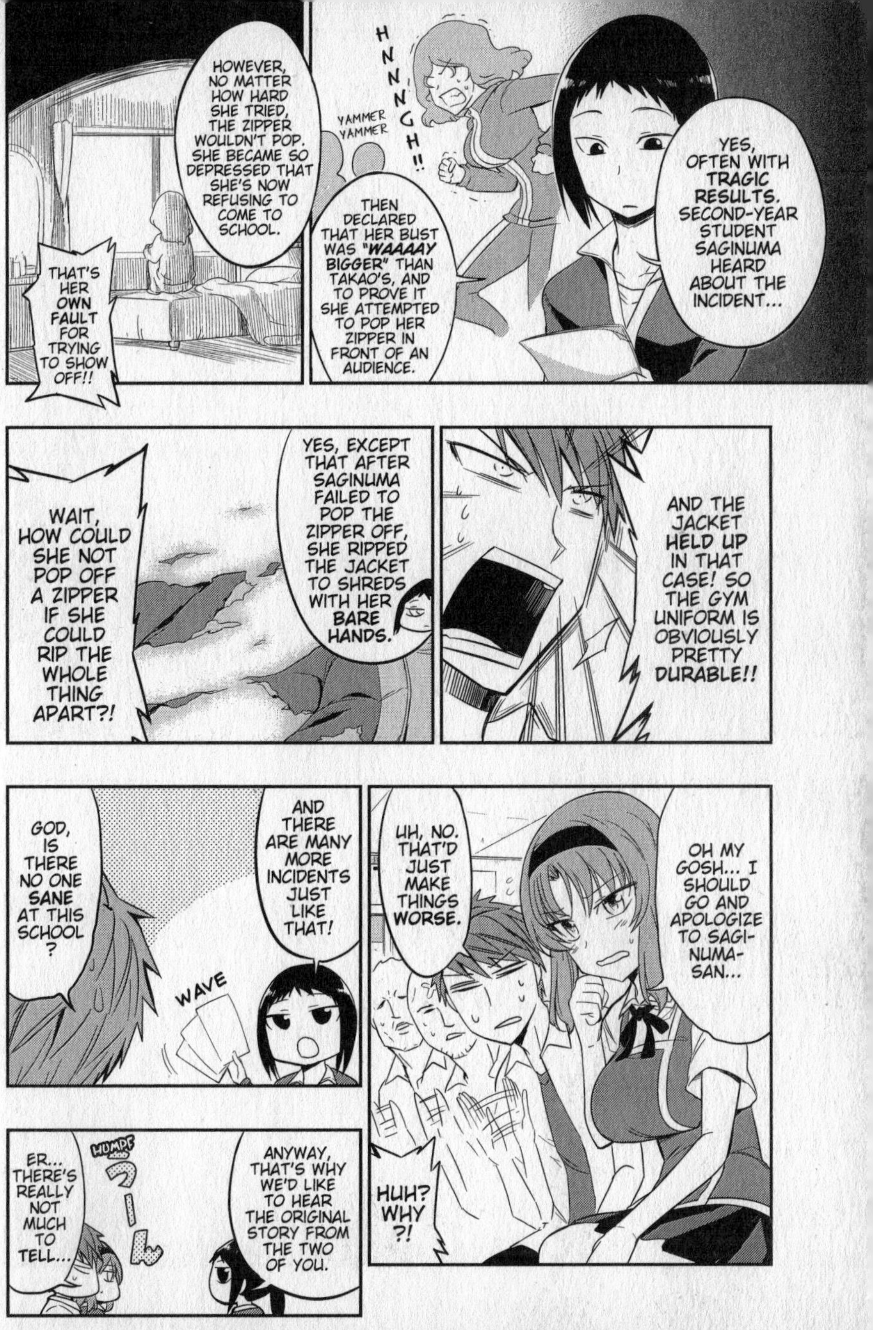
YES, OFTEN WITH TRAGIC RESULTS. SECOND-YEAR STUDENT SAGINUMA HEARD ABOUT THE INCIDENT...
HNNNGH!!
THEN DECLARED THAT HER BUST WAS "WAAAAY BIGGER" THAN TAKAO'S, AND TO PROVE IT SHE ATTEMPTED TO POP HER ZIPPER IN FRONT OF AN AUDIENCE.
YAMMER YAMMER
HOWEVER, NO MATTER HOW HARD SHE TRIED, THE ZIPPER WOULDN'T POP. SHE BECAME SO DEPRESSED THAT SHE'S NOW REFUSING TO COME TO SCHOOL.
THAT'S HER OWN FAULT FOR TRYING TO SHOW OFF!!
AND THE JACKET HELD UP IN THAT CASE! SO THE GYM UNIFORM IS OBVIOUSLY PRETTY DURABLE!!
YES, EXCEPT THAT AFTER SAGINUMA FAILED TO POP THE ZIPPER OFF, SHE RIPPED THE JACKET TO SHREDS WITH HER BARE HANDS.
WAIT, HOW COULD SHE NOT POP OFF A ZIPPER IF SHE COULD RIP THE WHOLE THING APART?!
OH MY GOSH... I SHOULD GO AND APOLOGIZE TO SAGINUMA-SAN...
UH, NO. THAT'D JUST MAKE THINGS WORSE.
HUH? WHY?!
AND THERE ARE MANY MORE INCIDENTS JUST LIKE THAT!
GOD, IS THERE NO ONE SANE AT THIS SCHOOL?
WAVE
ANYWAY, THAT'S WHY WE'D LIKE TO HEAR THE ORIGINAL STORY FROM THE TWO OF YOU.
HUMPF
ER... THERE'S REALLY NOT MUCH TO TELL...

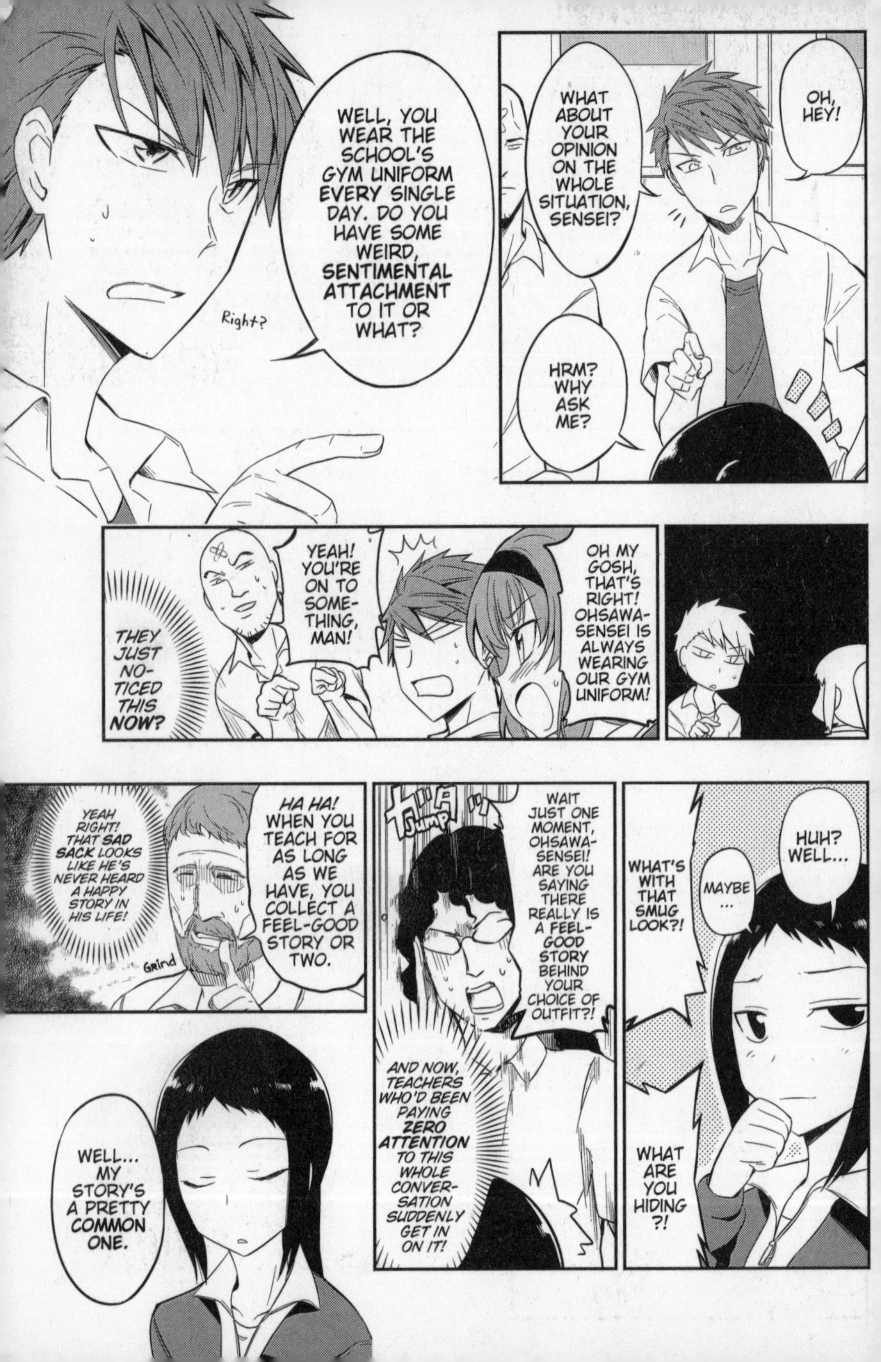
OH, HEY!
WHAT ABOUT YOUR OPINION ON THE WHOLE SITUATION, SENSEI?
HRM? WHY ASK ME?
WELL, YOU WEAR THE SCHOOL'S GYM UNIFORM EVERY SINGLE DAY. DO YOU HAVE SOME WEIRD, SENTIMENTAL ATTACHMENT TO IT OR WHAT?
Right?
OH MY GOSH, THAT'S RIGHT! OHSAWA-SENSEI IS ALWAYS WEARING OUR GYM UNIFORM!
YEAH! YOU'RE ON TO SOME-THING, MAN!
THEY JUST NO-TICED THIS NOW?
HUH? WELL...
MAYBE...
WHAT'S WITH THAT SMUG LOOK?!
WHAT ARE YOU HIDING?!
Jump
WAIT JUST ONE MOMENT, OHSAWA-SENSEI! ARE YOU SAYING THERE REALLY IS A FEEL-GOOD STORY BEHIND YOUR CHOICE OF OUTFIT?!
AND NOW, TEACHERS WHO'D BEEN PAYING ZERO ATTENTION TO THIS WHOLE CONVER-SATION SUDDENLY GET IN ON IT!
HA HA! WHEN YOU TEACH FOR AS LONG AS WE HAVE, YOU COLLECT A FEEL-GOOD STORY OR TWO.
YEAH RIGHT! THAT SAD SACK LOOKS LIKE HE'S NEVER HEARD A HAPPY STORY IN HIS LIFE!
Grind
WELL... MY STORY'S A PRETTY COMMON ONE.

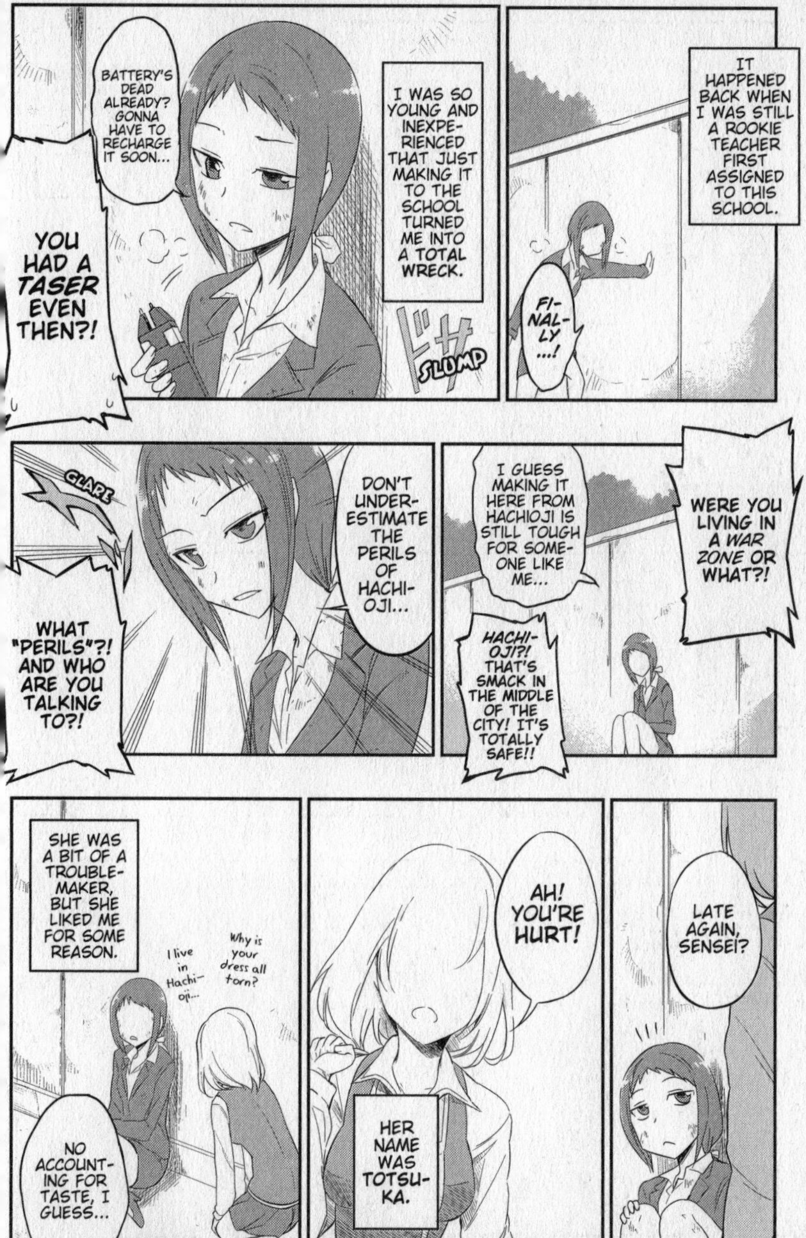
IT HAPPENED BACK WHEN I WAS STILL A ROOKIE TEACHER FIRST ASSIGNED TO THIS SCHOOL.
FINALLY...!
I WAS SO YOUNG AND INEXPERIENCED THAT JUST MAKING IT TO THE SCHOOL TURNED ME INTO A TOTAL WRECK.
ドサ
SLUMP
BATTERY'S DEAD ALREADY? GONNA HAVE TO RECHARGE IT SOON...
YOU HAD A *TASER* EVEN THEN?!
WERE YOU LIVING IN A *WAR ZONE* OR WHAT?!
I GUESS MAKING IT HERE FROM HACHIOJI IS STILL TOUGH FOR SOMEONE LIKE ME...
HACHIOJI?! THAT'S SMACK IN THE MIDDLE OF THE CITY! IT'S TOTALLY SAFE!!
GLARE
DON'T UNDERESTIMATE THE PERILS OF HACHIOJI...
WHAT "PERILS"?! AND WHO ARE YOU TALKING TO?!
LATE AGAIN, SENSEI?
AH! YOU'RE HURT!
HER NAME WAS TOTSUKA.
SHE WAS A BIT OF A TROUBLEMAKER, BUT SHE LIKED ME FOR SOME REASON.
Why is your dress all torn?
I live in Hachioji...
NO ACCOUNTING FOR TASTE, I GUESS...

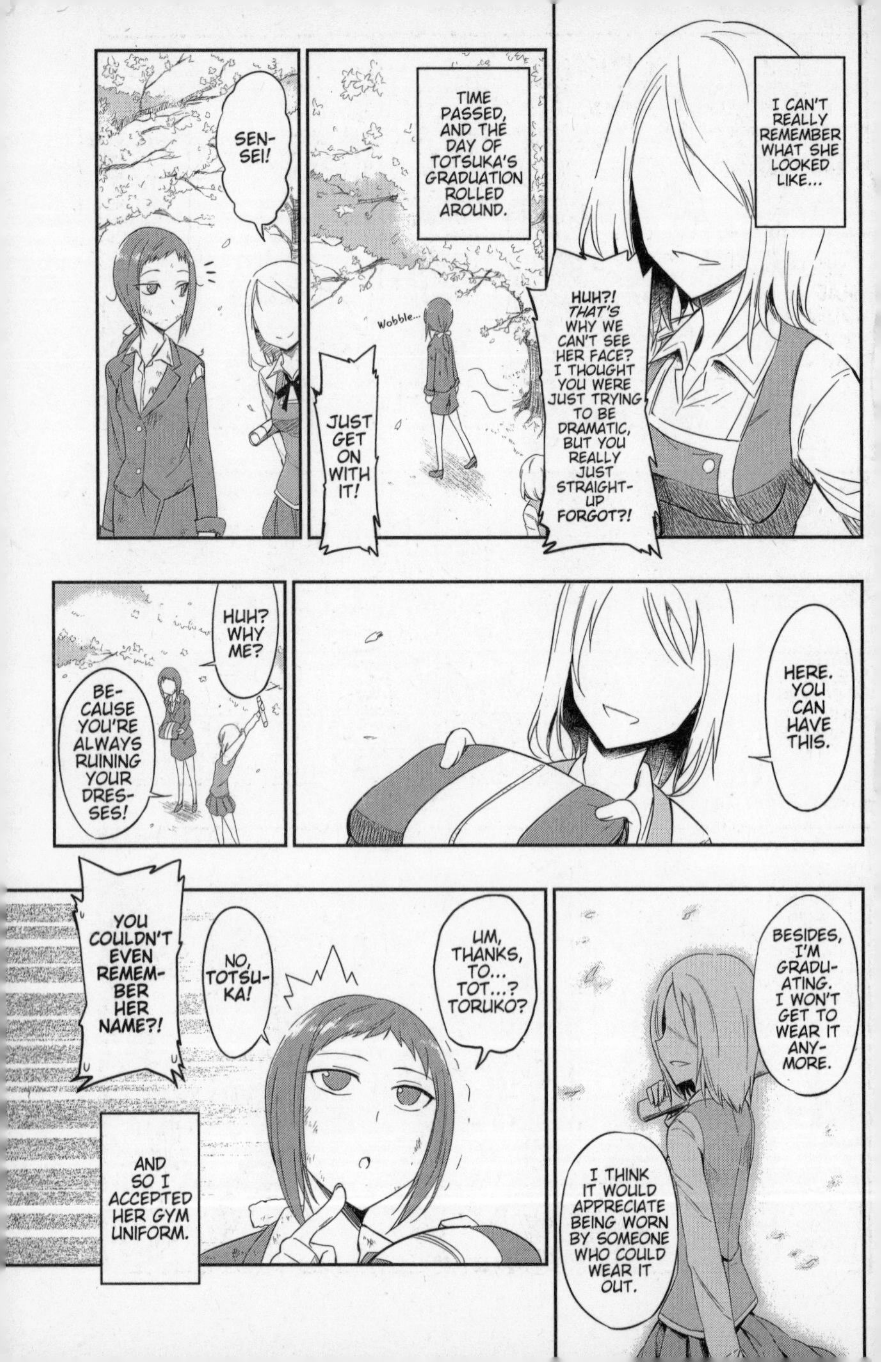
I CAN'T REALLY REMEMBER WHAT SHE LOOKED LIKE...
HUH?! *THAT'S* WHY WE CAN'T SEE HER FACE? I THOUGHT YOU WERE JUST TRYING TO BE DRAMATIC, BUT YOU REALLY JUST STRAIGHT-UP FORGOT?!
TIME PASSED, AND THE DAY OF TOTSUKA'S GRADUATION ROLLED AROUND.
Wobble...
JUST GET ON WITH IT!
SEN-SEI!
HERE. YOU CAN HAVE THIS.
HUH? WHY ME?
BE-CAUSE YOU'RE ALWAYS RUINING YOUR DRESSES!
BESIDES, I'M GRADU-ATING. I WON'T GET TO WEAR IT ANY-MORE.
I THINK IT WOULD APPRECIATE BEING WORN BY SOMEONE WHO COULD WEAR IT OUT.
UM, THANKS, TO... TOT...? TORUKO?
NO, TOTSU-KA!
YOU COULDN'T EVEN REMEM-BER HER NAME?!
AND SO I ACCEPTED HER GYM UNIFORM.

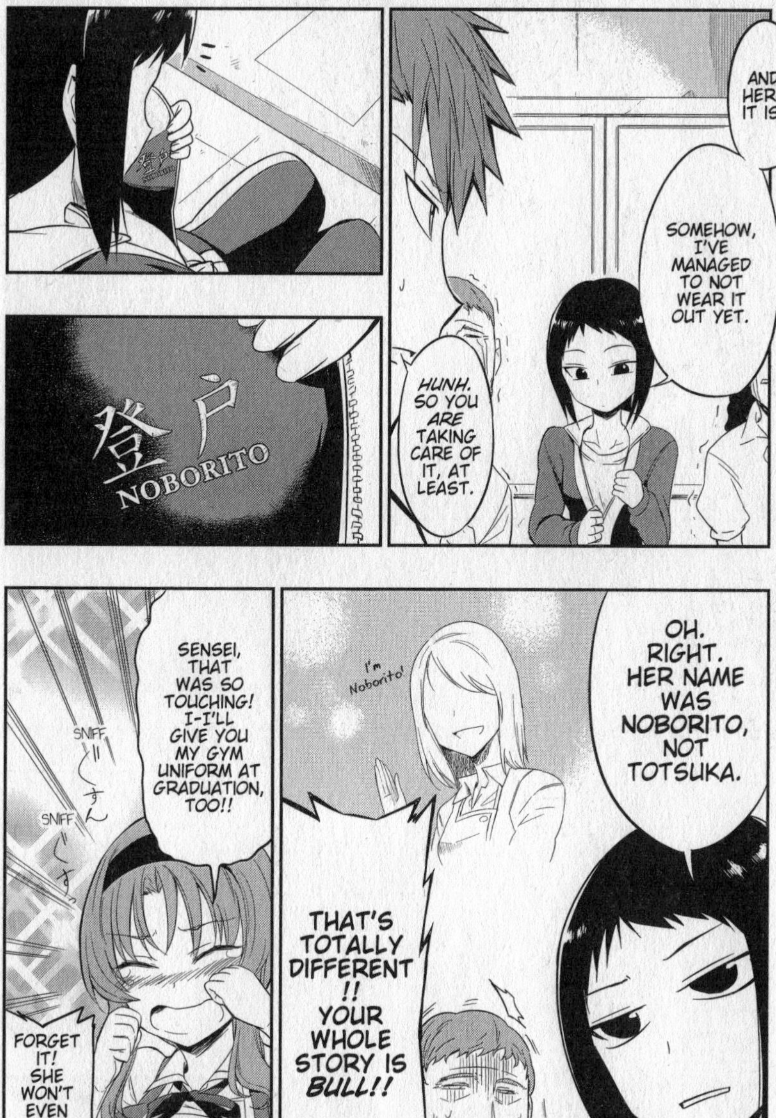
AND HERE IT IS.
SOMEHOW, I'VE MANAGED TO NOT WEAR IT OUT YET.
HUNH. SO YOU ARE TAKING CARE OF IT, AT LEAST.
登戸
登戸 NOBORITO
OH. RIGHT. HER NAME WAS NOBORITO, NOT TOTSUKA.
I'm Noborito!
THAT'S TOTALLY DIFFERENT!! YOUR WHOLE STORY IS *BULL!!*
SENSEI, THAT WAS SO TOUCHING! I-I'LL GIVE YOU MY GYM UNIFORM AT GRADUATION, TOO!!
SNIFF ぐすん
SNIFF ぐす
FORGET IT! SHE WON'T EVEN REMEMBER YOUR NAME!

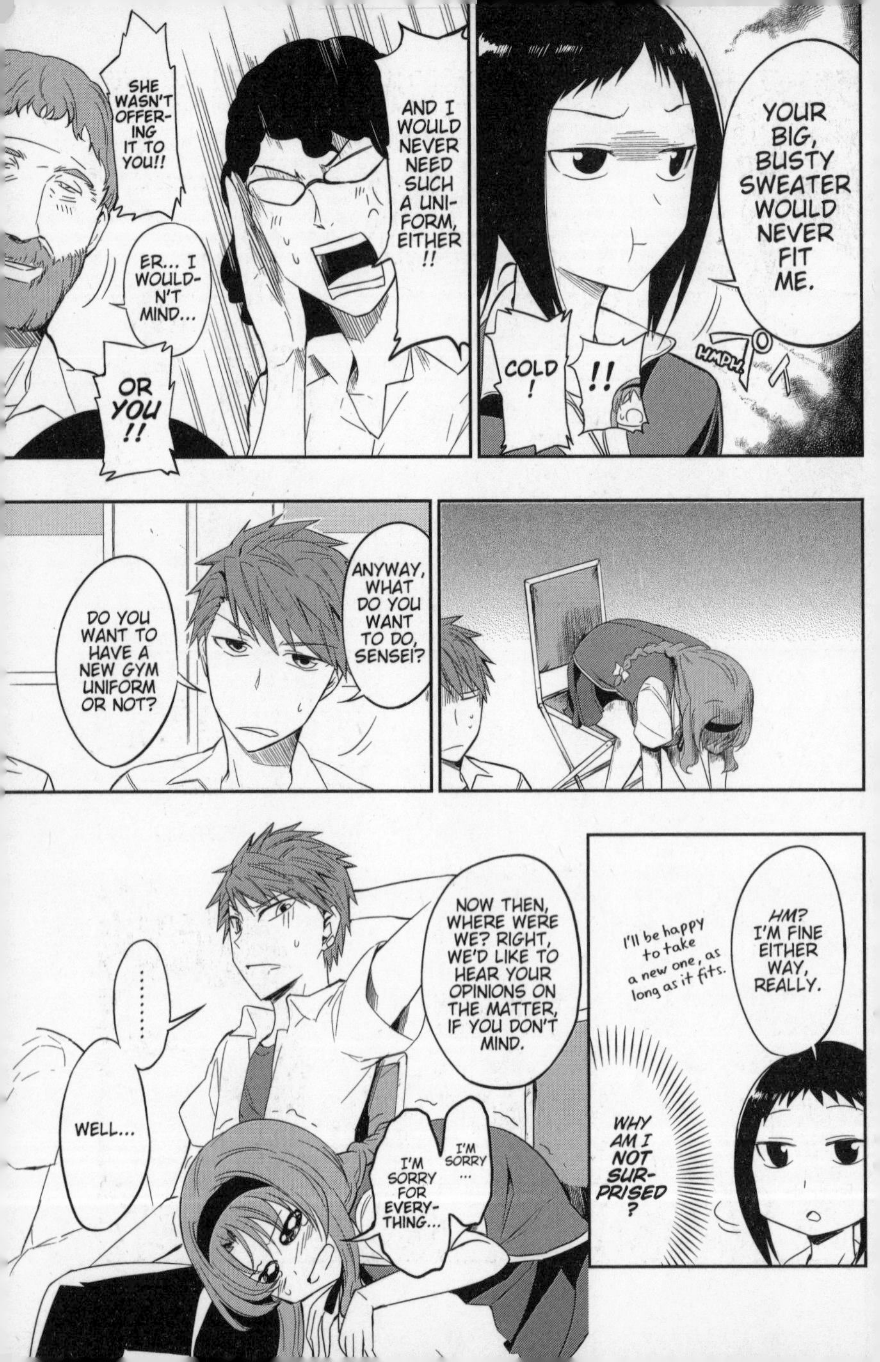
YOUR BIG, BUSTY SWEATER WOULD NEVER FIT ME.
HMPH
!!
COLD!
AND I WOULD NEVER NEED SUCH A UNIFORM, EITHER!!
SHE WASN'T OFFERING IT TO YOU!!
ER... I WOULDN'T MIND...
OR YOU!!
ANYWAY, WHAT DO YOU WANT TO DO, SENSEI?
DO YOU WANT TO HAVE A NEW GYM UNIFORM OR NOT?
HM? I'M FINE EITHER WAY, REALLY.
I'll be happy to take a new one, as long as it fits.
WHY AM I NOT SURPRISED?
NOW THEN, WHERE WERE WE? RIGHT, WE'D LIKE TO HEAR YOUR OPINIONS ON THE MATTER, IF YOU DON'T MIND.
......
I'M SORRY...
I'M SORRY FOR EVERYTHING...
WELL...

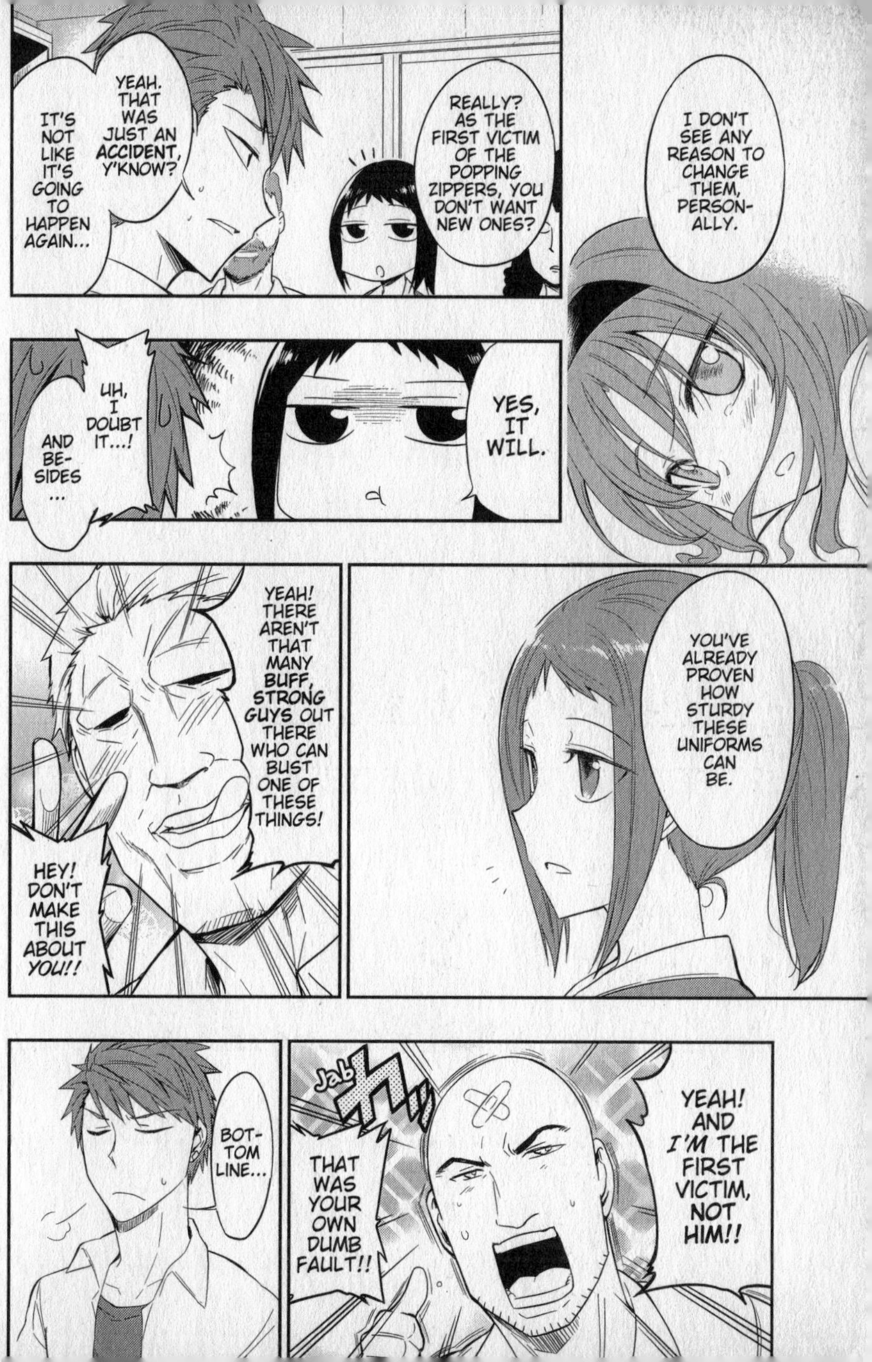
I DON'T SEE ANY REASON TO CHANGE THEM, PERSONALLY.
REALLY? AS THE FIRST VICTIM OF THE POPPING ZIPPERS, YOU DON'T WANT NEW ONES?
YEAH. THAT WAS JUST AN ACCIDENT, Y'KNOW?
IT'S NOT LIKE IT'S GOING TO HAPPEN AGAIN...
YES, IT WILL.
UH, I DOUBT IT...!
AND BE-SIDES...
YOU'VE ALREADY PROVEN HOW STURDY THESE UNIFORMS CAN BE.
YEAH! THERE AREN'T THAT MANY BUFF, STRONG GUYS OUT THERE WHO CAN BUST ONE OF THESE THINGS!
HEY! DON'T MAKE THIS ABOUT YOU!!
YEAH! AND I'M THE FIRST VICTIM, NOT HIM!!
Jab
THAT WAS YOUR OWN DUMB FAULT!!
BOT-TOM LINE...

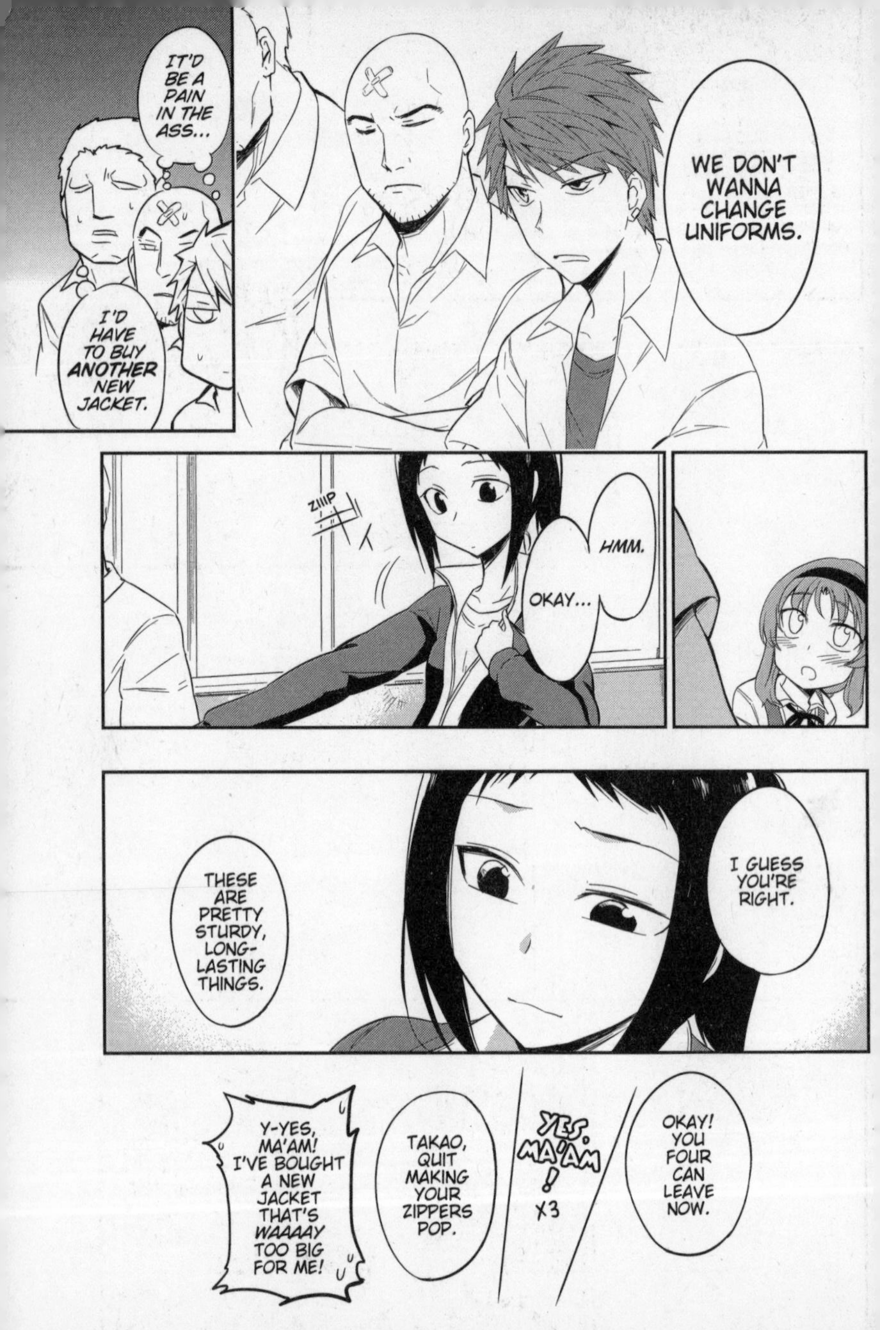
WE DON'T WANNA CHANGE UNIFORMS.
IT'D BE A PAIN IN THE ASS...
I'D HAVE TO BUY ANOTHER NEW JACKET.
HMM.
ZIIIP
OKAY...
I GUESS YOU'RE RIGHT.
THESE ARE PRETTY STURDY, LONG-LASTING THINGS.
OKAY! YOU FOUR CAN LEAVE NOW.
YES, MA'AM!
X3
TAKAO, QUIT MAKING YOUR ZIPPERS POP.
Y-YES, MA'AM! I'VE BOUGHT A NEW JACKET THAT'S WAAAAY TOO BIG FOR ME!

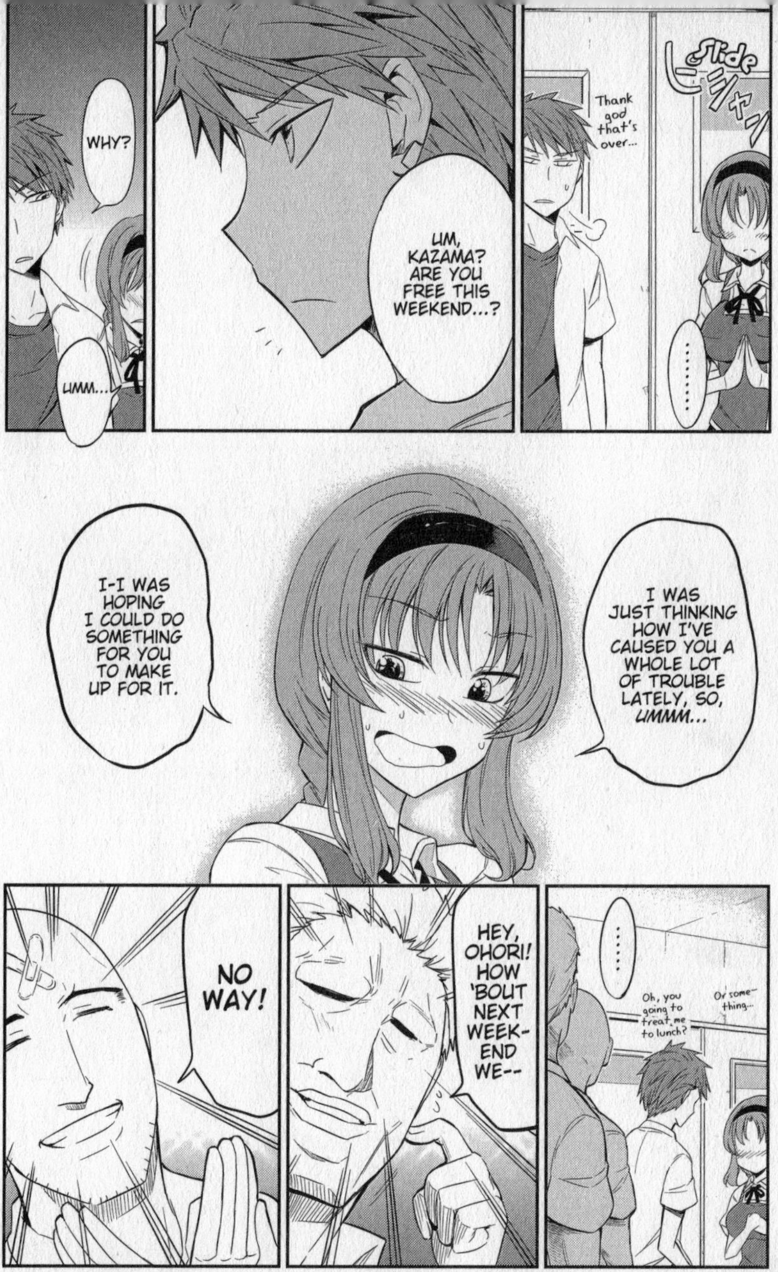
Slide
Thank god that's over...
......
UM, KAZAMA? ARE YOU FREE THIS WEEKEND...?
WHY?
UMM...
I WAS JUST THINKING HOW I'VE CAUSED YOU A WHOLE LOT OF TROUBLE LATELY, SO, UMMM...
I-I WAS HOPING I COULD DO SOMETHING FOR YOU TO MAKE UP FOR IT.
......
Or some-thing...
Oh, you going to treat me to lunch?
HEY, OHORI! HOW 'BOUT NEXT WEEK-END WE--
NO WAY!

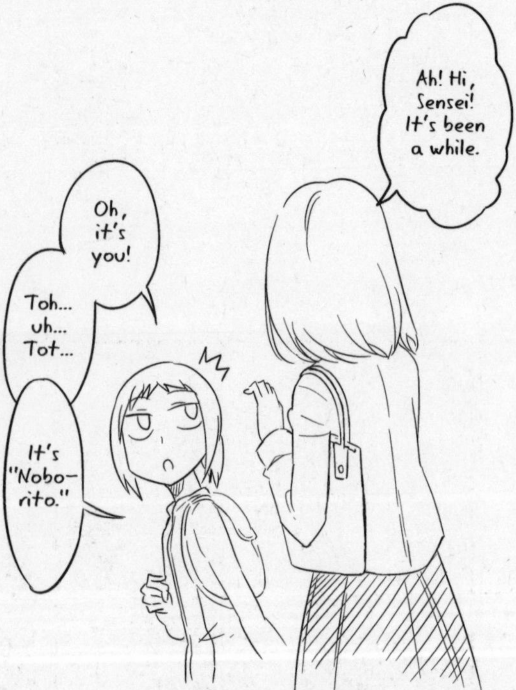
Ah! Hi, Sensei! It's been a while.
Oh, it's you!
Toh... uh... Tot...
It's "Nobo-rito."

D-FRAGMENTS ディーふらぐめんつ!

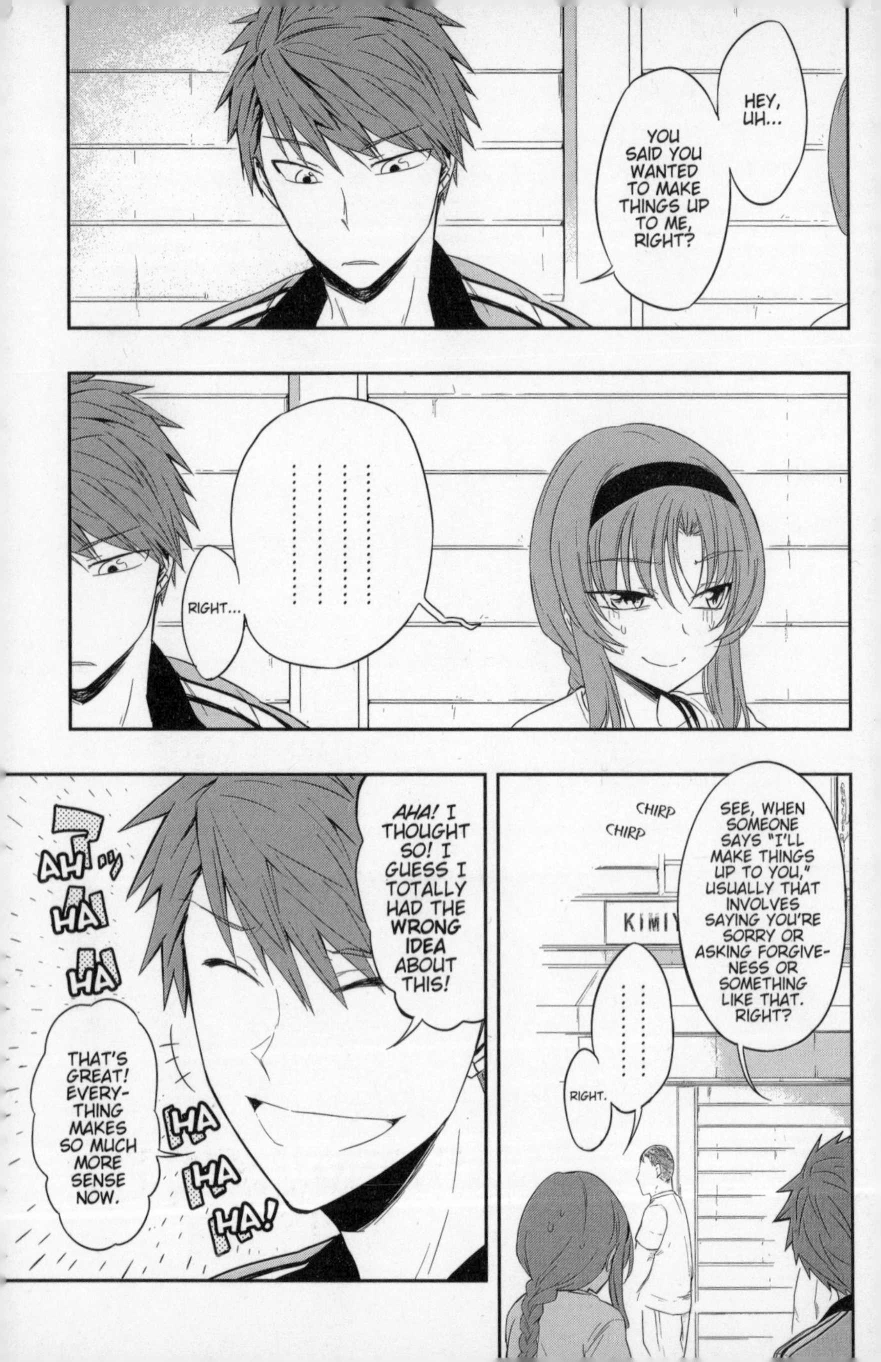
HEY, UH...
YOU SAID YOU WANTED TO MAKE THINGS UP TO ME, RIGHT?
......
RIGHT...
CHIRP
CHIRP
SEE, WHEN SOMEONE SAYS "I'LL MAKE THINGS UP TO YOU," USUALLY THAT INVOLVES SAYING YOU'RE SORRY OR ASKING FORGIVE-NESS OR SOMETHING LIKE THAT. RIGHT?
KIMIY
......
RIGHT.
AHA! I THOUGHT SO! I GUESS I TOTALLY HAD THE WRONG IDEA ABOUT THIS!
AH HA HA
THAT'S GREAT! EVERY-THING MAKES SO MUCH MORE SENSE NOW.
HA HA HA!

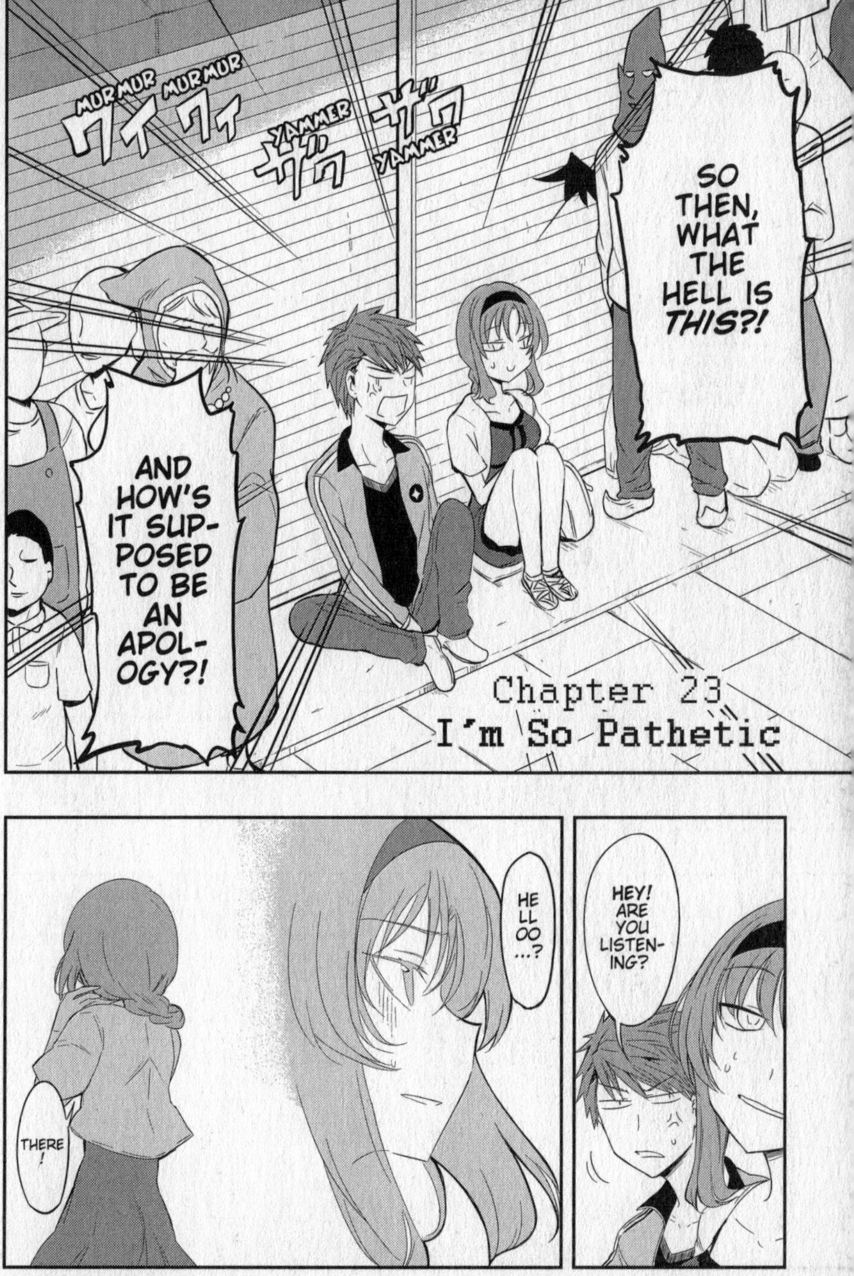
SO THEN, WHAT THE HELL IS *THIS?!*
ザワ ザワ
YAMMER YAMMER
ワィ ワィ
MURMUR MURMUR
AND HOW'S IT SUP-POSED TO BE AN APOL-OGY?!
Chapter 23
I'm So Pathetic
HEY! ARE YOU LISTEN-ING?
HELLOO...?
THERE!

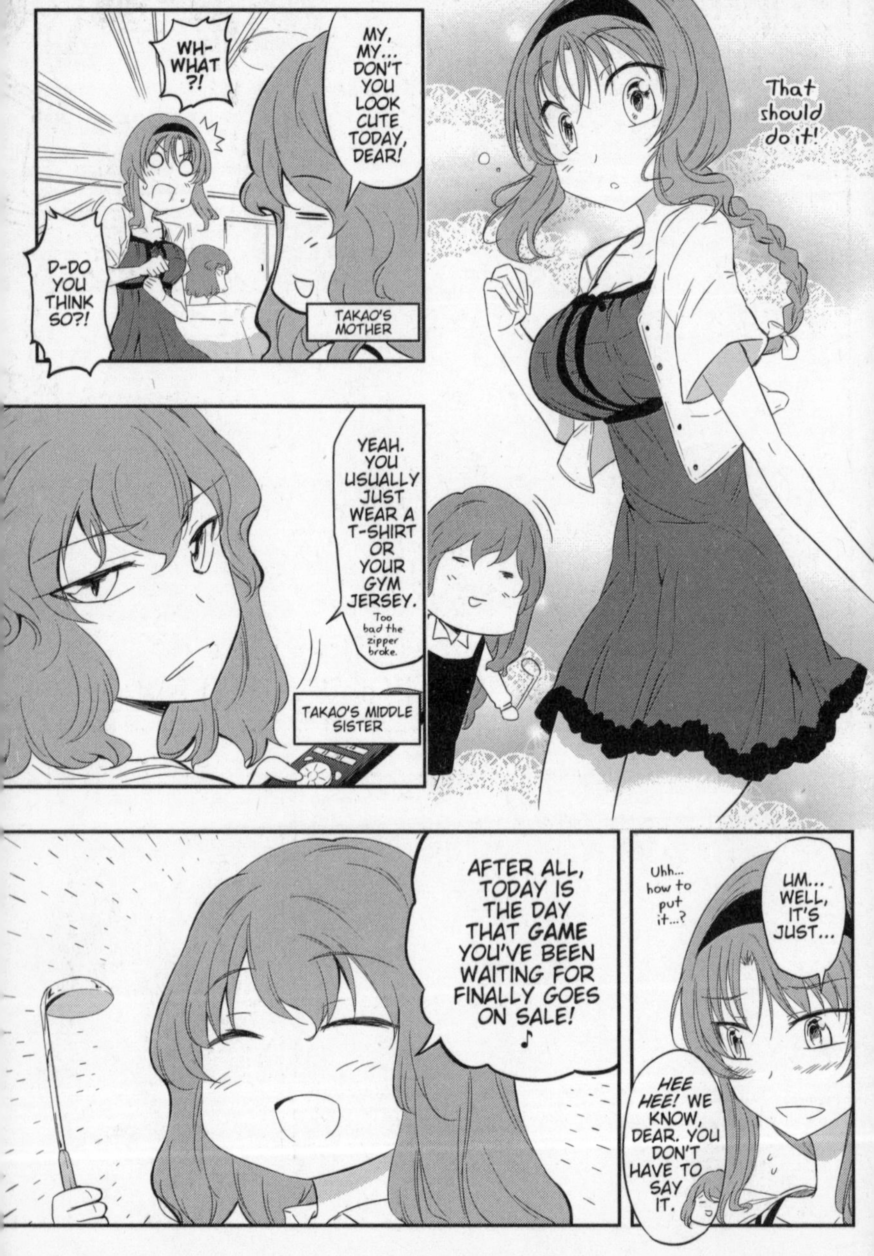

That should do it!
MY, MY... DON'T YOU LOOK CUTE TODAY, DEAR!
WH-WHAT?!
TAKAO'S MOTHER
D-DO YOU THINK SO?!
YEAH. YOU USUALLY JUST WEAR A T-SHIRT OR YOUR GYM JERSEY.
Too bad the zipper broke.
TAKAO'S MIDDLE SISTER
UM... WELL, IT'S JUST...
Uhh... how to put it...?
HEE HEE! WE KNOW, DEAR. YOU DON'T HAVE TO SAY IT.
AFTER ALL, TODAY IS THE DAY THAT GAME YOU'VE BEEN WAITING FOR FINALLY GOES ON SALE! ♪

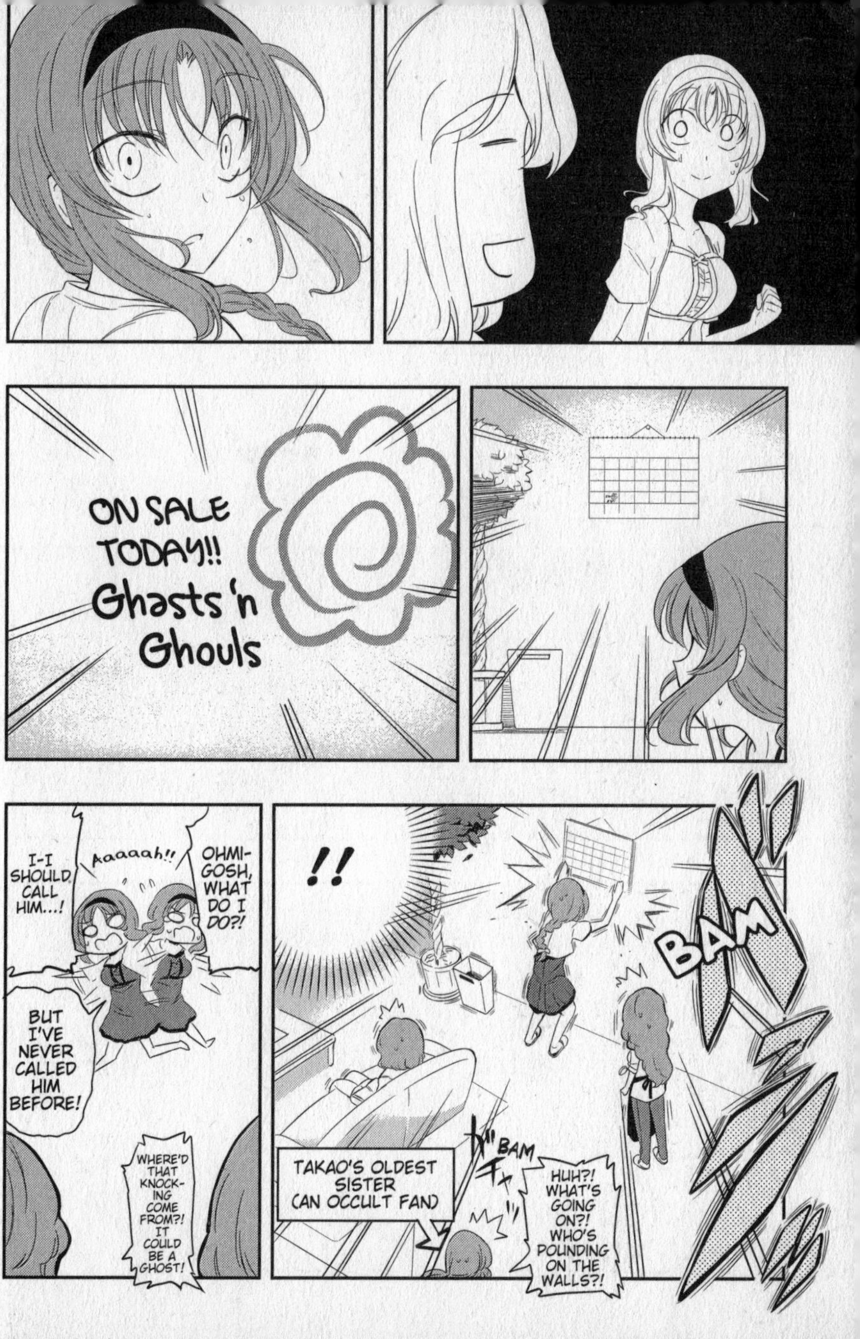
ON SALE TODAY!! Ghasts 'n Ghouls
BAM
!!
BAM
HUH?! WHAT'S GOING ON?! WHO'S POUNDING ON THE WALLS?!
TAKAO'S OLDEST SISTER (AN OCCULT FAN)
WHERE'D THAT KNOCKING COME FROM?! IT COULD BE A GHOST!
OHMI-GOSH, WHAT DO I DO?!
Aaaaah!!
I-I SHOULD CALL HIM...!
BUT I'VE NEVER CALLED HIM BEFORE!

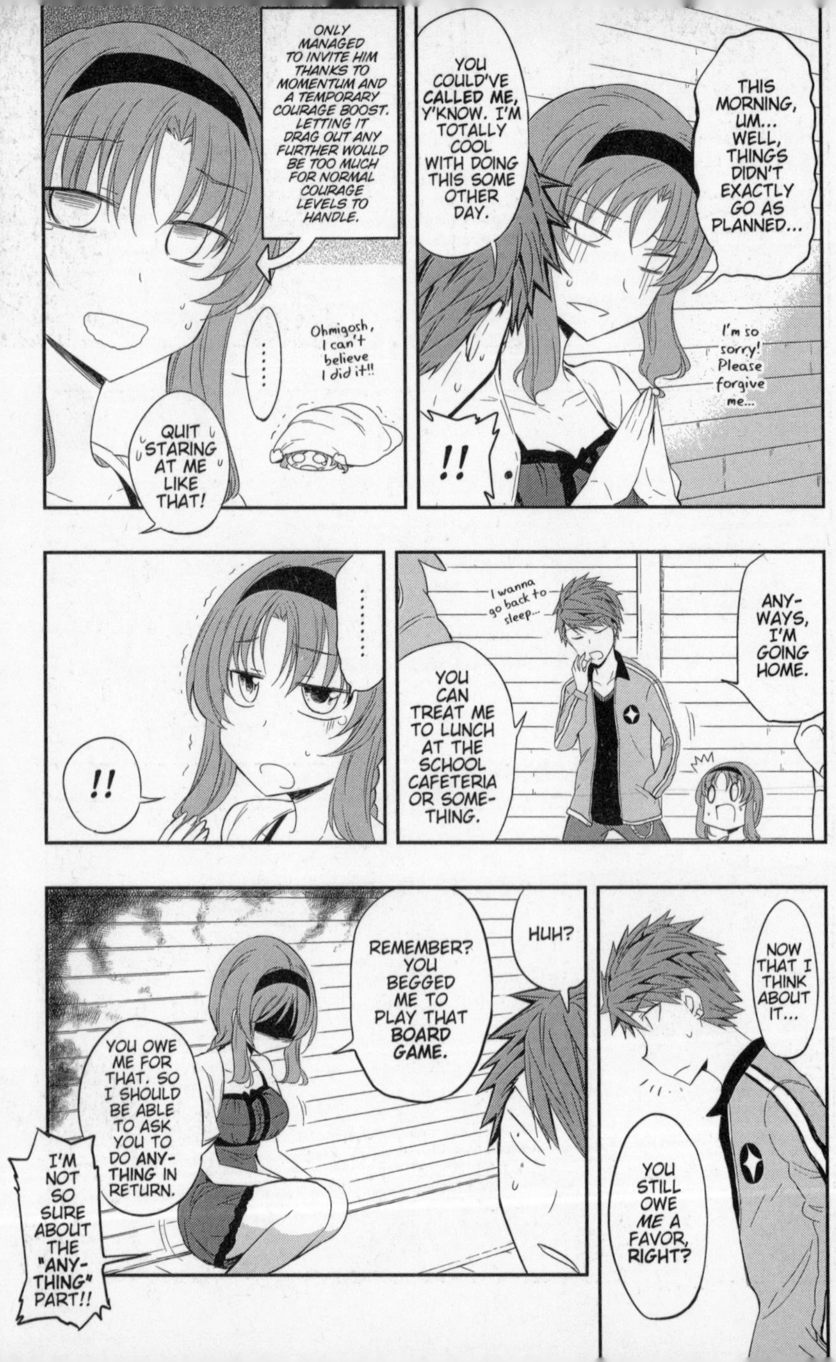
THIS MORNING, UM... WELL, THINGS DIDN'T EXACTLY GO AS PLANNED...
I'm so sorry! Please forgive me...
YOU COULD'VE CALLED ME, Y'KNOW. I'M TOTALLY COOL WITH DOING THIS SOME OTHER DAY.
!!
ONLY MANAGED TO INVITE HIM THANKS TO MOMENTUM AND A TEMPORARY COURAGE BOOST. LETTING IT DRAG OUT ANY FURTHER WOULD BE TOO MUCH FOR NORMAL COURAGE LEVELS TO HANDLE.
......
Ohmigosh, I can't believe I did it!!
QUIT STARING AT ME LIKE THAT!
ANYWAYS, I'M GOING HOME.
I wanna go back to sleep...
YOU CAN TREAT ME TO LUNCH AT THE SCHOOL CAFETERIA OR SOMETHING.
......
!!
NOW THAT I THINK ABOUT IT...
YOU STILL OWE ME A FAVOR, RIGHT?
HUH?
REMEMBER? YOU BEGGED ME TO PLAY THAT BOARD GAME.
YOU OWE ME FOR THAT. SO I SHOULD BE ABLE TO ASK YOU TO DO ANYTHING IN RETURN.
I'M NOT SO SURE ABOUT THE "ANYTHING" PART!!

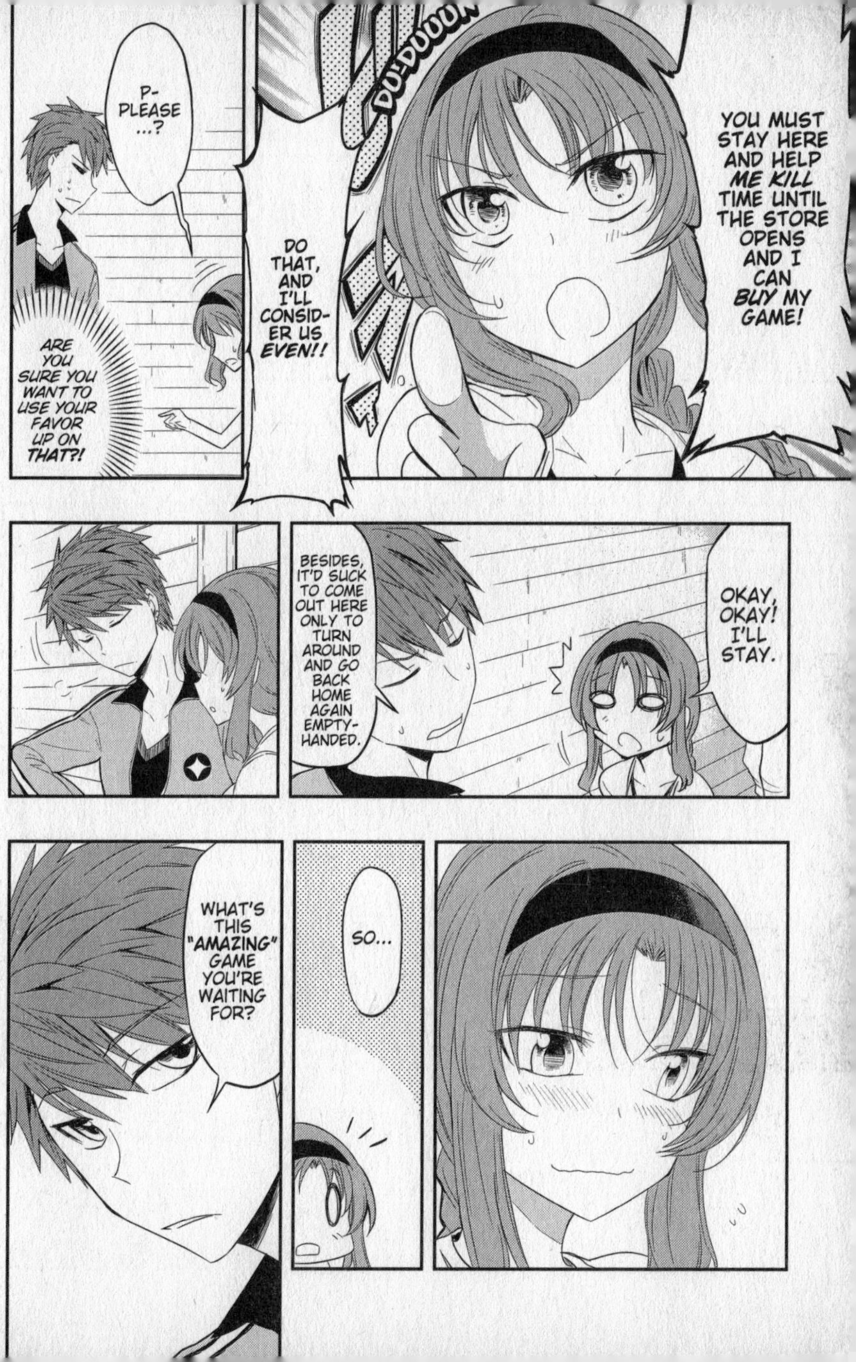
DU-DUUUN
YOU MUST STAY HERE AND HELP ME KILL TIME UNTIL THE STORE OPENS AND I CAN BUY MY GAME!
DO THAT, AND I'LL CONSIDER US EVEN!!
P-PLEASE ...?
ARE YOU SURE YOU WANT TO USE YOUR FAVOR UP ON THAT?!
OKAY, OKAY! I'LL STAY.
BESIDES, IT'D SUCK TO COME OUT HERE ONLY TO TURN AROUND AND GO BACK HOME AGAIN EMPTY-HANDED.
SO...
WHAT'S THIS "AMAZING" GAME YOU'RE WAITING FOR?

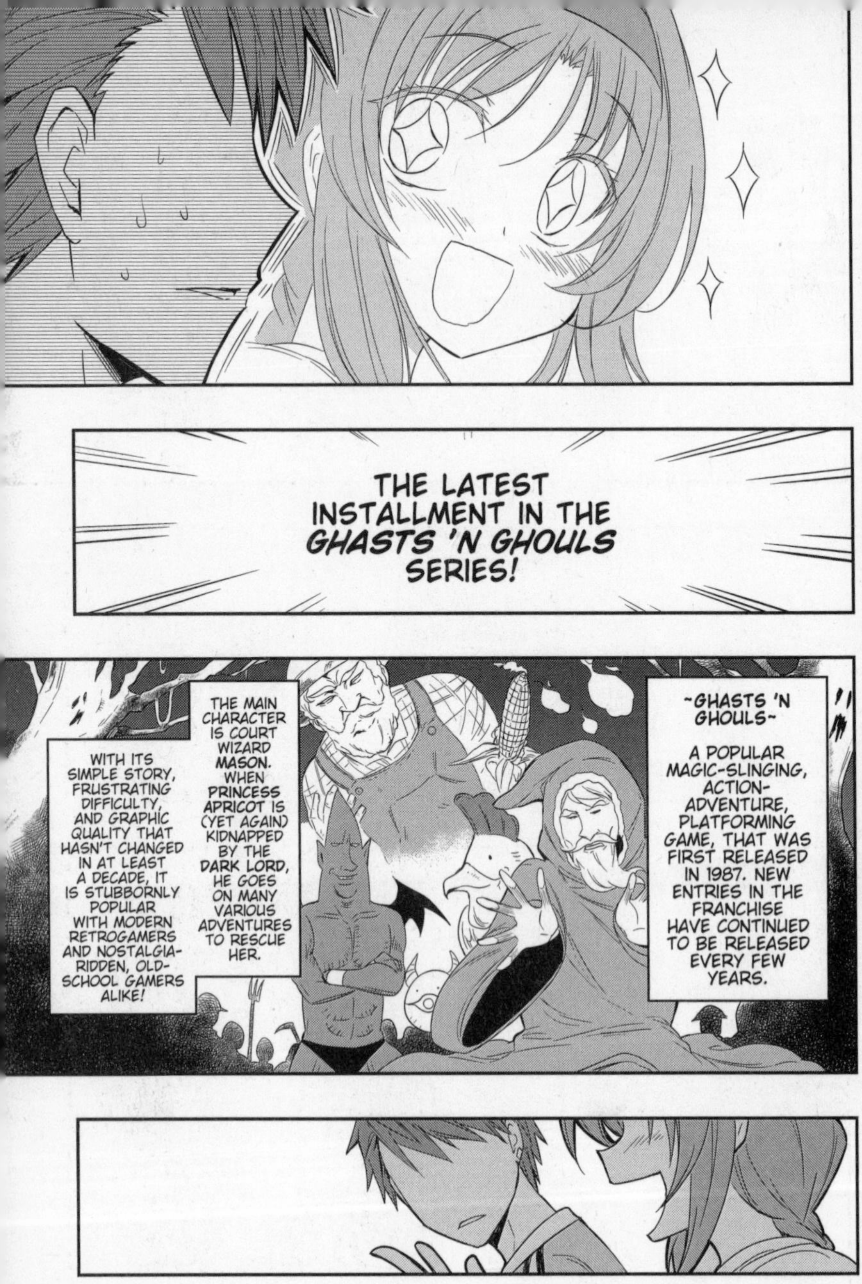
THE LATEST INSTALLMENT IN THE *GHASTS 'N GHOULS* SERIES!
~GHASTS 'N GHOULS~
A POPULAR MAGIC-SLINGING, ACTION-ADVENTURE, PLATFORMING GAME, THAT WAS FIRST RELEASED IN 1987. NEW ENTRIES IN THE FRANCHISE HAVE CONTINUED TO BE RELEASED EVERY FEW YEARS.
THE MAIN CHARACTER IS COURT WIZARD MASON. WHEN PRINCESS APRICOT IS (YET AGAIN) KIDNAPPED BY THE DARK LORD, HE GOES ON MANY VARIOUS ADVENTURES TO RESCUE HER.
WITH ITS SIMPLE STORY, FRUSTRATING DIFFICULTY, AND GRAPHIC QUALITY THAT HASN'T CHANGED IN AT LEAST A DECADE, IT IS STUBBORNLY POPULAR WITH MODERN RETROGAMERS AND NOSTALGIA-RIDDEN, OLD-SCHOOL GAMERS ALIKE!

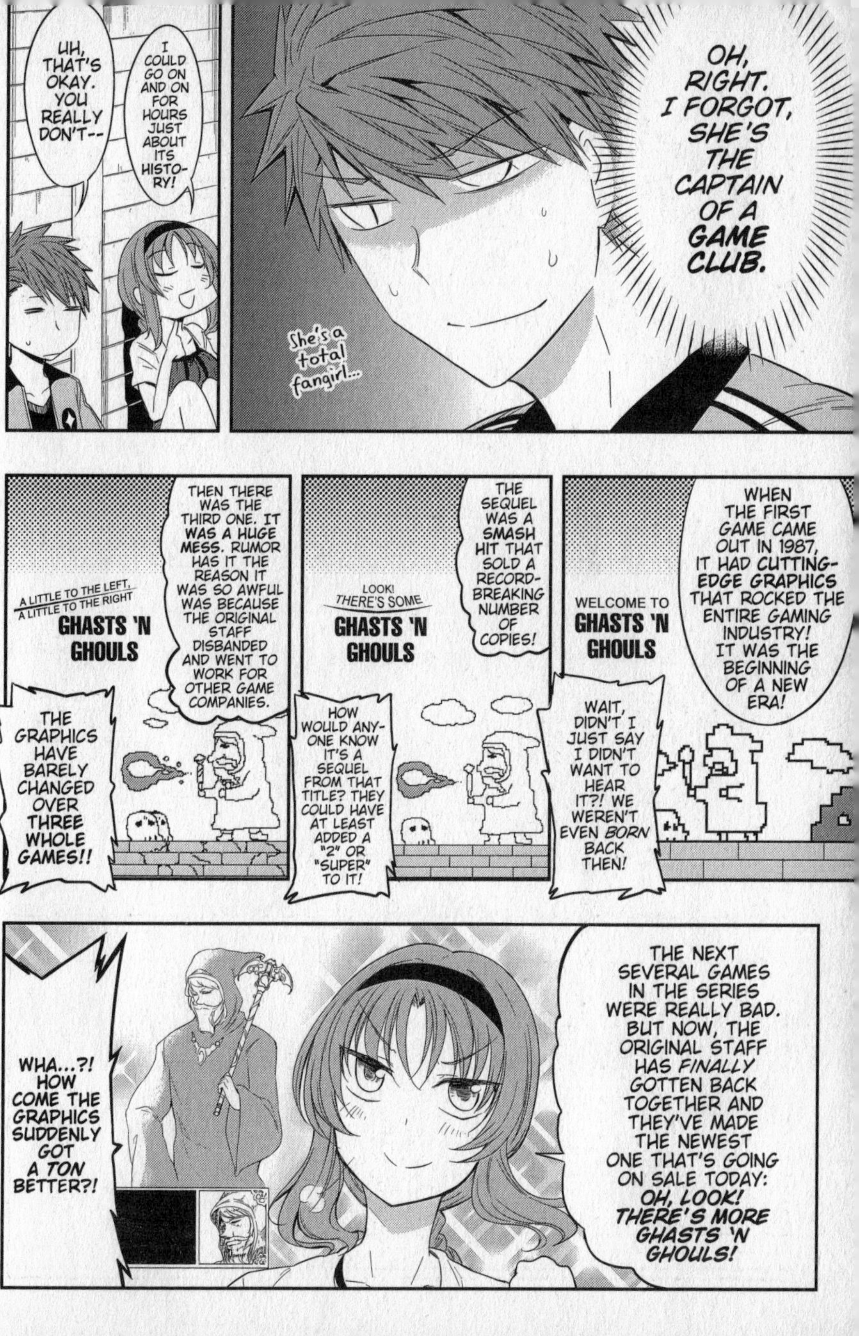
OH, RIGHT. I FORGOT, SHE'S THE CAPTAIN OF A GAME CLUB.
She's a total fangirl...
I COULD GO ON AND ON FOR HOURS JUST ABOUT ITS HISTORY!
UH, THAT'S OKAY. YOU REALLY DON'T--
WHEN THE FIRST GAME CAME OUT IN 1987, IT HAD CUTTING-EDGE GRAPHICS THAT ROCKED THE ENTIRE GAMING INDUSTRY! IT WAS THE BEGINNING OF A NEW ERA!
WELCOME TO GHASTS 'N GHOULS
WAIT, DIDN'T I JUST SAY I DIDN'T WANT TO HEAR IT?! WE WEREN'T EVEN BORN BACK THEN!
THE SEQUEL WAS A SMASH HIT THAT SOLD A RECORD-BREAKING NUMBER OF COPIES!
LOOK! THERE'S SOME GHASTS 'N GHOULS
HOW WOULD ANYONE KNOW IT'S A SEQUEL FROM THAT TITLE? THEY COULD HAVE AT LEAST ADDED A "2" OR "SUPER" TO IT!
THEN THERE WAS THE THIRD ONE. IT WAS A HUGE MESS. RUMOR HAS IT THE REASON IT WAS SO AWFUL WAS BECAUSE THE ORIGINAL STAFF DISBANDED AND WENT TO WORK FOR OTHER GAME COMPANIES.
A LITTLE TO THE LEFT, A LITTLE TO THE RIGHT GHASTS 'N GHOULS
THE GRAPHICS HAVE BARELY CHANGED OVER THREE WHOLE GAMES!!
THE NEXT SEVERAL GAMES IN THE SERIES WERE REALLY BAD. BUT NOW, THE ORIGINAL STAFF HAS FINALLY GOTTEN BACK TOGETHER AND THEY'VE MADE THE NEWEST ONE THAT'S GOING ON SALE TODAY: OH, LOOK! THERE'S MORE GHASTS 'N GHOULS!
WHA...?! HOW COME THE GRAPHICS SUDDENLY GOT A TON BETTER?!

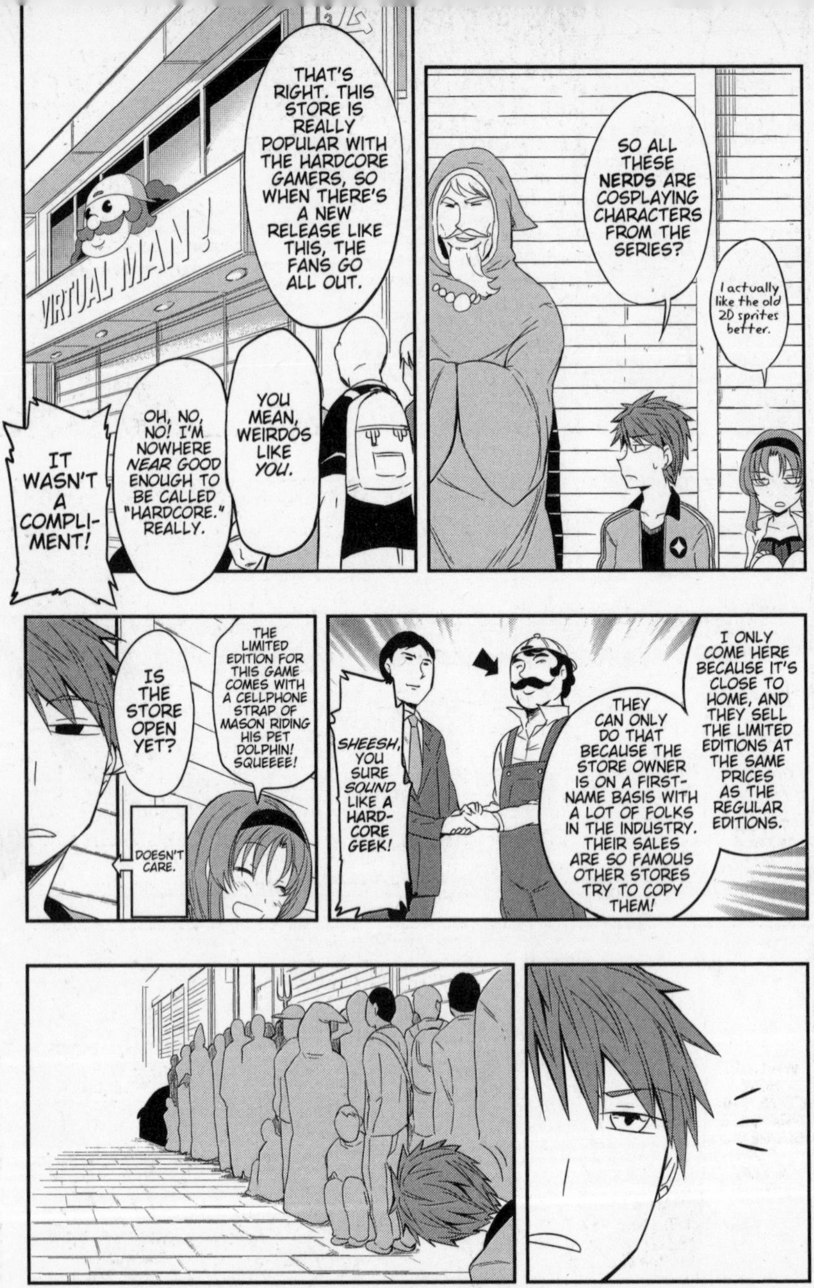
SO ALL THESE NERDS ARE COSPLAYING CHARACTERS FROM THE SERIES?
I actually like the old 2D sprites better.
VIRTUAL MAN!
THAT'S RIGHT. THIS STORE IS REALLY POPULAR WITH THE HARDCORE GAMERS, SO WHEN THERE'S A NEW RELEASE LIKE THIS, THE FANS GO ALL OUT.
YOU MEAN, WEIRDOS LIKE *YOU.*
OH, NO, NO! I'M NOWHERE *NEAR* GOOD ENOUGH TO BE CALLED "HARDCORE." REALLY.
IT WASN'T A COMPLIMENT!
I ONLY COME HERE BECAUSE IT'S CLOSE TO HOME, AND THEY SELL THE LIMITED EDITIONS AT THE SAME PRICES AS THE REGULAR EDITIONS.
THEY CAN ONLY DO THAT BECAUSE THE STORE OWNER IS ON A FIRST-NAME BASIS WITH A LOT OF FOLKS IN THE INDUSTRY. THEIR SALES ARE SO FAMOUS OTHER STORES TRY TO COPY THEM!
SHEESH, YOU SURE *SOUND* LIKE A HARD-CORE GEEK!
THE LIMITED EDITION FOR THIS GAME COMES WITH A CELLPHONE STRAP OF MASON RIDING HIS PET DOLPHIN! SQUEEEE!
IS THE STORE OPEN YET?
DOESN'T CARE.

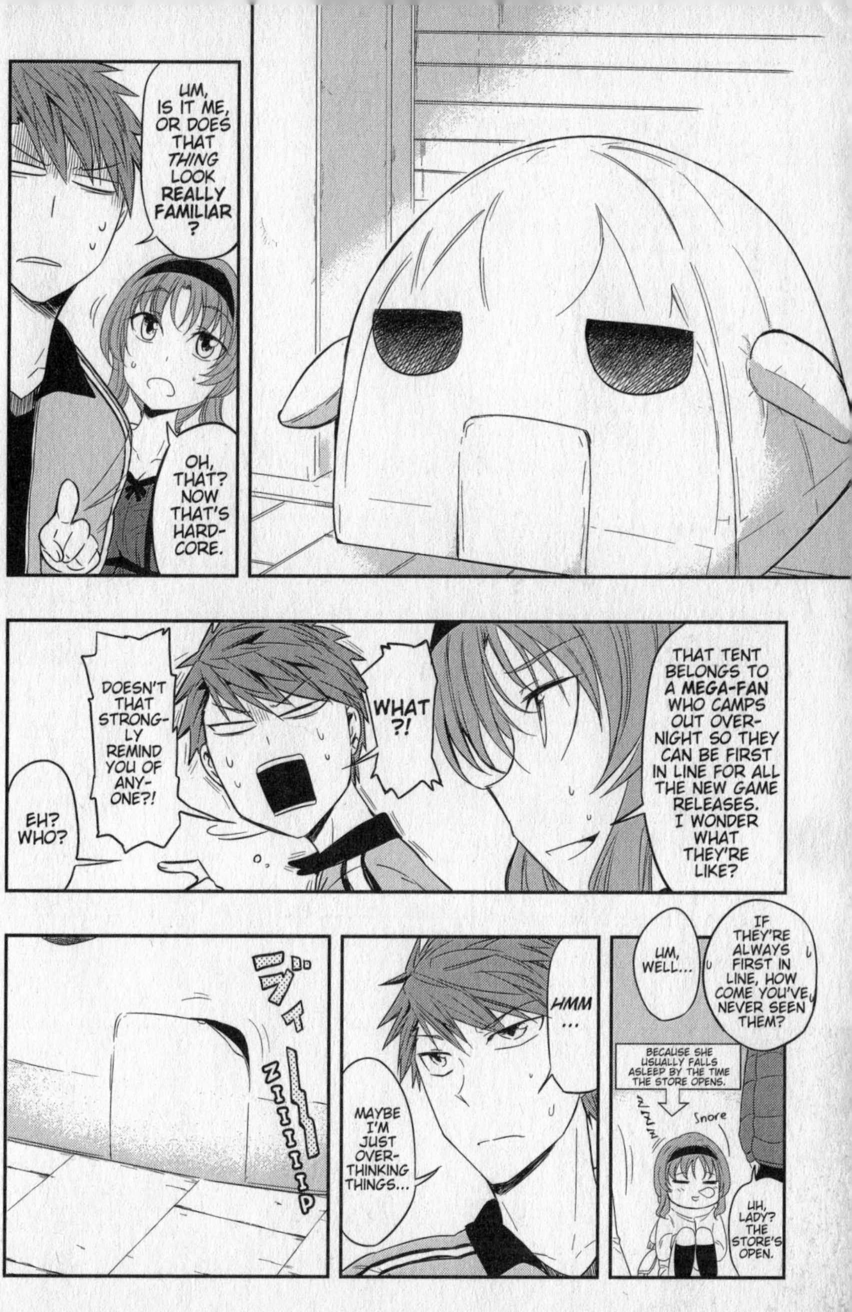
UM, IS IT ME, OR DOES THAT *THING* LOOK REALLY FAMILIAR?
OH, THAT? NOW THAT'S HARDCORE.
THAT TENT BELONGS TO A MEGA-FAN WHO CAMPS OUT OVERNIGHT SO THEY CAN BE FIRST IN LINE FOR ALL THE NEW GAME RELEASES. I WONDER WHAT THEY'RE LIKE?
WHAT?!
DOESN'T THAT STRONGLY REMIND YOU OF ANYONE?!
EH? WHO?
IF THEY'RE ALWAYS FIRST IN LINE, HOW COME YOU'VE NEVER SEEN THEM?
UM, WELL...
BECAUSE SHE USUALLY FALLS ASLEEP BY THE TIME THE STORE OPENS.
Snore
UH, LADY? THE STORE'S OPEN.
HMM...
MAYBE I'M JUST OVER-THINKING THINGS...
ZIIIIIIP

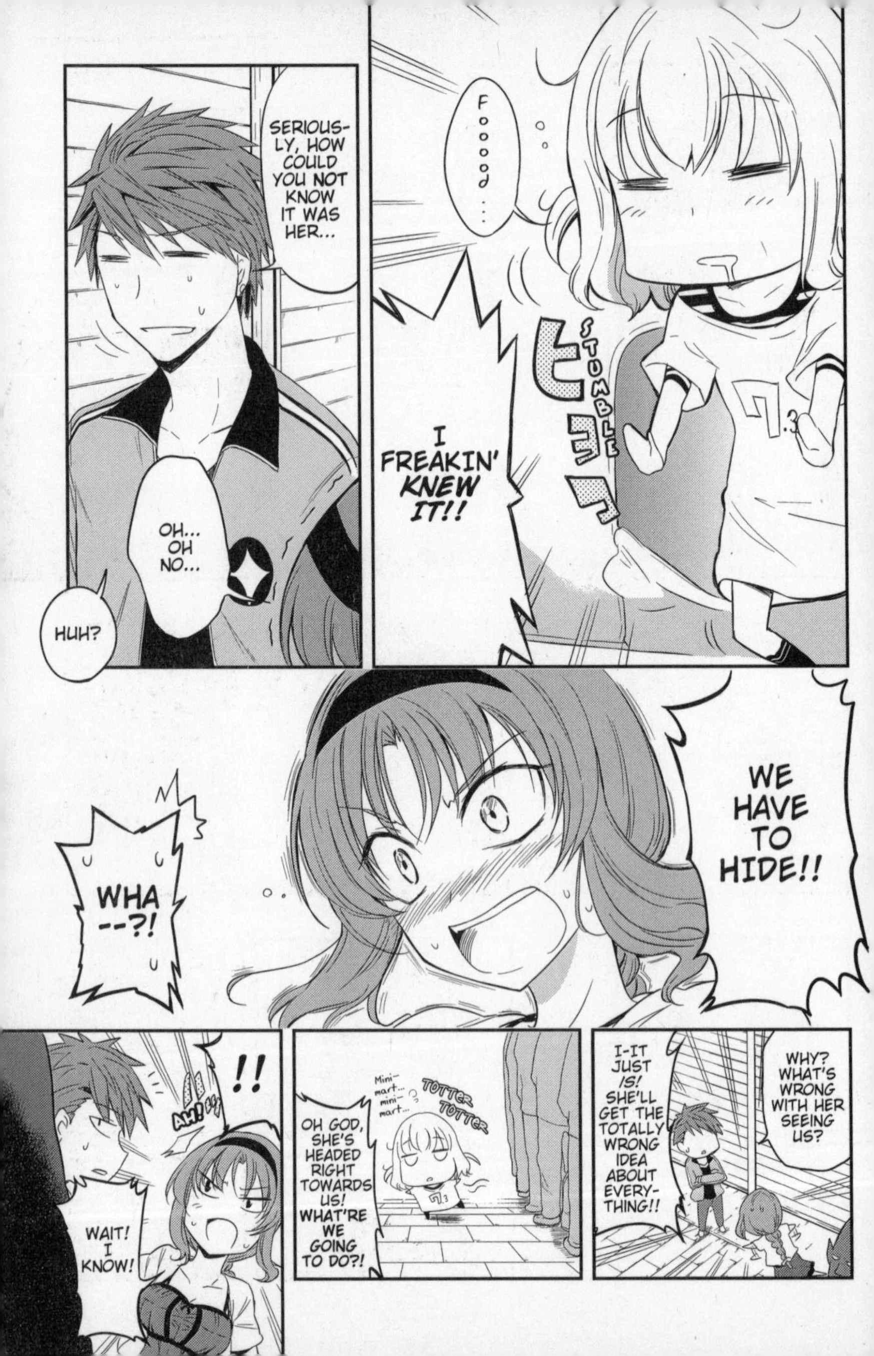
Foooood...
STUMBLE
I FREAKIN' KNEW IT!!
SERIOUSLY, HOW COULD YOU NOT KNOW IT WAS HER...
OH... OH NO...
HUH?
WE HAVE TO HIDE!!
WHA--?!
WHY? WHAT'S WRONG WITH HER SEEING US?
I-IT JUST IS! SHE'LL GET THE TOTALLY WRONG IDEA ABOUT EVERYTHING!!
TOTTER TOTTER
Mini-mart... mini-mart...
OH GOD, SHE'S HEADED RIGHT TOWARDS US! WHAT'RE WE GOING TO DO?!
!!
AH!
WAIT! I KNOW!

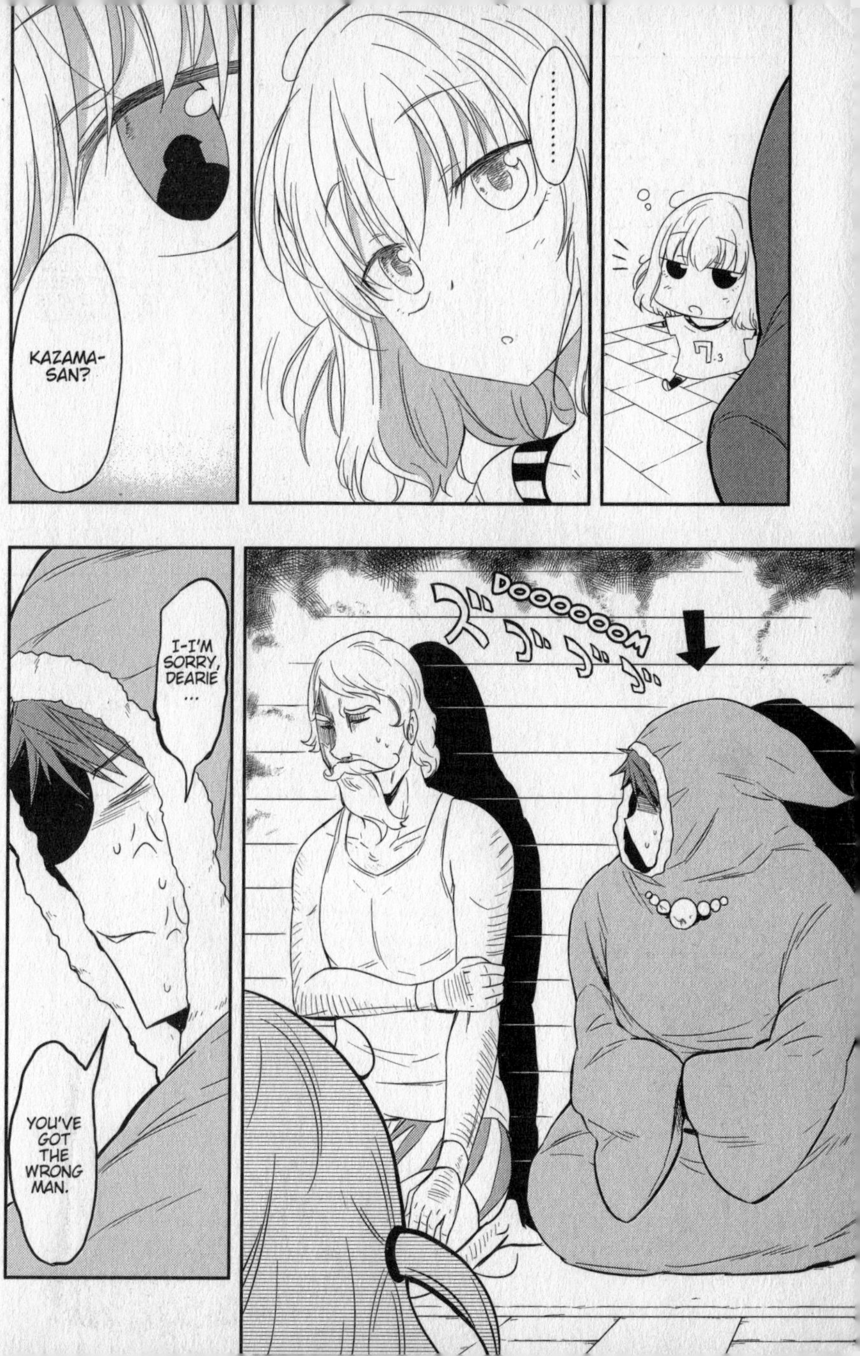

......
KAZAMA-SAN?
DOOOOOOOM
I-I'M SORRY, DEARIE ...
YOU'VE GOT THE WRONG MAN.

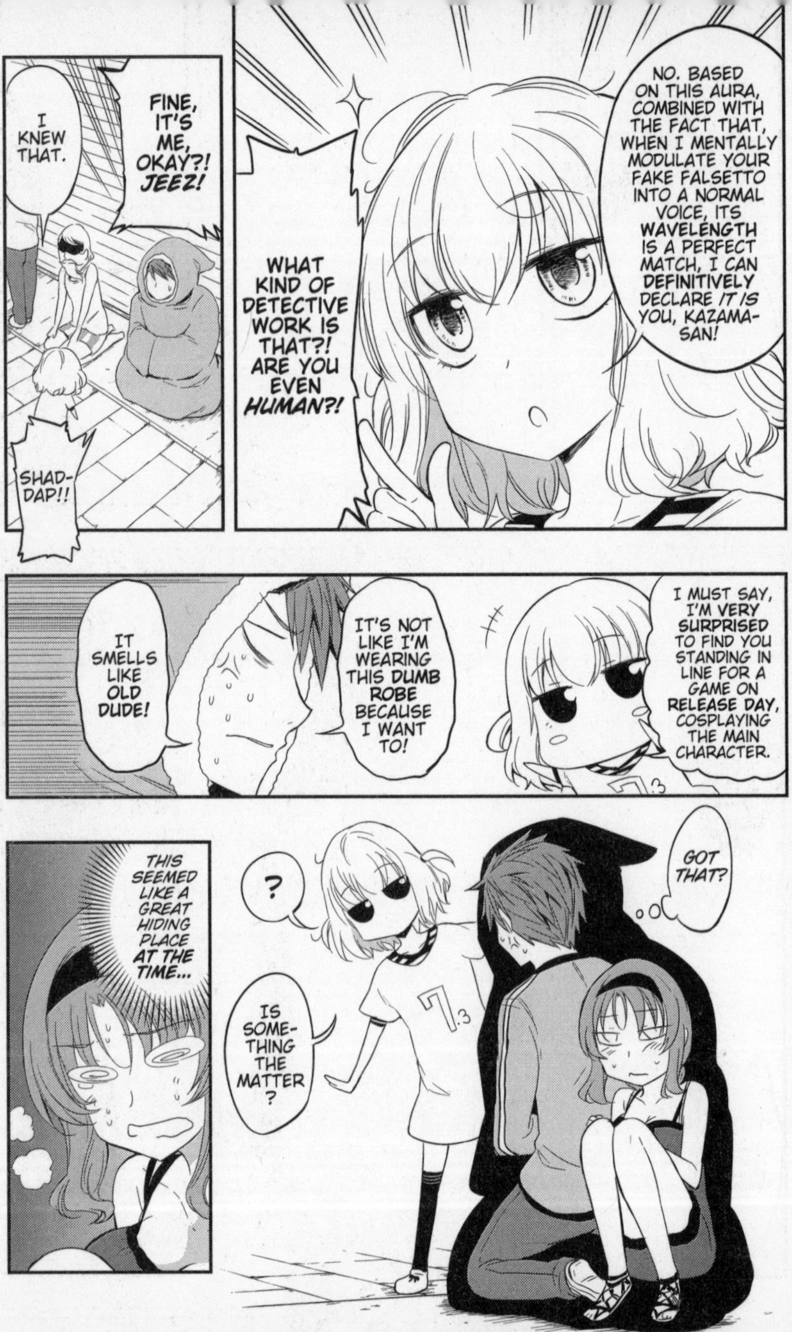
NO. BASED ON THIS AURA, COMBINED WITH THE FACT THAT, WHEN I MENTALLY MODULATE YOUR FAKE FALSETTO INTO A NORMAL VOICE, ITS WAVELENGTH IS A PERFECT MATCH, I CAN DEFINITIVELY DECLARE *IT IS* YOU, KAZAMA-SAN!
WHAT KIND OF DETECTIVE WORK IS THAT?! ARE YOU EVEN *HUMAN?!*
FINE, IT'S ME, OKAY?! *JEEZ!*
I KNEW THAT.
SHAD-DAP!!
I MUST SAY, I'M VERY SURPRISED TO FIND YOU STANDING IN LINE FOR A GAME ON RELEASE DAY, COSPLAYING THE MAIN CHARACTER.
IT'S NOT LIKE I'M WEARING THIS DUMB ROBE BECAUSE I WANT TO!
IT SMELLS LIKE OLD DUDE!
GOT THAT?
?
IS SOMETHING THE MATTER?
THIS SEEMED LIKE A GREAT HIDING PLACE AT THE TIME...

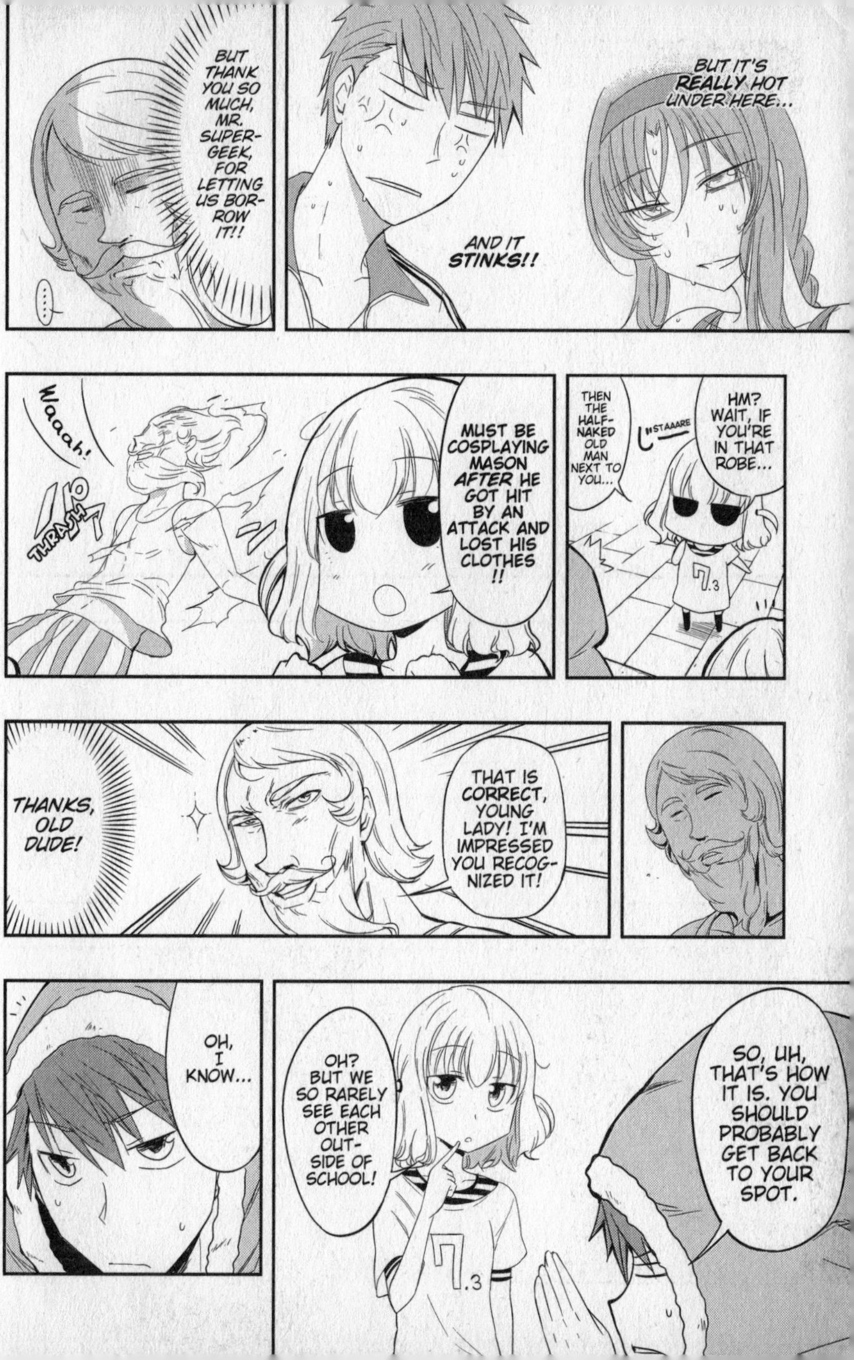
BUT IT'S REALLY HOT UNDER HERE...
AND IT STINKS!!
BUT THANK YOU SO MUCH, MR. SUPER-GEEK, FOR LETTING US BORROW IT!!
......
HM? WAIT, IF YOU'RE IN THAT ROBE...
STAAARE
THEN THE HALF-NAKED OLD MAN NEXT TO YOU...
MUST BE COSPLAYING MASON AFTER HE GOT HIT BY AN ATTACK AND LOST HIS CLOTHES!!
Waaaah!
THRASH
THAT IS CORRECT, YOUNG LADY! I'M IMPRESSED YOU RECOGNIZED IT!
THANKS, OLD DUDE!
SO, UH, THAT'S HOW IT IS. YOU SHOULD PROBABLY GET BACK TO YOUR SPOT.
OH? BUT WE SO RARELY SEE EACH OTHER OUTSIDE OF SCHOOL!
OH, I KNOW...

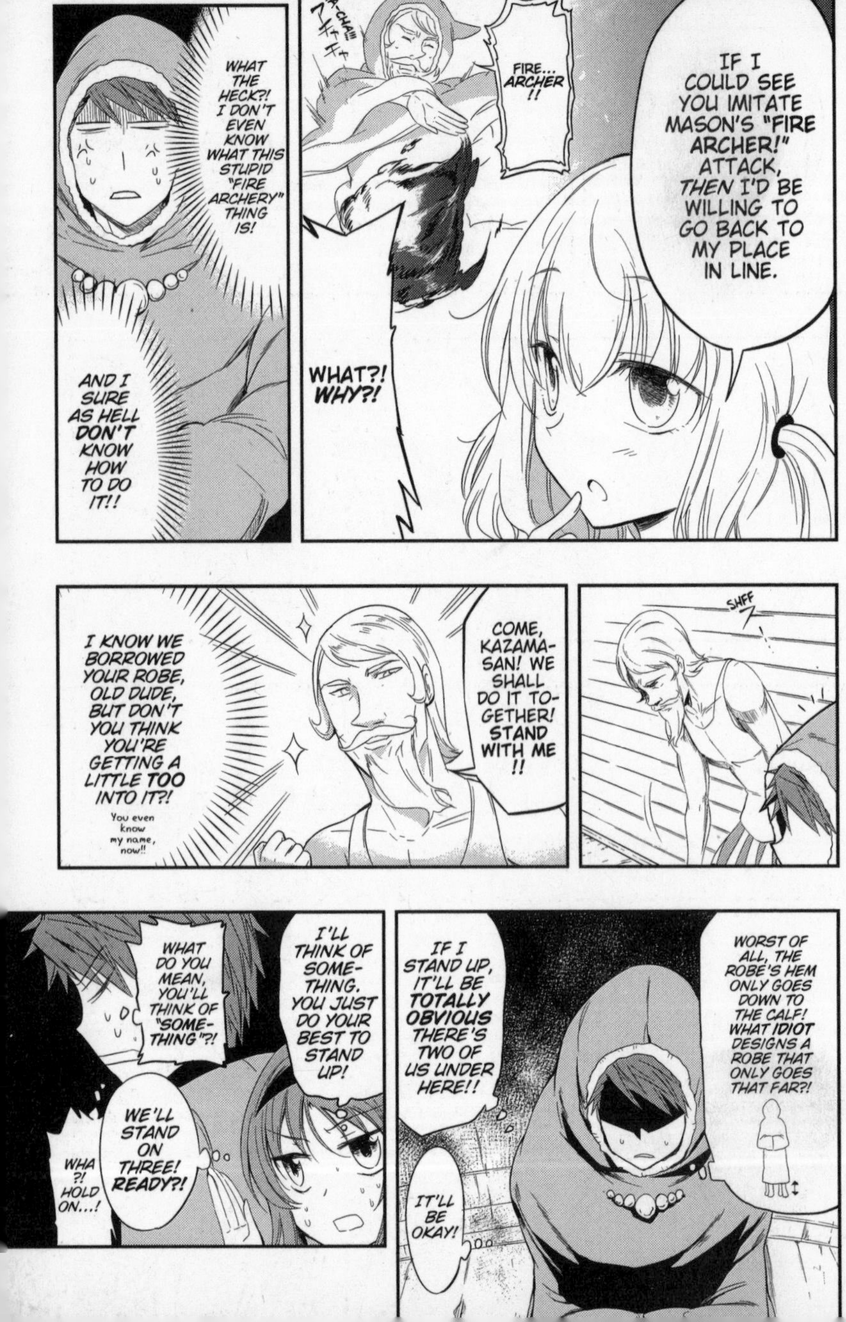
IF I COULD SEE YOU IMITATE MASON'S "FIRE ARCHER!" ATTACK, THEN I'D BE WILLING TO GO BACK TO MY PLACE IN LINE.
HA-CHA!!
FIRE... ARCHER!!
WHAT?! WHY?!
WHAT THE HECK?! I DON'T EVEN KNOW WHAT THIS STUPID "FIRE ARCHERY" THING IS!
AND I SURE AS HELL DON'T KNOW HOW TO DO IT!!
SHFF
COME, KAZAMA-SAN! WE SHALL DO IT TOGETHER! STAND WITH ME!!
I KNOW WE BORROWED YOUR ROBE, OLD DUDE, BUT DON'T YOU THINK YOU'RE GETTING A LITTLE TOO INTO IT?!
You even know my name, now!!
WORST OF ALL, THE ROBE'S HEM ONLY GOES DOWN TO THE CALF! WHAT IDIOT DESIGNS A ROBE THAT ONLY GOES THAT FAR?!
IF I STAND UP, IT'LL BE TOTALLY OBVIOUS THERE'S TWO OF US UNDER HERE!!
IT'LL BE OKAY!
I'LL THINK OF SOMETHING. YOU JUST DO YOUR BEST TO STAND UP!
WHAT DO YOU MEAN, YOU'LL THINK OF "SOMETHING"?!
WE'LL STAND ON THREE! READY?!
WHA?! HOLD ON...!

ONE!

TWO!

THREE!!

HRAAAAGH!!

STAND

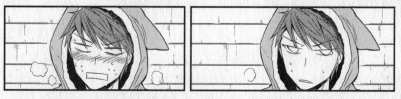

UUUM...

squiiish

I'M SORRY! I KNOW I'M REALLY HEAVY!

UM, IT'S NOT YOUR *WEIGHT* THAT'S THE PROBLEM. HOO BOY...

UHH... THIS IS A LITTLE, UM...

SQUEEE

EEE

EEEZ

OH, JEEZ, HIS SPIKY HAIR IS PRICK-ING ME...

FI-YAAAAH... ARCHER!!

COME ON, EVERYONE! DO IT TOGETHER WITH ME!

FWOOOOO

FWOOOOO

FWOOOO

!!

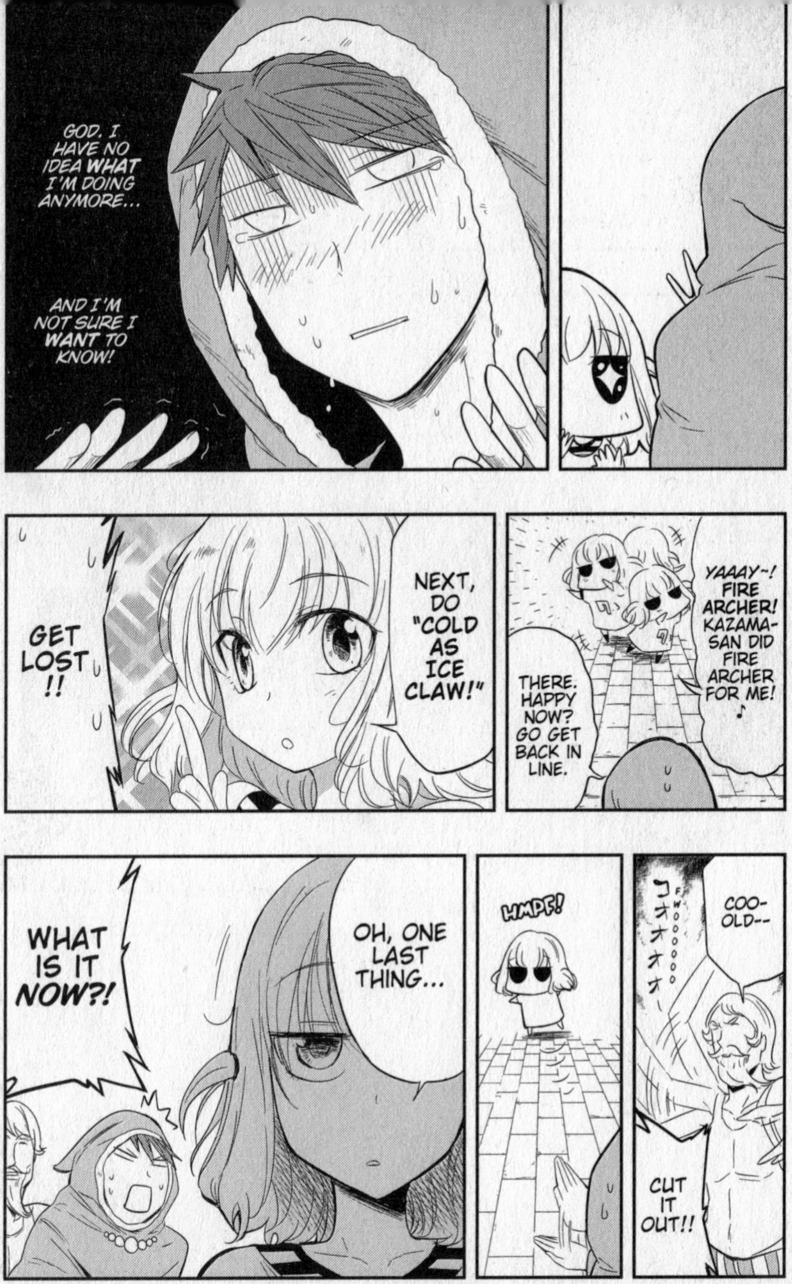
GOD. I HAVE NO IDEA WHAT I'M DOING ANYMORE...
AND I'M NOT SURE I WANT TO KNOW!
YAAAY~! FIRE ARCHER! KAZAMA-SAN DID FIRE ARCHER FOR ME! ♪
THERE. HAPPY NOW? GO GET BACK IN LINE.
NEXT, DO "COLD AS ICE CLAW!"
GET LOST!!
COO-OLD--
FWOOOOOOO
CUT IT OUT!!
HMPF!
OH, ONE LAST THING...
WHAT IS IT NOW?!

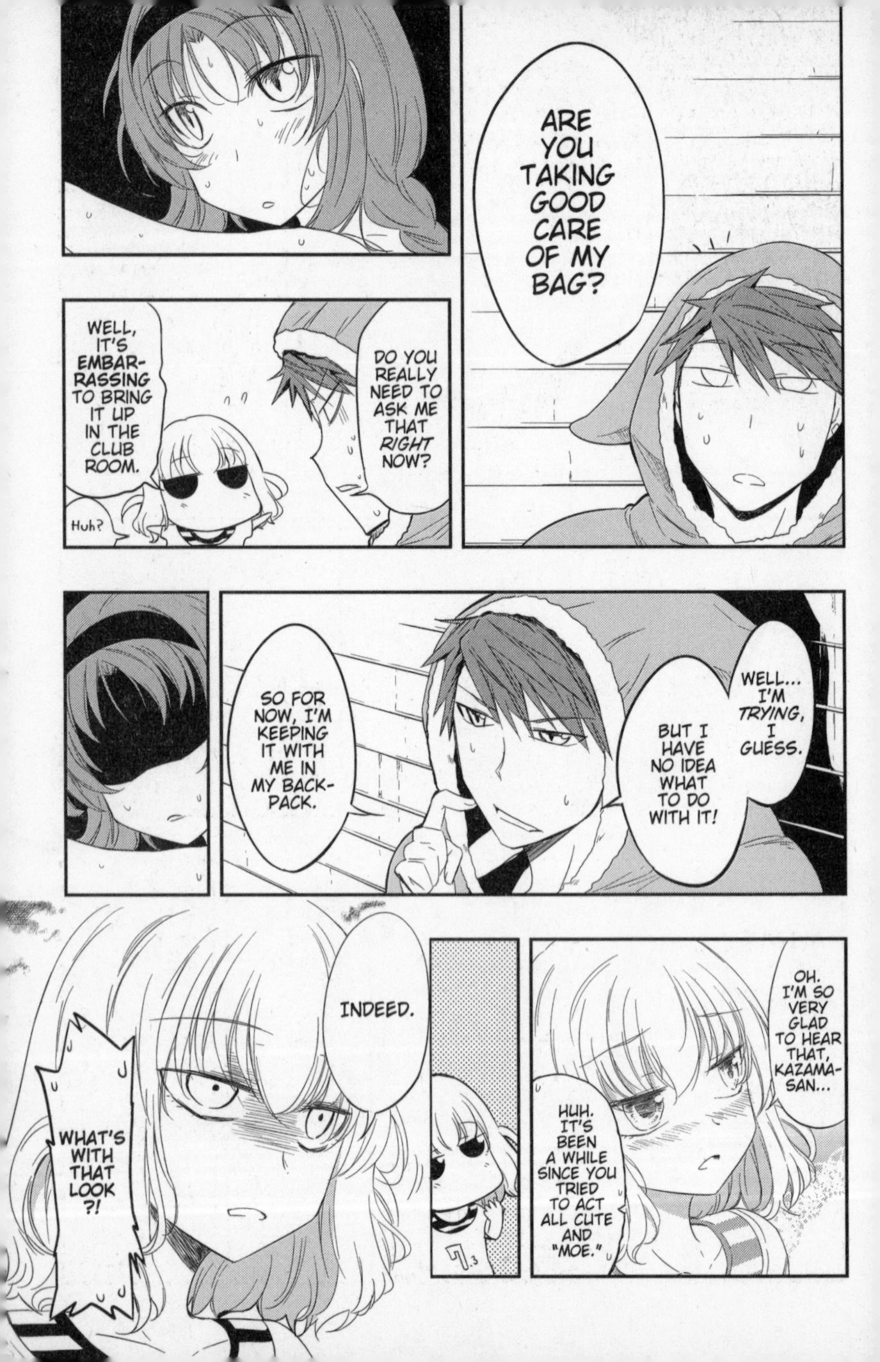
ARE YOU TAKING GOOD CARE OF MY BAG?
DO YOU REALLY NEED TO ASK ME THAT *RIGHT* NOW?
WELL, IT'S EMBARRASSING TO BRING IT UP IN THE CLUB ROOM.
Huh?
WELL... I'M *TRYING*, I GUESS.
BUT I HAVE NO IDEA WHAT TO DO WITH IT!
SO FOR NOW, I'M KEEPING IT WITH ME IN MY BACKPACK.
OH. I'M SO VERY GLAD TO HEAR THAT, KAZAMA-SAN...
HUH. IT'S BEEN A WHILE SINCE YOU TRIED TO ACT ALL CUTE AND "MOE."
INDEED.
WHAT'S WITH THAT LOOK?!

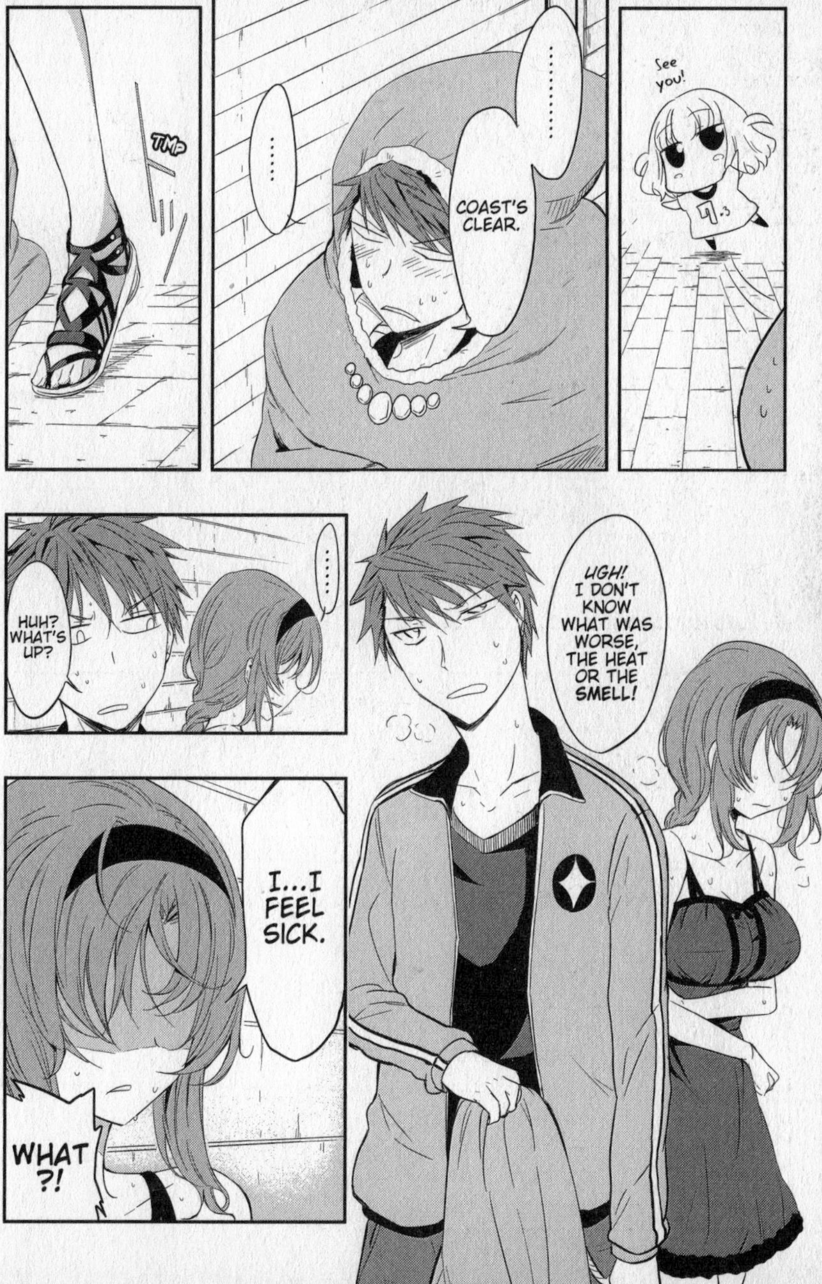
See you!
......
COAST'S CLEAR.
......
TMP
UGH! I DON'T KNOW WHAT WAS WORSE, THE HEAT OR THE SMELL!
......
HUH? WHAT'S UP?
I...I FEEL SICK.
WHAT?!

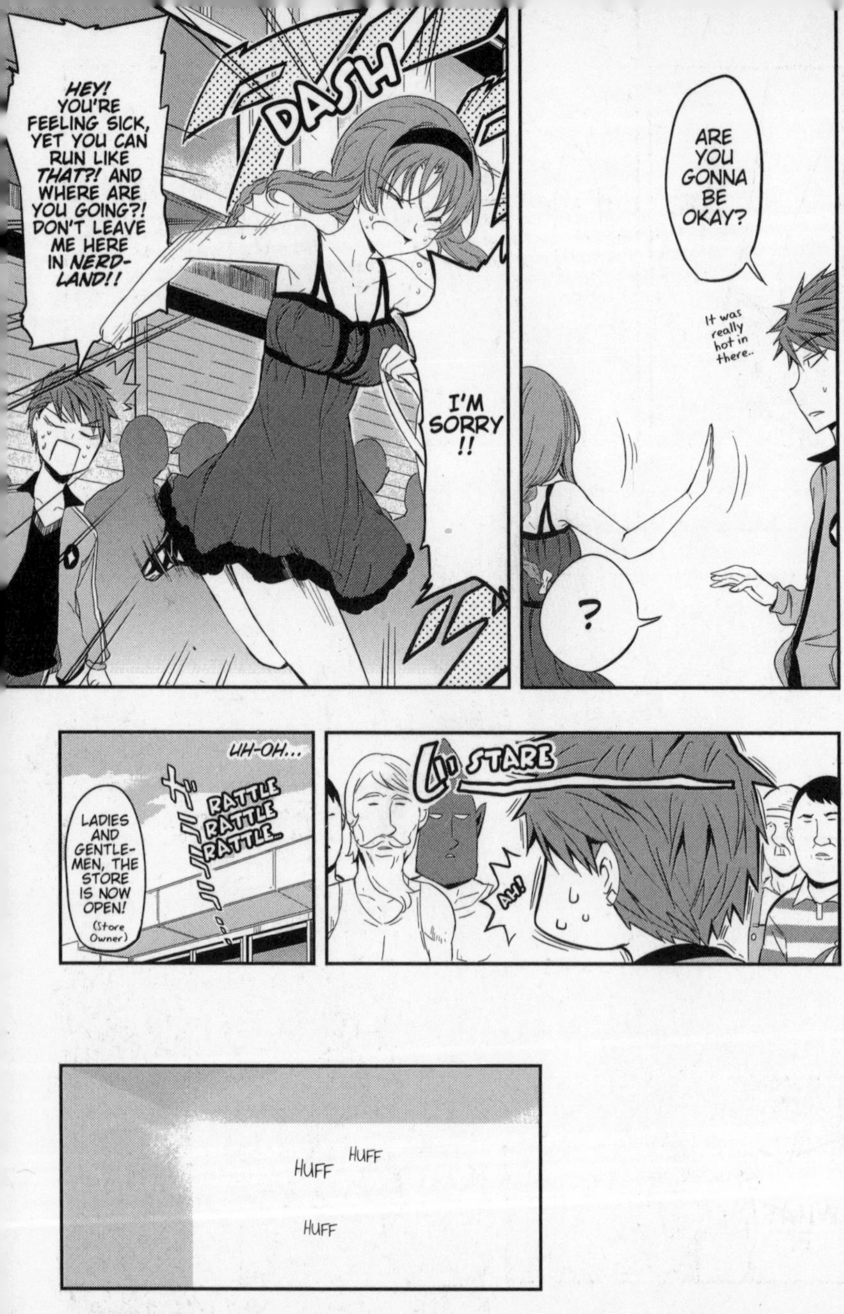
ARE YOU GONNA BE OKAY?
It was really hot in there..
?
DASH
HEY! YOU'RE FEELING SICK, YET YOU CAN RUN LIKE THAT?! AND WHERE ARE YOU GOING?! DON'T LEAVE ME HERE IN NERD-LAND!!
I'M SORRY!!
STARE
AH!
UH-OH...
RATTLE RATTLE RATTLE...
LADIES AND GENTLE-MEN, THE STORE IS NOW OPEN! (Store Owner)
HUFF
HUFF
HUFF

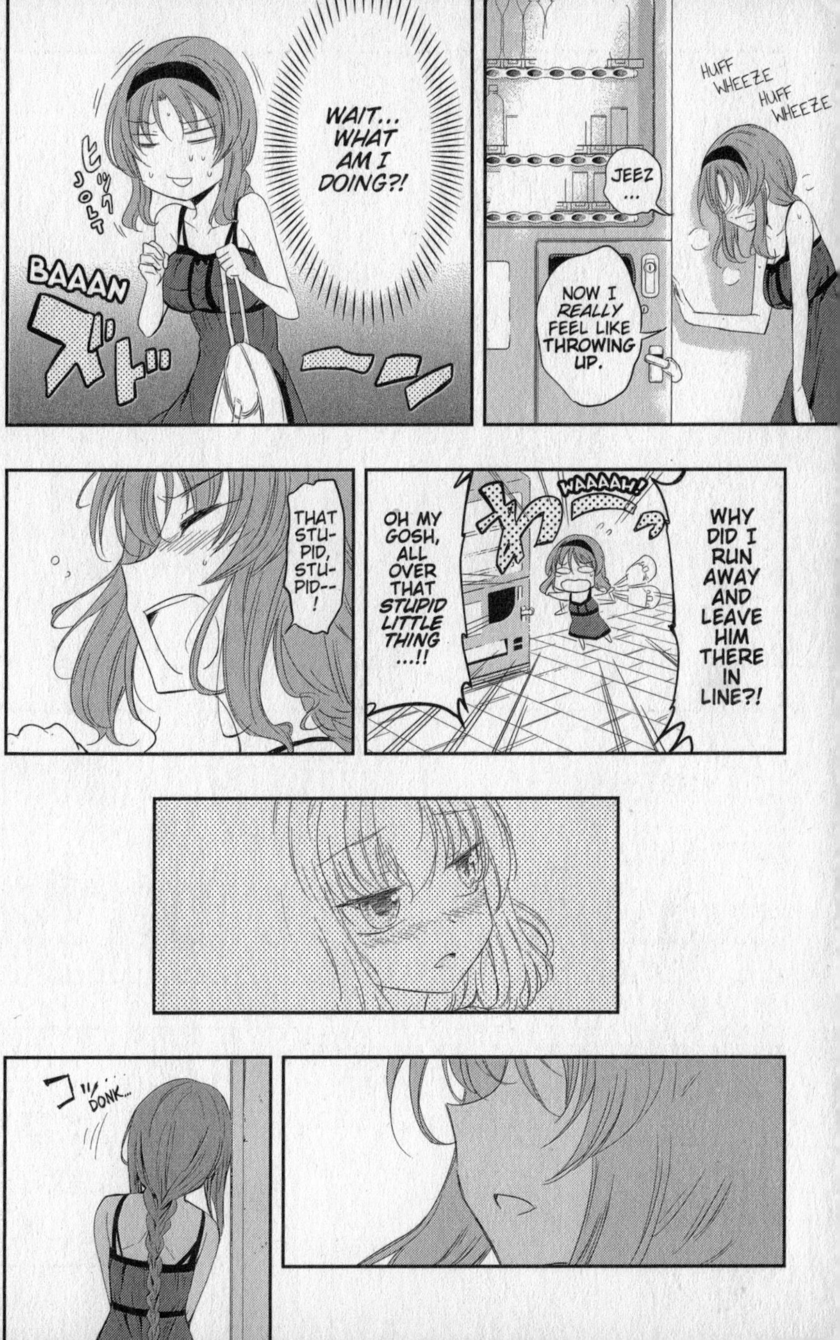
HUFF WHEEZE HUFF WHEEZE
JEEZ...
NOW I REALLY FEEL LIKE THROWING UP.
JOLT
WAIT... WHAT AM I DOING?!
BAAAN
WHY DID I RUN AWAY AND LEAVE HIM THERE IN LINE?!
WAAAAH!
OH MY GOSH, ALL OVER THAT STUPID LITTLE THING...!!
THAT STU-PID, STU-PID--!
DONK...

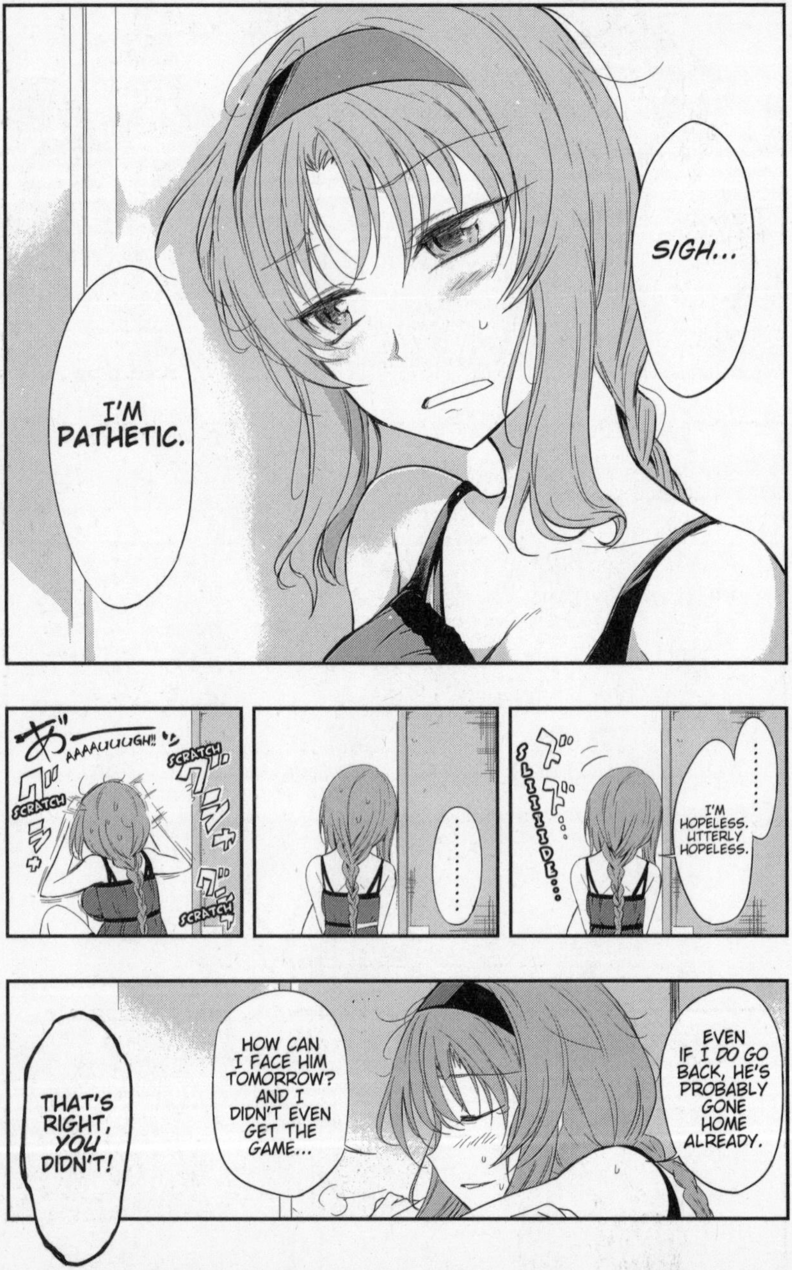
SIGH...
I'M PATHETIC.
......
I'M HOPELESS. UTTERLY HOPELESS.
SLIIIIIDE...
....
AAAAUUUGH!!
SCRATCH
SCRATCH
SCRATCH
EVEN IF I *DO* GO BACK, HE'S PROBABLY GONE HOME ALREADY.
HOW CAN I FACE HIM TOMORROW? AND I DIDN'T EVEN GET THE GAME...
THAT'S RIGHT, *YOU* DIDN'T!

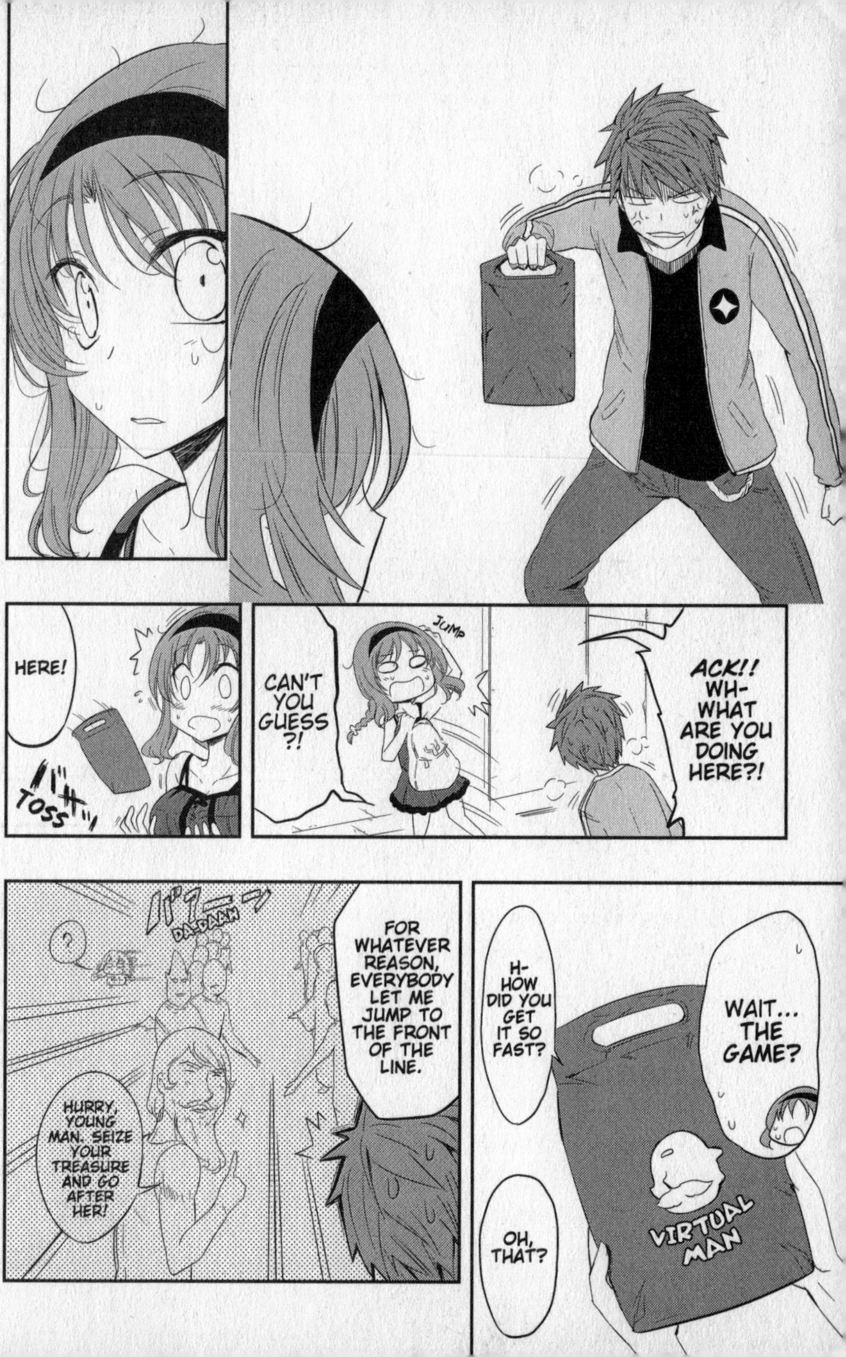
ACK!! WH-WHAT ARE YOU DOING HERE?!
JUMP
CAN'T YOU GUESS?!
HERE!
TOSS
WAIT... THE GAME?
H-HOW DID YOU GET IT SO FAST?
VIRTUAL MAN
OH, THAT?
FOR WHATEVER REASON, EVERYBODY LET ME JUMP TO THE FRONT OF THE LINE.
DA-DAAAH
?
HURRY, YOUNG MAN. SEIZE YOUR TREASURE AND GO AFTER HER!

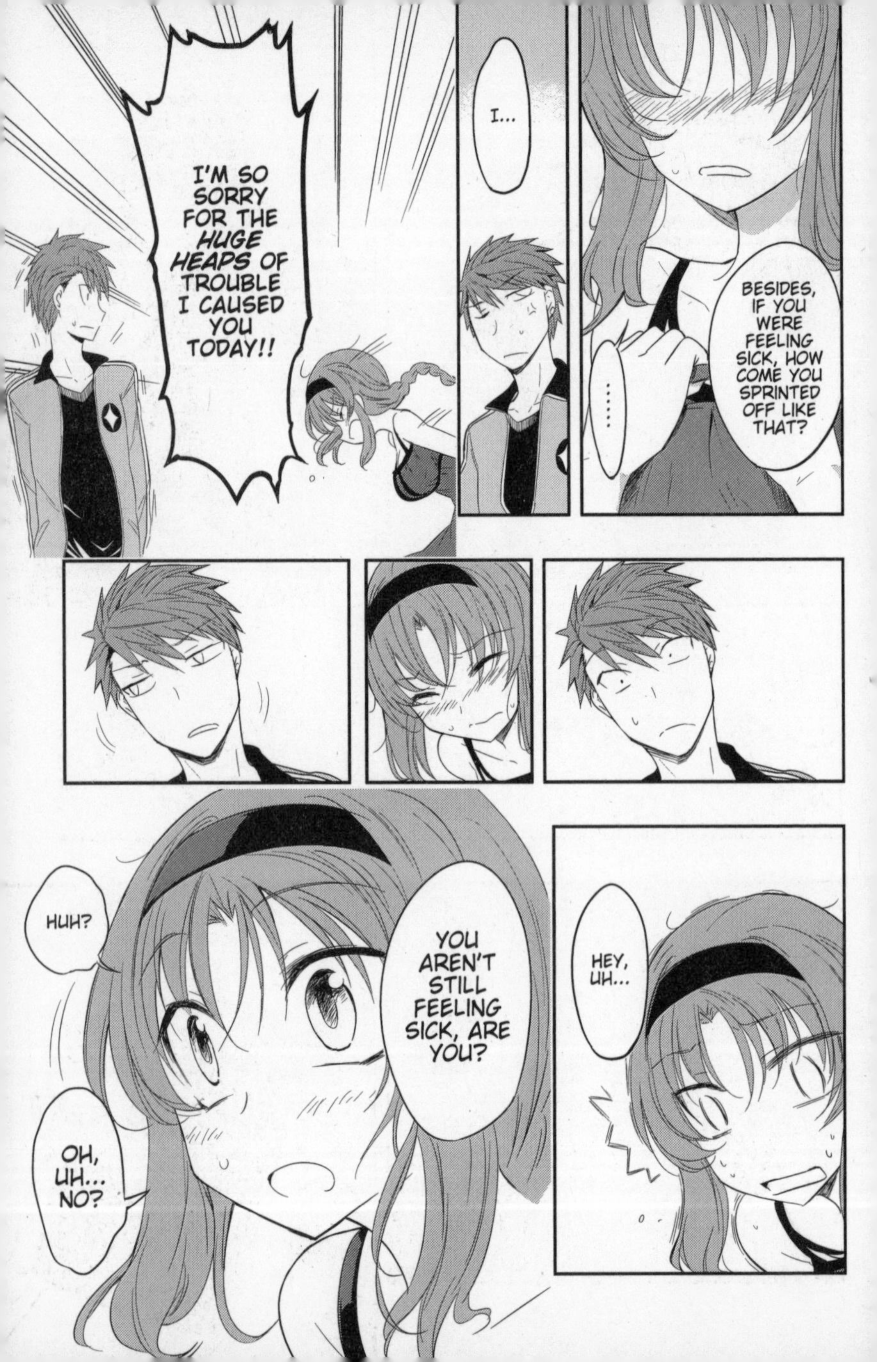
BESIDES, IF YOU WERE FEELING SICK, HOW COME YOU SPRINTED OFF LIKE THAT?
......
I...
I'M SO SORRY FOR THE HUGE HEAPS OF TROUBLE I CAUSED YOU TODAY!!
HEY, UH...
YOU AREN'T STILL FEELING SICK, ARE YOU?
HUH?
OH, UH... NO?

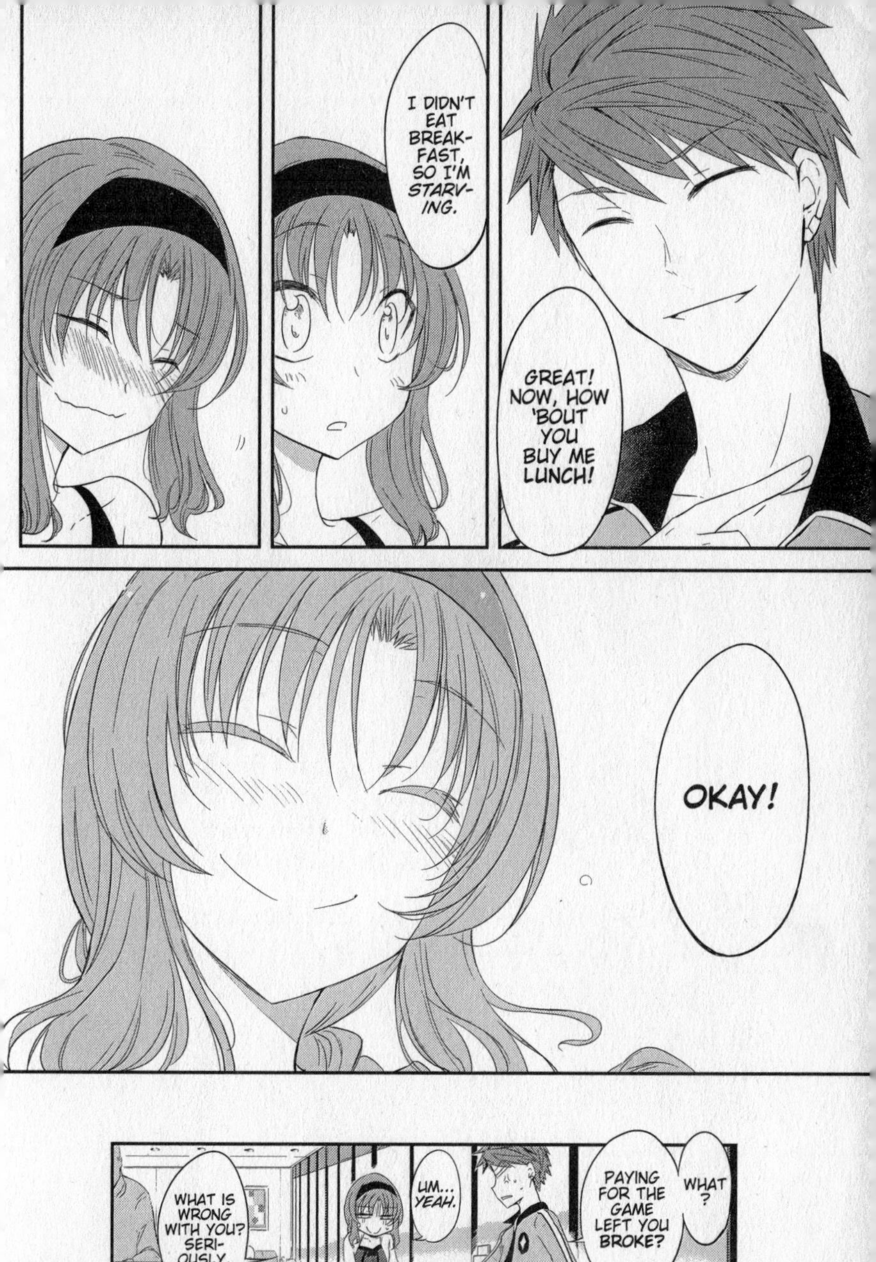
GREAT! NOW, HOW 'BOUT YOU BUY ME LUNCH!
I DIDN'T EAT BREAK-FAST, SO I'M STARV-ING.
OKAY!
WHAT?
PAYING FOR THE GAME LEFT YOU BROKE?
UM... YEAH.
WHAT IS WRONG WITH YOU? SERI-OUSLY.

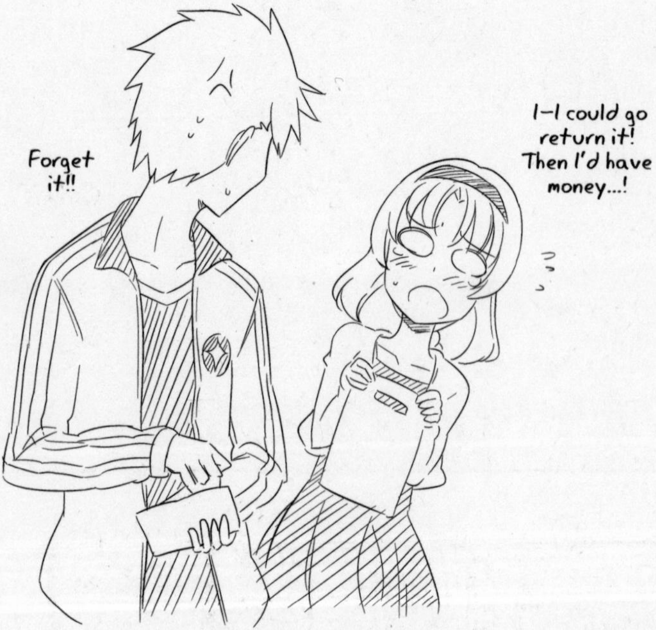
I-I could go return it! Then I'd have money...!
Forget it!!

D-FRAGMENTS
ディーふらぐ!

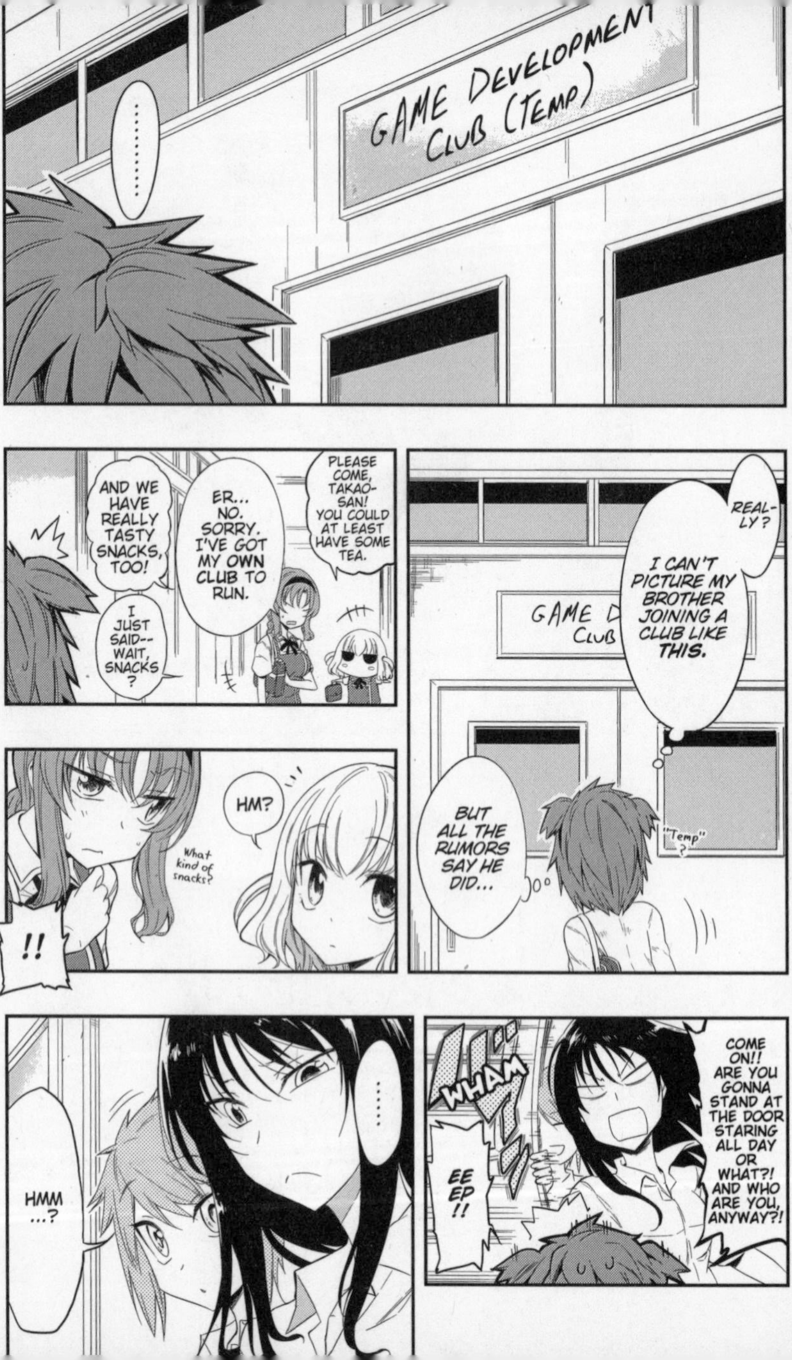
GAME DEVELOPMENT CLUB (TEMP)
......
REAL-LY?
I CAN'T PICTURE MY BROTHER JOINING A CLUB LIKE THIS.
BUT ALL THE RUMORS SAY HE DID...
"Temp"?
PLEASE COME, TAKAO-SAN! YOU COULD AT LEAST HAVE SOME TEA.
ER... NO. SORRY. I'VE GOT MY OWN CLUB TO RUN.
AND WE HAVE REALLY TASTY SNACKS, TOO!
I JUST SAID-- WAIT, SNACKS?
HM?
What kind of snacks?
!!
COME ON!! ARE YOU GONNA STAND AT THE DOOR STARING ALL DAY OR WHAT?! AND WHO ARE YOU, ANYWAY?!
WHAM
EEEP!!
......
HMM ...?

Chapter 24
Really Incredible

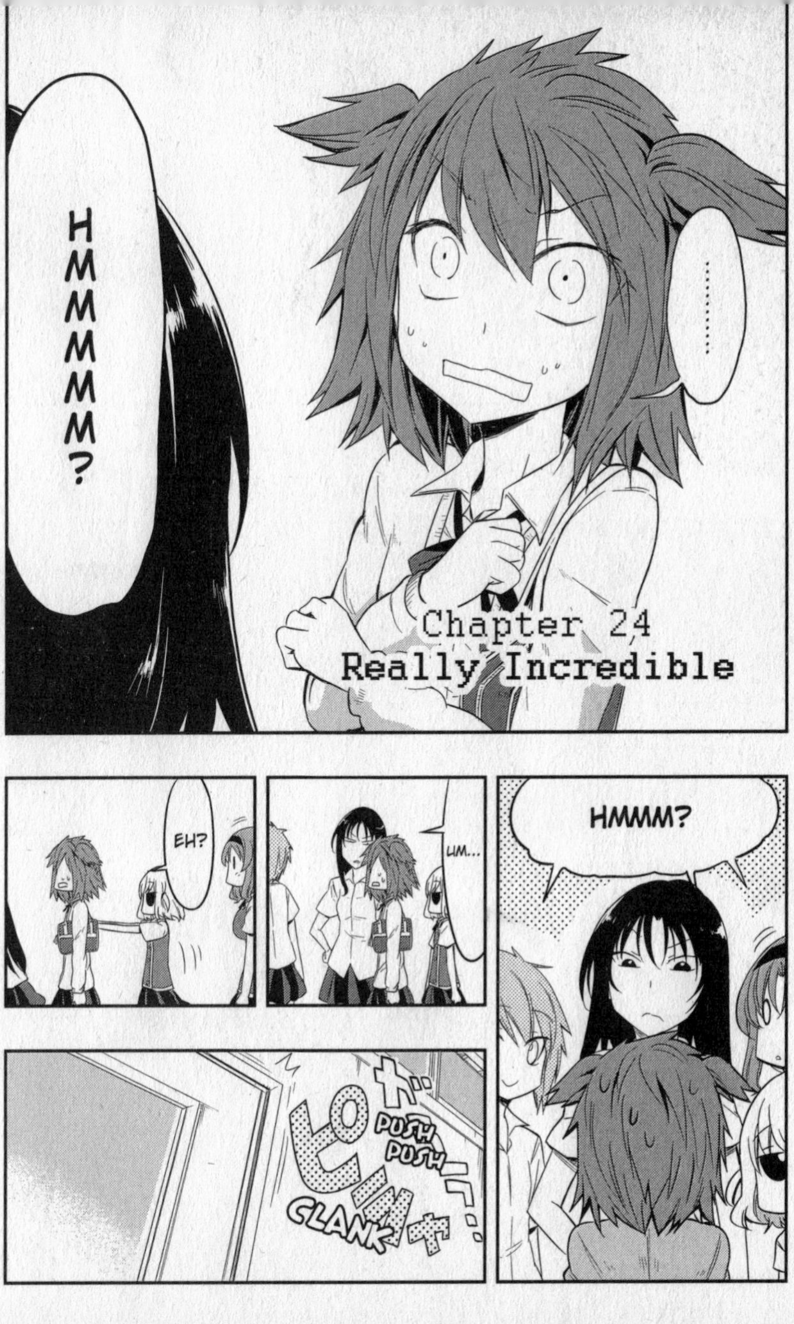
......
HMMMMMM?
HMMM?
UM...
EH?
PUSH
PUSH
CLANK

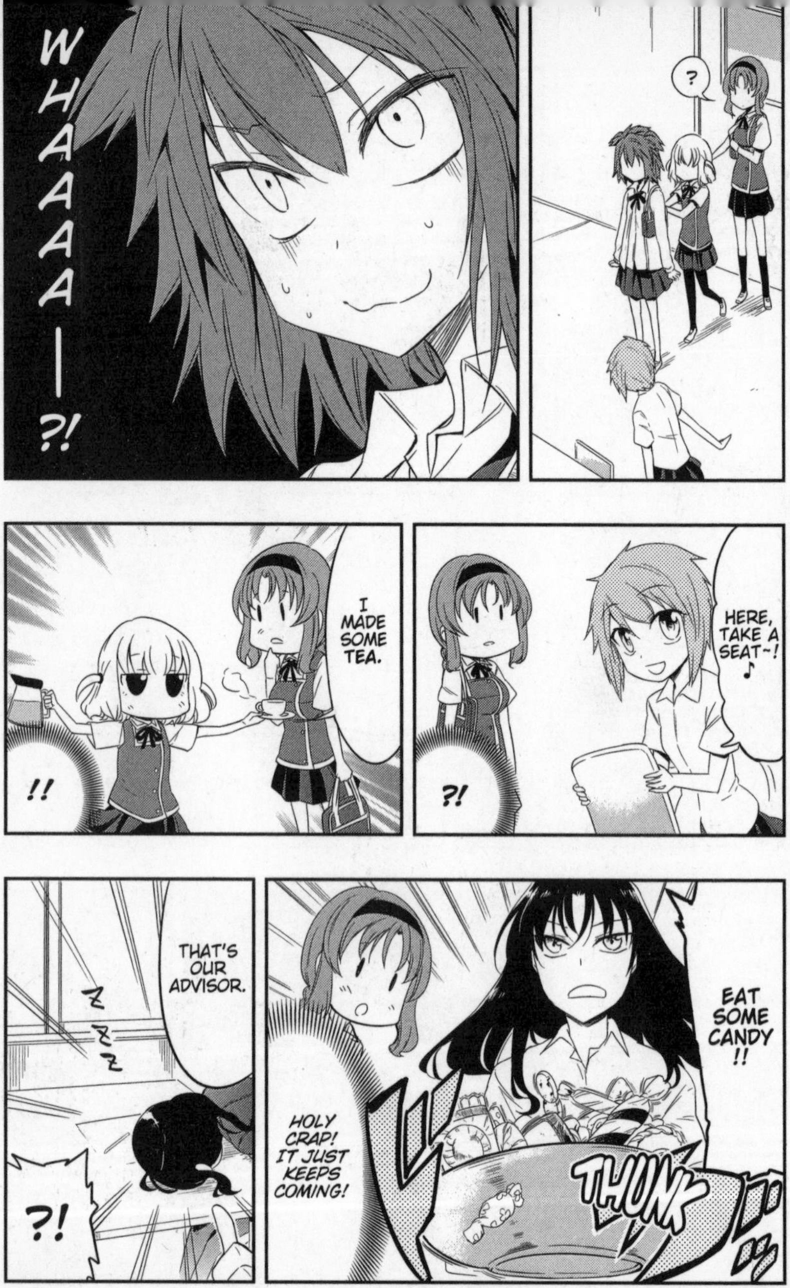
?
WHAAAAA—?!
HERE, TAKE A SEAT~! ♪
?!
I MADE SOME TEA.
!!
EAT SOME CANDY!!
THUNK
HOLY CRAP! IT JUST KEEPS COMING!
THAT'S OUR ADVISOR.
Z Z Z
?!

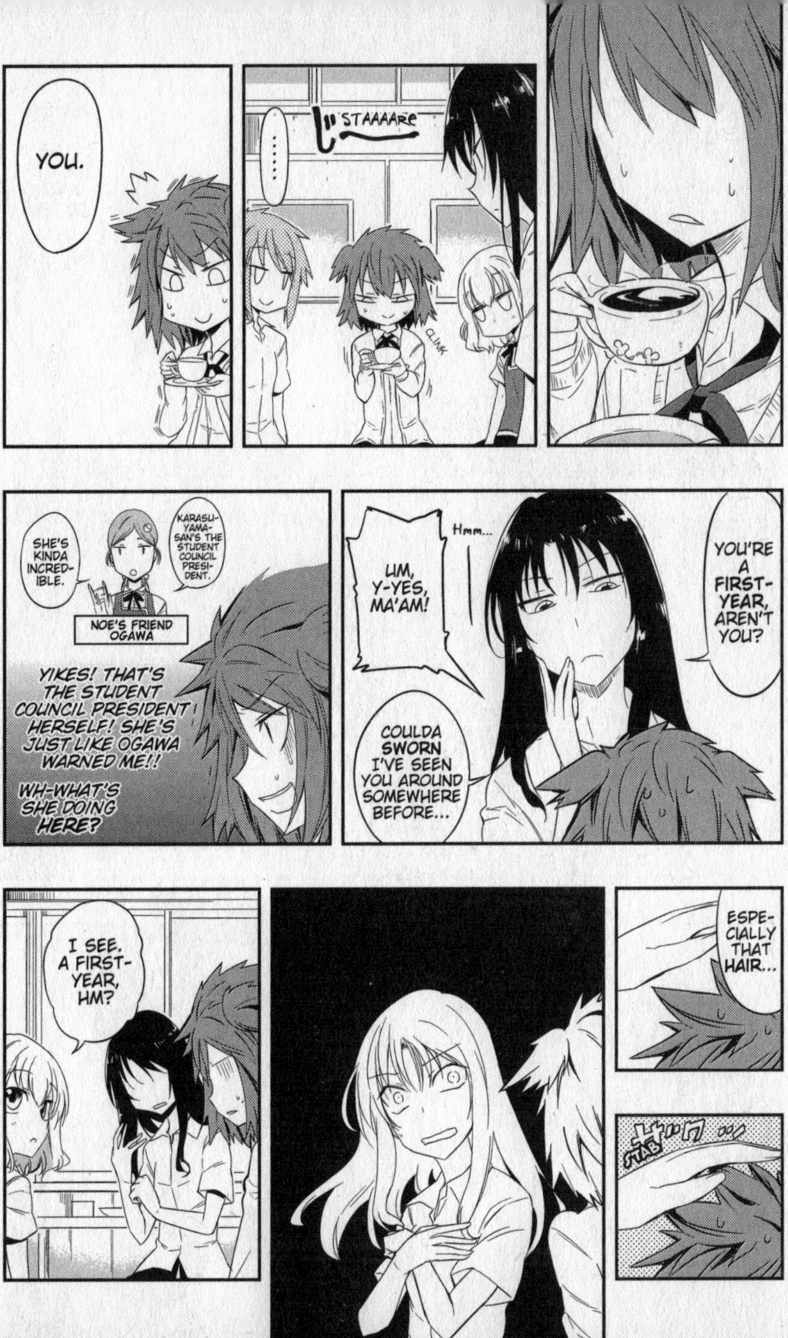
STAAAARE
......
CLINK
YOU.
YOU'RE A FIRST-YEAR, AREN'T YOU?
Hmm...
UM, Y-YES, MA'AM!
COULDA SWORN I'VE SEEN YOU AROUND SOMEWHERE BEFORE...
KARASUYAMA-SAN'S THE STUDENT COUNCIL PRESIDENT.
SHE'S KINDA INCREDIBLE.
NOE'S FRIEND OGAWA
YIKES! THAT'S THE STUDENT COUNCIL PRESIDENT HERSELF! SHE'S JUST LIKE OGAWA WARNED ME!!
WH-WHAT'S SHE DOING HERE?
ESPECIALLY THAT HAIR...
STAB
I SEE. A FIRST-YEAR, HM?

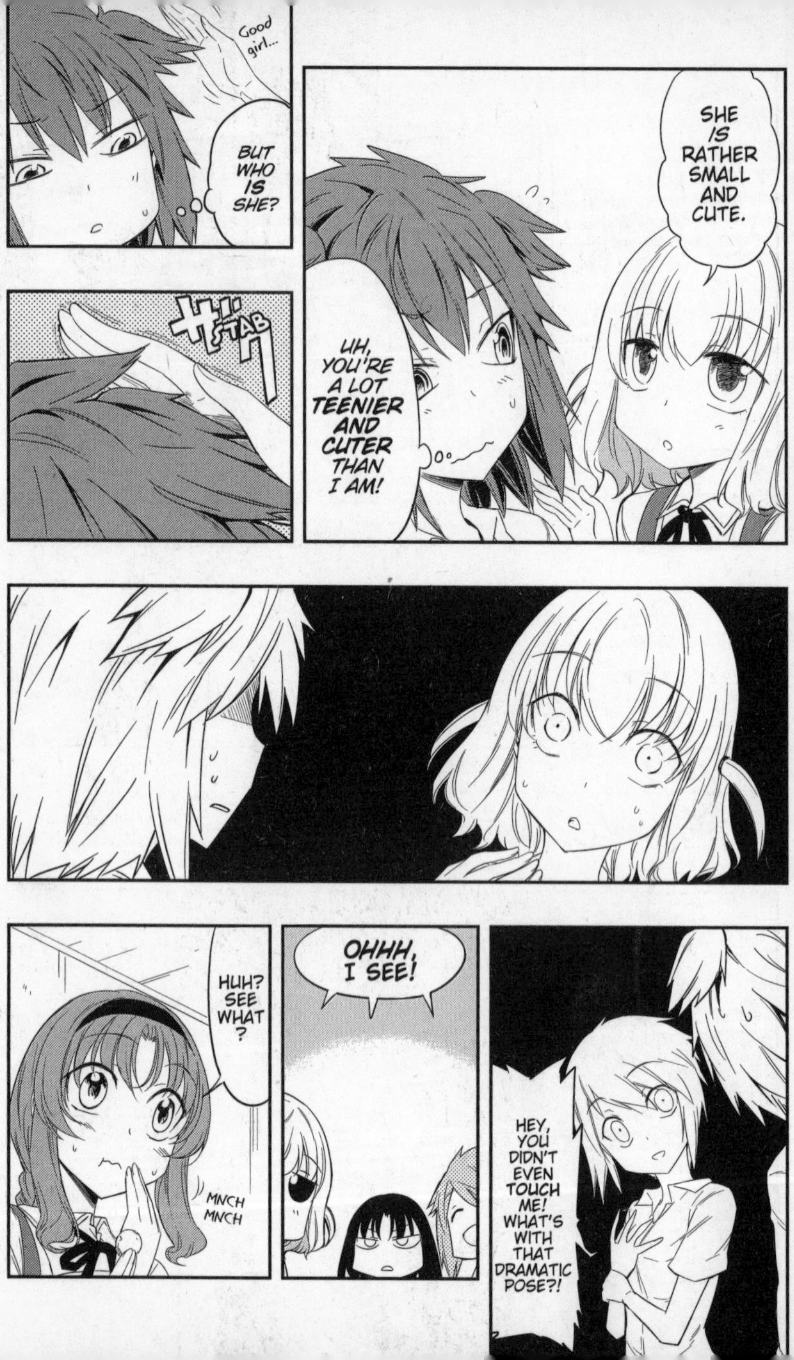
SHE IS RATHER SMALL AND CUTE.
UH, YOU'RE A LOT TEENIER AND CUTER THAN I AM!
Good girl...
BUT WHO IS SHE?
STAB
HEY, YOU DIDN'T EVEN TOUCH ME! WHAT'S WITH THAT DRAMATIC POSE?!
OHHH, I SEE!
HUH? SEE WHAT?
MNCH MNCH

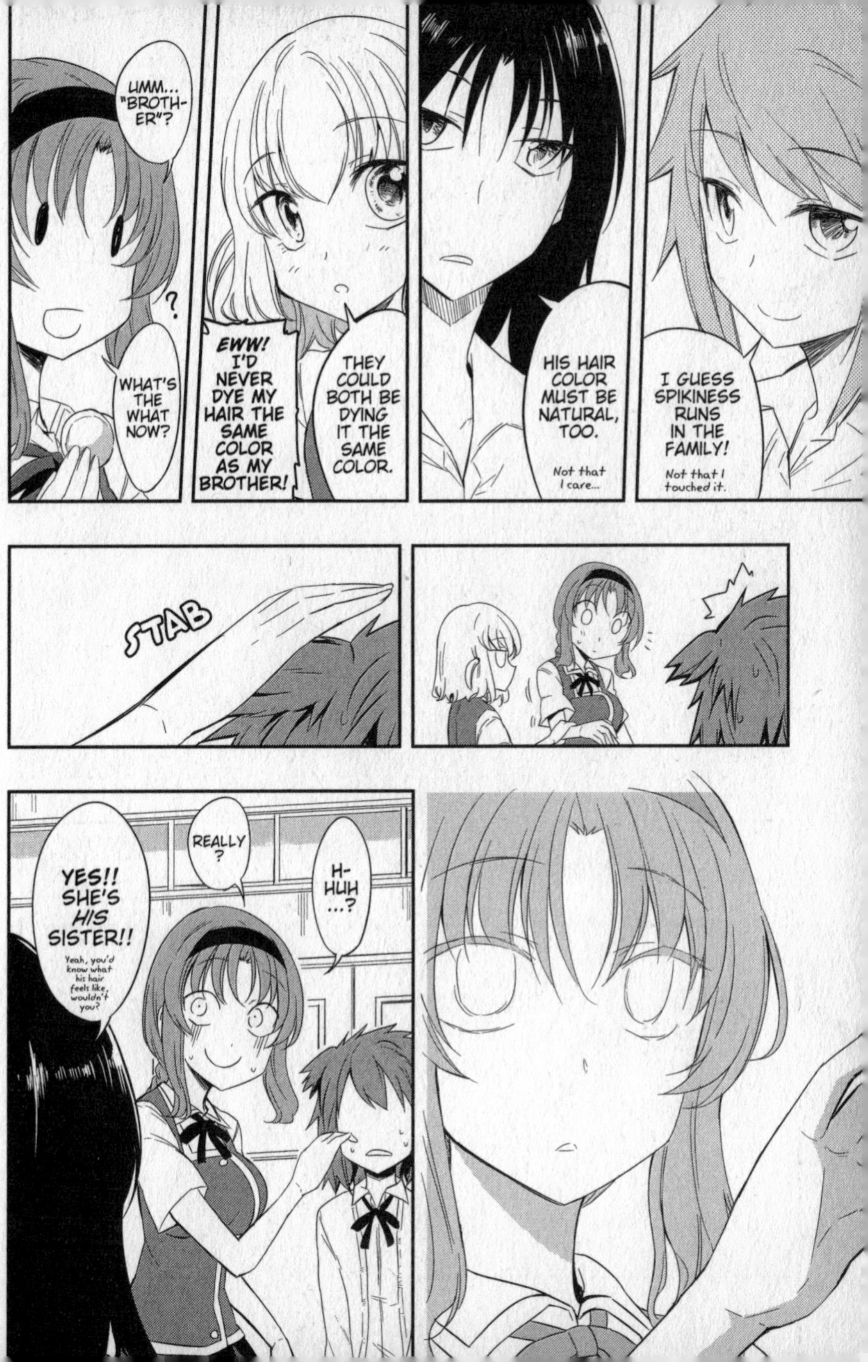
I GUESS SPIKINESS RUNS IN THE FAMILY!
Not that I touched it.
HIS HAIR COLOR MUST BE NATURAL, TOO.
Not that I care...
THEY COULD BOTH BE DYING IT THE SAME COLOR.
EWW! I'D NEVER DYE MY HAIR THE SAME COLOR AS MY BROTHER!
UMMM... "BROTHER"?
?
WHAT'S THE WHAT NOW?
STAB
H-HUH...?
REALLY?
YES!! SHE'S HIS SISTER!!
Yeah, you'd know what his hair feels like, wouldn't you?

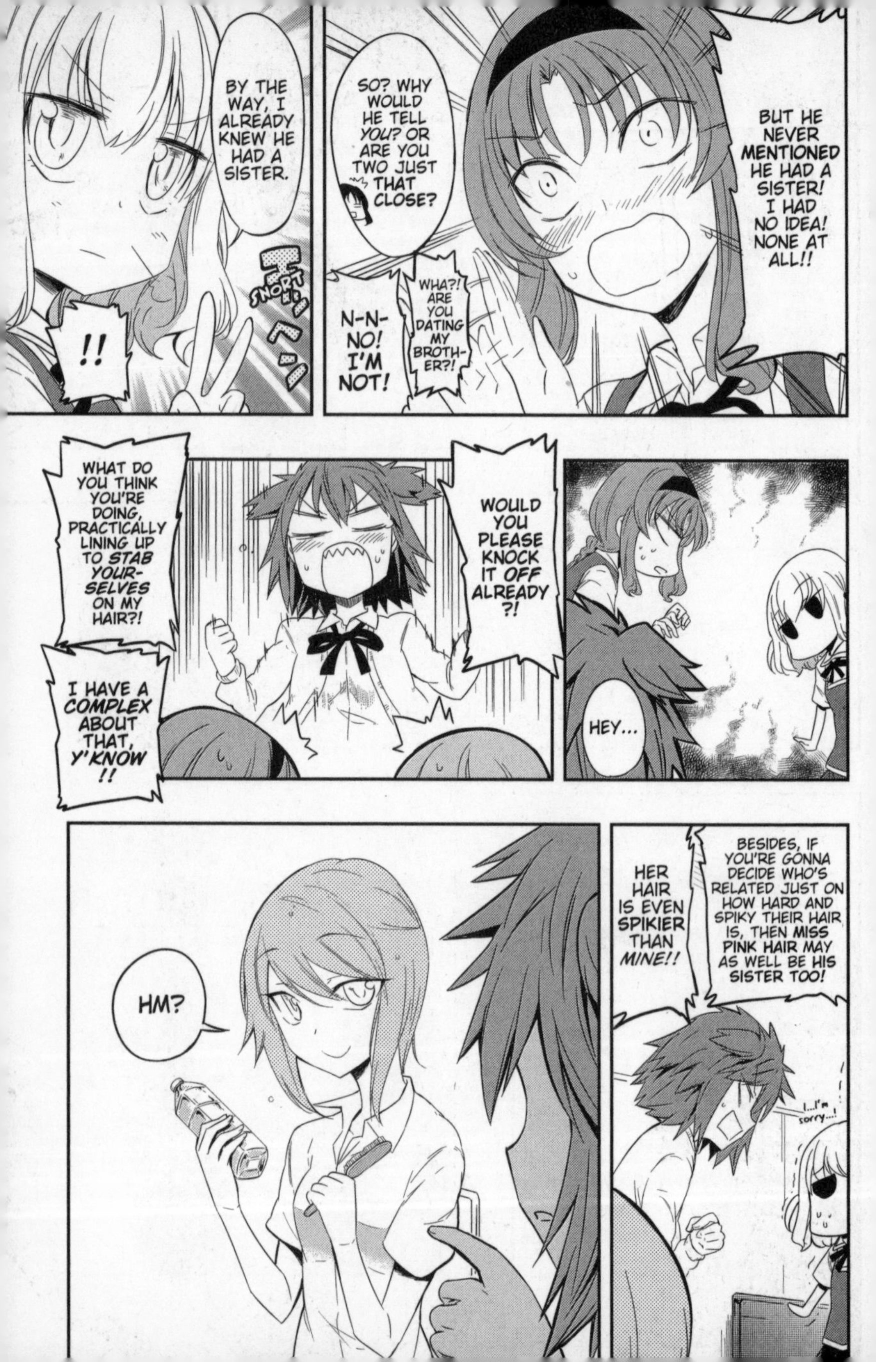
BUT HE NEVER MENTIONED HE HAD A SISTER! I HAD NO IDEA! NONE AT ALL!!
SO? WHY WOULD HE TELL YOU? OR ARE YOU TWO JUST THAT CLOSE?
WHA?! ARE YOU DATING MY BROTHER?!
N-N-NO! I'M NOT!
BY THE WAY, I ALREADY KNEW HE HAD A SISTER.
SNORT
!!
HEY...
WOULD YOU PLEASE KNOCK IT OFF ALREADY?!
WHAT DO YOU THINK YOU'RE DOING, PRACTICALLY LINING UP TO STAB YOURSELVES ON MY HAIR?!
I HAVE A COMPLEX ABOUT THAT, Y'KNOW!!
BESIDES, IF YOU'RE GONNA DECIDE WHO'S RELATED JUST ON HOW HARD AND SPIKY THEIR HAIR IS, THEN MISS PINK HAIR MAY AS WELL BE HIS SISTER TOO!
HER HAIR IS EVEN SPIKIER THAN MINE!!
I...I'm sorry...!
HM?

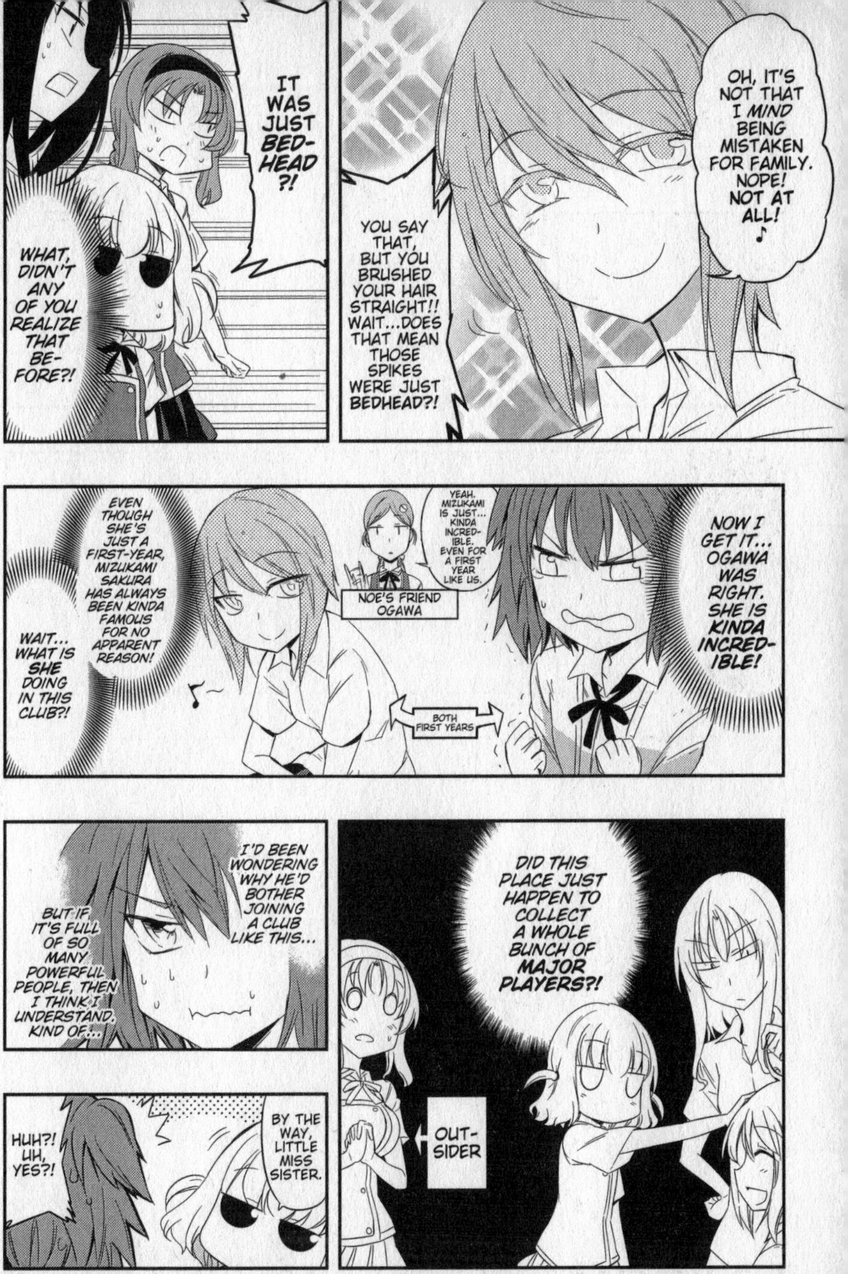
OH, IT'S NOT THAT I MIND BEING MISTAKEN FOR FAMILY. NOPE! NOT AT ALL! ♪
YOU SAY THAT, BUT YOU BRUSHED YOUR HAIR STRAIGHT!! WAIT...DOES THAT MEAN THOSE SPIKES WERE JUST BEDHEAD?!
IT WAS JUST BED-HEAD?!
WHAT, DIDN'T ANY OF YOU REALIZE THAT BE-FORE?!
NOW I GET IT... OGAWA WAS RIGHT. SHE IS KINDA INCRED-IBLE!
YEAH. MIZUKAMI IS JUST... KINDA INCRED-IBLE. EVEN FOR A FIRST YEAR LIKE US.
NOE'S FRIEND OGAWA
EVEN THOUGH SHE'S JUST A FIRST-YEAR, MIZUKAMI SAKURA HAS ALWAYS BEEN KINDA FAMOUS FOR NO APPARENT REASON!
WAIT... WHAT IS SHE DOING IN THIS CLUB?!
BOTH FIRST YEARS
♪~
DID THIS PLACE JUST HAPPEN TO COLLECT A WHOLE BUNCH OF MAJOR PLAYERS?!
OUT-SIDER
I'D BEEN WONDERING WHY HE'D BOTHER JOINING A CLUB LIKE THIS...
BUT IF IT'S FULL OF SO MANY POWERFUL PEOPLE, THEN I THINK I UNDERSTAND. KIND OF...
BY THE WAY, LITTLE MISS SISTER.
HUH?! UH, YES?!

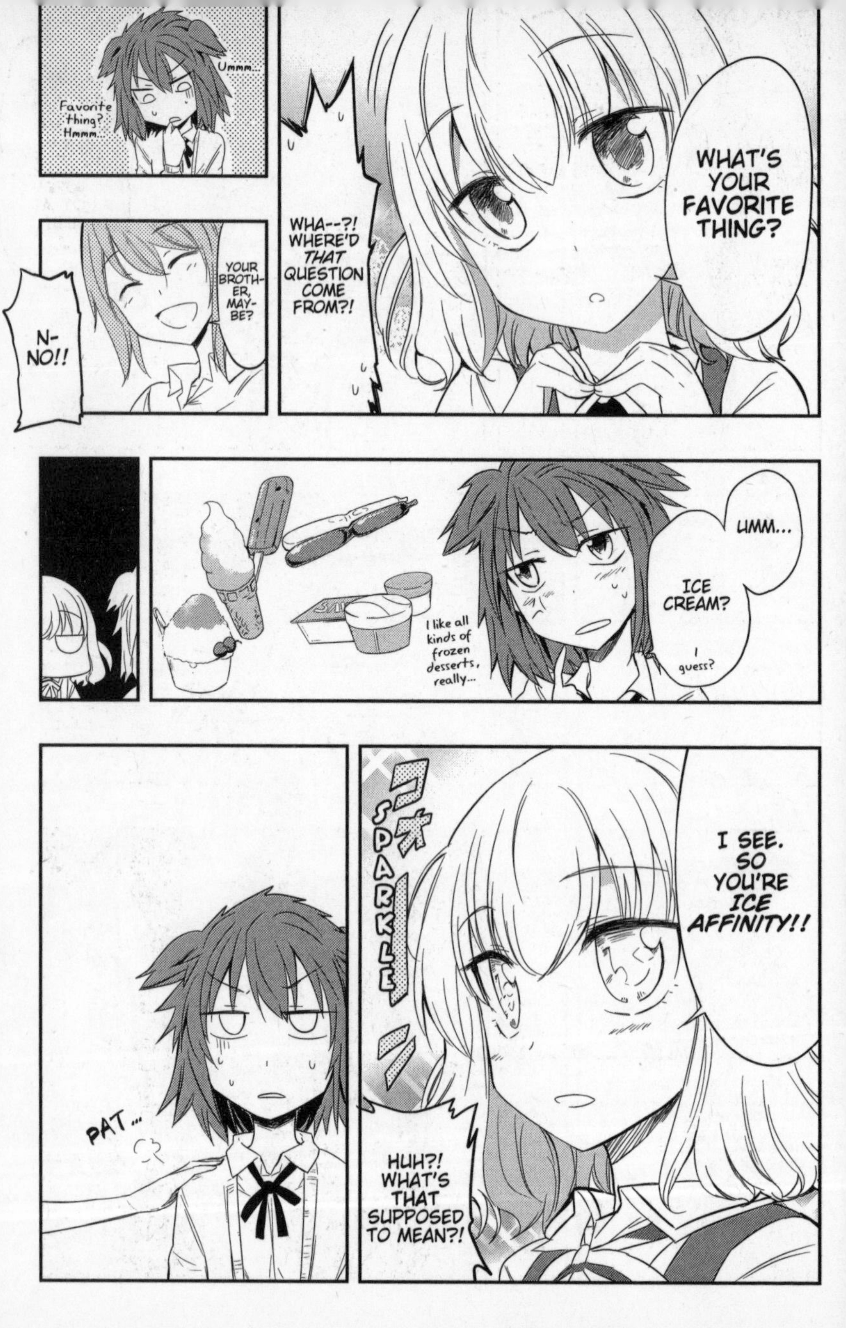
WHAT'S YOUR FAVORITE THING?
WHA--?! WHERE'D THAT QUESTION COME FROM?!
Ummm...
Favorite thing? Hmmm...
YOUR BROTHER, MAYBE?
N-NO!!
UMMM...
ICE CREAM?
I guess?
I like all kinds of frozen desserts, really...
I SEE. SO YOU'RE ICE AFFINITY!!
SPARKLE
HUH?! WHAT'S THAT SUPPOSED TO MEAN?!
PAT...

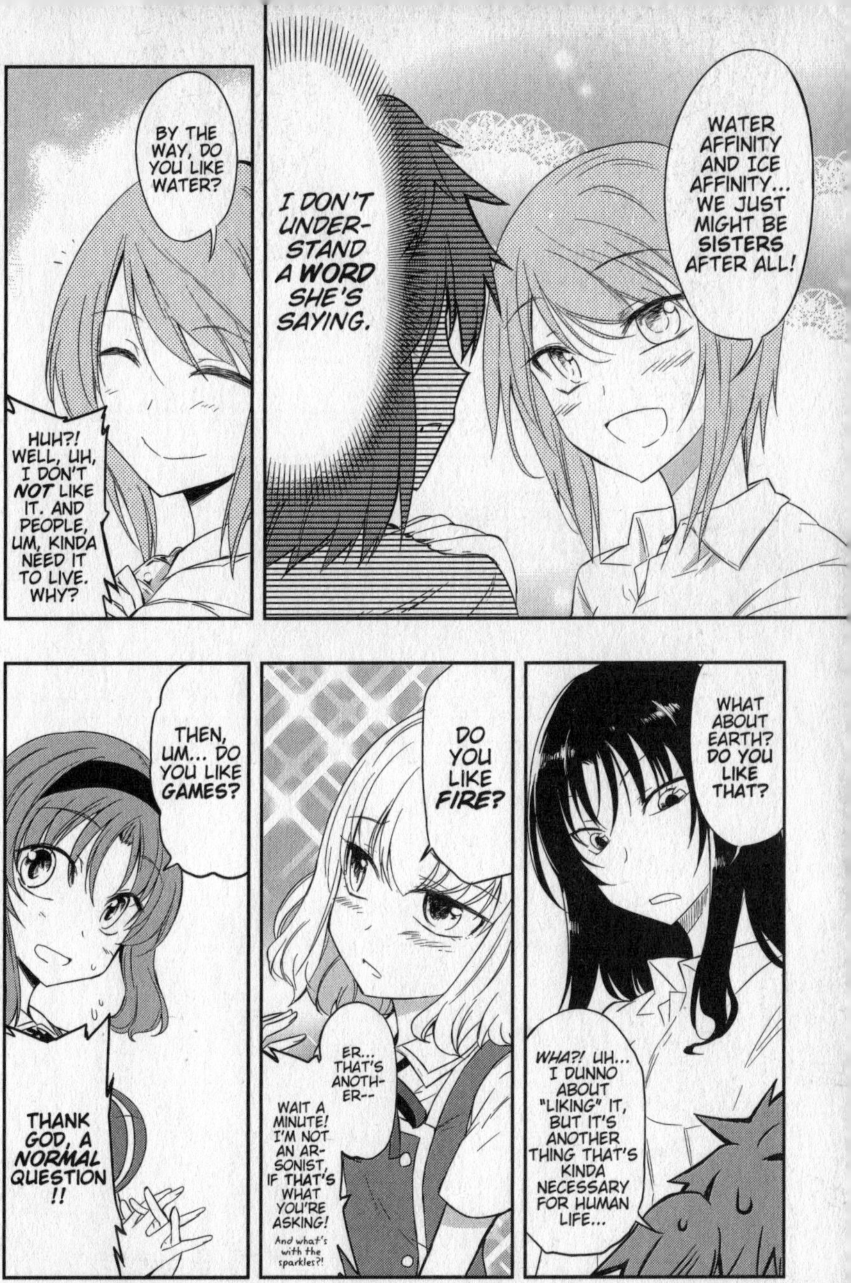
WATER AFFINITY AND ICE AFFINITY... WE JUST MIGHT BE SISTERS AFTER ALL!
I DON'T UNDER-STAND A WORD SHE'S SAYING.
BY THE WAY, DO YOU LIKE WATER?
HUH?! WELL, UH, I DON'T NOT LIKE IT. AND PEOPLE, UM, KINDA NEED IT TO LIVE. WHY?
WHAT ABOUT EARTH? DO YOU LIKE THAT?
WHA?! UH... I DUNNO ABOUT "LIKING" IT, BUT IT'S ANOTHER THING THAT'S KINDA NECESSARY FOR HUMAN LIFE...
DO YOU LIKE FIRE?
ER... THAT'S ANOTH-ER--
WAIT A MINUTE! I'M NOT AN AR-SONIST, IF THAT'S WHAT YOU'RE ASKING!
And what's with the sparkles?!
THEN, UM... DO YOU LIKE GAMES?
THANK GOD, A NORMAL QUESTION !!

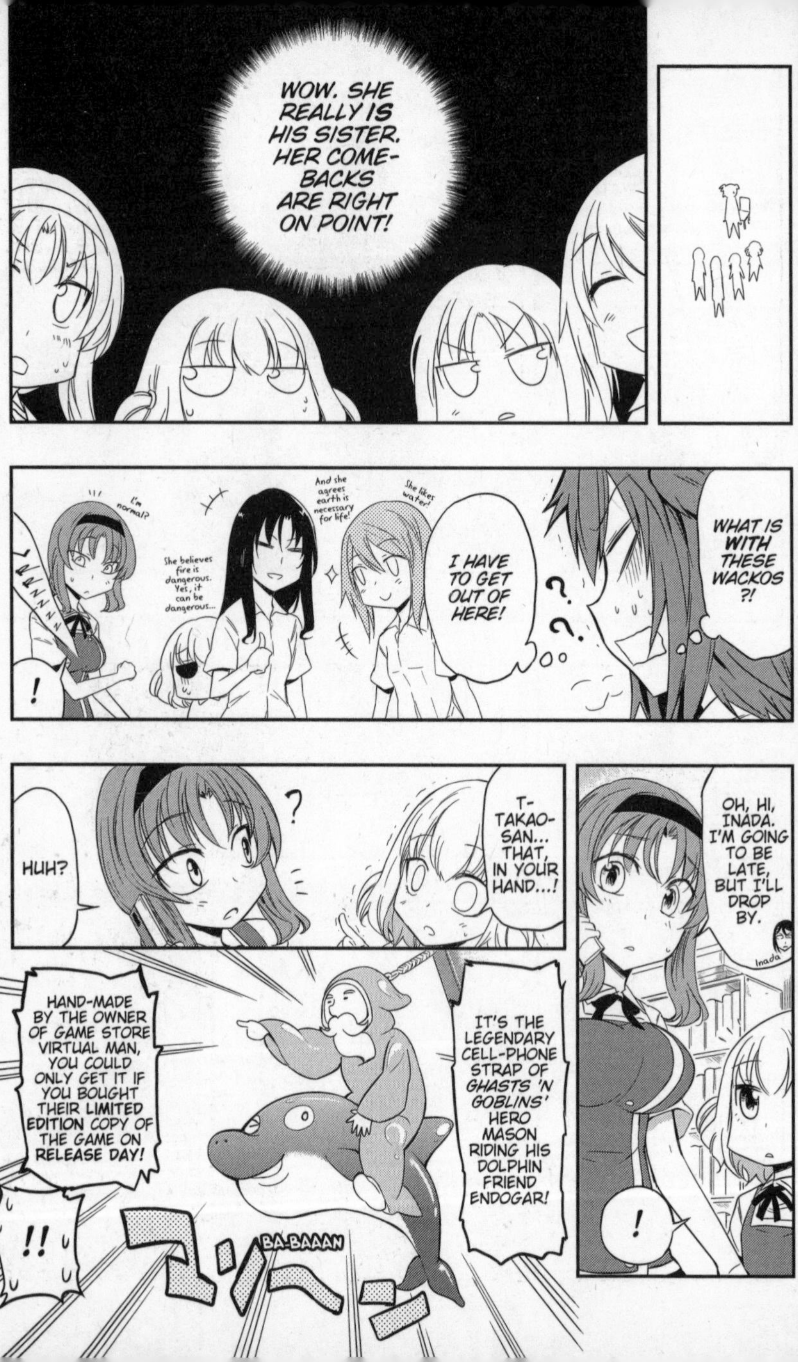
WOW. SHE REALLY IS HIS SISTER. HER COME-BACKS ARE RIGHT ON POINT!
WHAT IS WITH THESE WACKOS?!
I HAVE TO GET OUT OF HERE!
She likes water!
And she agrees earth is necessary for life!
She believes fire is dangerous. Yes, it can be dangerous...
I'm normal?
!
OH, HI, INADA. I'M GOING TO BE LATE, BUT I'LL DROP BY.
Inada
!
T-TAKAO-SAN... THAT, IN YOUR HAND...!
?
HUH?
IT'S THE LEGENDARY CELL-PHONE STRAP OF GHASTS 'N GOBLINS' HERO MASON RIDING HIS DOLPHIN FRIEND ENDOGAR!
HAND-MADE BY THE OWNER OF GAME STORE VIRTUAL MAN, YOU COULD ONLY GET IT IF YOU BOUGHT THEIR LIMITED EDITION COPY OF THE GAME ON RELEASE DAY!
BA-BAAAN
!!

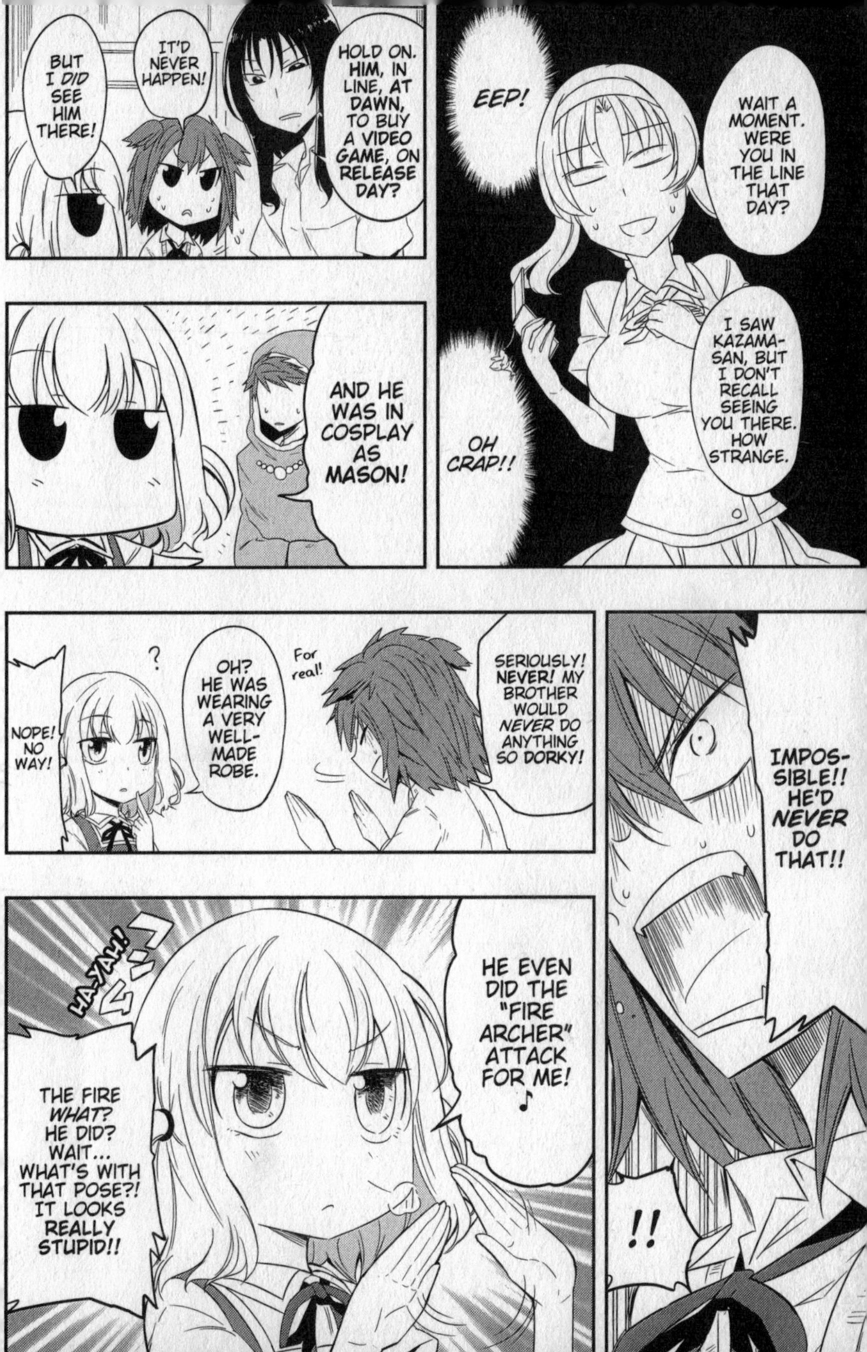
WAIT A MOMENT. WERE YOU IN THE LINE THAT DAY?
EEP!
I SAW KAZAMA-SAN, BUT I DON'T RECALL SEEING YOU THERE. HOW STRANGE.
OH CRAP!!
HOLD ON. HIM, IN LINE, AT DAWN, TO BUY A VIDEO GAME, ON RELEASE DAY?
IT'D NEVER HAPPEN!
BUT I *DID* SEE HIM THERE!
AND HE WAS IN COSPLAY AS MASON!
IMPOSSIBLE!! HE'D *NEVER* DO THAT!!
!!
SERIOUSLY! NEVER! MY BROTHER WOULD *NEVER* DO ANYTHING SO DORKY!
For real!
OH? HE WAS WEARING A VERY WELL-MADE ROBE.
?
NOPE! NO WAY!
HE EVEN DID THE "FIRE ARCHER" ATTACK FOR ME! ♪
HA-YAH!
THE FIRE *WHAT*? HE DID? WAIT... WHAT'S WITH THAT POSE?! IT LOOKS REALLY STUPID!!

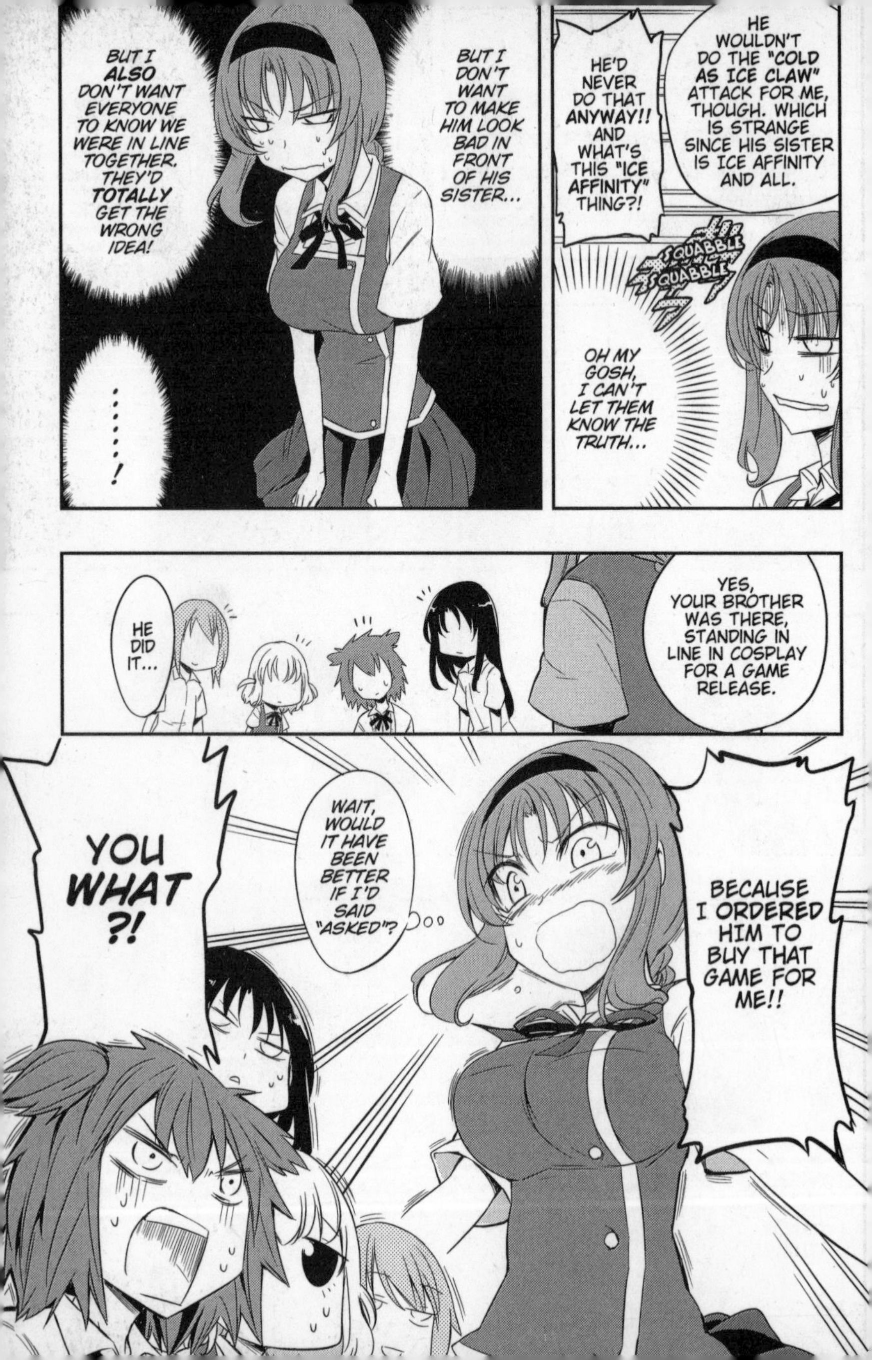
HE WOULDN'T DO THE "COLD AS ICE CLAW" ATTACK FOR ME, THOUGH. WHICH IS STRANGE SINCE HIS SISTER IS ICE AFFINITY AND ALL.
HE'D NEVER DO THAT ANYWAY!! AND WHAT'S THIS "ICE AFFINITY" THING?!
SQUABBLE SQUABBLE
OH MY GOSH, I CAN'T LET THEM KNOW THE TRUTH...
BUT I DON'T WANT TO MAKE HIM LOOK BAD IN FRONT OF HIS SISTER...
BUT I ALSO DON'T WANT EVERYONE TO KNOW WE WERE IN LINE TOGETHER. THEY'D TOTALLY GET THE WRONG IDEA!
......!
YES, YOUR BROTHER WAS THERE, STANDING IN LINE IN COSPLAY FOR A GAME RELEASE.
HE DID IT...
BECAUSE I ORDERED HIM TO BUY THAT GAME FOR ME!!
WAIT, WOULD IT HAVE BEEN BETTER IF I'D SAID "ASKED"?
YOU WHAT?!

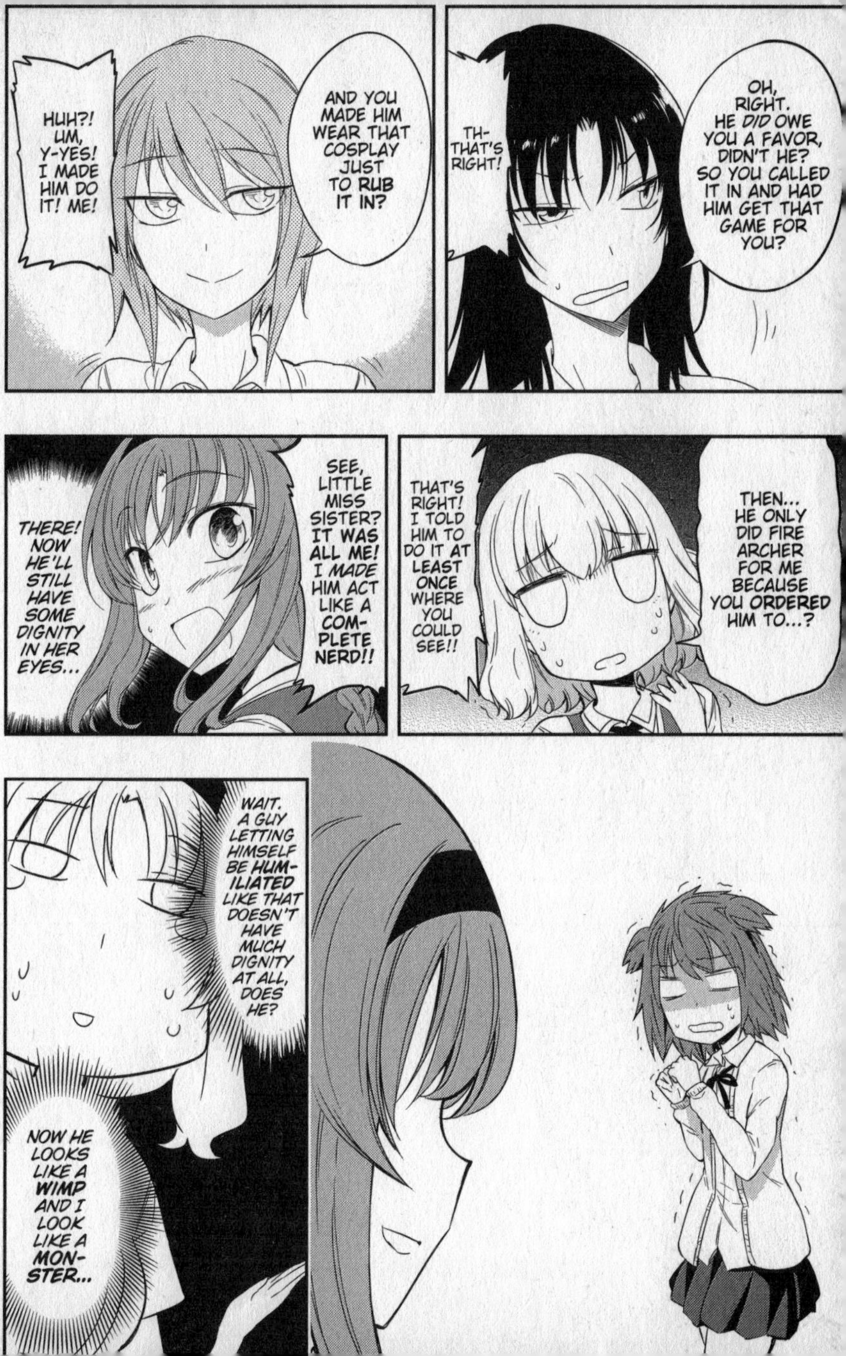
OH, RIGHT. HE DID OWE YOU A FAVOR, DIDN'T HE? SO YOU CALLED IT IN AND HAD HIM GET THAT GAME FOR YOU?
TH-THAT'S RIGHT!
AND YOU MADE HIM WEAR THAT COSPLAY JUST TO RUB IT IN?
HUH?! UM, Y-YES! I MADE HIM DO IT! ME!
THEN... HE ONLY DID FIRE ARCHER FOR ME BECAUSE YOU ORDERED HIM TO...?
THAT'S RIGHT! I TOLD HIM TO DO IT AT LEAST ONCE WHERE YOU COULD SEE!!
SEE, LITTLE MISS SISTER? IT WAS ALL ME! I MADE HIM ACT LIKE A COMPLETE NERD!!
THERE! NOW HE'LL STILL HAVE SOME DIGNITY IN HER EYES...
WAIT. A GUY LETTING HIMSELF BE HUMILIATED LIKE THAT DOESN'T HAVE MUCH DIGNITY AT ALL, DOES HE?
NOW HE LOOKS LIKE A WIMP AND I LOOK LIKE A MONSTER...

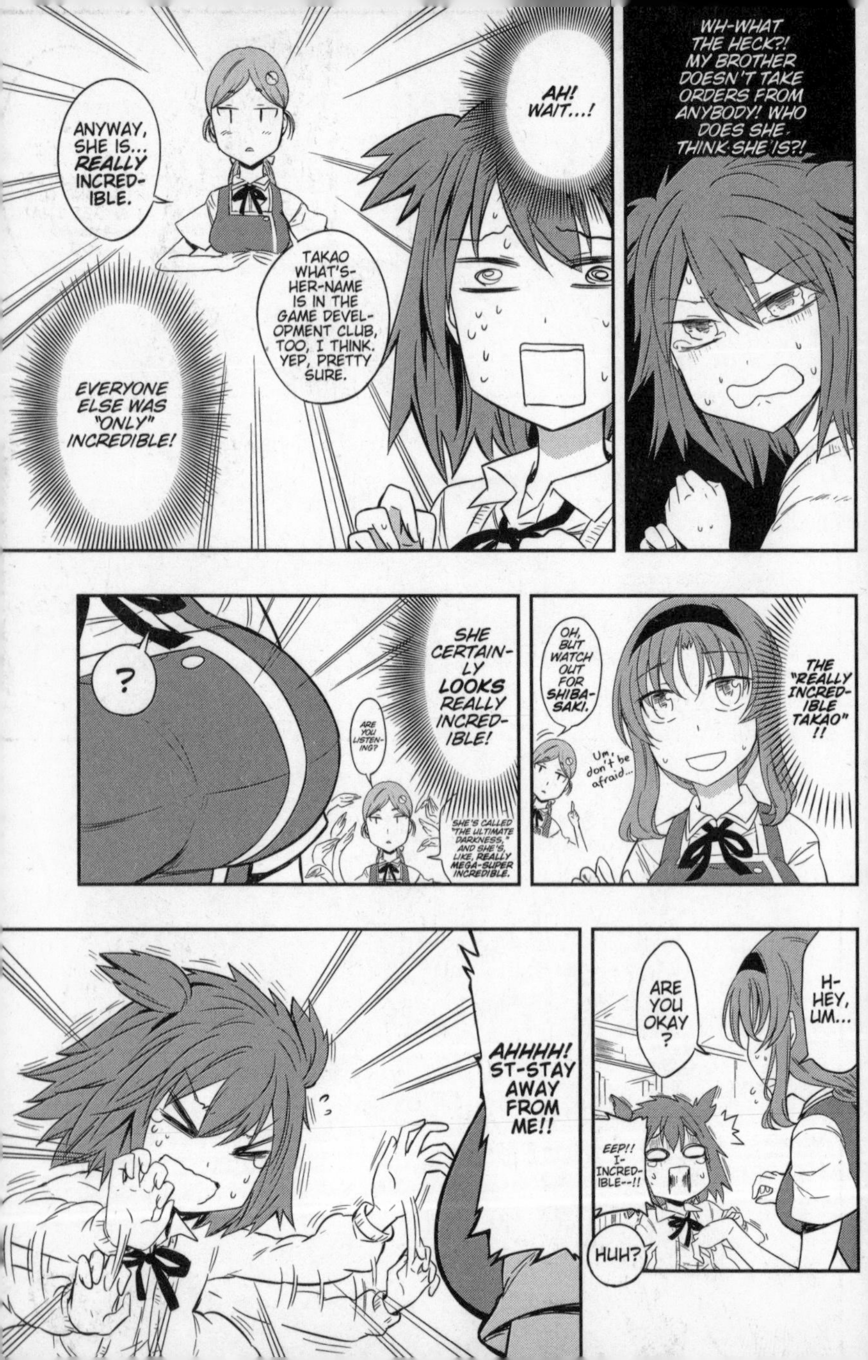
WH-WHAT THE HECK?! MY BROTHER DOESN'T TAKE ORDERS FROM ANYBODY! WHO DOES SHE THINK SHE IS?!
AH! WAIT...!
ANYWAY, SHE IS... REALLY INCREDIBLE.
TAKAO WHAT'S-HER-NAME IS IN THE GAME DEVELOPMENT CLUB, TOO, I THINK. YEP, PRETTY SURE.
EVERYONE ELSE WAS "ONLY" INCREDIBLE!
THE "REALLY INCREDIBLE TAKAO" !!
OH, BUT WATCH OUT FOR SHIBASAKI.
Um, don't be afraid...
SHE CERTAINLY LOOKS REALLY INCREDIBLE!
?
ARE YOU LISTENING?
SHE'S CALLED "THE ULTIMATE DARKNESS," AND SHE'S, LIKE, REALLY MEGA-SUPER INCREDIBLE.
H-HEY, UM...
ARE YOU OKAY?
EEP!! I-INCREDIBLE--!!
HUH?
AHHHH! ST-STAY AWAY FROM ME!!

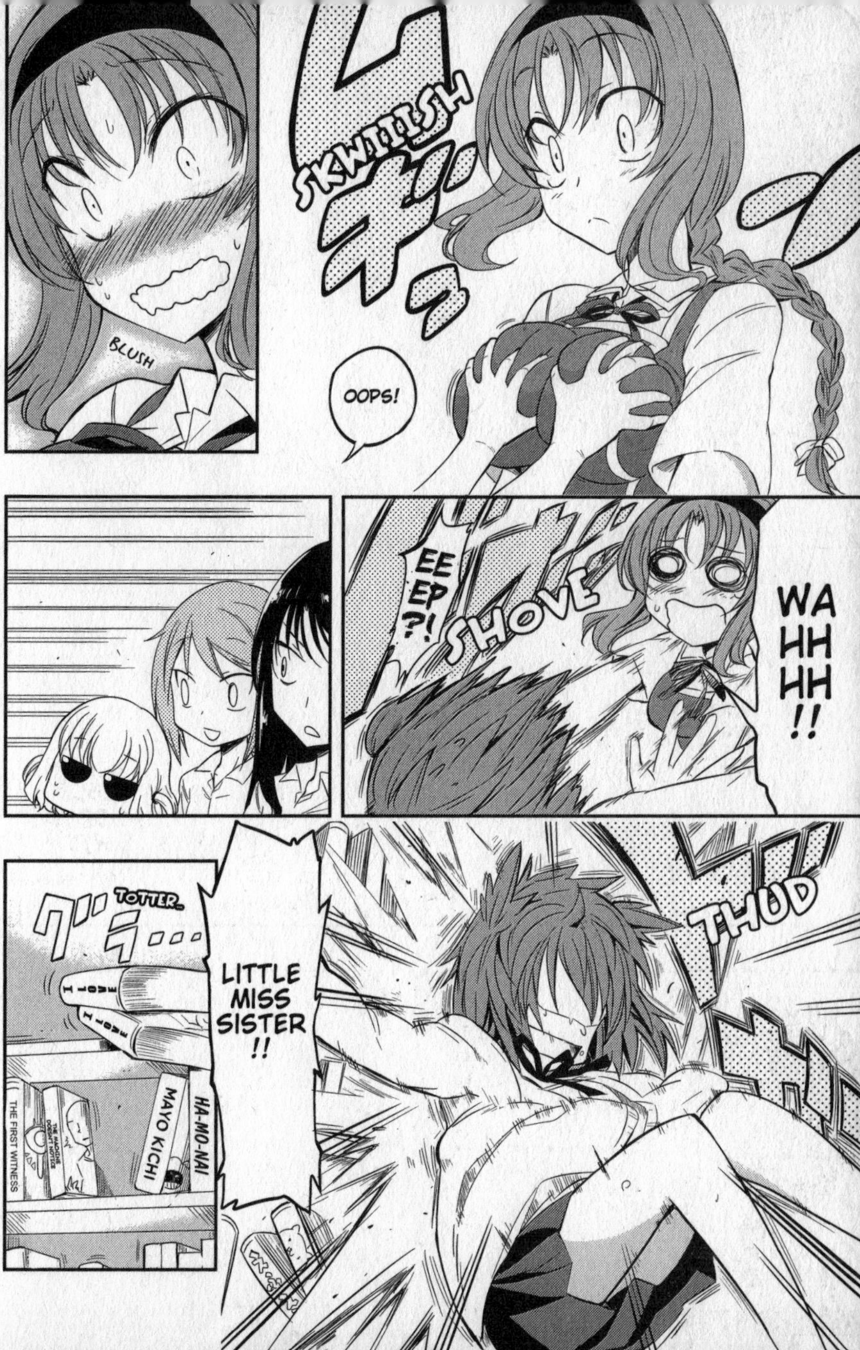
SKWIIISH
OOPS!
BLUSH
EEEP?!
SHOVE
WAHHHH!!
THUD
LITTLE MISS SISTER!!
TOTTER...
HA-MO-NAI
MAYO KICHI
THE MACHINE DOESN'T NOTICE
THE FIRST WITNESS

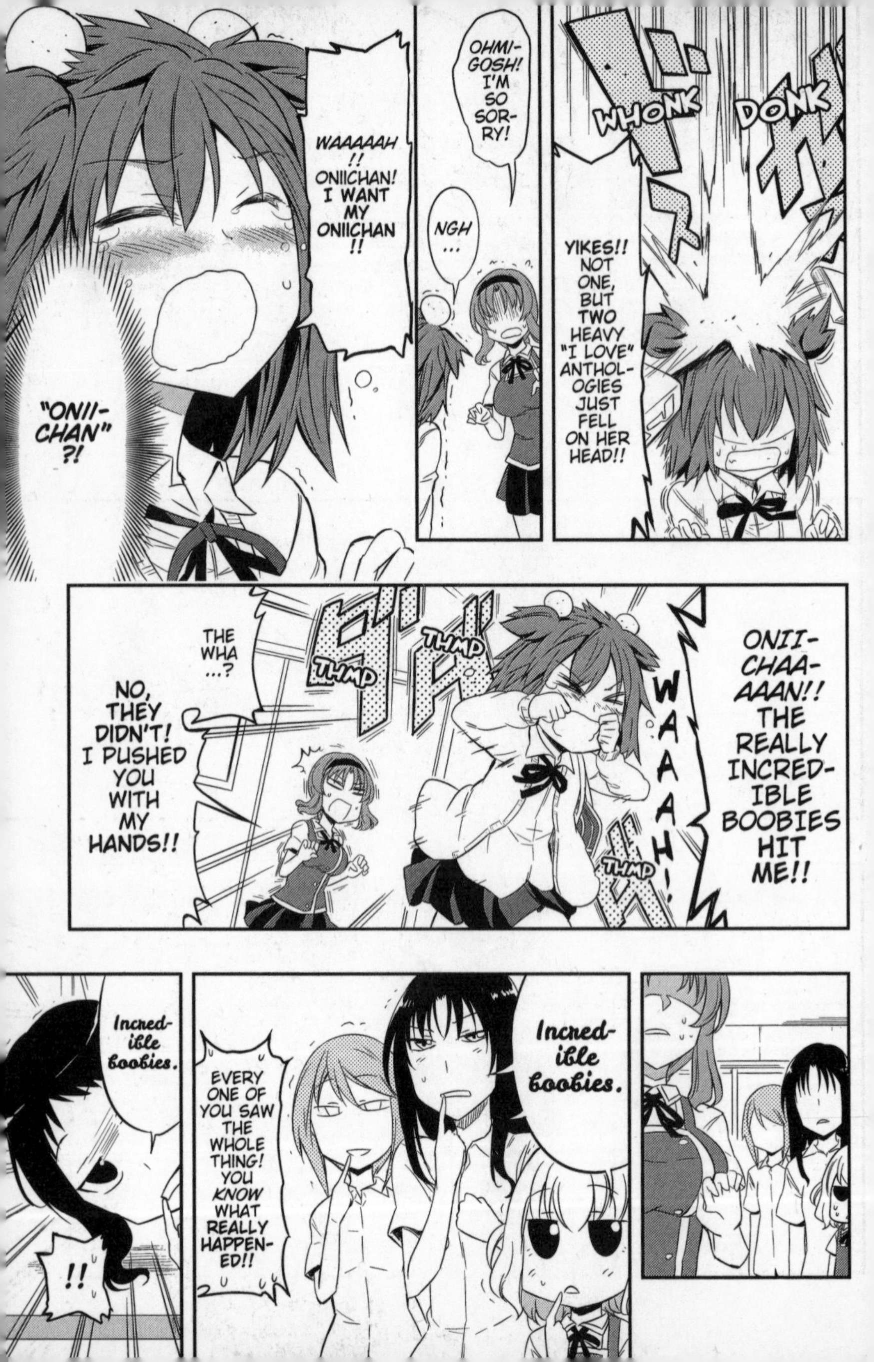

WHONK
DONK
YIKES!! NOT ONE, BUT TWO HEAVY "I LOVE" ANTHOLOGIES JUST FELL ON HER HEAD!!
OHMI-GOSH! I'M SO SORRY!
NGH...
WAAAAAH!! ONIICHAN! I WANT MY ONIICHAN!!
"ONII-CHAN"?!
ONII-CHAAAAAN!! THE REALLY INCREDIBLE BOOBIES HIT ME!!
WAAAAH!
THMP
THMP
THMP
THE WHA...?
NO, THEY DIDN'T! I PUSHED YOU WITH MY HANDS!!
Incredible boobies.
EVERY ONE OF YOU SAW THE WHOLE THING! YOU KNOW WHAT REALLY HAPPENED!!
Incredible boobies.
!!

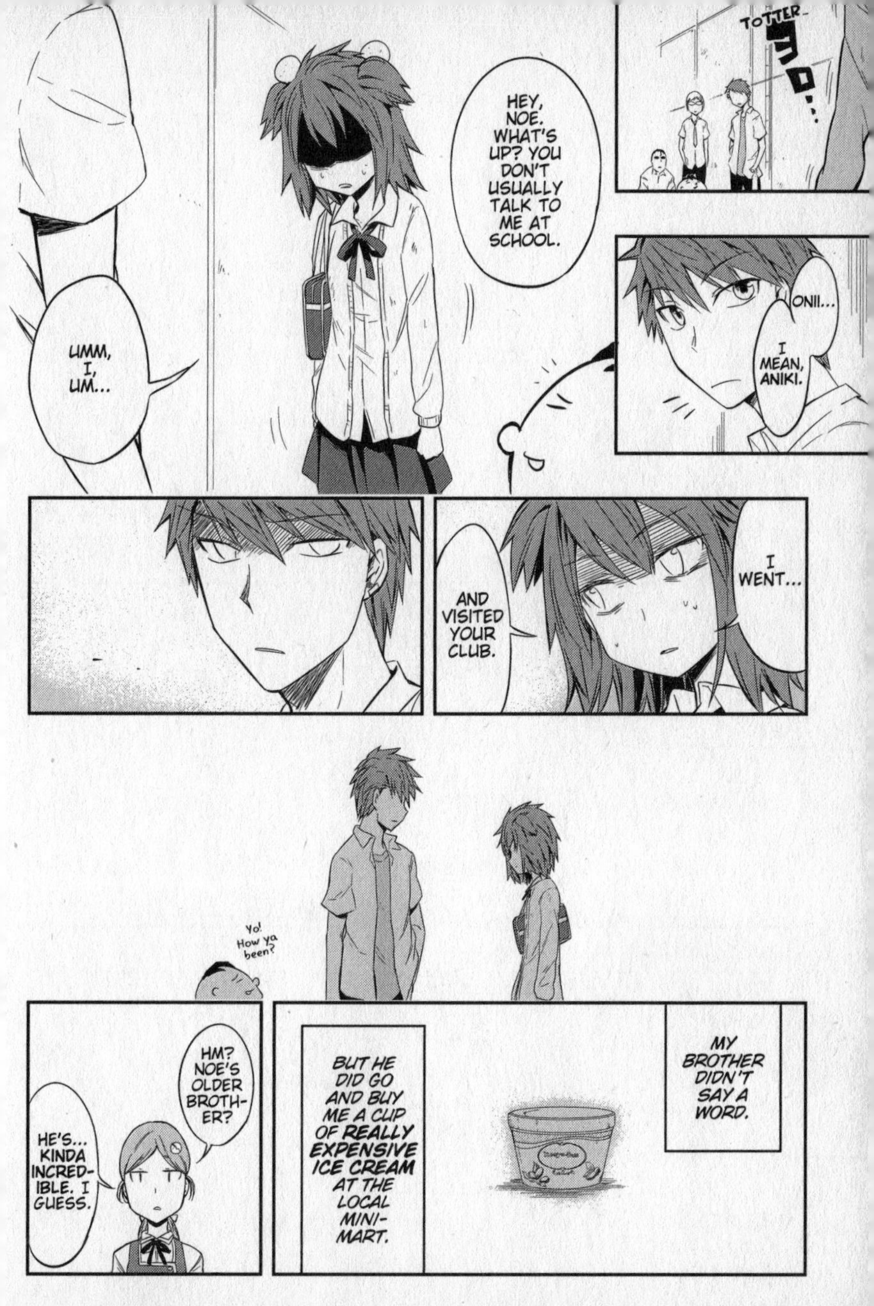
TOTTER
ヨロ…
ONII... I MEAN, ANIKI.
HEY, NOE. WHAT'S UP? YOU DON'T USUALLY TALK TO ME AT SCHOOL.
UMM, I, UM...
I WENT...
AND VISITED YOUR CLUB.
Yo! How ya been?
MY BROTHER DIDN'T SAY A WORD.
BUT HE DID GO AND BUY ME A CUP OF **REALLY EXPENSIVE ICE CREAM** AT THE LOCAL MINI-MART.
HM? NOE'S OLDER BROTHER?
HE'S... KINDA INCREDIBLE. I GUESS.

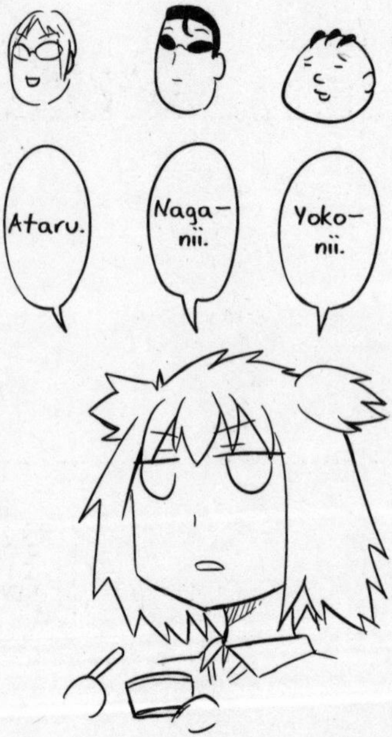
Yoko-nii.
Naga-nii.
Ataru.

D-FRAGMENTS

ディーふらぐ!

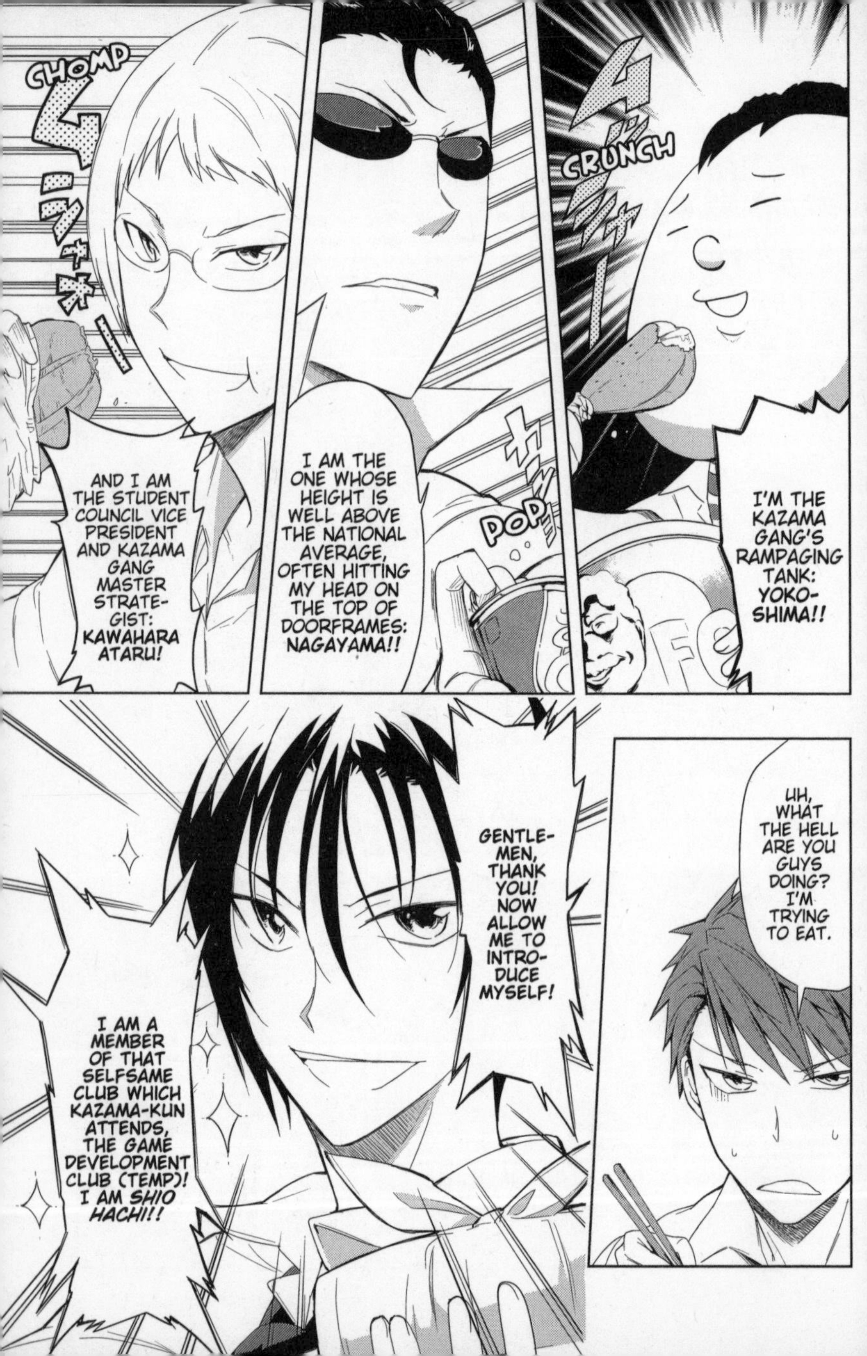
CRUNCH
I'M THE KAZAMA GANG'S RAMPAGING TANK: YOKO-SHIMA!!
POP
I AM THE ONE WHOSE HEIGHT IS WELL ABOVE THE NATIONAL AVERAGE, OFTEN HITTING MY HEAD ON THE TOP OF DOORFRAMES: NAGAYAMA!!
CHOMP
AND I AM THE STUDENT COUNCIL VICE PRESIDENT AND KAZAMA GANG MASTER STRATE-GIST: KAWAHARA ATARU!
UH, WHAT THE HELL ARE YOU GUYS DOING? I'M TRYING TO EAT.
GENTLE-MEN, THANK YOU! NOW ALLOW ME TO INTRO-DUCE MYSELF!
I AM A MEMBER OF THAT SELFSAME CLUB WHICH KAZAMA-KUN ATTENDS, THE GAME DEVELOPMENT CLUB (TEMP)! I AM *SHIO HACHI*!!

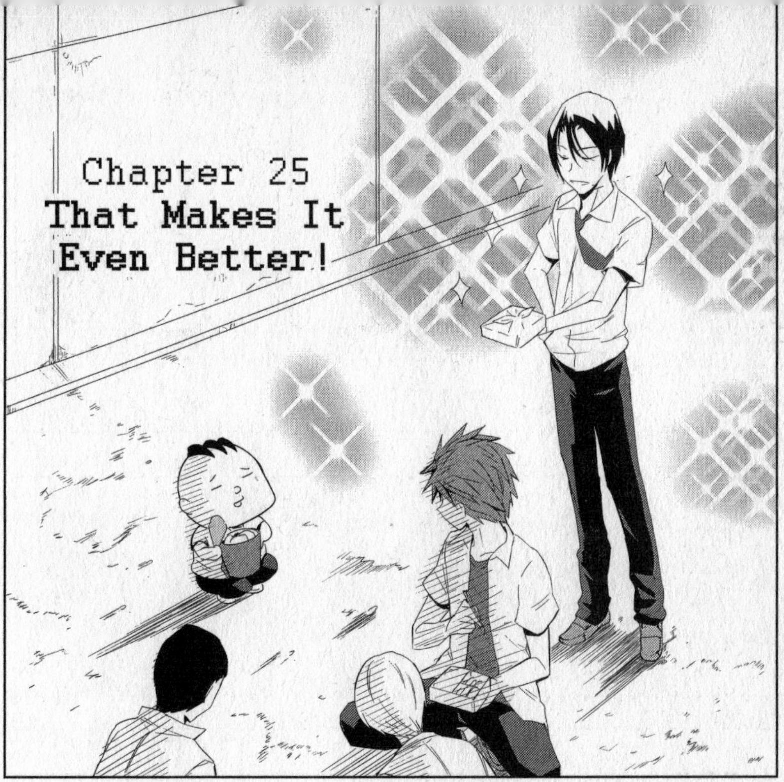
Chapter 25
That Makes It Even Better!

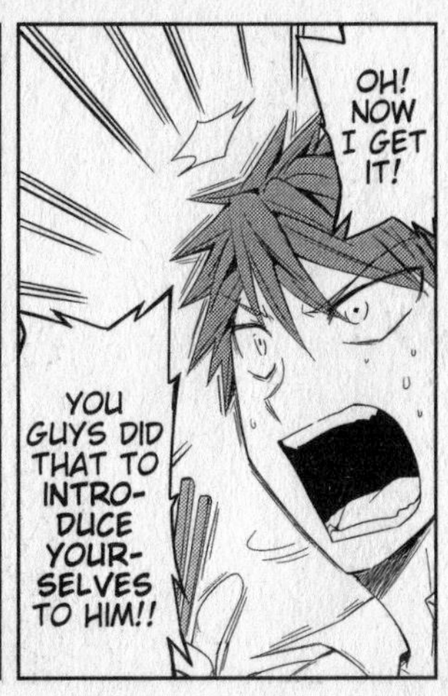
OH! NOW I GET IT!
YOU GUYS DID THAT TO INTRO-DUCE YOUR-SELVES TO HIM!!

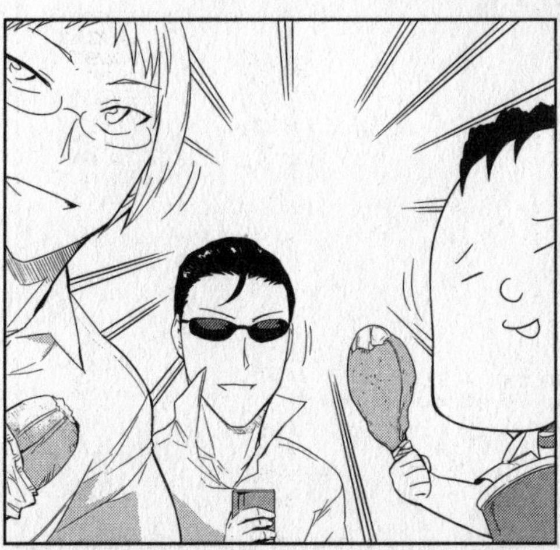

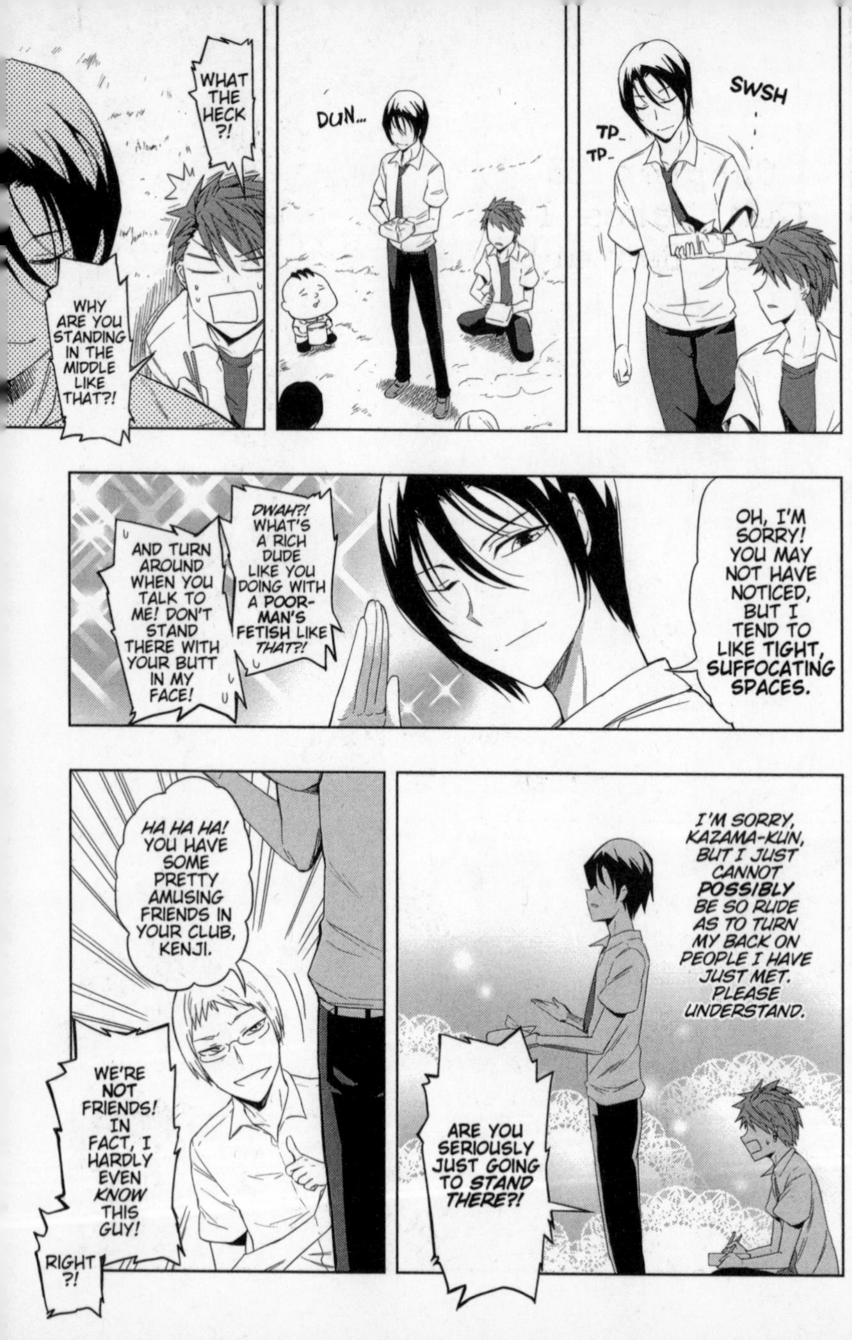
SWSH
TP_ TP_
DUN...
WHAT THE HECK?!
WHY ARE YOU STANDING IN THE MIDDLE LIKE THAT?!
OH, I'M SORRY! YOU MAY NOT HAVE NOTICED, BUT I TEND TO LIKE TIGHT, SUFFOCATING SPACES.
DWAH?! WHAT'S A RICH DUDE LIKE YOU DOING WITH A POOR-MAN'S FETISH LIKE *THAT?!*
AND TURN AROUND WHEN YOU TALK TO ME! DON'T STAND THERE WITH YOUR BUTT IN MY FACE!
I'M SORRY, KAZAMA-KUN, BUT I JUST CANNOT **POSSIBLY** *BE SO RUDE AS TO TURN MY BACK ON PEOPLE I HAVE JUST MET. PLEASE UNDERSTAND.*
ARE YOU SERIOUSLY JUST GOING TO *STAND THERE?!*
HA HA HA! YOU HAVE SOME PRETTY AMUSING FRIENDS IN YOUR CLUB, KENJI.
WE'RE NOT FRIENDS! IN FACT, I HARDLY EVEN *KNOW* THIS GUY!
RIGHT?!

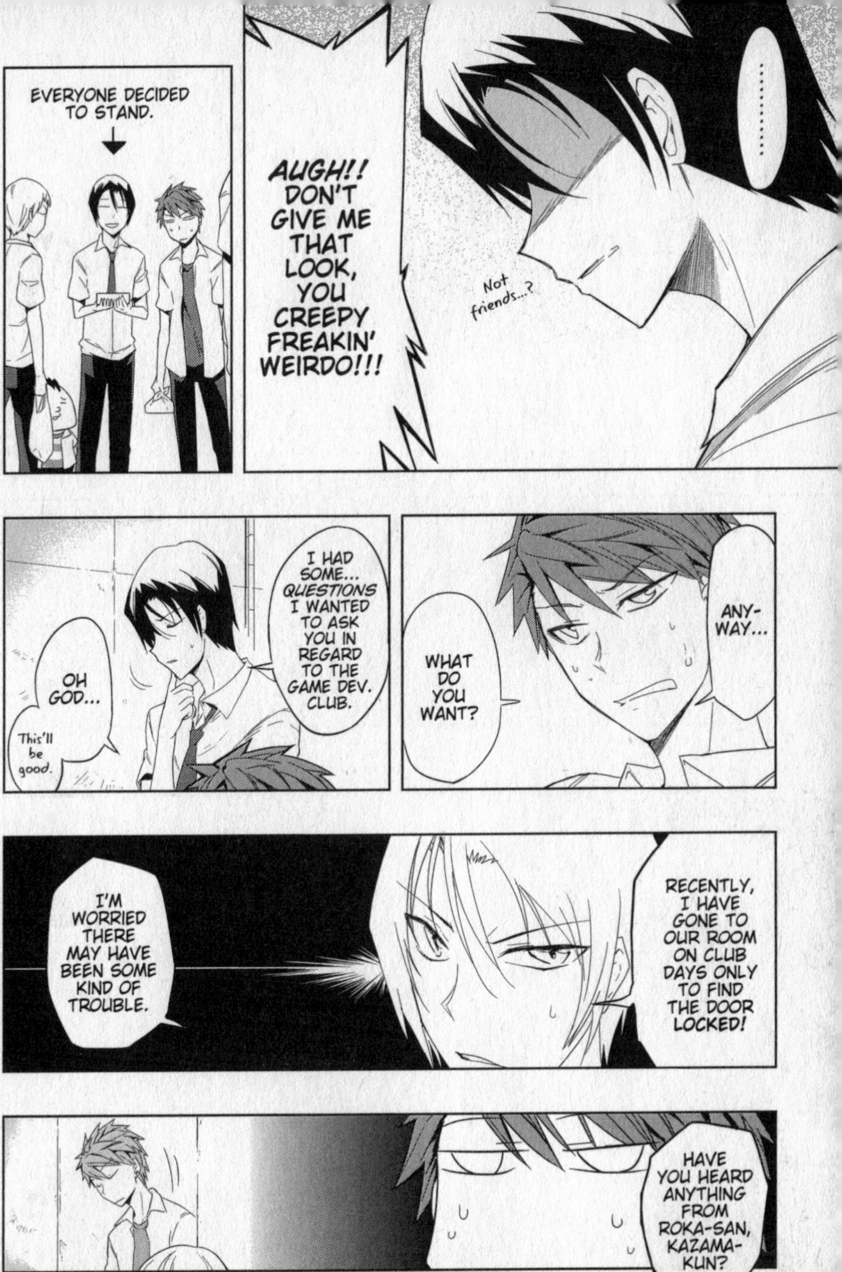
......
Not friends...?
AUGH!! DON'T GIVE ME THAT LOOK, YOU CREEPY FREAKIN' WEIRDO!!!
EVERYONE DECIDED TO STAND.
ANY-WAY...
WHAT DO YOU WANT?
I HAD SOME... *QUESTIONS* I WANTED TO ASK YOU IN REGARD TO THE GAME DEV. CLUB.
OH GOD...
This'll be good.
RECENTLY, I HAVE GONE TO OUR ROOM ON CLUB DAYS ONLY TO FIND THE DOOR LOCKED!
I'M WORRIED THERE MAY HAVE BEEN SOME KIND OF TROUBLE.
HAVE YOU HEARD ANYTHING FROM ROKA-SAN, KAZAMA-KUN?

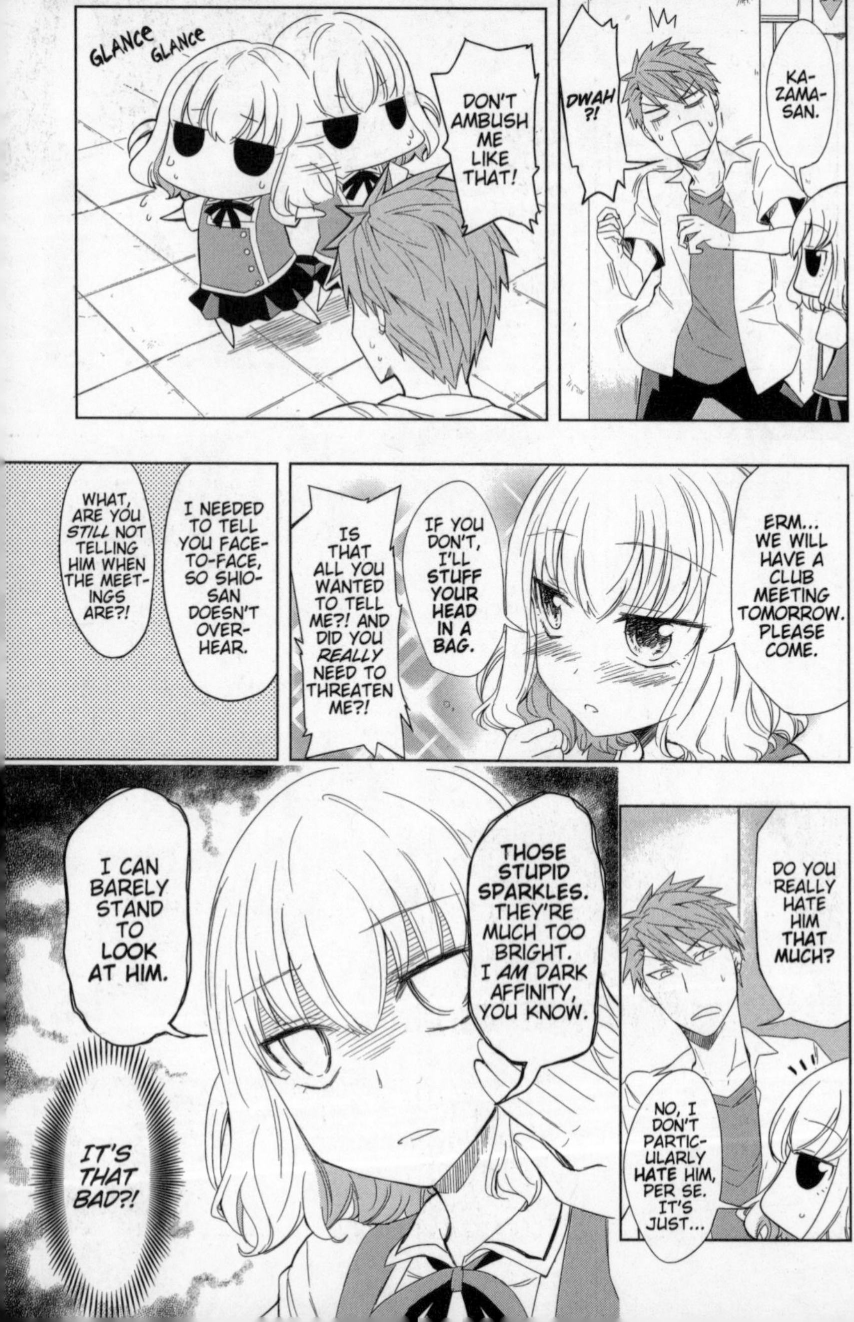
KA-ZAMA-SAN.
DWAH?!
DON'T AMBUSH ME LIKE THAT!
GLANCE GLANCE
ERM... WE WILL HAVE A CLUB MEETING TOMORROW. PLEASE COME.
IF YOU DON'T, I'LL STUFF YOUR HEAD IN A BAG.
IS THAT ALL YOU WANTED TO TELL ME?! AND DID YOU *REALLY* NEED TO THREATEN ME?!
I NEEDED TO TELL YOU FACE-TO-FACE, SO SHIO-SAN DOESN'T OVER-HEAR.
WHAT, ARE YOU *STILL* NOT TELLING HIM WHEN THE MEET-INGS ARE?!
DO YOU REALLY HATE HIM THAT MUCH?
NO, I DON'T PARTIC-ULARLY HATE HIM, PER SE. IT'S JUST...
THOSE STUPID SPARKLES. THEY'RE MUCH TOO BRIGHT. I *AM* DARK AFFINITY, YOU KNOW.
I CAN BARELY STAND TO LOOK AT HIM.
IT'S THAT BAD?!

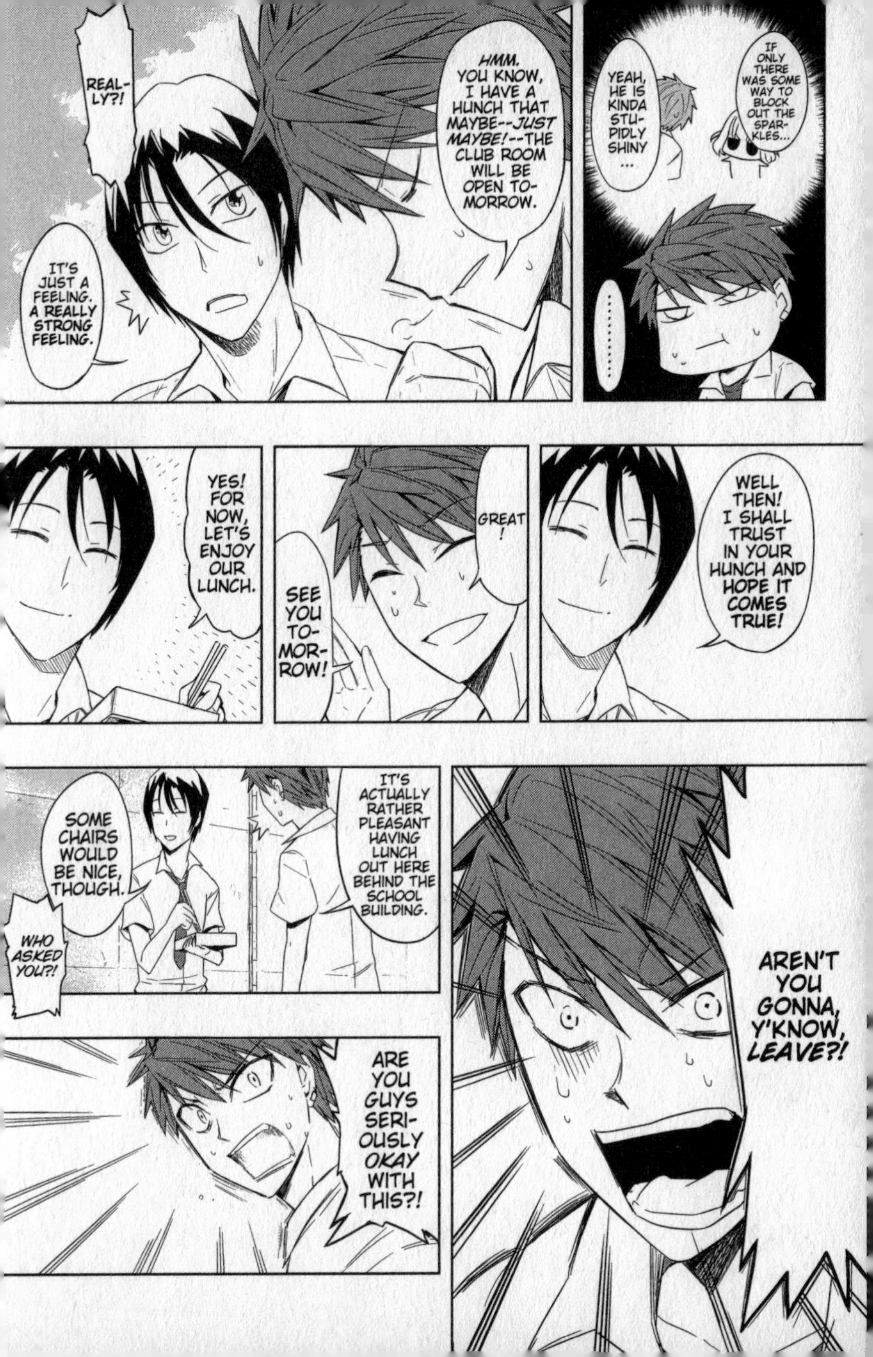
IF ONLY THERE WAS SOME WAY TO BLOCK OUT THE SPARKLES...
YEAH, HE IS KINDA STUPIDLY SHINY ...
......
HMM. YOU KNOW, I HAVE A HUNCH THAT MAYBE--*JUST MAYBE!*--THE CLUB ROOM WILL BE OPEN TOMORROW.
REALLY?!
IT'S JUST A FEELING. A REALLY STRONG FEELING.
WELL THEN! I SHALL TRUST IN YOUR HUNCH AND HOPE IT COMES TRUE!
GREAT!
SEE YOU TOMORROW!
YES! FOR NOW, LET'S ENJOY OUR LUNCH.
AREN'T YOU GONNA, Y'KNOW, *LEAVE?!*
IT'S ACTUALLY RATHER PLEASANT HAVING LUNCH OUT HERE BEHIND THE SCHOOL BUILDING.
SOME CHAIRS WOULD BE NICE, THOUGH.
WHO ASKED YOU?!
ARE YOU GUYS SERIOUSLY *OKAY* WITH THIS?!

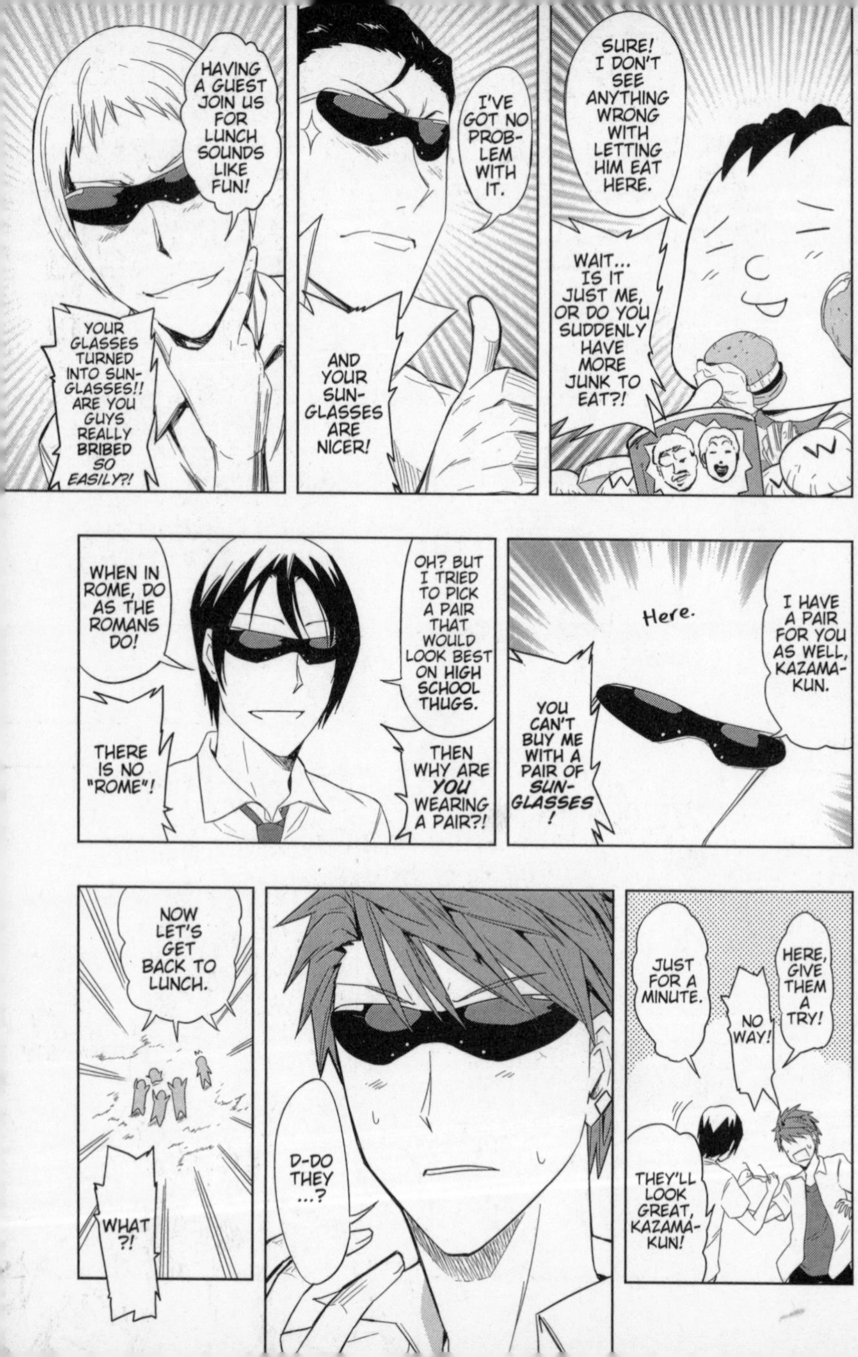
SURE! I DON'T SEE ANYTHING WRONG WITH LETTING HIM EAT HERE.
WAIT... IS IT JUST ME, OR DO YOU SUDDENLY HAVE MORE JUNK TO EAT?!
I'VE GOT NO PROBLEM WITH IT.
AND YOUR SUNGLASSES ARE NICER!
HAVING A GUEST JOIN US FOR LUNCH SOUNDS LIKE FUN!
YOUR GLASSES TURNED INTO SUNGLASSES!! ARE YOU GUYS REALLY BRIBED *SO EASILY*?!
I HAVE A PAIR FOR YOU AS WELL, KAZAMA-KUN.
Here.
YOU CAN'T BUY ME WITH A PAIR OF *SUNGLASSES*!
OH? BUT I TRIED TO PICK A PAIR THAT WOULD LOOK BEST ON HIGH SCHOOL THUGS.
THEN WHY ARE *YOU* WEARING A PAIR?!
WHEN IN ROME, DO AS THE ROMANS DO!
THERE IS NO "ROME"!
HERE, GIVE THEM A TRY!
NO WAY!
JUST FOR A MINUTE.
THEY'LL LOOK GREAT, KAZAMA-KUN!
D-DO THEY ...?
NOW LET'S GET BACK TO LUNCH.
WHAT?!

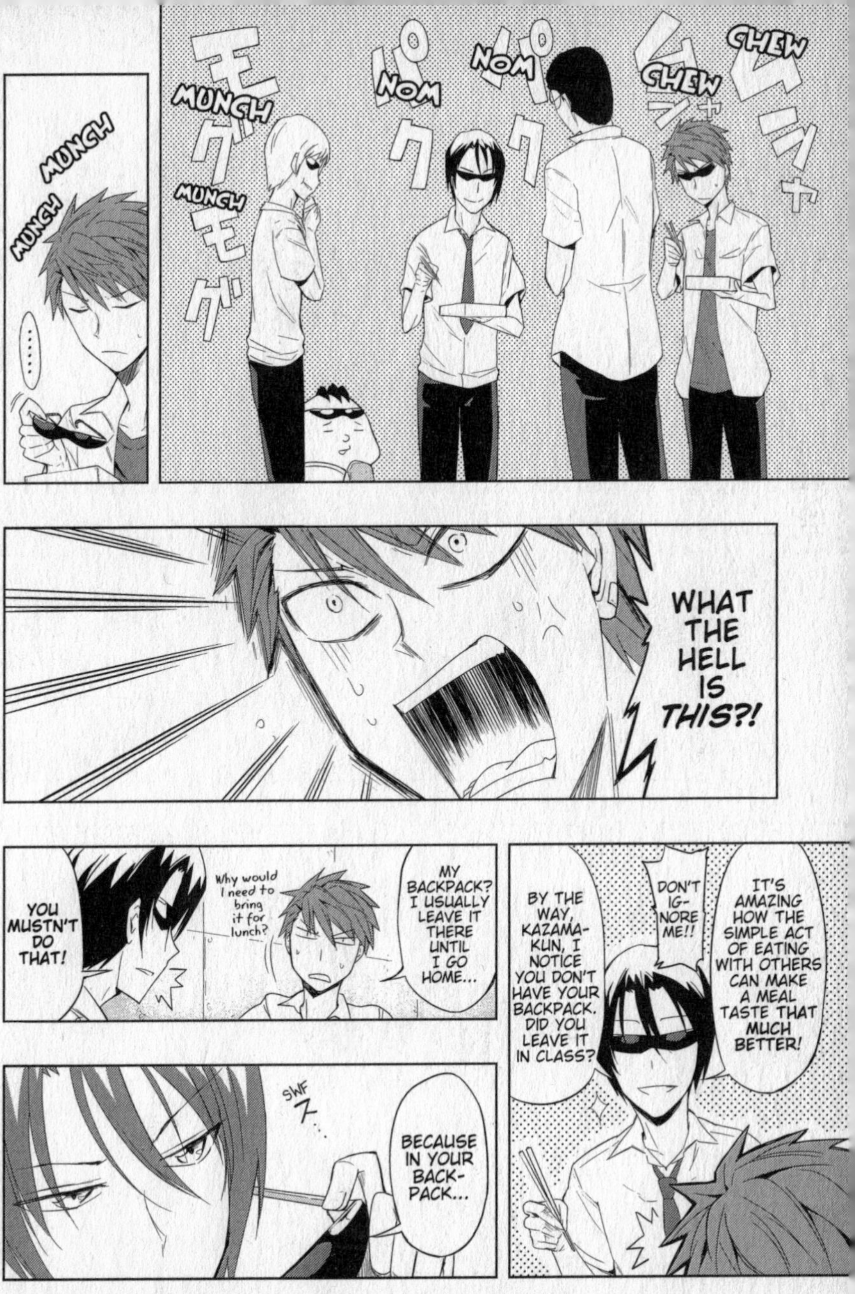
CHEW
CHEW
ムシャムシャ
NOM
NOM
パクパク
MUNCH
MUNCH
モグモグ
MUNCH
MUNCH
......
WHAT THE HELL IS THIS?!
IT'S AMAZING HOW THE SIMPLE ACT OF EATING WITH OTHERS CAN MAKE A MEAL TASTE THAT MUCH BETTER!
DON'T IG-NORE ME!!
BY THE WAY, KAZAMA-KUN, I NOTICE YOU DON'T HAVE YOUR BACKPACK. DID YOU LEAVE IT IN CLASS?
MY BACKPACK? I USUALLY LEAVE IT THERE UNTIL I GO HOME...
Why would I need to bring it for lunch?
YOU MUSTN'T DO THAT!
BECAUSE IN YOUR BACK-PACK...
SWF

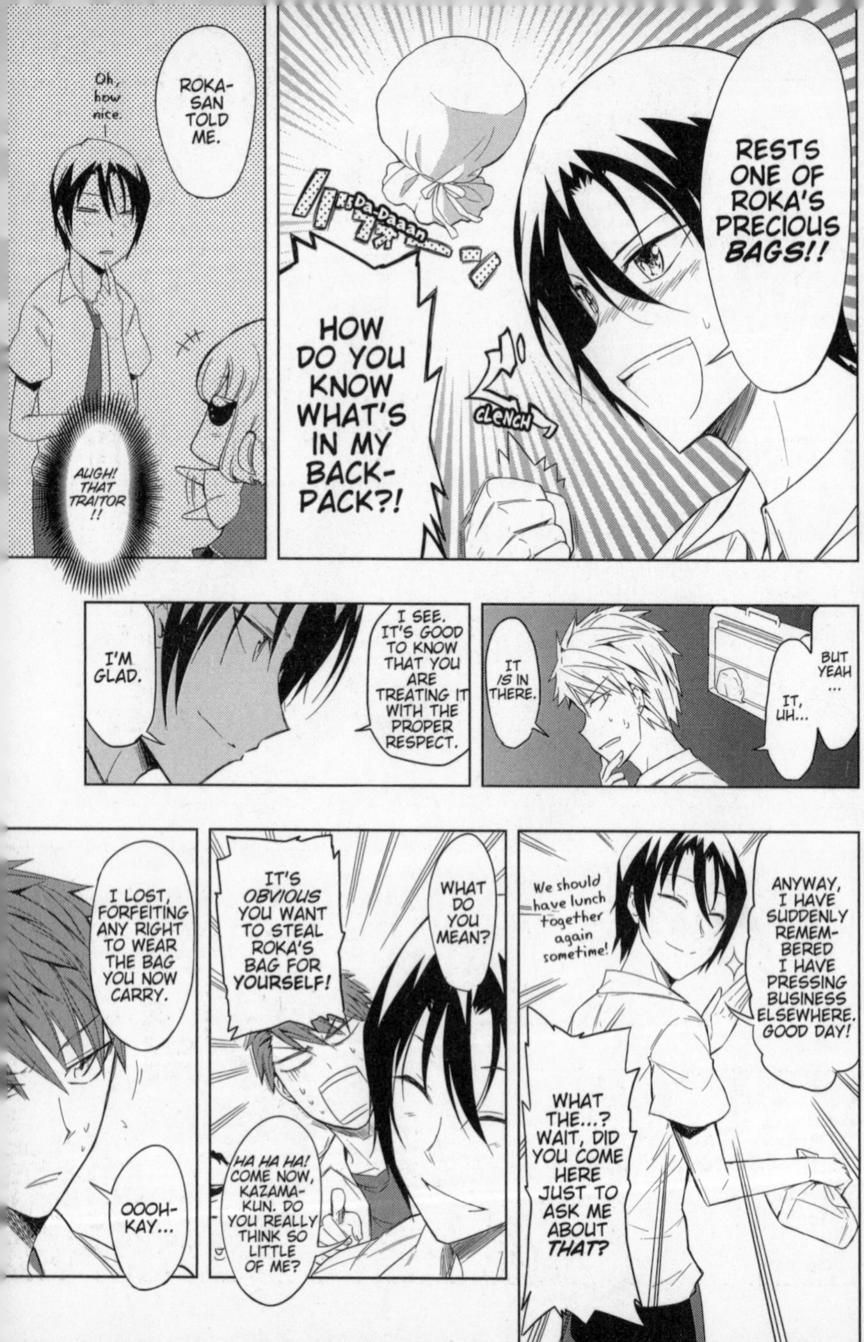
RESTS ONE OF ROKA'S PRECIOUS BAGS!!
Da-Daaan
HOW DO YOU KNOW WHAT'S IN MY BACK-PACK?!
CLENCH
ROKA-SAN TOLD ME.
Oh, how nice.
AUGH! THAT TRAITOR!!
BUT YEAH...
IT, UH...
IT IS IN THERE.
I SEE. IT'S GOOD TO KNOW THAT YOU ARE TREATING IT WITH THE PROPER RESPECT.
I'M GLAD.
ANYWAY, I HAVE SUDDENLY REMEM-BERED I HAVE PRESSING BUSINESS ELSEWHERE. GOOD DAY!
We should have lunch together again sometime!
WHAT THE...? WAIT, DID YOU COME HERE JUST TO ASK ME ABOUT THAT?
WHAT DO YOU MEAN?
IT'S OBVIOUS YOU WANT TO STEAL ROKA'S BAG FOR YOURSELF!
HA HA HA! COME NOW, KAZAMA-KUN. DO YOU REALLY THINK SO LITTLE OF ME?
I LOST, FORFEITING ANY RIGHT TO WEAR THE BAG YOU NOW CARRY.
OOOH-KAY...

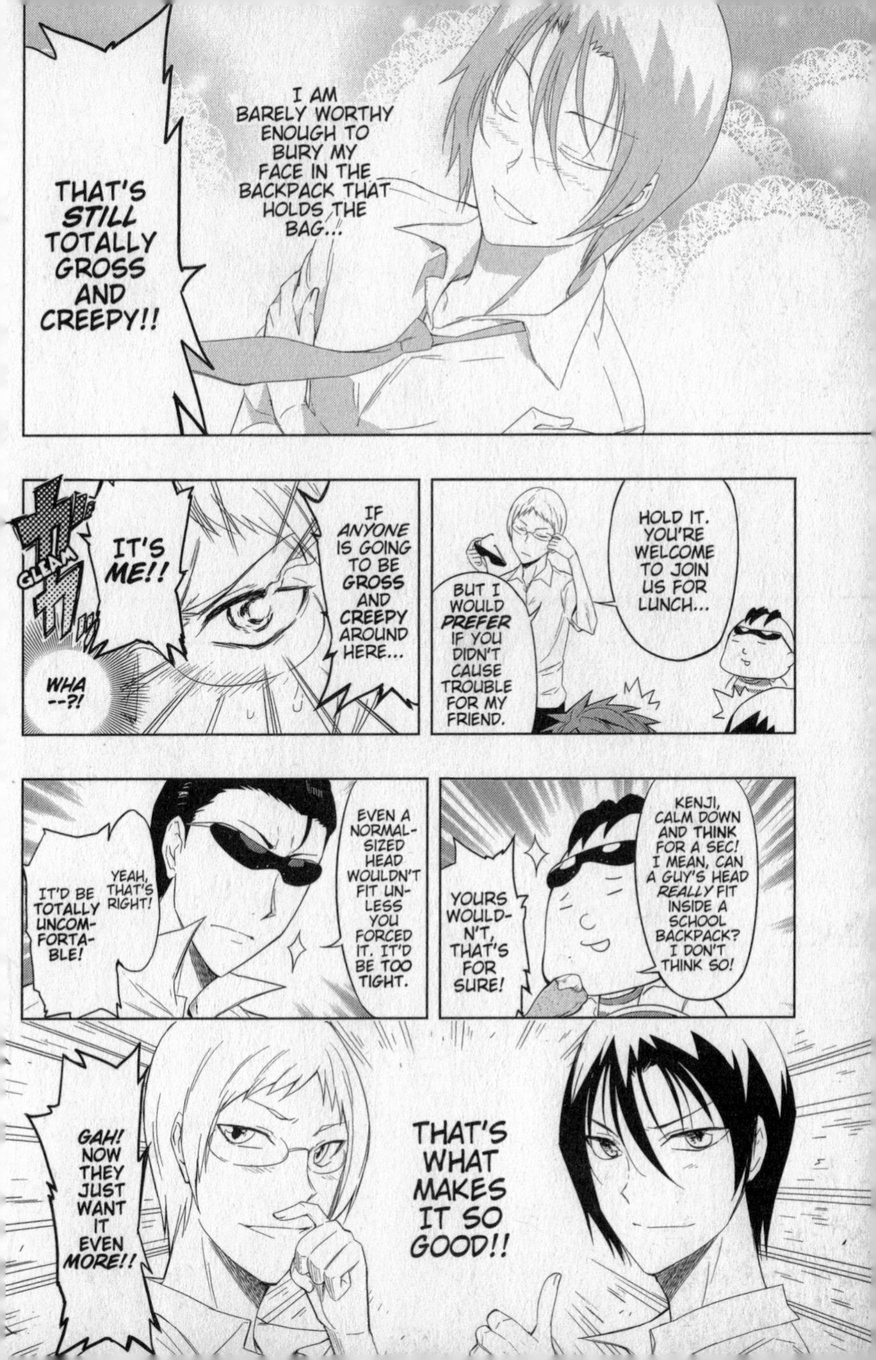
I AM BARELY WORTHY ENOUGH TO BURY MY FACE IN THE BACKPACK THAT HOLDS THE BAG...
THAT'S *STILL* TOTALLY GROSS AND CREEPY!!
HOLD IT. YOU'RE WELCOME TO JOIN US FOR LUNCH...
BUT I WOULD *PREFER* IF YOU DIDN'T CAUSE TROUBLE FOR MY FRIEND.
IF *ANYONE* IS GOING TO BE GROSS AND CREEPY AROUND HERE...
IT'S *ME!!*
GLEAM
WHA--?!
KENJI, CALM DOWN AND THINK FOR A SEC! I MEAN, CAN A GUY'S HEAD *REALLY* FIT INSIDE A SCHOOL BACKPACK? I DON'T THINK SO!
YOURS WOULDN'T, THAT'S FOR SURE!
EVEN A NORMAL-SIZED HEAD WOULDN'T FIT UNLESS YOU FORCED IT. IT'D BE TOO TIGHT.
YEAH, THAT'S RIGHT!
IT'D BE TOTALLY UNCOMFORTABLE!
THAT'S WHAT MAKES IT SO GOOD!!
GAH! NOW THEY JUST WANT IT EVEN MORE!!

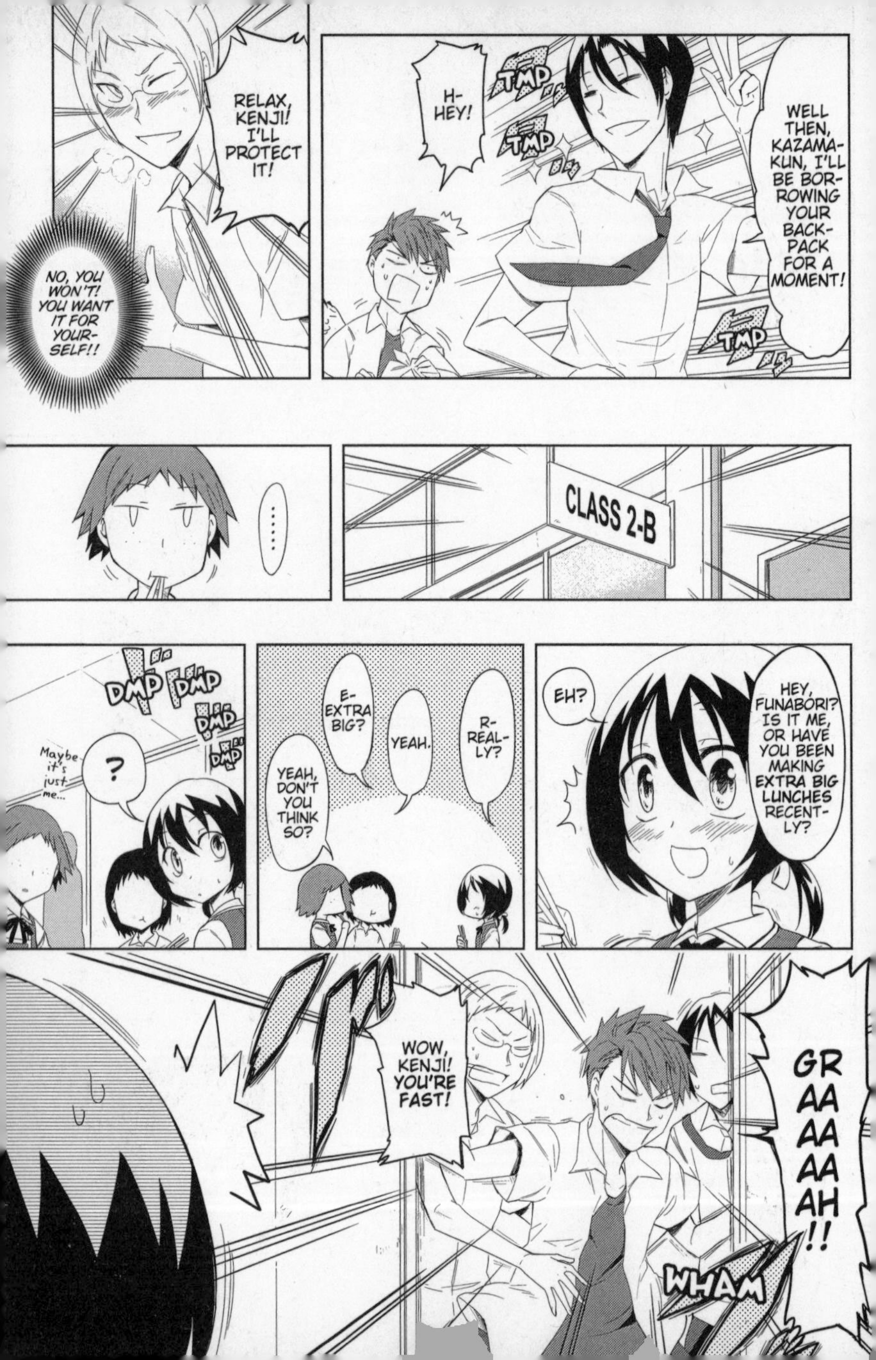
WELL THEN, KAZAMA-KUN, I'LL BE BORROWING YOUR BACKPACK FOR A MOMENT!
TMP
TMP
TMP
H-HEY!
RELAX, KENJI! I'LL PROTECT IT!
NO, YOU WON'T! YOU WANT IT FOR YOURSELF!!
CLASS 2-B
......
HEY, FUNABORI? IS IT ME, OR HAVE YOU BEEN MAKING EXTRA BIG LUNCHES RECENTLY?
EH?
R-REALLY?
YEAH.
E-EXTRA BIG?
YEAH, DON'T YOU THINK SO?
DMP DMP
DMP
DMP
?
Maybe it's just me...
GRAAAAAAAAAH!!
WHAM
WOW, KENJI! YOU'RE FAST!

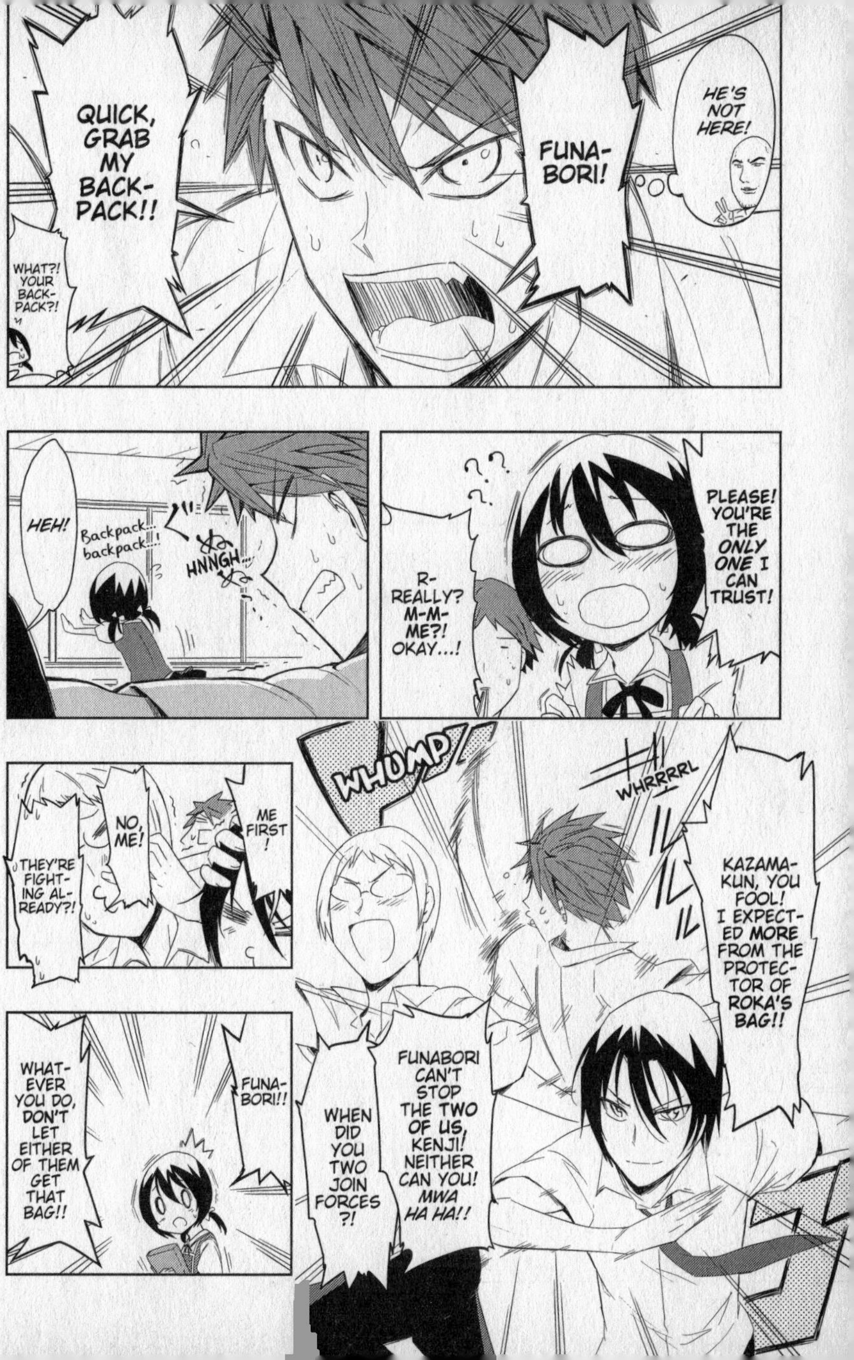
FUNA-BORI!
HE'S NOT HERE!
QUICK, GRAB MY BACK-PACK!!
WHAT?! YOUR BACK-PACK?!
PLEASE! YOU'RE THE *ONLY ONE* I CAN TRUST!
R-REALLY? M-M-ME?! OKAY...!
HEH!
Backpack... backpack...!
HNNGH...
WHUMP
WHRRRRL
KAZAMA-KUN, YOU FOOL! I EXPECTED MORE FROM THE PROTECTOR OF ROKA'S BAG!!
FUNABORI CAN'T STOP THE TWO OF US, KENJI! NEITHER CAN YOU! *MWA HA HA!!*
WHEN DID YOU TWO JOIN FORCES?!
ME FIRST!
NO, ME!
THEY'RE FIGHTING ALREADY?!
FUNA-BORI!!
WHAT-EVER YOU DO, DON'T LET EITHER OF THEM GET THAT BAG!!

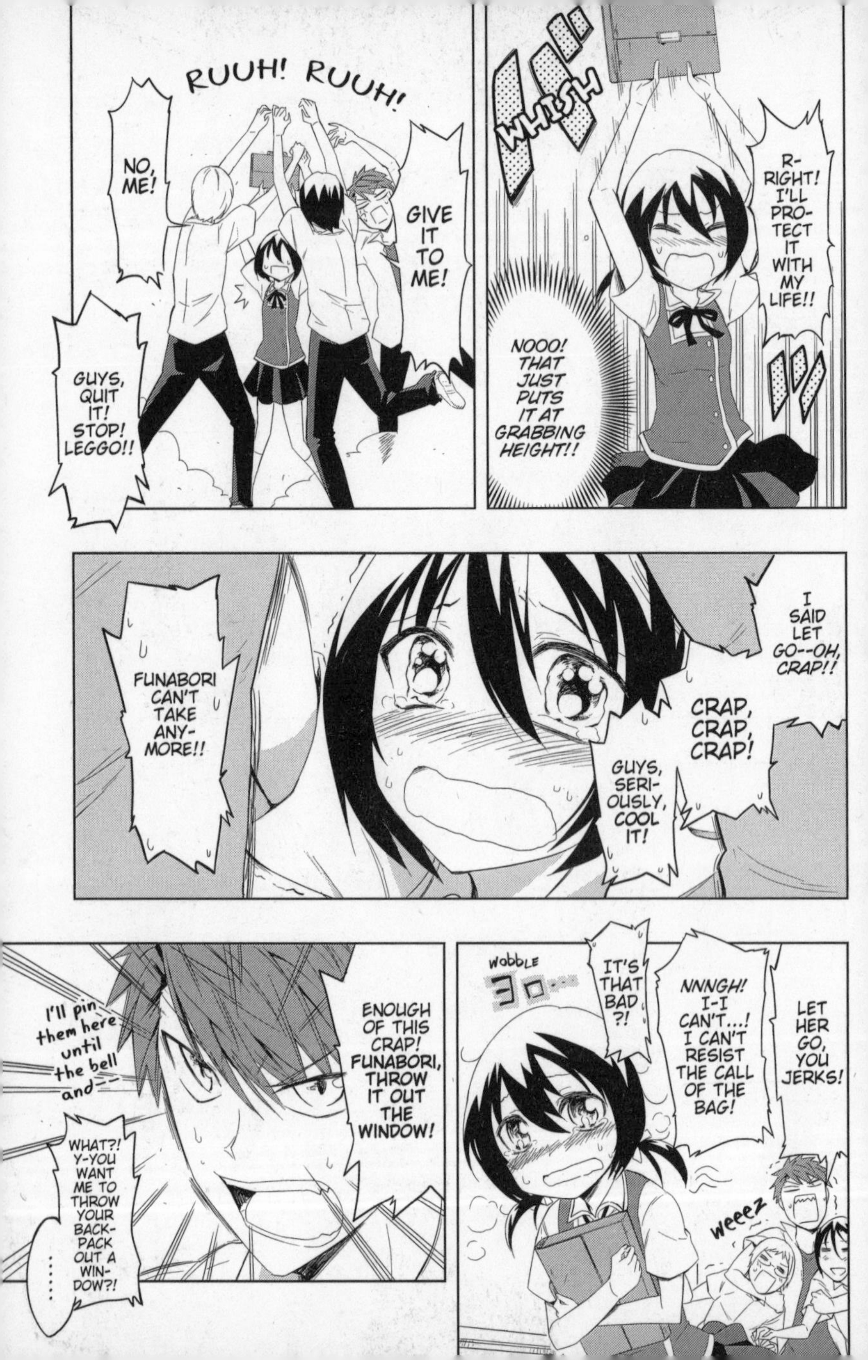
WHISH
R-RIGHT! I'LL PROTECT IT WITH MY LIFE!!
NOOO! THAT JUST PUTS IT AT GRABBING HEIGHT!!
RUUH! RUUH!
GIVE IT TO ME!
NO, ME!
GUYS, QUIT IT! STOP! LEGGO!!
I SAID LET GO--OH, CRAP!!
CRAP, CRAP, CRAP!
GUYS, SERIOUSLY, COOL IT!
FUNABORI CAN'T TAKE ANYMORE!!
LET HER GO, YOU JERKS!
NNNGH! I-I CAN'T...! I CAN'T RESIST THE CALL OF THE BAG!
IT'S THAT BAD?!
wobble
ヨロ・・・
weeez
ENOUGH OF THIS CRAP! FUNABORI, THROW IT OUT THE WINDOW!
I'll pin them here until the bell and--
WHAT?! Y-YOU WANT ME TO THROW YOUR BACKPACK OUT A WINDOW?!
......

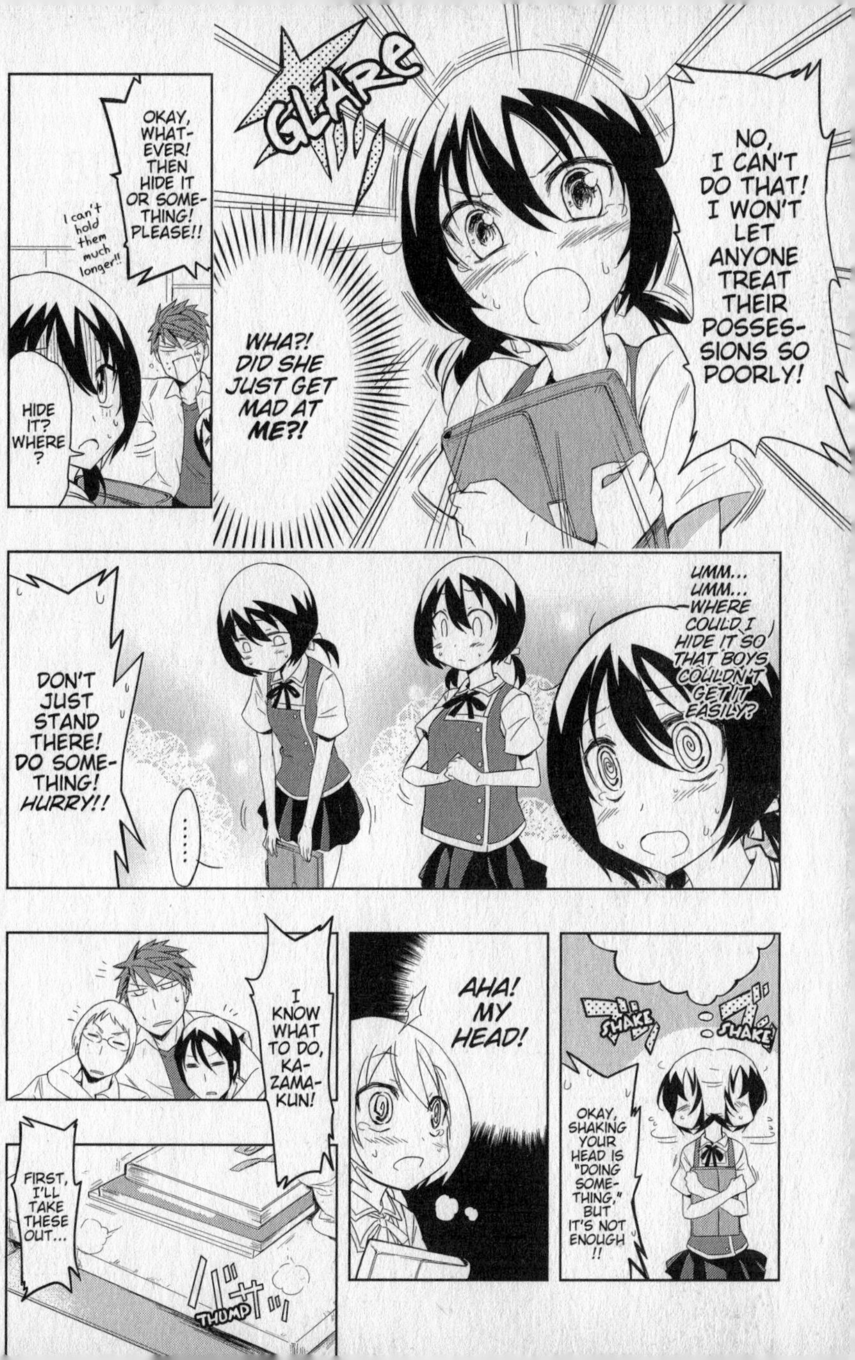
GLARE
NO, I CAN'T DO THAT! I WON'T LET ANYONE TREAT THEIR POSSESSIONS SO POORLY!
WHA?! DID SHE JUST GET MAD AT ME?!
OKAY, WHATEVER! THEN HIDE IT OR SOMETHING! PLEASE!!
I can't hold them much longer!!
HIDE IT? WHERE?
UMM... UMM... WHERE COULD I HIDE IT SO THAT BOYS COULDN'T GET IT EASILY?
DON'T JUST STAND THERE! DO SOMETHING! HURRY!!
......
SHAKE
SHAKE
OKAY, SHAKING YOUR HEAD IS "DOING SOMETHING," BUT IT'S NOT ENOUGH!!
AHA! MY HEAD!
I KNOW WHAT TO DO, KAZAMA-KUN!
FIRST, I'LL TAKE THESE OUT...
THUMP

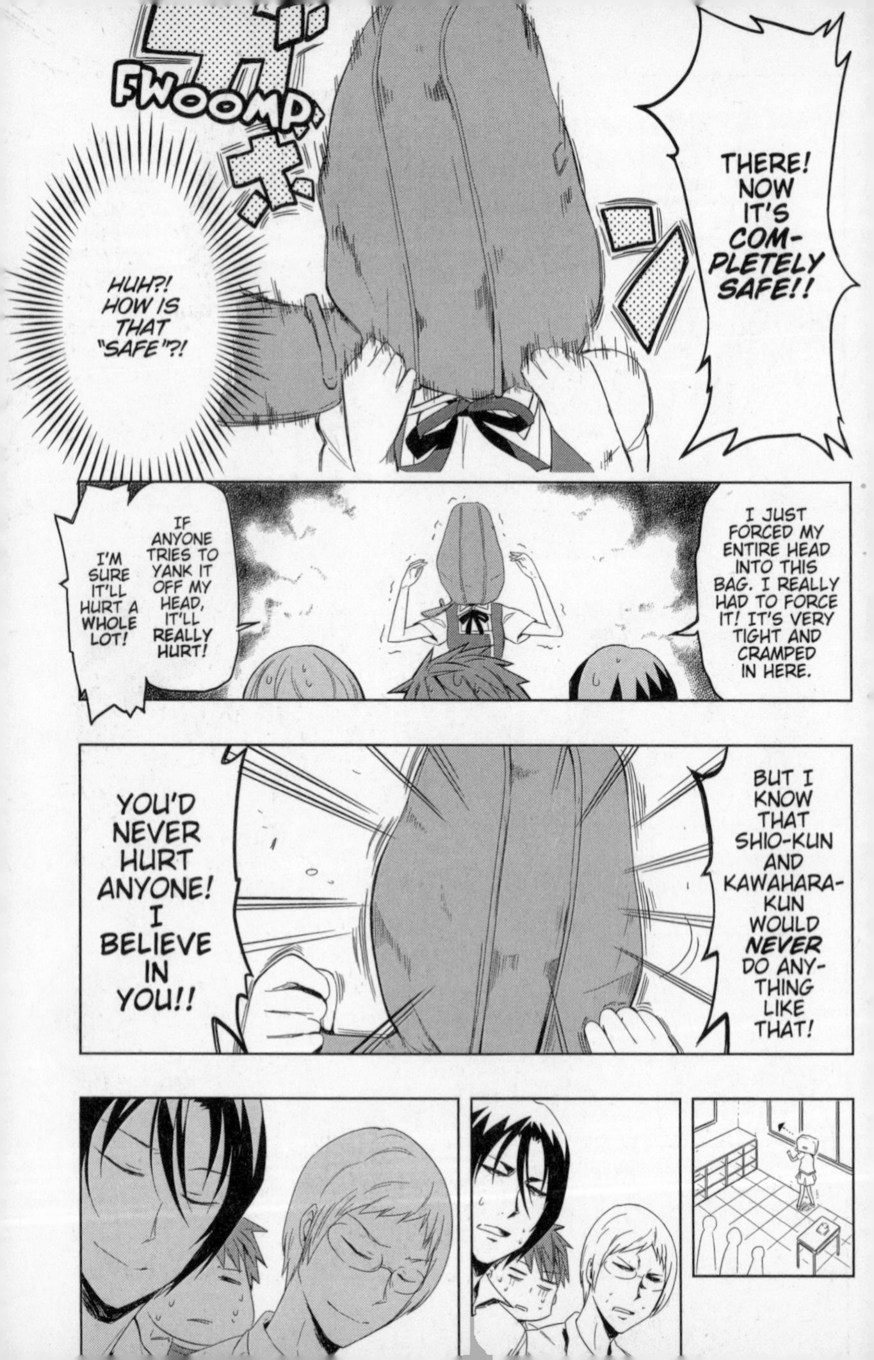
THERE! NOW IT'S COMPLETELY SAFE!!
FWOOMP
HUH?! HOW IS THAT "SAFE"?!
I JUST FORCED MY ENTIRE HEAD INTO THIS BAG. I REALLY HAD TO FORCE IT! IT'S VERY TIGHT AND CRAMPED IN HERE.
IF ANYONE TRIES TO YANK IT OFF MY HEAD, IT'LL REALLY HURT!
I'M SURE IT'LL HURT A WHOLE LOT!
BUT I KNOW THAT SHIO-KUN AND KAWAHARA-KUN WOULD NEVER DO ANYTHING LIKE THAT!
YOU'D NEVER HURT ANYONE! I BELIEVE IN YOU!!

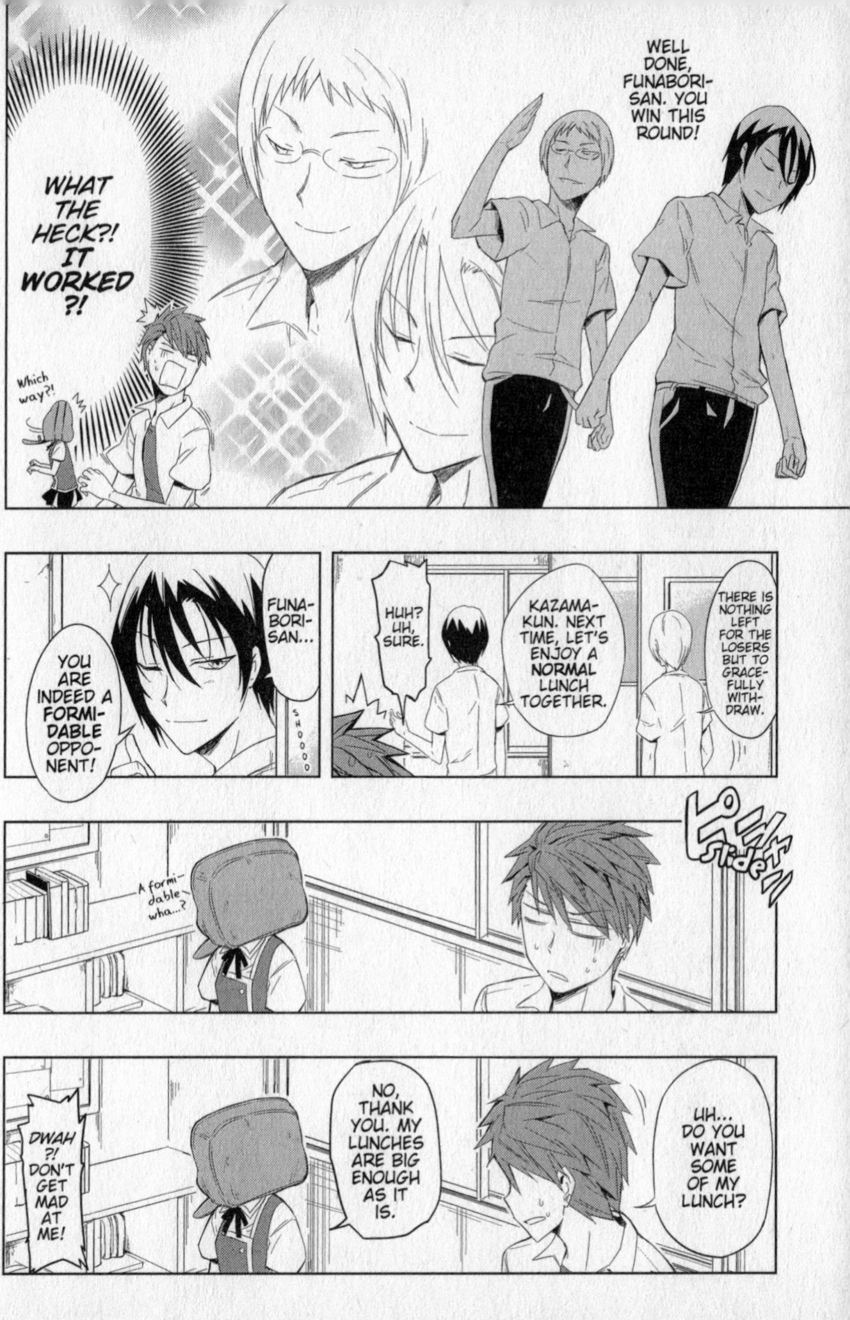
WELL DONE, FUNABORI-SAN. YOU WIN THIS ROUND!
WHAT THE HECK?! IT WORKED?!
Which way?!
THERE IS NOTHING LEFT FOR THE LOSERS BUT TO GRACEFULLY WITHDRAW.
KAZAMA-KUN. NEXT TIME, LET'S ENJOY A NORMAL LUNCH TOGETHER.
HUH? UH, SURE.
FUNABORI-SAN...
YOU ARE INDEED A FORMIDABLE OPPONENT!
slide
A formidable wha...?
UH... DO YOU WANT SOME OF MY LUNCH?
NO, THANK YOU. MY LUNCHES ARE BIG ENOUGH AS IT IS.
DWAH?! DON'T GET MAD AT ME!

ディーふらぐ!
D-FRAGMENTS

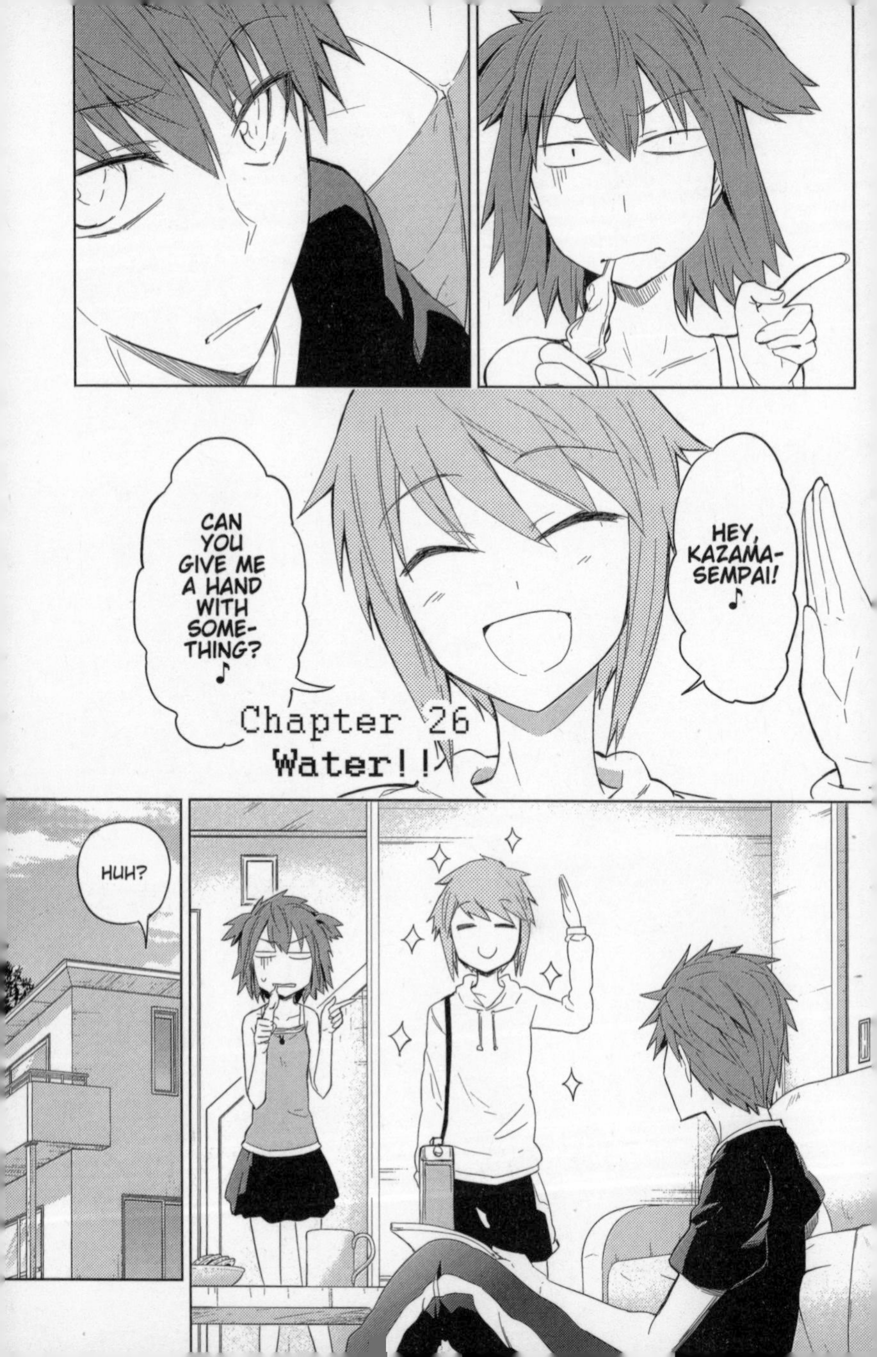
HEY, KAZAMA-SEMPAI! ♪
CAN YOU GIVE ME A HAND WITH SOME-THING? ♪
Chapter 26
Water!!
HUH?

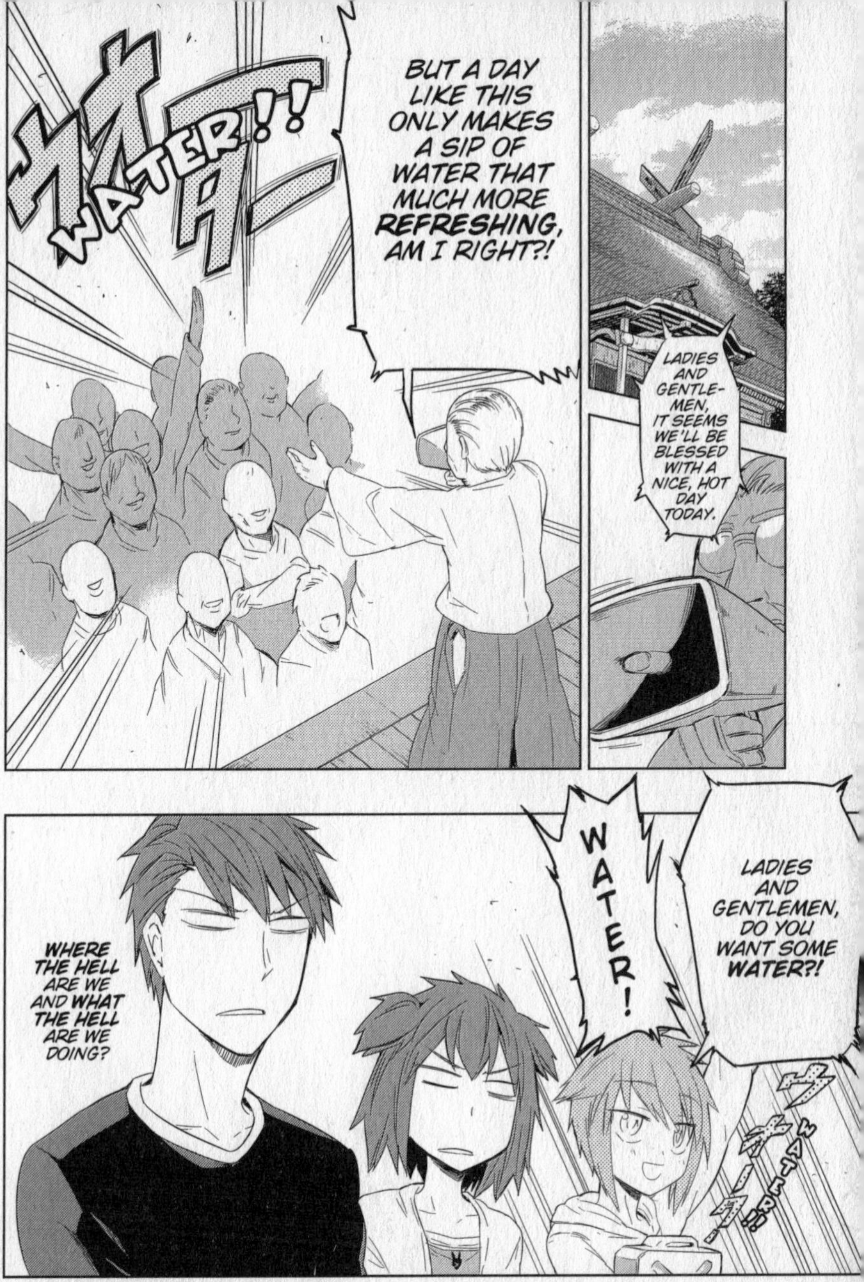
LADIES AND GENTLEMEN, IT SEEMS WE'LL BE BLESSED WITH A NICE, HOT DAY TODAY.
BUT A DAY LIKE THIS ONLY MAKES A SIP OF WATER THAT MUCH MORE REFRESHING, AM I RIGHT?!
WATER!!
LADIES AND GENTLEMEN, DO YOU WANT SOME WATER?!
WATER!
WATER?!
WHERE THE HELL ARE WE AND WHAT THE HELL ARE WE DOING?

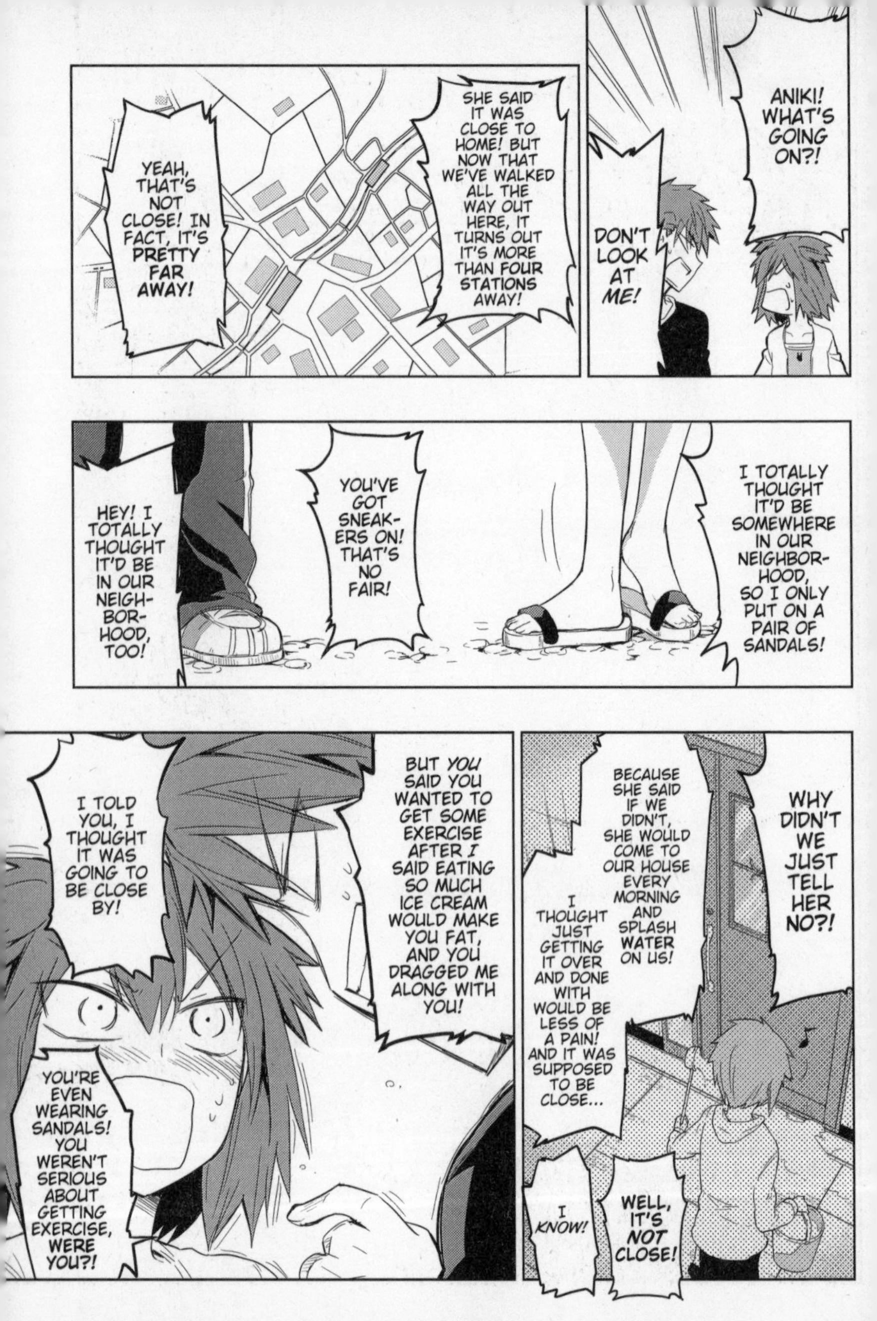
ANIKI! WHAT'S GOING ON?!
DON'T LOOK AT ME!
SHE SAID IT WAS CLOSE TO HOME! BUT NOW THAT WE'VE WALKED ALL THE WAY OUT HERE, IT TURNS OUT IT'S MORE THAN FOUR STATIONS AWAY!
YEAH, THAT'S NOT CLOSE! IN FACT, IT'S PRETTY FAR AWAY!
I TOTALLY THOUGHT IT'D BE SOMEWHERE IN OUR NEIGHBOR-HOOD, SO I ONLY PUT ON A PAIR OF SANDALS!
YOU'VE GOT SNEAK-ERS ON! THAT'S NO FAIR!
HEY! I TOTALLY THOUGHT IT'D BE IN OUR NEIGH-BOR-HOOD, TOO!
WHY DIDN'T WE JUST TELL HER NO?!
BECAUSE SHE SAID IF WE DIDN'T, SHE WOULD COME TO OUR HOUSE EVERY MORNING AND SPLASH WATER ON US!
I THOUGHT JUST GETTING IT OVER AND DONE WITH WOULD BE LESS OF A PAIN! AND IT WAS SUPPOSED TO BE CLOSE...
WELL, IT'S *NOT* CLOSE!
I *KNOW*!
BUT *YOU* SAID YOU WANTED TO GET SOME EXERCISE AFTER *I* SAID EATING SO MUCH ICE CREAM WOULD MAKE YOU FAT, AND YOU DRAGGED ME ALONG WITH YOU!
I TOLD YOU, I THOUGHT IT WAS GOING TO BE CLOSE BY!
YOU'RE EVEN WEARING SANDALS! YOU WEREN'T SERIOUS ABOUT GETTING EXERCISE, WERE YOU?!

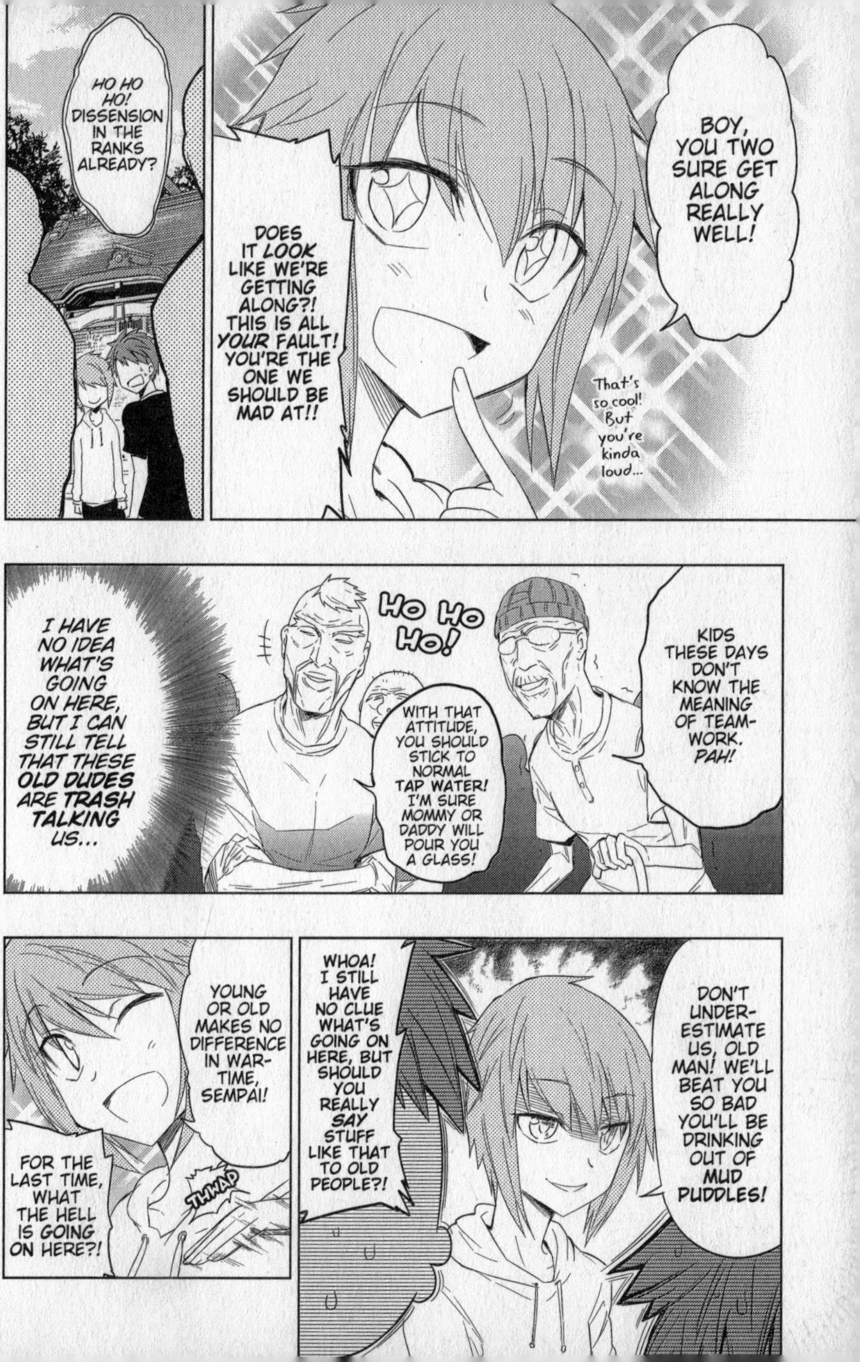
BOY, YOU TWO SURE GET ALONG REALLY WELL!
That's so cool! But you're kinda loud...
DOES IT LOOK LIKE WE'RE GETTING ALONG?! THIS IS ALL YOUR FAULT! YOU'RE THE ONE WE SHOULD BE MAD AT!!
HO HO HO! DISSENSION IN THE RANKS ALREADY?
KIDS THESE DAYS DON'T KNOW THE MEANING OF TEAM-WORK. PAH!
HO HO HO!
WITH THAT ATTITUDE, YOU SHOULD STICK TO NORMAL TAP WATER! I'M SURE MOMMY OR DADDY WILL POUR YOU A GLASS!
I HAVE NO IDEA WHAT'S GOING ON HERE, BUT I CAN STILL TELL THAT THESE OLD DUDES ARE TRASH TALKING US...
DON'T UNDER-ESTIMATE US, OLD MAN! WE'LL BEAT YOU SO BAD YOU'LL BE DRINKING OUT OF MUD PUDDLES!
WHOA! I STILL HAVE NO CLUE WHAT'S GOING ON HERE, BUT SHOULD YOU REALLY SAY STUFF LIKE THAT TO OLD PEOPLE?!
YOUNG OR OLD MAKES NO DIFFERENCE IN WAR-TIME, SEMPAI!
THWAP
FOR THE LAST TIME, WHAT THE HELL IS GOING ON HERE?!

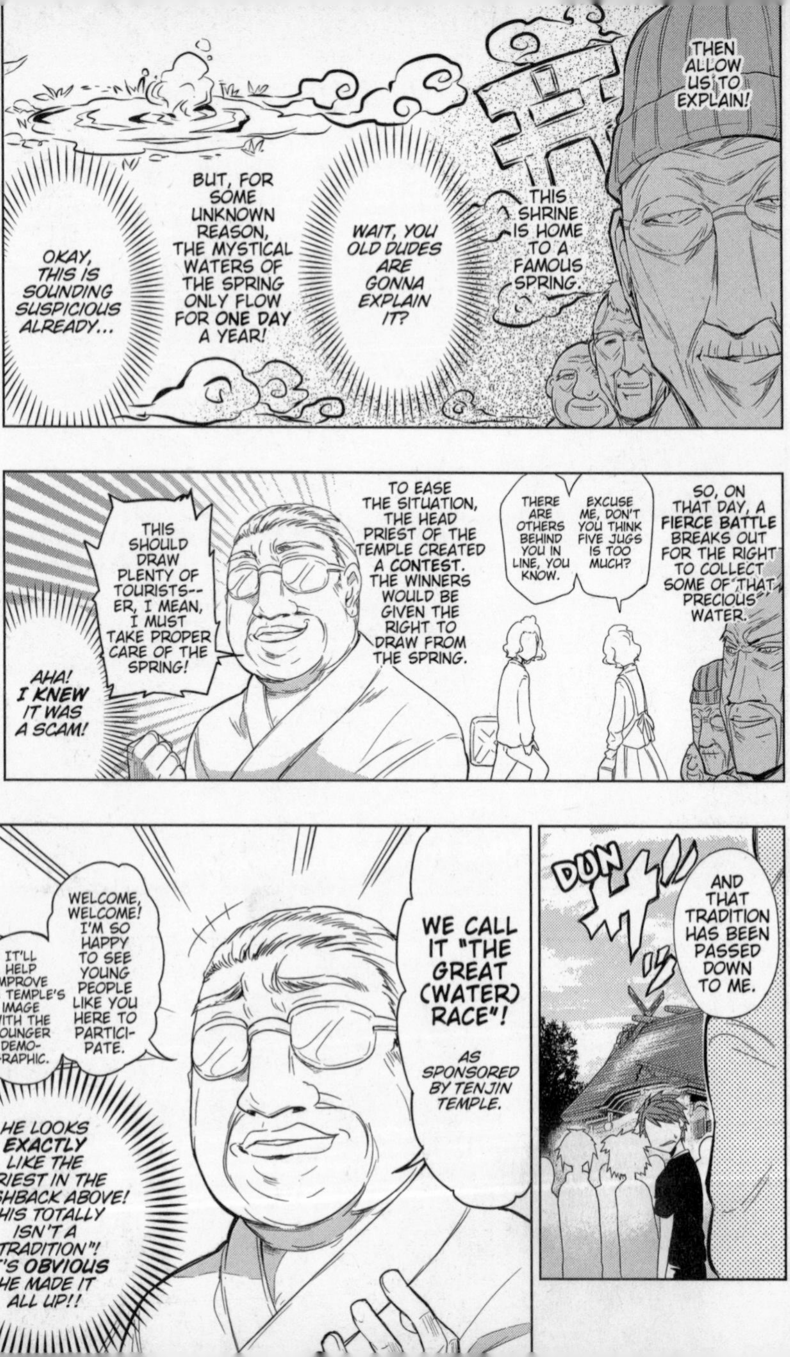
THEN ALLOW US TO EXPLAIN!
THIS SHRINE IS HOME TO A FAMOUS SPRING.
WAIT, YOU OLD DUDES ARE GONNA EXPLAIN IT?
BUT, FOR SOME UNKNOWN REASON, THE MYSTICAL WATERS OF THE SPRING ONLY FLOW FOR ONE DAY A YEAR!
OKAY, THIS IS SOUNDING SUSPICIOUS ALREADY...
SO, ON THAT DAY, A FIERCE BATTLE BREAKS OUT FOR THE RIGHT TO COLLECT SOME OF THAT PRECIOUS WATER.
EXCUSE ME, DON'T YOU THINK FIVE JUGS IS TOO MUCH?
THERE ARE OTHERS BEHIND YOU IN LINE, YOU KNOW.
TO EASE THE SITUATION, THE HEAD PRIEST OF THE TEMPLE CREATED A CONTEST. THE WINNERS WOULD BE GIVEN THE RIGHT TO DRAW FROM THE SPRING.
THIS SHOULD DRAW PLENTY OF TOURISTS-- ER, I MEAN, I MUST TAKE PROPER CARE OF THE SPRING!
AHA! I KNEW IT WAS A SCAM!
DON
AND THAT TRADITION HAS BEEN PASSED DOWN TO ME.
WE CALL IT "THE GREAT (WATER) RACE"!
AS SPONSORED BY TENJIN TEMPLE.
WELCOME, WELCOME! I'M SO HAPPY TO SEE YOUNG PEOPLE LIKE YOU HERE TO PARTICI-PATE.
IT'LL HELP IMPROVE THE TEMPLE'S IMAGE WITH THE YOUNGER DEMO-GRAPHIC.
HE LOOKS EXACTLY LIKE THE PRIEST IN THE FLASHBACK ABOVE! THIS TOTALLY ISN'T A "TRADITION"! IT'S OBVIOUS HE MADE IT ALL UP!!

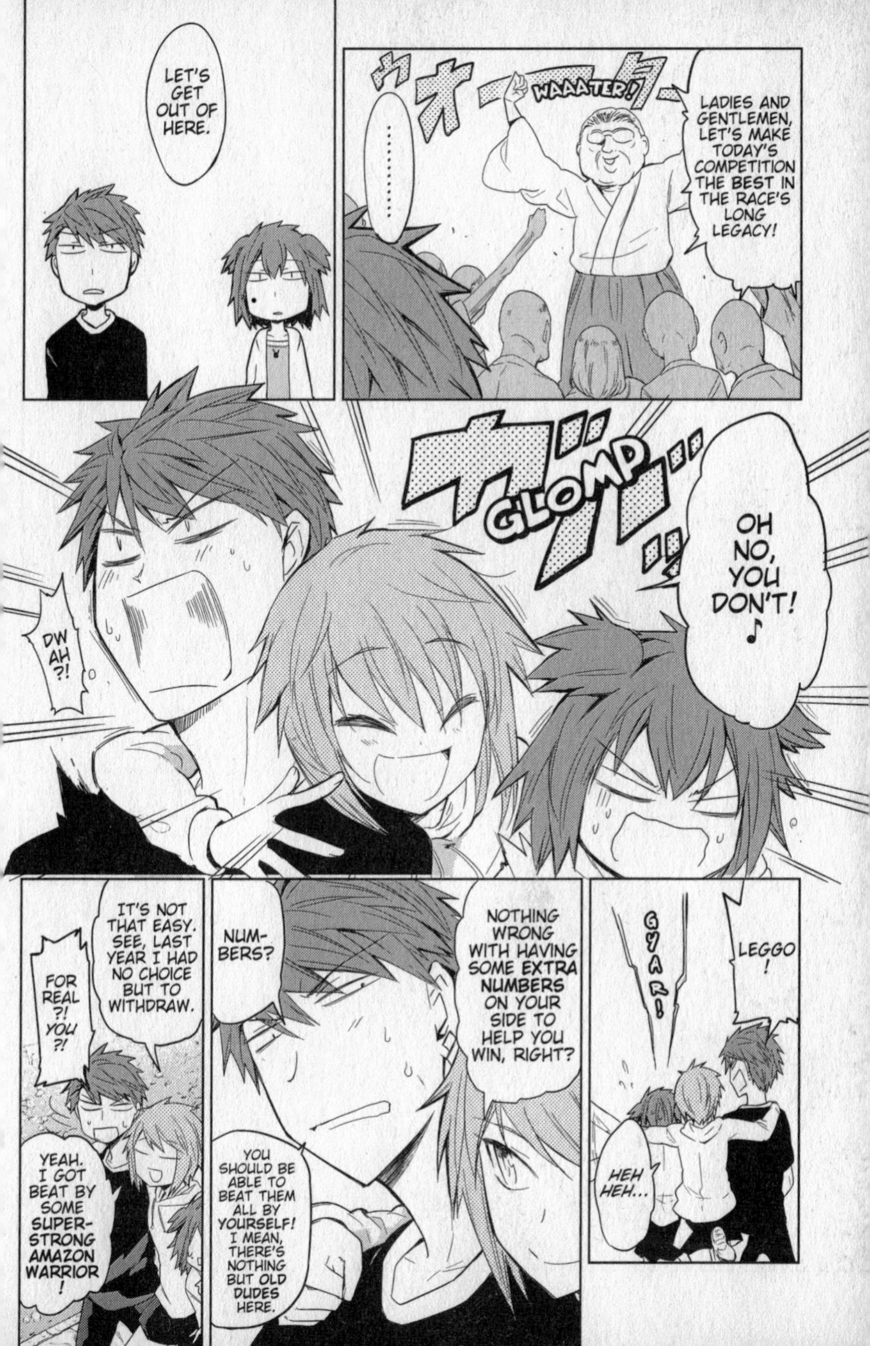
WAAATER!
LADIES AND GENTLEMEN, LET'S MAKE TODAY'S COMPETITION THE BEST IN THE RACE'S LONG LEGACY!
......
LET'S GET OUT OF HERE.
GLOMP
OH NO, YOU DON'T! ♪
DWAH?!
LEGGO!
GYAR!
HEH HEH...
NOTHING WRONG WITH HAVING SOME EXTRA NUMBERS ON YOUR SIDE TO HELP YOU WIN, RIGHT?
NUM-BERS?
YOU SHOULD BE ABLE TO BEAT THEM ALL BY YOURSELF! I MEAN, THERE'S NOTHING BUT OLD DUDES HERE.
IT'S NOT THAT EASY. SEE, LAST YEAR I HAD NO CHOICE BUT TO WITHDRAW.
FOR REAL?! YOU?!
YEAH. I GOT BEAT BY SOME SUPER-STRONG AMAZON WARRIOR!

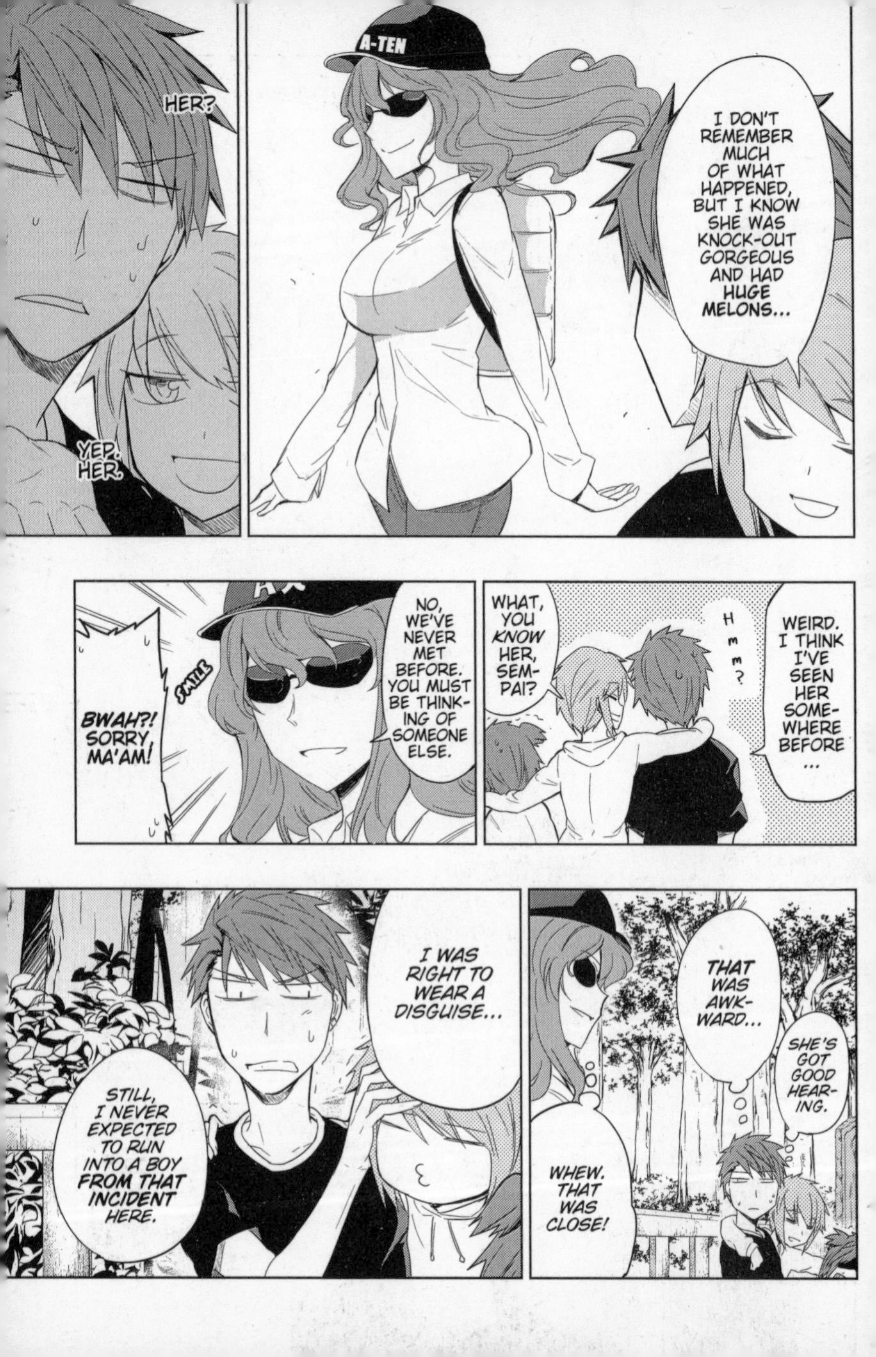

I DON'T REMEMBER MUCH OF WHAT HAPPENED, BUT I KNOW SHE WAS KNOCK-OUT GORGEOUS AND HAD HUGE MELONS...
A-TEN
HER?
YEP. HER.
WEIRD. I THINK I'VE SEEN HER SOMEWHERE BEFORE...
Hmm?
WHAT, YOU KNOW HER, SEMPAI?
NO, WE'VE NEVER MET BEFORE. YOU MUST BE THINKING OF SOMEONE ELSE.
SMILE
BWAH?! SORRY, MA'AM!
THAT WAS AWKWARD...
SHE'S GOT GOOD HEARING.
WHEW. THAT WAS CLOSE!
I WAS RIGHT TO WEAR A DISGUISE...
STILL, I NEVER EXPECTED TO RUN INTO A BOY FROM THAT INCIDENT HERE.

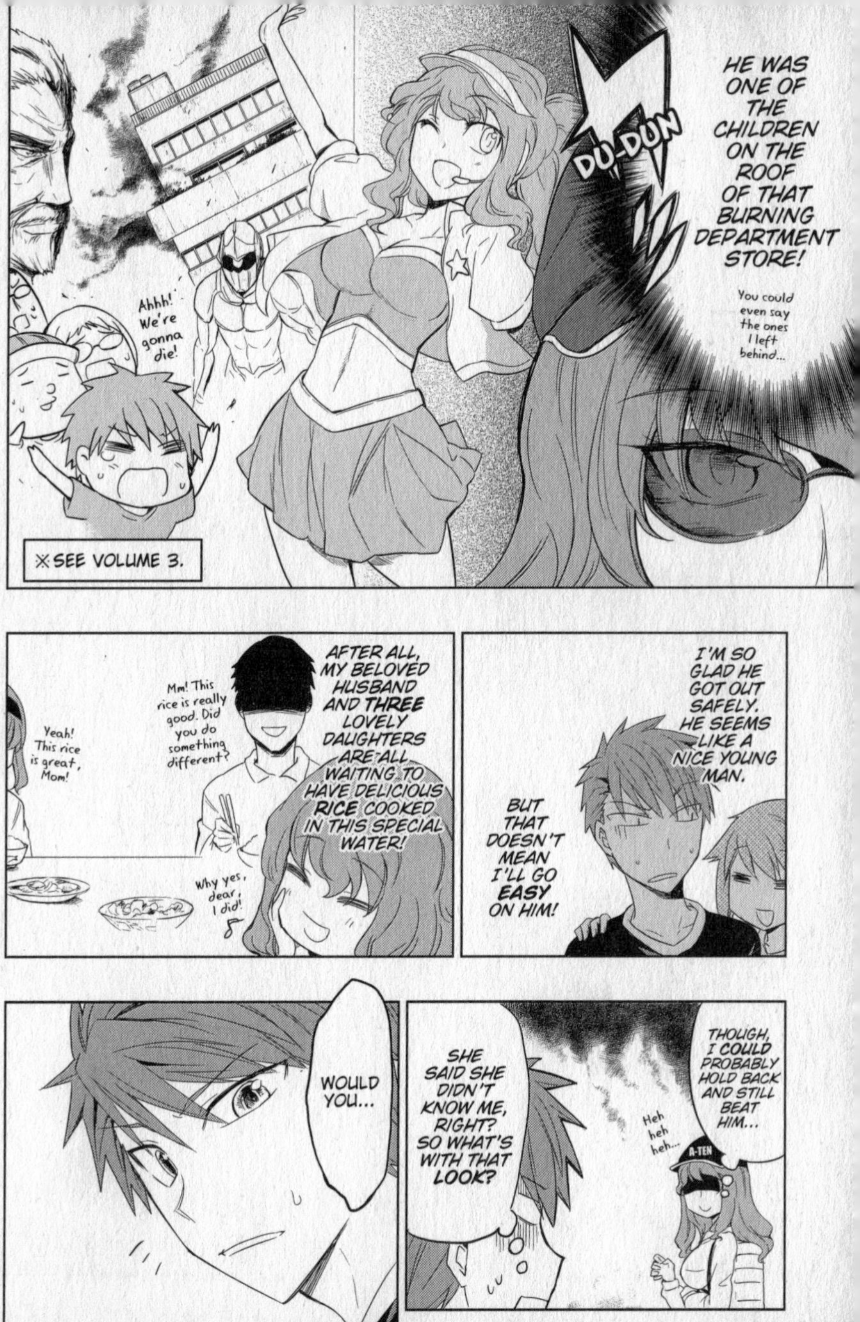
HE WAS ONE OF THE CHILDREN ON THE ROOF OF THAT BURNING DEPARTMENT STORE!
DU-DUN
You could even say the ones I left behind...
Ahhh! We're gonna die!
※SEE VOLUME 3.
I'M SO GLAD HE GOT OUT SAFELY. HE SEEMS LIKE A NICE YOUNG MAN.
BUT THAT DOESN'T MEAN I'LL GO EASY ON HIM!
AFTER ALL, MY BELOVED HUSBAND AND THREE LOVELY DAUGHTERS ARE ALL WAITING TO HAVE DELICIOUS RICE COOKED IN THIS SPECIAL WATER!
Mm! This rice is really good. Did you do something different?
Yeah! This rice is great, Mom!
Why yes, dear, I did!
THOUGH, I COULD PROBABLY HOLD BACK AND STILL BEAT HIM...
Heh heh heh...
A-TEN
SHE SAID SHE DIDN'T KNOW ME, RIGHT? SO WHAT'S WITH THAT LOOK?
WOULD YOU...

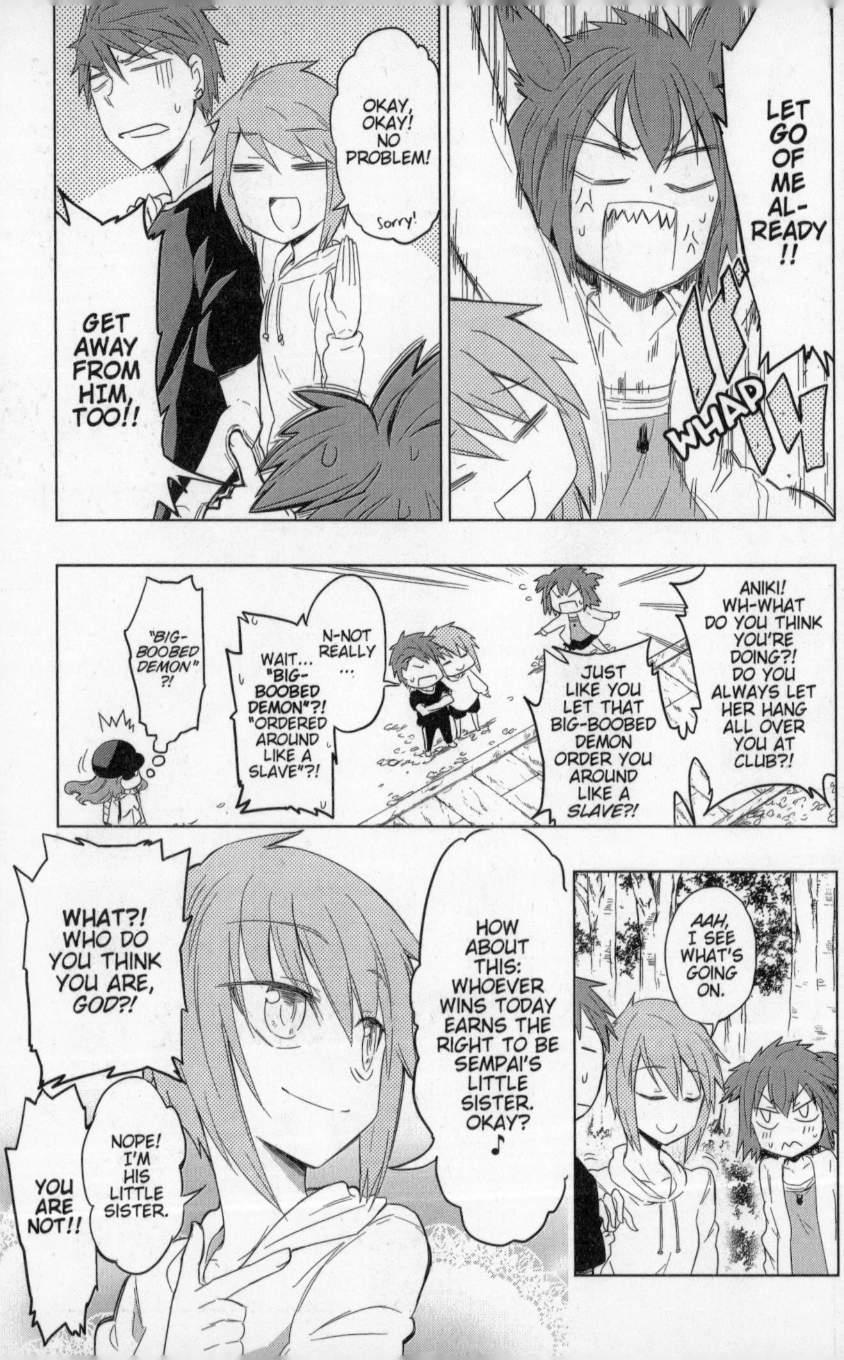
LET GO OF ME AL-READY!!
WHAP
OKAY, OKAY! NO PROBLEM!
Sorry!
GET AWAY FROM HIM, TOO!!
ANIKI! WH-WHAT DO YOU THINK YOU'RE DOING?! DO YOU ALWAYS LET HER HANG ALL OVER YOU AT CLUB?!
JUST LIKE YOU LET THAT BIG-BOOBED DEMON ORDER YOU AROUND LIKE A *SLAVE*?!
N-NOT REALLY ...
WAIT... "BIG-BOOBED DEMON"?! "ORDERED AROUND LIKE A SLAVE"?!
"BIG-BOOBED DEMON"?!
AAH, I SEE WHAT'S GOING ON.
HOW ABOUT THIS: WHOEVER WINS TODAY EARNS THE RIGHT TO BE SEMPAI'S LITTLE SISTER. OKAY? ♪
WHAT?! WHO DO YOU THINK YOU ARE, *GOD*?!
NOPE! I'M HIS LITTLE SISTER.
YOU ARE NOT!!

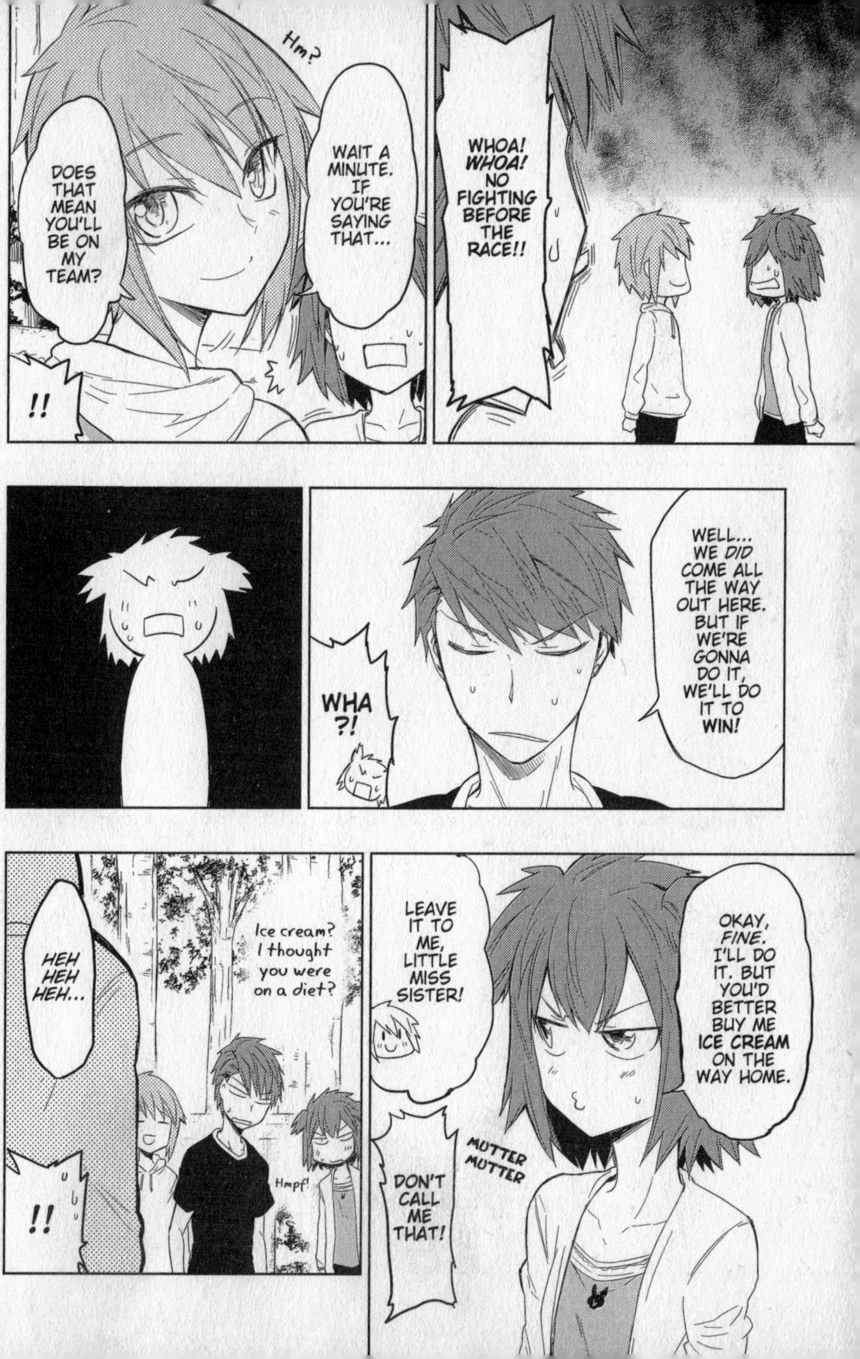
WHOA! WHOA! NO FIGHTING BEFORE THE RACE!!
Hm?
WAIT A MINUTE. IF YOU'RE SAYING THAT...
DOES THAT MEAN YOU'LL BE ON MY TEAM?
!!
WELL... WE DID COME ALL THE WAY OUT HERE. BUT IF WE'RE GONNA DO IT, WE'LL DO IT TO WIN!
WHA ?!
OKAY, FINE. I'LL DO IT. BUT YOU'D BETTER BUY ME ICE CREAM ON THE WAY HOME.
LEAVE IT TO ME, LITTLE MISS SISTER!
MUTTER MUTTER
DON'T CALL ME THAT!
Ice cream? I thought you were on a diet?
HEH HEH HEH...
Hmpf!
!!

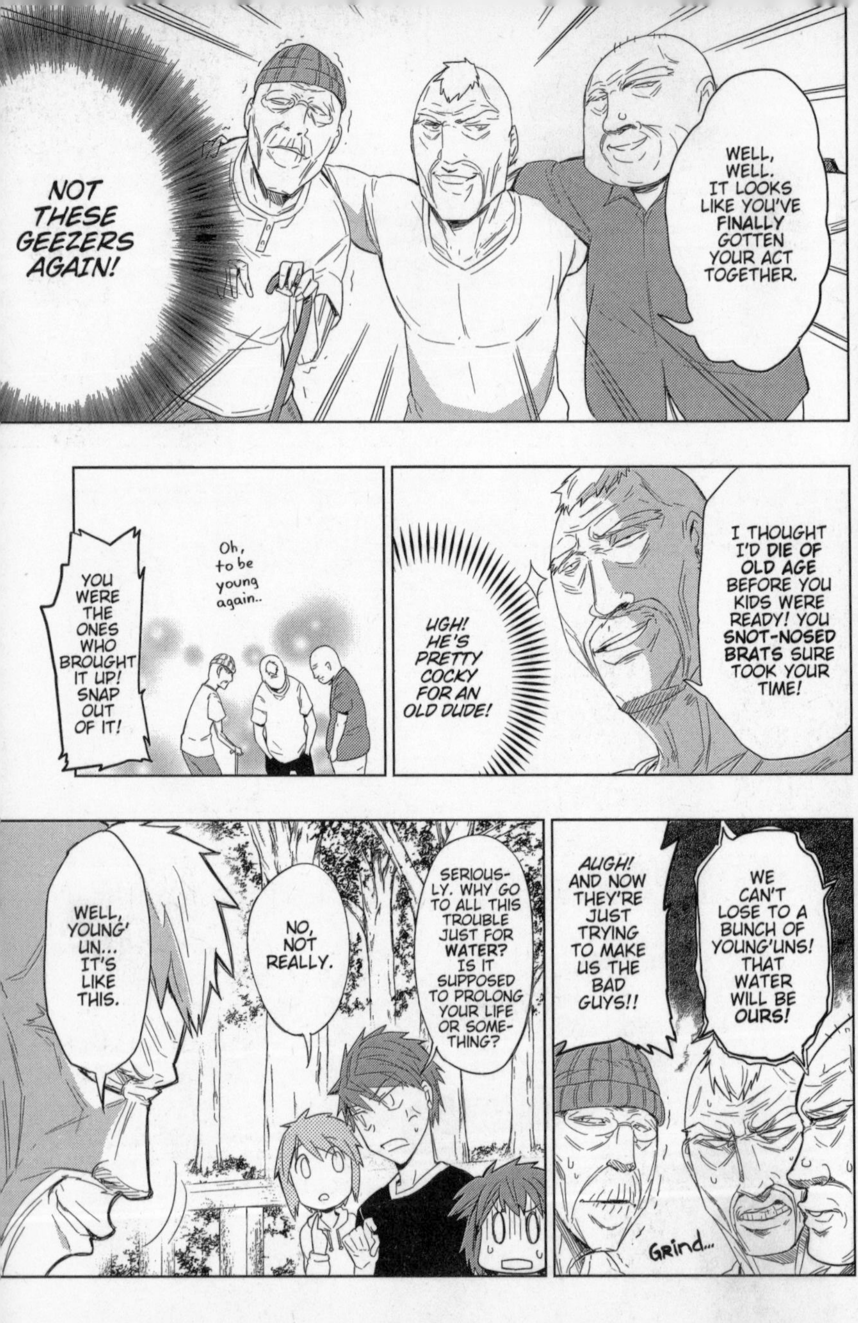
WELL, WELL. IT LOOKS LIKE YOU'VE FINALLY GOTTEN YOUR ACT TOGETHER.
NOT THESE GEEZERS AGAIN!
I THOUGHT I'D DIE OF OLD AGE BEFORE YOU KIDS WERE READY! YOU SNOT-NOSED BRATS SURE TOOK YOUR TIME!
UGH! HE'S PRETTY COCKY FOR AN OLD DUDE!
Oh, to be young again..
YOU WERE THE ONES WHO BROUGHT IT UP! SNAP OUT OF IT!
WE CAN'T LOSE TO A BUNCH OF YOUNG'UNS! THAT WATER WILL BE OURS!
AUGH! AND NOW THEY'RE JUST TRYING TO MAKE US THE BAD GUYS!!
Grind...
SERIOUS-LY. WHY GO TO ALL THIS TROUBLE JUST FOR WATER? IS IT SUPPOSED TO PROLONG YOUR LIFE OR SOME-THING?
NO, NOT REALLY.
WELL, YOUNG' UN... IT'S LIKE THIS.

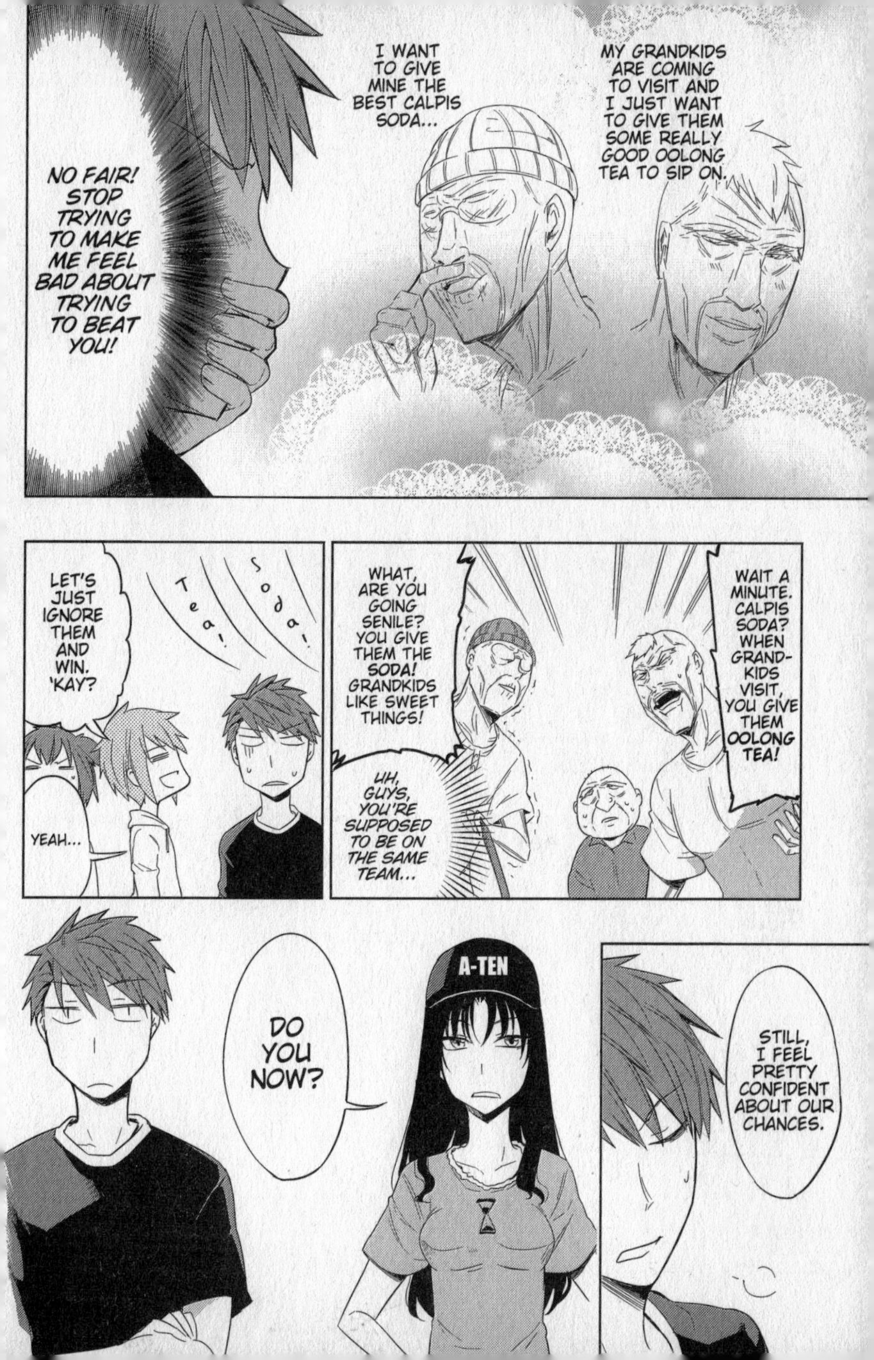
MY GRANDKIDS ARE COMING TO VISIT AND I JUST WANT TO GIVE THEM SOME REALLY GOOD OOLONG TEA TO SIP ON.
I WANT TO GIVE MINE THE BEST CALPIS SODA...
NO FAIR! STOP TRYING TO MAKE ME FEEL BAD ABOUT TRYING TO BEAT YOU!
WAIT A MINUTE. CALPIS SODA? WHEN GRAND-KIDS VISIT, YOU GIVE THEM OOLONG TEA!
WHAT, ARE YOU GOING SENILE? YOU GIVE THEM THE SODA! GRANDKIDS LIKE SWEET THINGS!
UH, GUYS, YOU'RE SUPPOSED TO BE ON THE SAME TEAM...
Soda!
Tea!
LET'S JUST IGNORE THEM AND WIN. 'KAY?
YEAH...
STILL, I FEEL PRETTY CONFIDENT ABOUT OUR CHANCES.
A-TEN
DO YOU NOW?

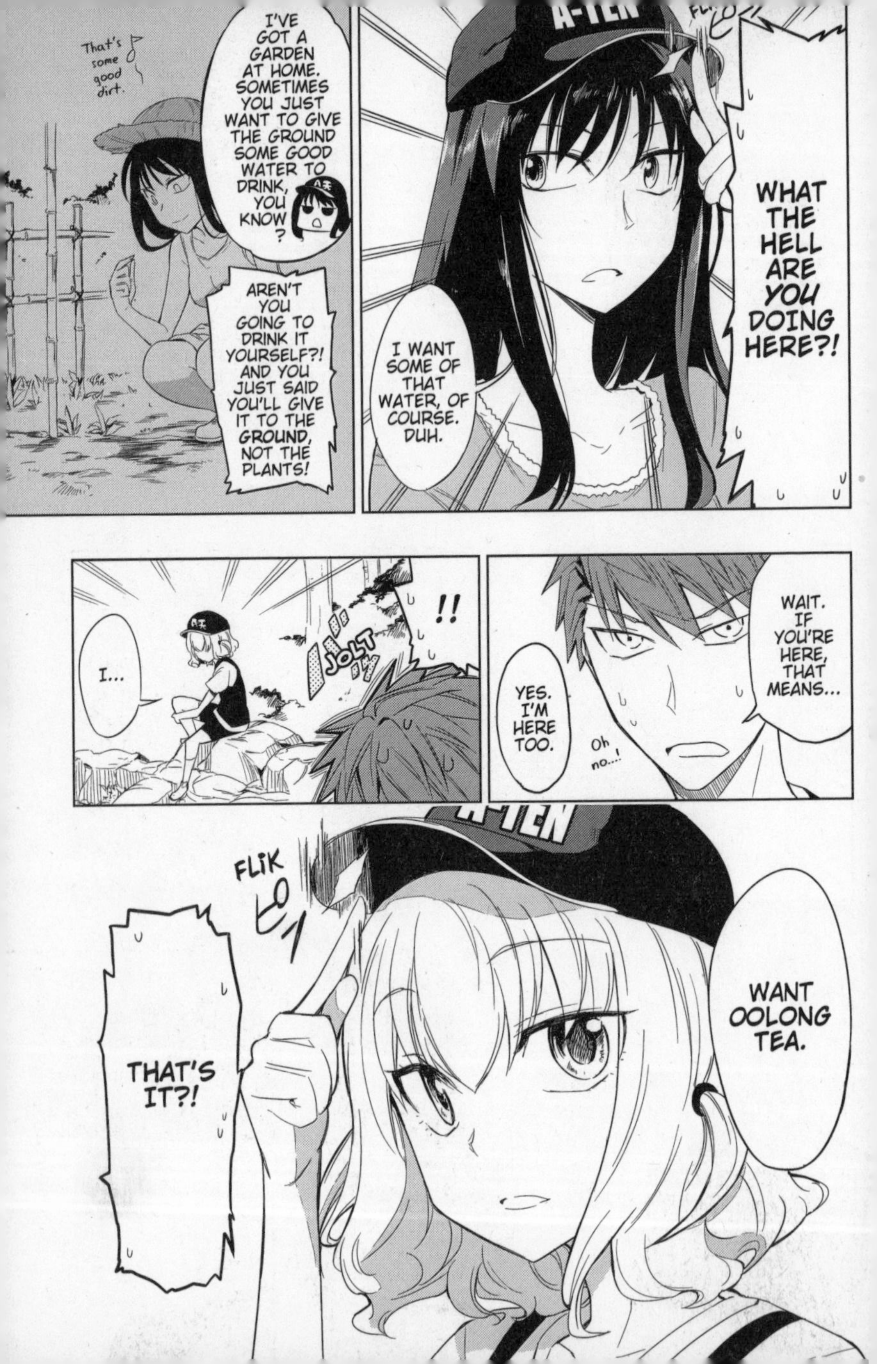
WHAT THE HELL ARE YOU DOING HERE?!
I WANT SOME OF THAT WATER, OF COURSE. DUH.
I'VE GOT A GARDEN AT HOME. SOMETIMES YOU JUST WANT TO GIVE THE GROUND SOME GOOD WATER TO DRINK, YOU KNOW?
That's some good dirt.
AREN'T YOU GOING TO DRINK IT YOURSELF?! AND YOU JUST SAID YOU'LL GIVE IT TO THE GROUND, NOT THE PLANTS!
WAIT. IF YOU'RE HERE, THAT MEANS...
YES. I'M HERE TOO.
Oh no...!
!!
JOLT
I...
WANT OOLONG TEA.
FLIK
THAT'S IT?!

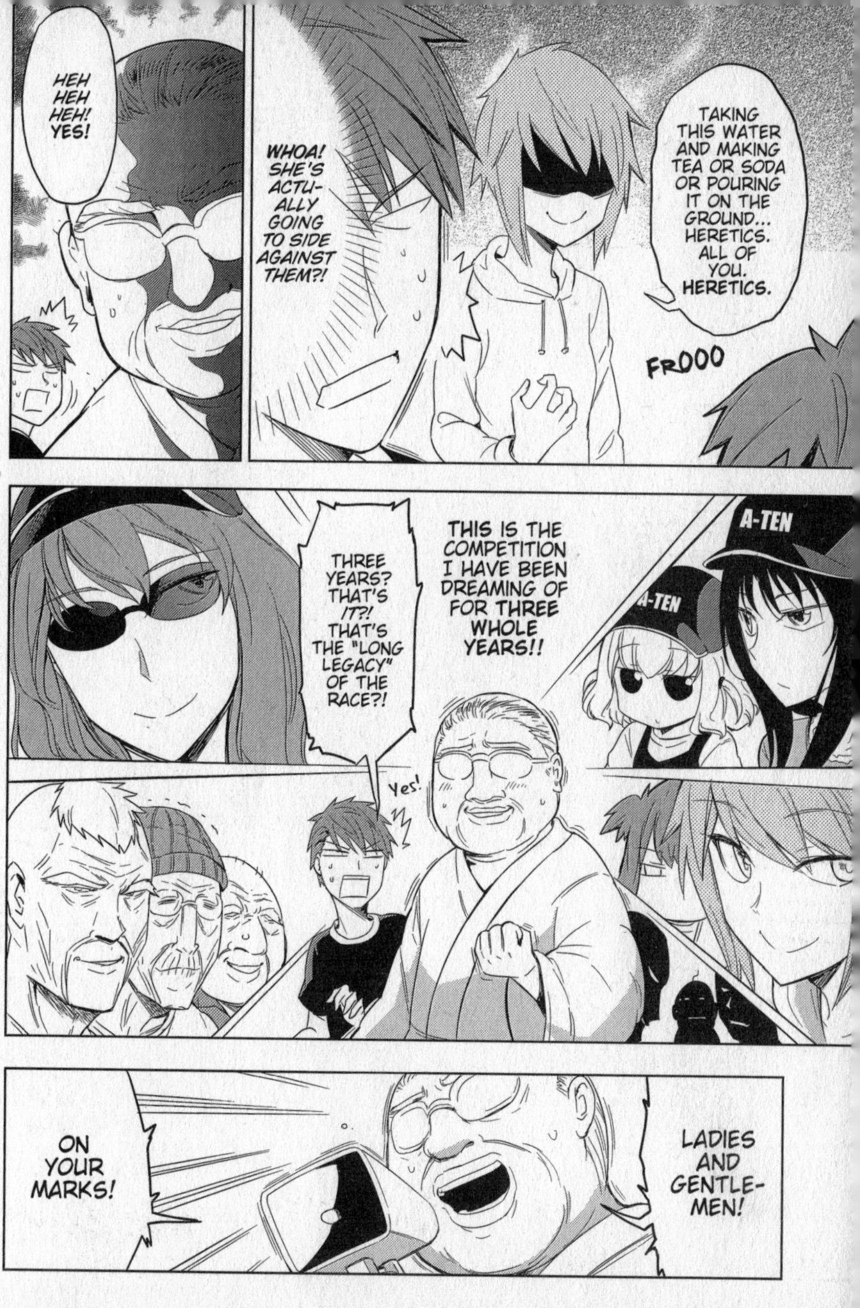
TAKING THIS WATER AND MAKING TEA OR SODA OR POURING IT ON THE GROUND... HERETICS. ALL OF YOU. HERETICS.
WHOA! SHE'S ACTU-ALLY GOING TO SIDE AGAINST THEM?!
FROOO
HEH HEH HEH! YES!
A-TEN
A-TEN
THIS IS THE COMPETITION I HAVE BEEN DREAMING OF FOR THREE WHOLE YEARS!!
THREE YEARS? THAT'S IT?! THAT'S THE "LONG LEGACY" OF THE RACE?!
Yes!
LADIES AND GENTLE-MEN!
ON YOUR MARKS!

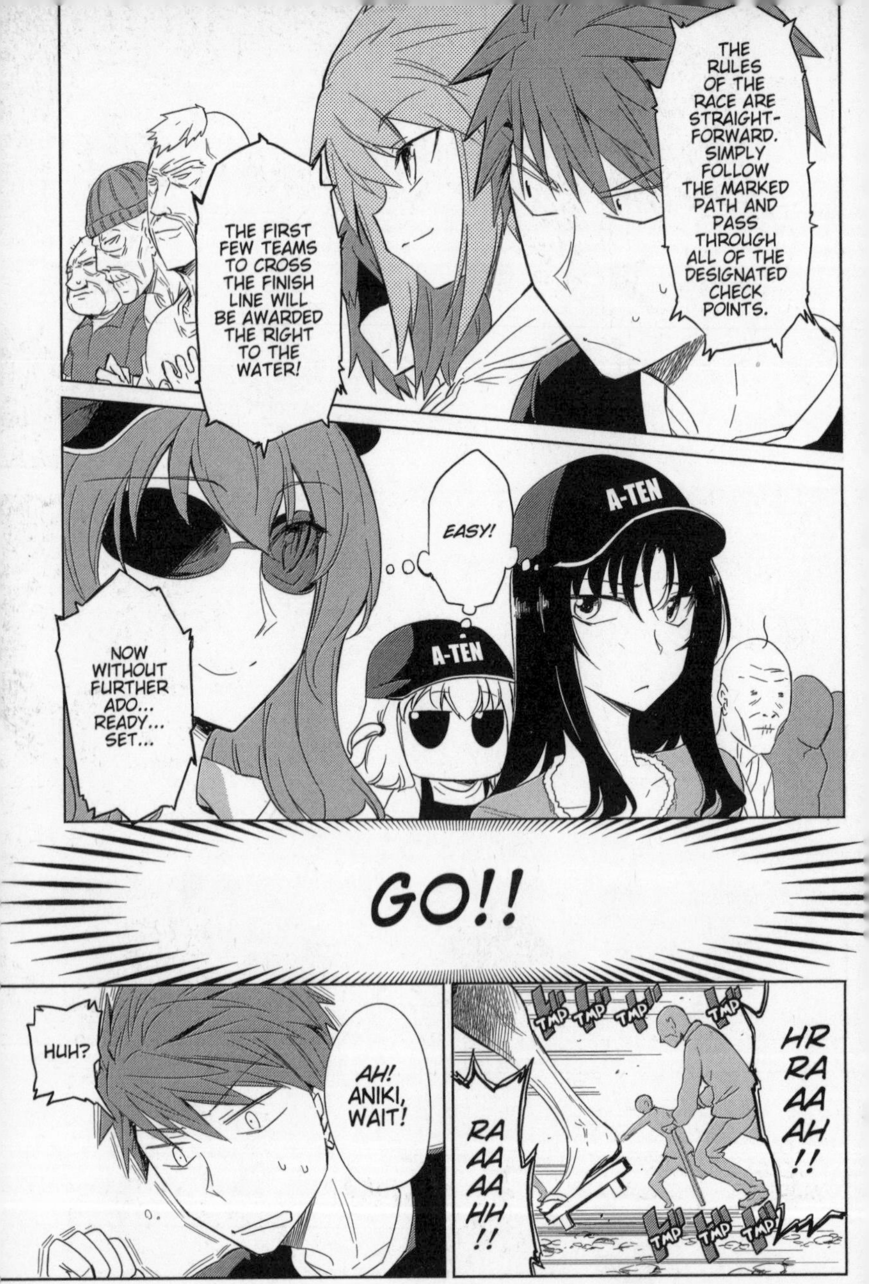
THE RULES OF THE RACE ARE STRAIGHT-FORWARD. SIMPLY FOLLOW THE MARKED PATH AND PASS THROUGH ALL OF THE DESIGNATED CHECK POINTS.
THE FIRST FEW TEAMS TO CROSS THE FINISH LINE WILL BE AWARDED THE RIGHT TO THE WATER!
A-TEN
EASY!
A-TEN
NOW WITHOUT FURTHER ADO... READY... SET...
GO!!
TMP TMP TMP TMP
HR RA AA AH!!
RA AA AA HH!!
TMP TMP TMP
AH! ANIKI, WAIT!
HUH?

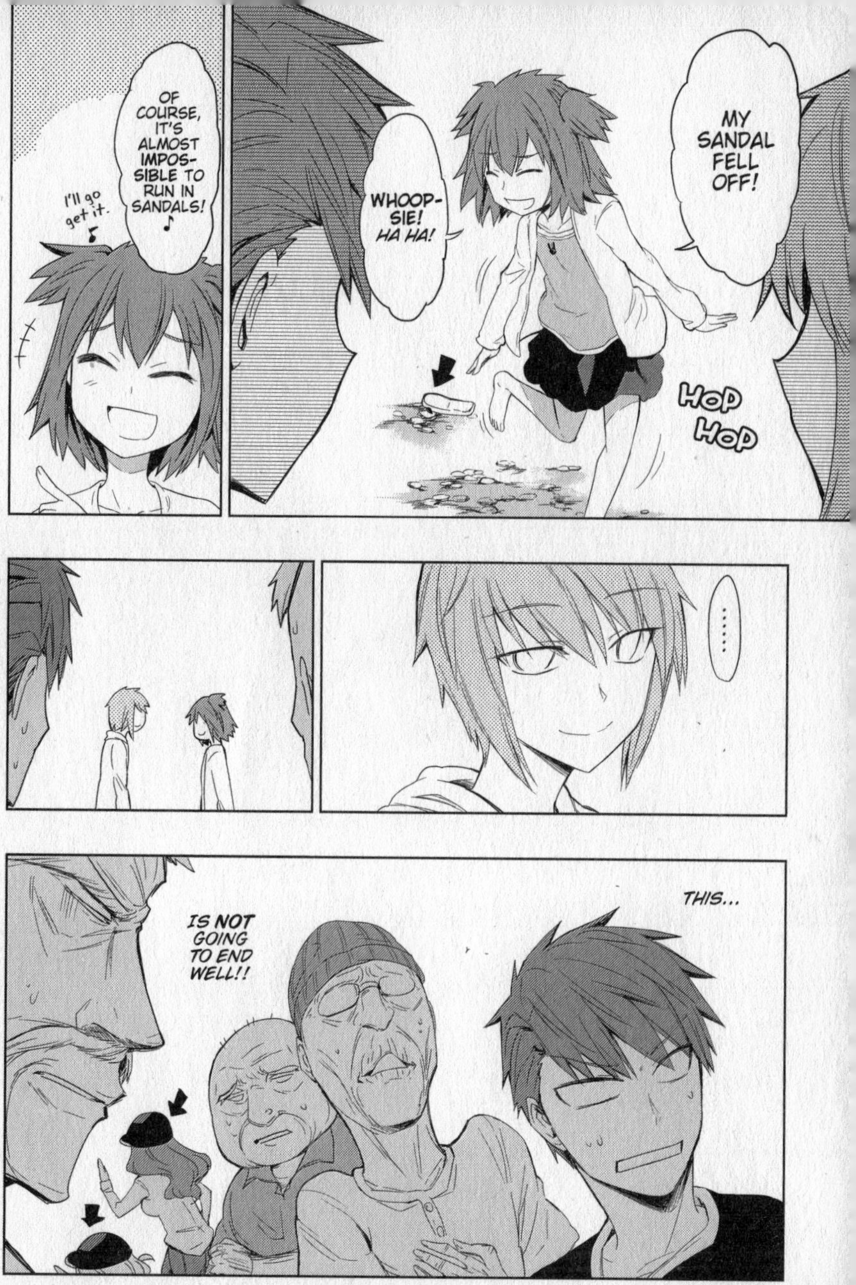
MY SANDAL FELL OFF!
WHOOP-SIE! HA HA!
HOP HOP
OF COURSE, IT'S ALMOST IMPOS-SIBLE TO RUN IN SANDALS! ♪
I'll go get it. ♪
......
THIS...
IS NOT GOING TO END WELL!!

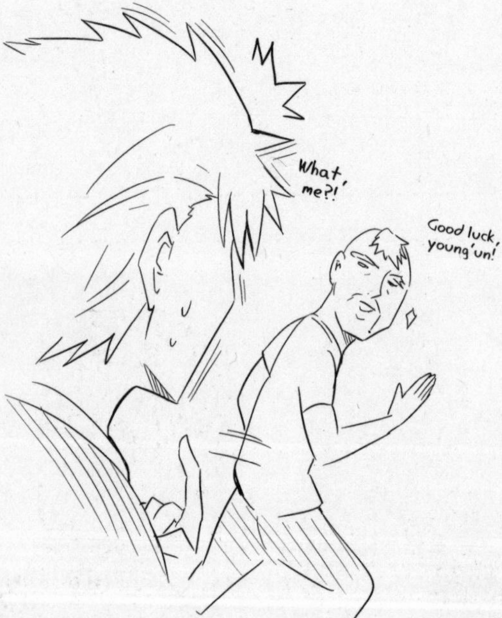
What, me?!
Good luck, young'un!

D-FRAGMENTS

ディーふらぐ!

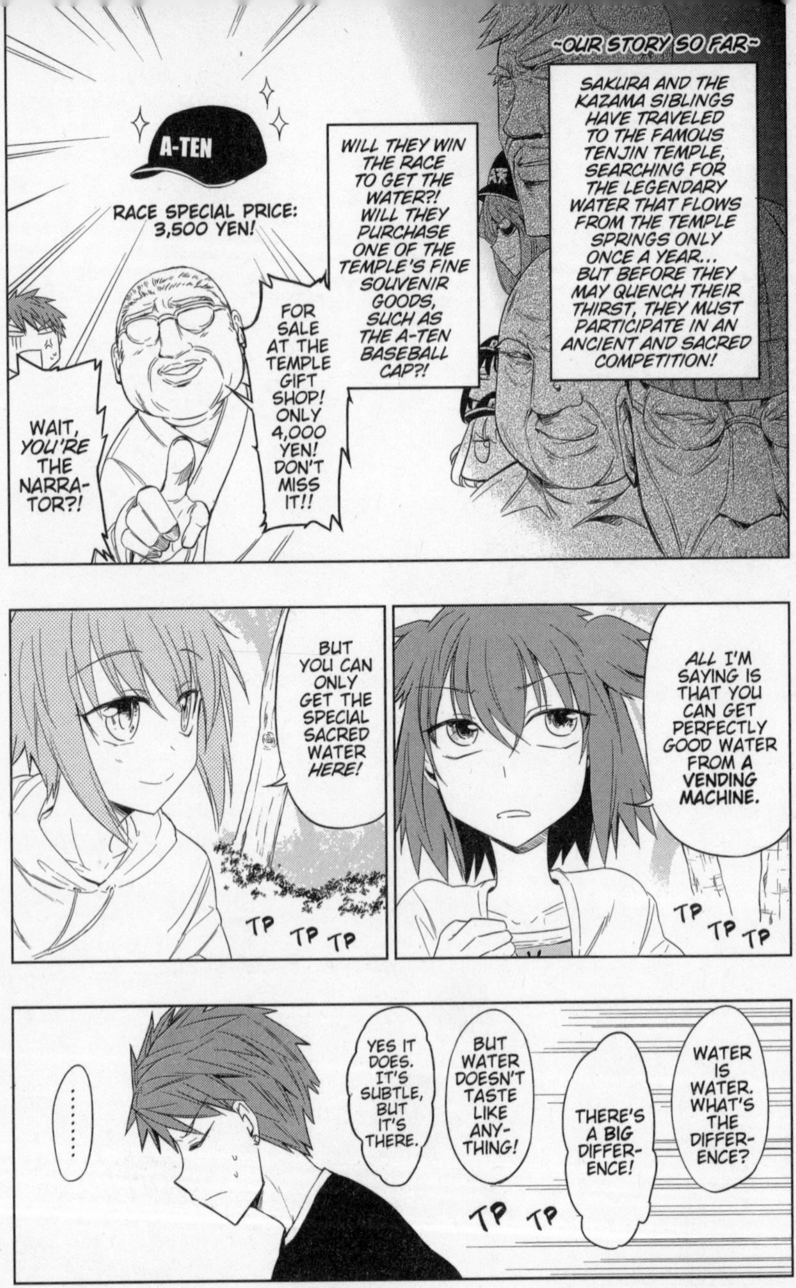
~OUR STORY SO FAR~
SAKURA AND THE KAZAMA SIBLINGS HAVE TRAVELED TO THE FAMOUS TENJIN TEMPLE, SEARCHING FOR THE LEGENDARY WATER THAT FLOWS FROM THE TEMPLE SPRINGS ONLY ONCE A YEAR... BUT BEFORE THEY MAY QUENCH THEIR THIRST, THEY MUST PARTICIPATE IN AN ANCIENT AND SACRED COMPETITION!
WILL THEY WIN THE RACE TO GET THE WATER?! WILL THEY PURCHASE ONE OF THE TEMPLE'S FINE SOUVENIR GOODS, SUCH AS THE A-TEN BASEBALL CAP?!
FOR SALE AT THE TEMPLE GIFT SHOP! ONLY 4,000 YEN! DON'T MISS IT!!
A-TEN
RACE SPECIAL PRICE: 3,500 YEN!
WAIT, YOU'RE THE NARRATOR?!
ALL I'M SAYING IS THAT YOU CAN GET PERFECTLY GOOD WATER FROM A VENDING MACHINE.
TP TP TP
BUT YOU CAN ONLY GET THE SPECIAL SACRED WATER HERE!
TP TP TP
WATER IS WATER. WHAT'S THE DIFFERENCE?
THERE'S A BIG DIFFERENCE!
BUT WATER DOESN'T TASTE LIKE ANYTHING!
YES IT DOES. IT'S SUBTLE, BUT IT'S THERE.
TP TP
....

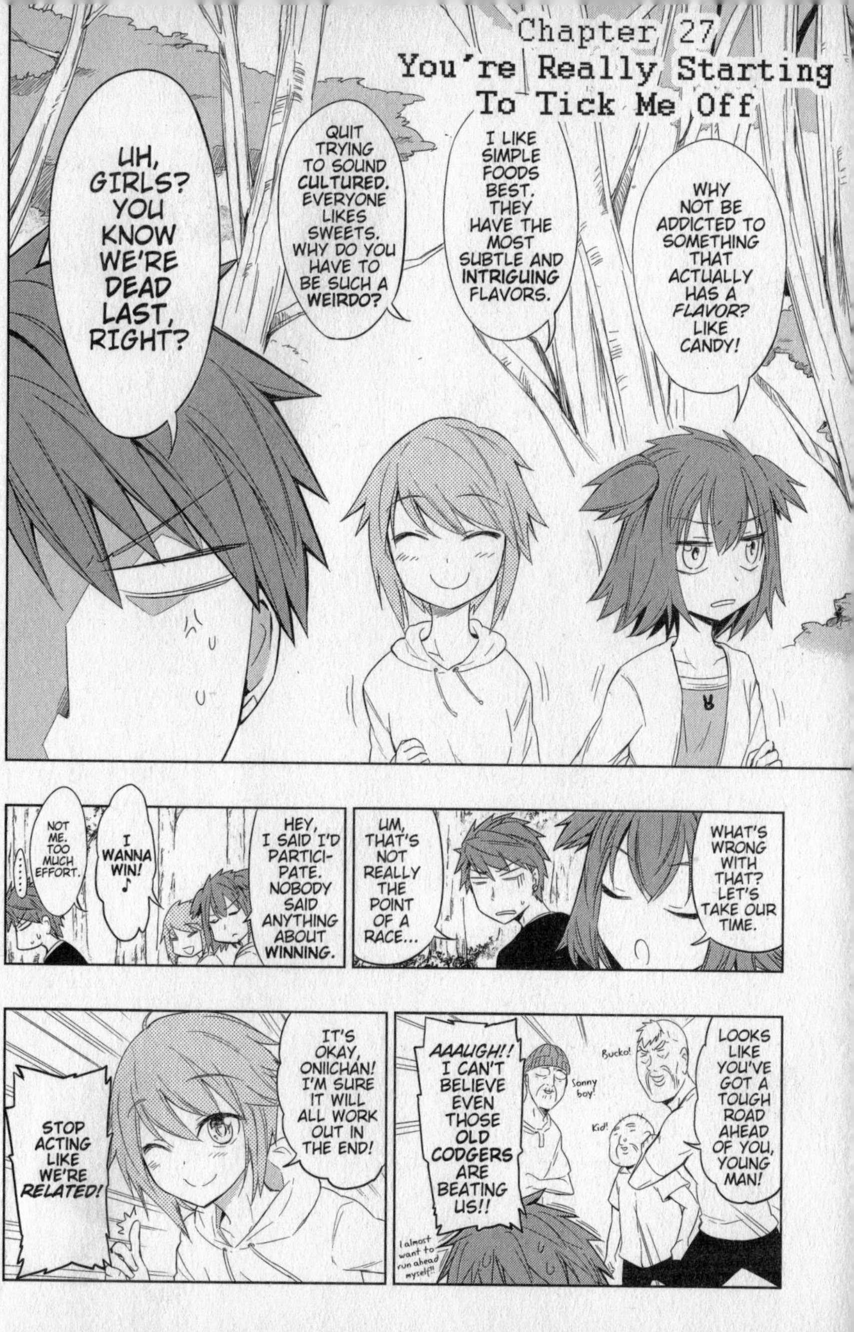
Chapter 27
You're Really Starting To Tick Me Off
WHY NOT BE ADDICTED TO SOMETHING THAT ACTUALLY HAS A *FLAVOR*? LIKE CANDY!
I LIKE SIMPLE FOODS BEST. THEY HAVE THE MOST SUBTLE AND INTRIGUING FLAVORS.
QUIT TRYING TO SOUND CULTURED. EVERYONE LIKES SWEETS. WHY DO YOU HAVE TO BE SUCH A WEIRDO?
UH, GIRLS? YOU KNOW WE'RE DEAD LAST, RIGHT?
WHAT'S WRONG WITH THAT? LET'S TAKE OUR TIME.
UM, THAT'S NOT REALLY THE POINT OF A RACE...
HEY, I SAID I'D PARTICIPATE. NOBODY SAID ANYTHING ABOUT WINNING.
I WANNA WIN! ♪
NOT ME. TOO MUCH EFFORT.
...
LOOKS LIKE YOU'VE GOT A TOUGH ROAD AHEAD OF YOU, YOUNG MAN!
Bucko!
Sonny boy!
Kid!
AAAUGH!! I CAN'T BELIEVE EVEN THOSE OLD CODGERS ARE BEATING US!!
I almost want to run ahead myself!!
IT'S OKAY, ONIICHAN! I'M SURE IT WILL ALL WORK OUT IN THE END!
STOP ACTING LIKE WE'RE *RELATED*!

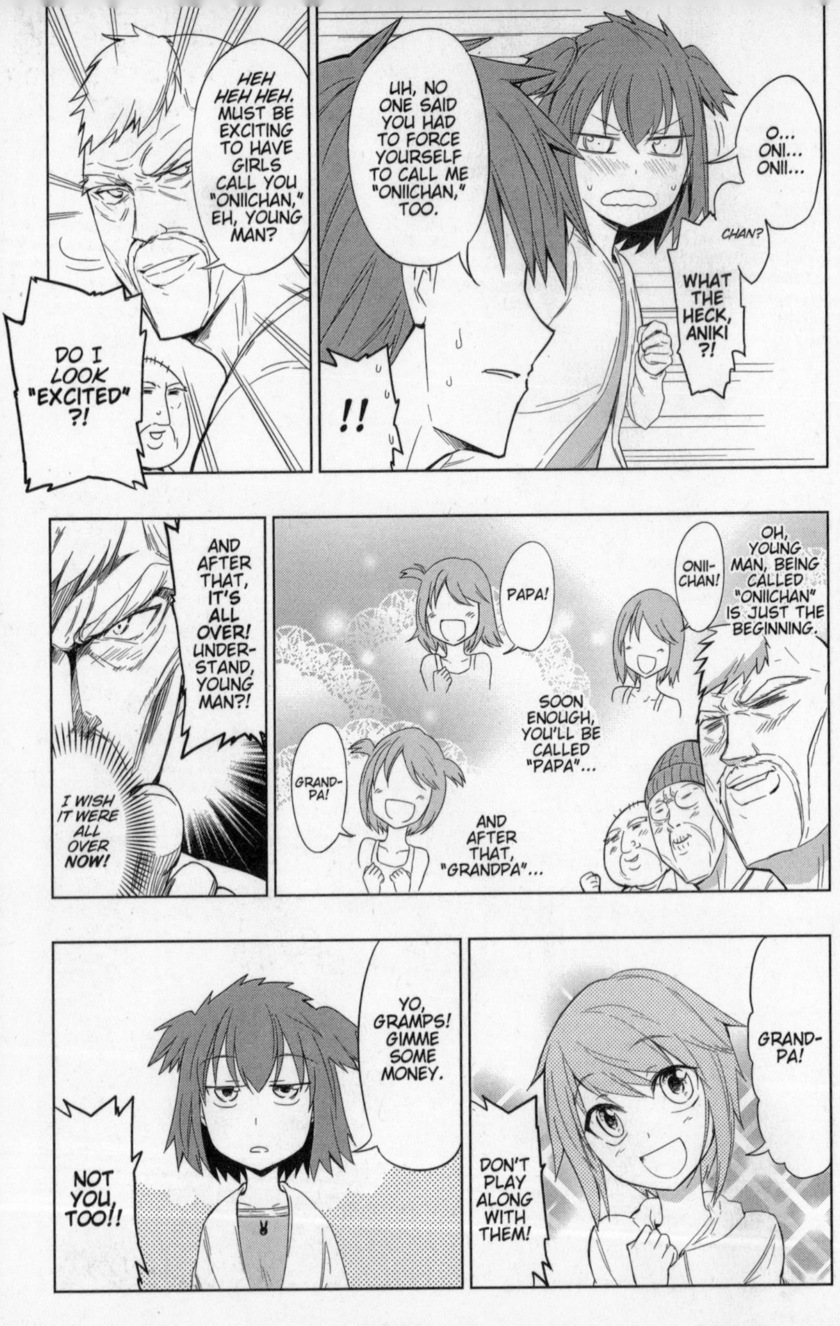
O... ONII... ONII... CHAN?
WHAT THE HECK, ANIKI?!
UH, NO ONE SAID YOU HAD TO FORCE YOURSELF TO CALL ME "ONIICHAN," TOO.
!!
HEH HEH HEH. MUST BE EXCITING TO HAVE GIRLS CALL YOU "ONIICHAN," EH, YOUNG MAN?
DO I LOOK "EXCITED"?!
OH, YOUNG MAN, BEING CALLED "ONIICHAN" IS JUST THE BEGINNING.
ONII-CHAN!
PAPA!
SOON ENOUGH, YOU'LL BE CALLED "PAPA"...
GRAND-PA!
AND AFTER THAT, "GRANDPA"...
AND AFTER THAT, IT'S ALL OVER! UNDER-STAND, YOUNG MAN?!
I WISH IT WERE ALL OVER NOW!
GRAND-PA!
DON'T PLAY ALONG WITH THEM!
YO, GRAMPS! GIMME SOME MONEY.
NOT YOU, TOO!!

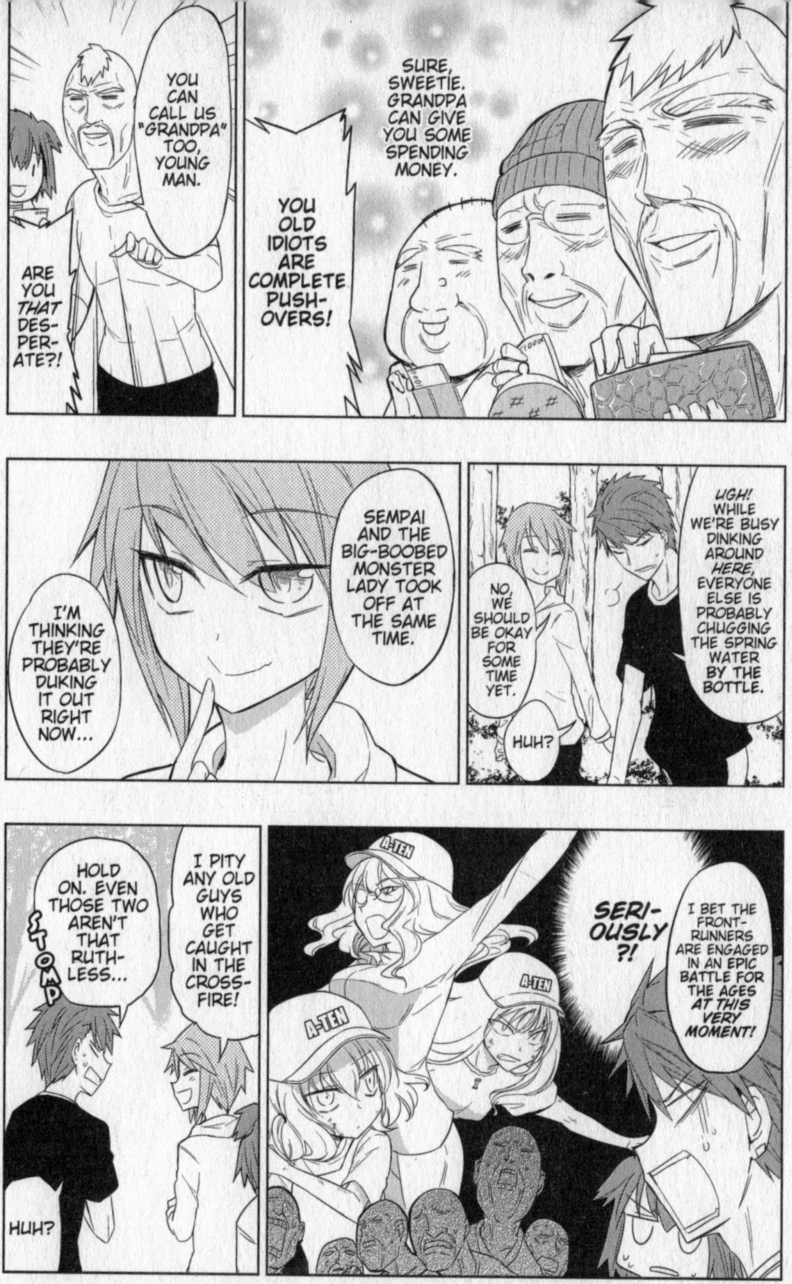
SURE, SWEETIE. GRANDPA CAN GIVE YOU SOME SPENDING MONEY.
YOU OLD IDIOTS ARE COMPLETE PUSH-OVERS!
YOU CAN CALL US "GRANDPA" TOO, YOUNG MAN.
ARE YOU *THAT* DESPERATE?!
UGH! WHILE WE'RE BUSY DINKING AROUND *HERE*, EVERYONE ELSE IS PROBABLY CHUGGING THE SPRING WATER BY THE BOTTLE.
NO, WE SHOULD BE OKAY FOR SOME TIME YET.
HUH?
SEMPAI AND THE BIG-BOOBED MONSTER LADY TOOK OFF AT THE SAME TIME.
I'M THINKING THEY'RE PROBABLY DUKING IT OUT RIGHT NOW...
I BET THE FRONT-RUNNERS ARE ENGAGED IN AN EPIC BATTLE FOR THE AGES *AT THIS VERY MOMENT!*
SERI-OUSLY?!
A-TEN
A-TEN
A-TEN
I PITY ANY OLD GUYS WHO GET CAUGHT IN THE CROSS-FIRE!
HOLD ON. EVEN THOSE TWO AREN'T THAT RUTH-LESS...
STOMP
HUH?

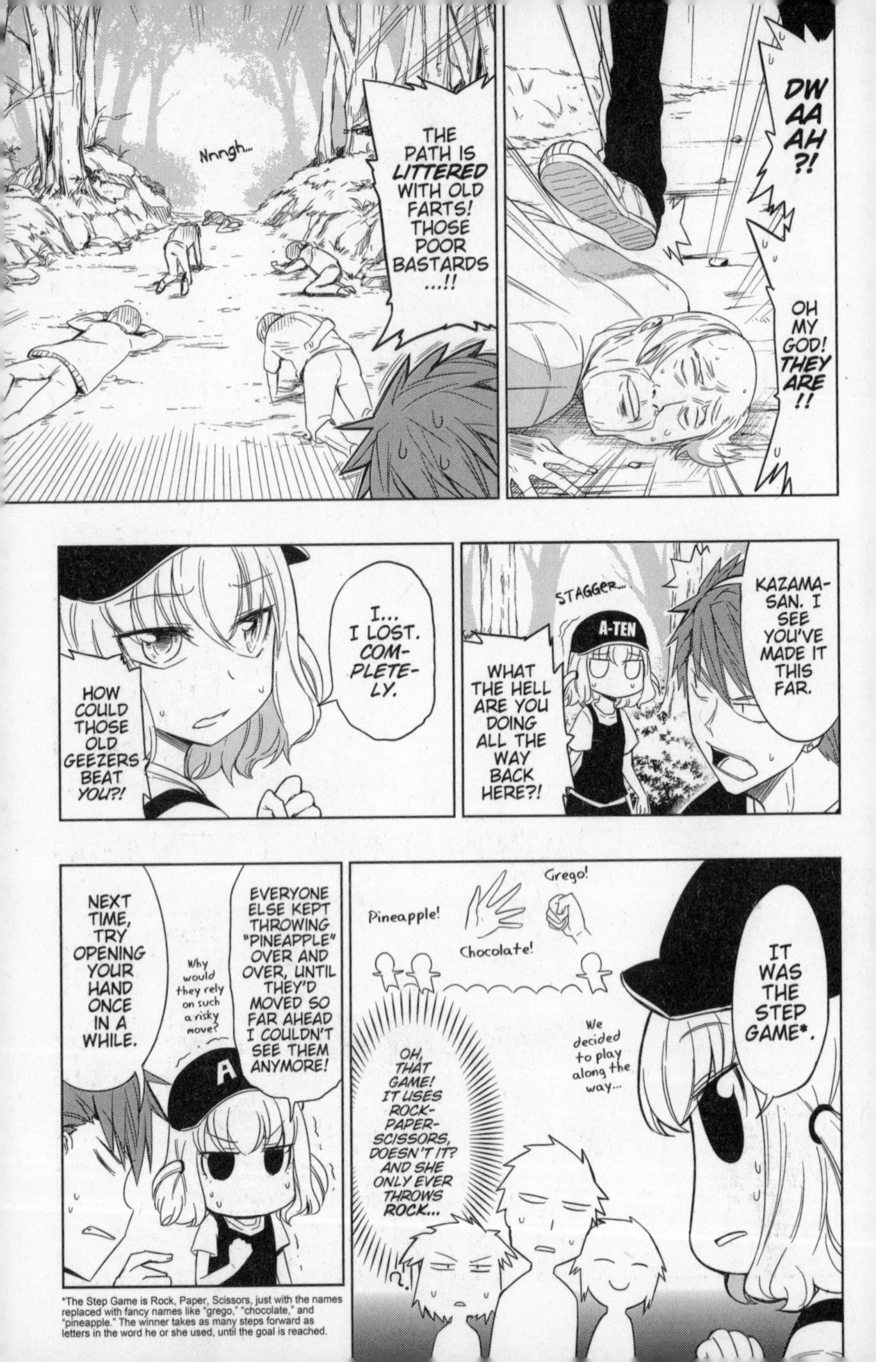
DWAAAH?!
OH MY GOD! THEY ARE!!
THE PATH IS LITTERED WITH OLD FARTS! THOSE POOR BASTARDS...!!
Nnngh...
KAZAMA-SAN. I SEE YOU'VE MADE IT THIS FAR.
STAGGER...
A-TEN
WHAT THE HELL ARE YOU DOING ALL THE WAY BACK HERE?!
I... I LOST. COMPLETELY.
HOW COULD THOSE OLD GEEZERS BEAT YOU?!
IT WAS THE STEP GAME*.
Grego!
Pineapple!
Chocolate!
We decided to play along the way...
OH, THAT GAME! IT USES ROCK-PAPER-SCISSORS, DOESN'T IT? AND SHE ONLY EVER THROWS ROCK...
EVERYONE ELSE KEPT THROWING "PINEAPPLE" OVER AND OVER, UNTIL THEY'D MOVED SO FAR AHEAD I COULDN'T SEE THEM ANYMORE!
Why would they rely on such a risky move?
A
NEXT TIME, TRY OPENING YOUR HAND ONCE IN A WHILE.

*The Step Game is Rock, Paper, Scissors, just with the names replaced with fancy names like "grego," "chocolate," and "pineapple." The winner takes as many steps forward as letters in the word he or she used, until the goal is reached.

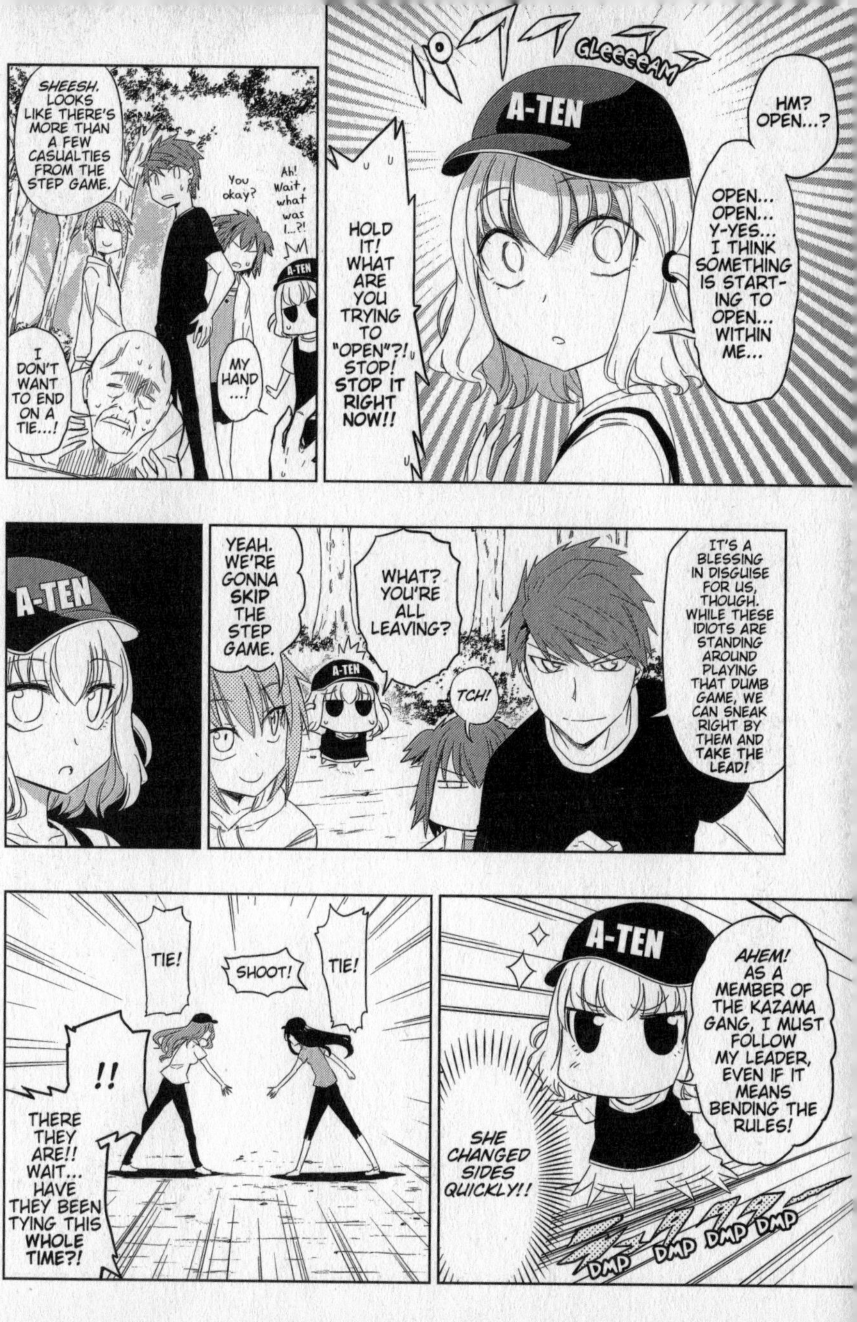
GLEEEEAM
HM? OPEN...?
OPEN... OPEN... Y-YES... I THINK SOMETHING IS STARTING TO OPEN... WITHIN ME...
HOLD IT! WHAT ARE YOU TRYING TO "OPEN"?! STOP! STOP IT RIGHT NOW!!
SHEESH. LOOKS LIKE THERE'S MORE THAN A FEW CASUALTIES FROM THE STEP GAME.
Ah! Wait, what was I...?!
You okay?
MY HAND...!
I DON'T WANT TO END ON A TIE...!
IT'S A BLESSING IN DISGUISE FOR US, THOUGH. WHILE THESE IDIOTS ARE STANDING AROUND PLAYING THAT DUMB GAME, WE CAN SNEAK RIGHT BY THEM AND TAKE THE LEAD!
TCH!
WHAT? YOU'RE ALL LEAVING?
YEAH. WE'RE GONNA SKIP THE STEP GAME.
A-TEN
AHEM! AS A MEMBER OF THE KAZAMA GANG, I MUST FOLLOW MY LEADER, EVEN IF IT MEANS BENDING THE RULES!
SHE CHANGED SIDES QUICKLY!!
DMP DMP DMP DMP DMP
TIE!
SHOOT!
TIE!
!!
THERE THEY ARE!! WAIT... HAVE THEY BEEN TYING THIS WHOLE TIME?!

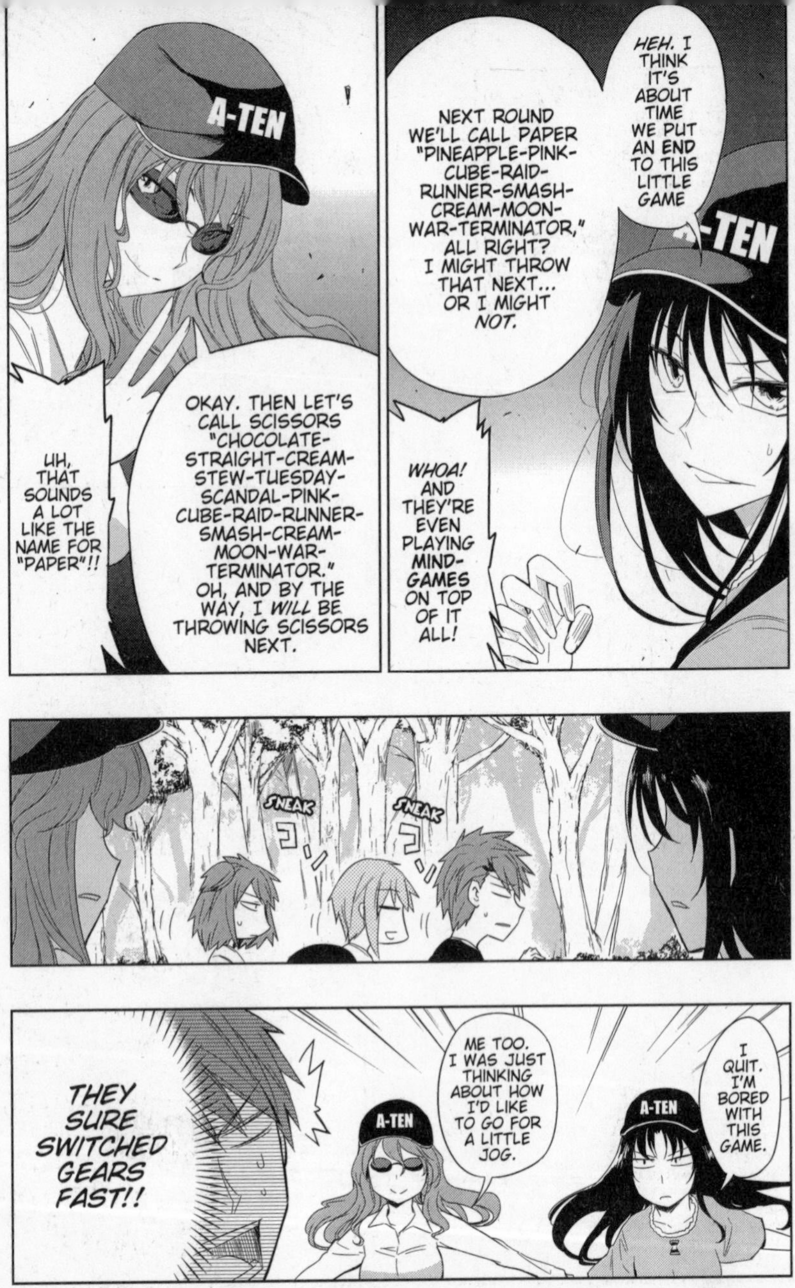
HEH. I THINK IT'S ABOUT TIME WE PUT AN END TO THIS LITTLE GAME
A-TEN
NEXT ROUND WE'LL CALL PAPER "PINEAPPLE-PINK-CUBE-RAID-RUNNER-SMASH-CREAM-MOON-WAR-TERMINATOR," ALL RIGHT? I MIGHT THROW THAT NEXT... OR I MIGHT *NOT.*
WHOA! AND THEY'RE EVEN PLAYING MIND-GAMES ON TOP OF IT ALL!
A-TEN
OKAY. THEN LET'S CALL SCISSORS "CHOCOLATE-STRAIGHT-CREAM-STEW-TUESDAY-SCANDAL-PINK-CUBE-RAID-RUNNER-SMASH-CREAM-MOON-WAR-TERMINATOR." OH, AND BY THE WAY, I *WILL* BE THROWING SCISSORS NEXT.
UH, THAT SOUNDS A LOT LIKE THE NAME FOR "PAPER"!!
SNEAK
SNEAK
I QUIT. I'M BORED WITH THIS GAME.
A-TEN
ME TOO. I WAS JUST THINKING ABOUT HOW I'D LIKE TO GO FOR A LITTLE JOG.
A-TEN
THEY SURE SWITCHED GEARS FAST!!

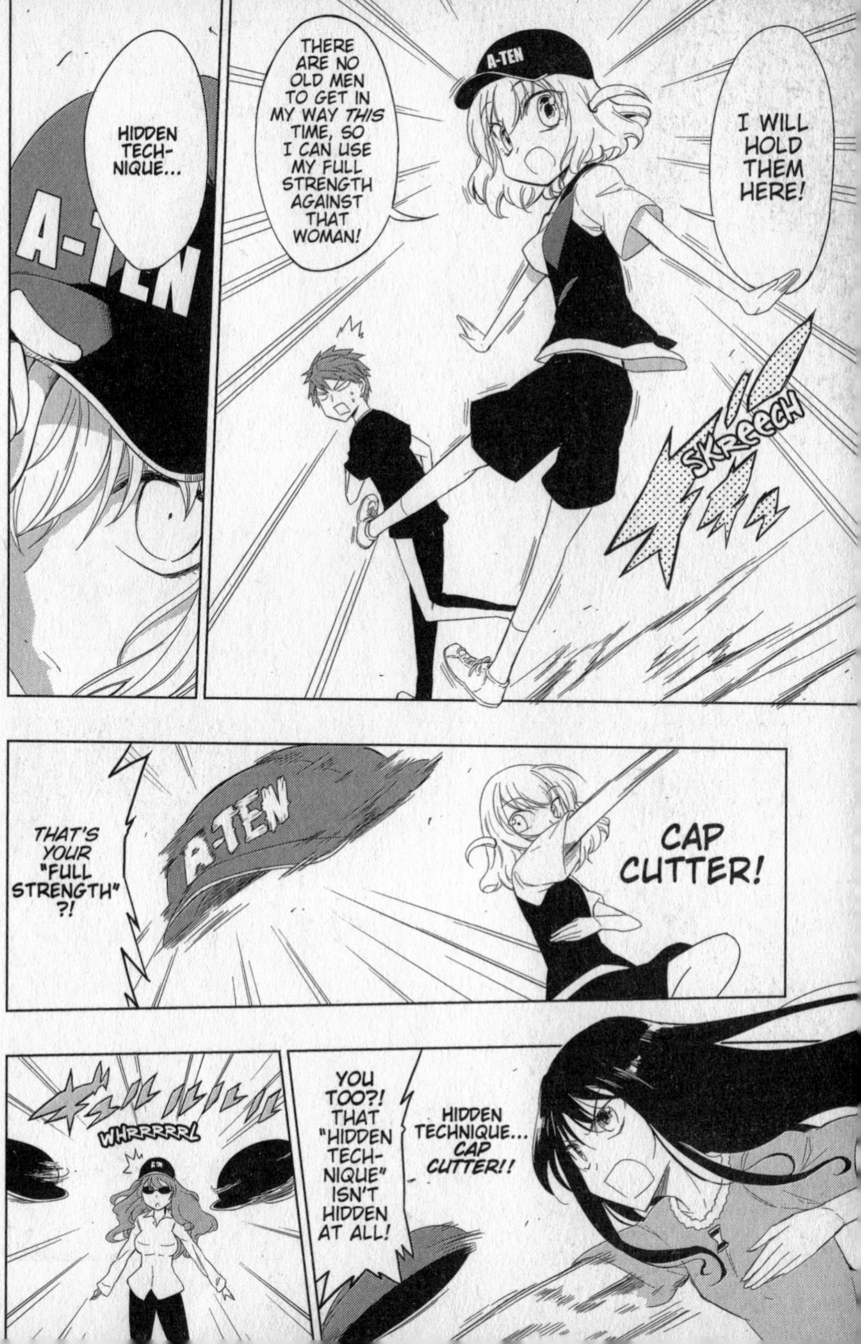
I WILL HOLD THEM HERE!
THERE ARE NO OLD MEN TO GET IN MY WAY *THIS* TIME, SO I CAN USE MY FULL STRENGTH AGAINST THAT WOMAN!
SKREECH
HIDDEN TECH-NIQUE...
CAP CUTTER!
THAT'S YOUR "FULL STRENGTH" ?!
HIDDEN TECHNIQUE... CAP CUTTER!!
YOU TOO?! THAT "HIDDEN TECH-NIQUE" ISN'T HIDDEN AT ALL!
WHRRRRRL

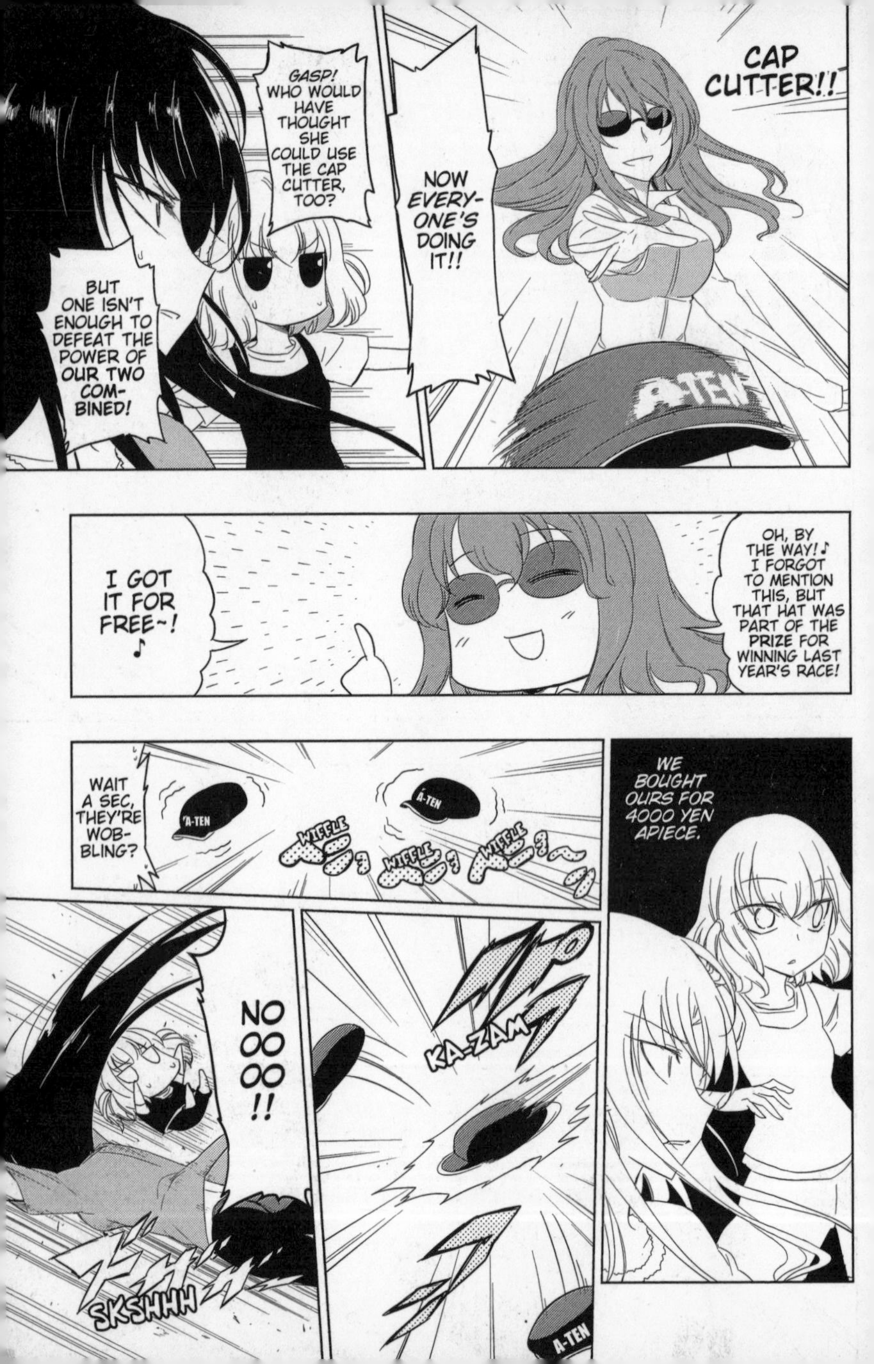
CAP CUTTER!!
A-TEN
GASP! WHO WOULD HAVE THOUGHT SHE COULD USE THE CAP CUTTER, TOO?
NOW EVERYONE'S DOING IT!!
BUT ONE ISN'T ENOUGH TO DEFEAT THE POWER OF OUR TWO COMBINED!
OH, BY THE WAY! ♪ I FORGOT TO MENTION THIS, BUT THAT HAT WAS PART OF THE PRIZE FOR WINNING LAST YEAR'S RACE!
I GOT IT FOR FREE~! ♪
WE BOUGHT OURS FOR 4000 YEN APIECE.
A-TEN
WIFFLE
WIFFLE
WIFFLE
A-TEN
WAIT A SEC, THEY'RE WOBBLING?
KA-ZAM
A-TEN
NOOOOO!!
SKSHHH

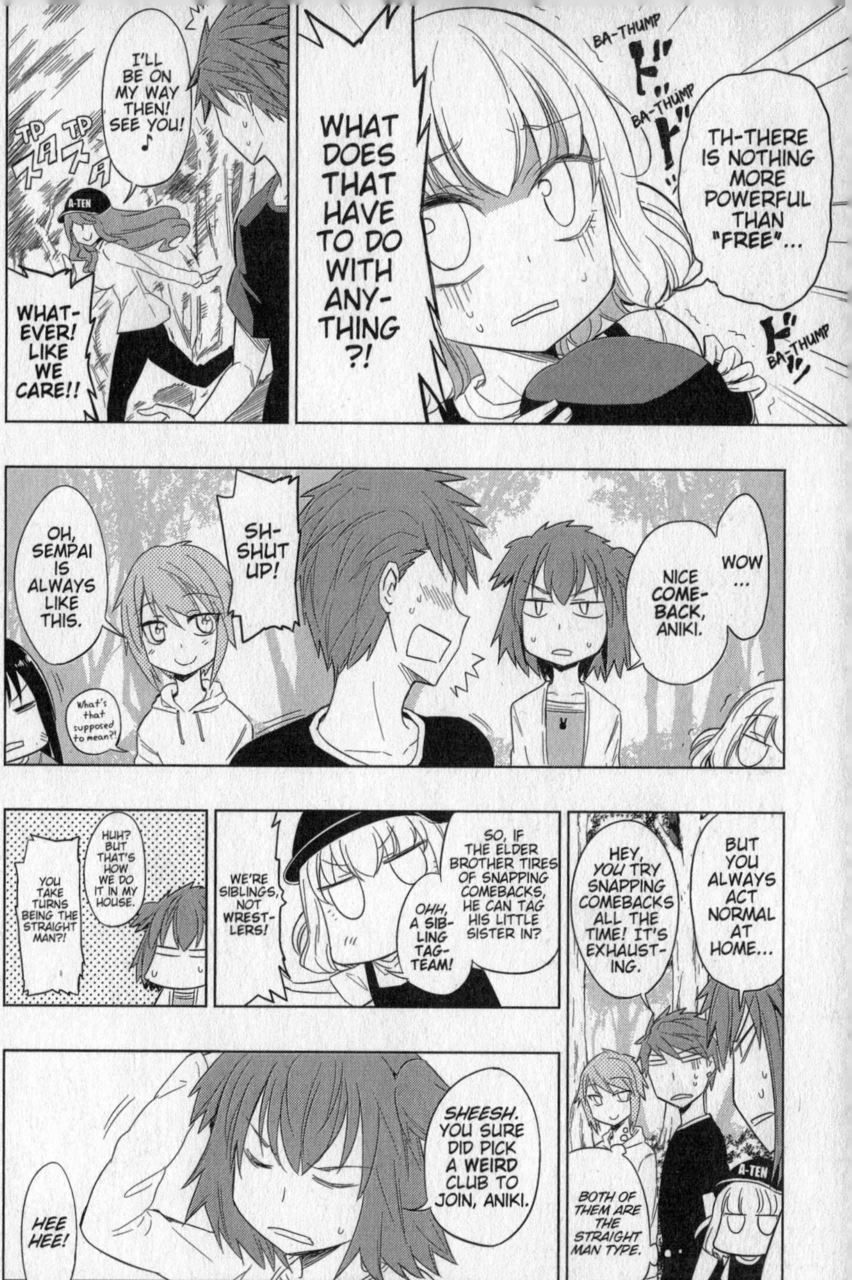
BA-THUMP
BA-THUMP
TH-THERE IS NOTHING MORE POWERFUL THAN "FREE"...
BA-THUMP
WHAT DOES THAT HAVE TO DO WITH ANYTHING?!
I'LL BE ON MY WAY THEN! SEE YOU! ♪
TP TP
A-TEN
WHATEVER! LIKE WE CARE!!
WOW...
NICE COMEBACK, ANIKI.
SH-SHUT UP!
OH, SEMPAI IS ALWAYS LIKE THIS.
What's that supposed to mean?!
BUT YOU ALWAYS ACT NORMAL AT HOME...
HEY, YOU TRY SNAPPING COMEBACKS ALL THE TIME! IT'S EXHAUSTING.
A-TEN
BOTH OF THEM ARE THE STRAIGHT MAN TYPE.
SO, IF THE ELDER BROTHER TIRES OF SNAPPING COMEBACKS, HE CAN TAG HIS LITTLE SISTER IN?
OHH, A SIBLING TAG-TEAM!
WE'RE SIBLINGS, NOT WRESTLERS!
HUH? BUT THAT'S HOW WE DO IT IN MY HOUSE.
YOU TAKE TURNS BEING THE STRAIGHT MAN?!
SHEESH. YOU SURE DID PICK A WEIRD CLUB TO JOIN, ANIKI.
HEE HEE!

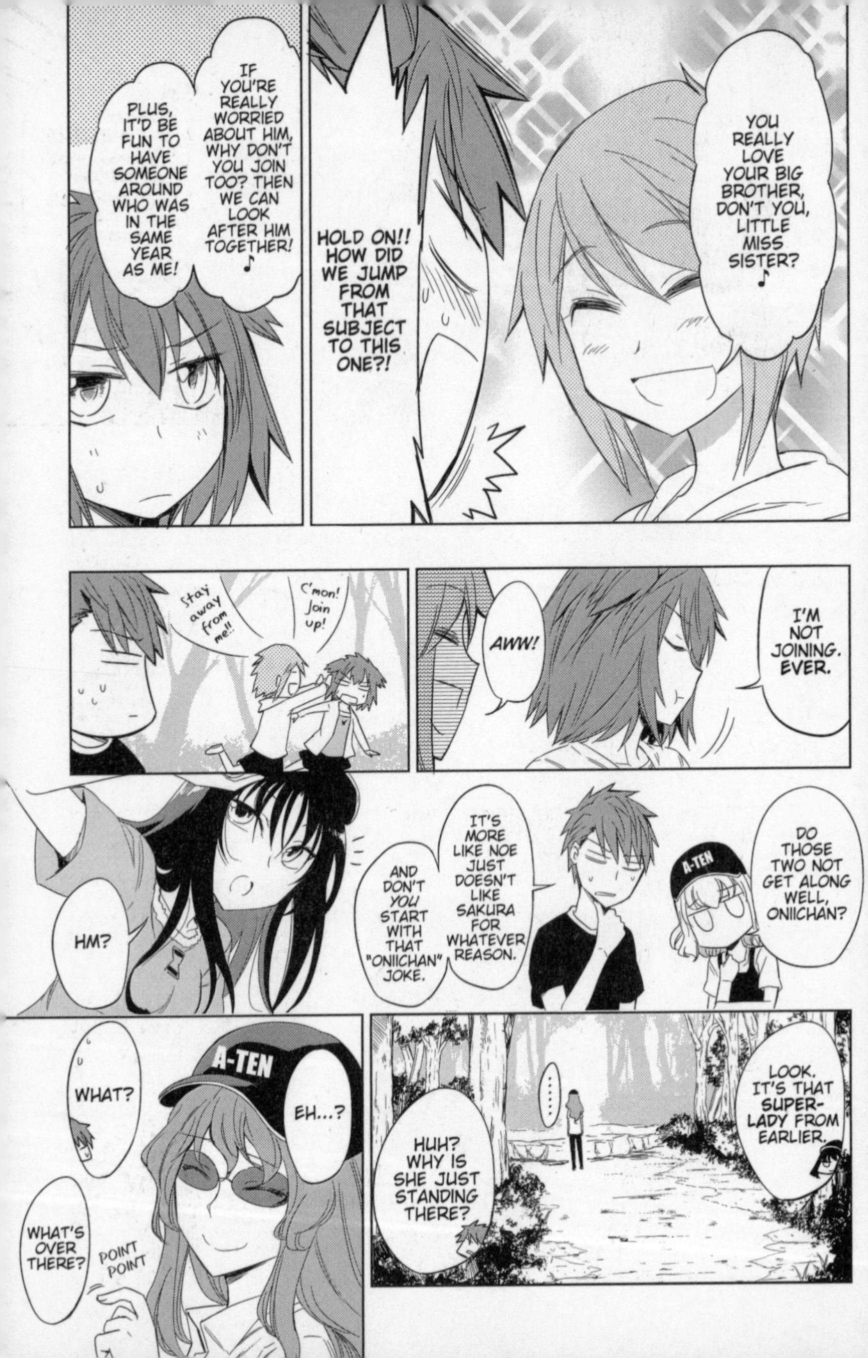
YOU REALLY LOVE YOUR BIG BROTHER, DON'T YOU, LITTLE MISS SISTER? ♪
HOLD ON!! HOW DID WE JUMP FROM THAT SUBJECT TO THIS ONE?!
IF YOU'RE REALLY WORRIED ABOUT HIM, WHY DON'T YOU JOIN TOO? THEN WE CAN LOOK AFTER HIM TOGETHER! ♪
PLUS, IT'D BE FUN TO HAVE SOMEONE AROUND WHO WAS IN THE SAME YEAR AS ME!
I'M NOT JOINING. EVER.
AWW!
C'mon! Join up!
Stay away from me!!
DO THOSE TWO NOT GET ALONG WELL, ONIICHAN?
A-TEN
IT'S MORE LIKE NOE JUST DOESN'T LIKE SAKURA FOR WHATEVER REASON.
AND DON'T YOU START WITH THAT "ONIICHAN" JOKE.
HM?
LOOK. IT'S THAT SUPER-LADY FROM EARLIER.
......
HUH? WHY IS SHE JUST STANDING THERE?
EH...?
A-TEN
WHAT?
WHAT'S OVER THERE?
POINT POINT

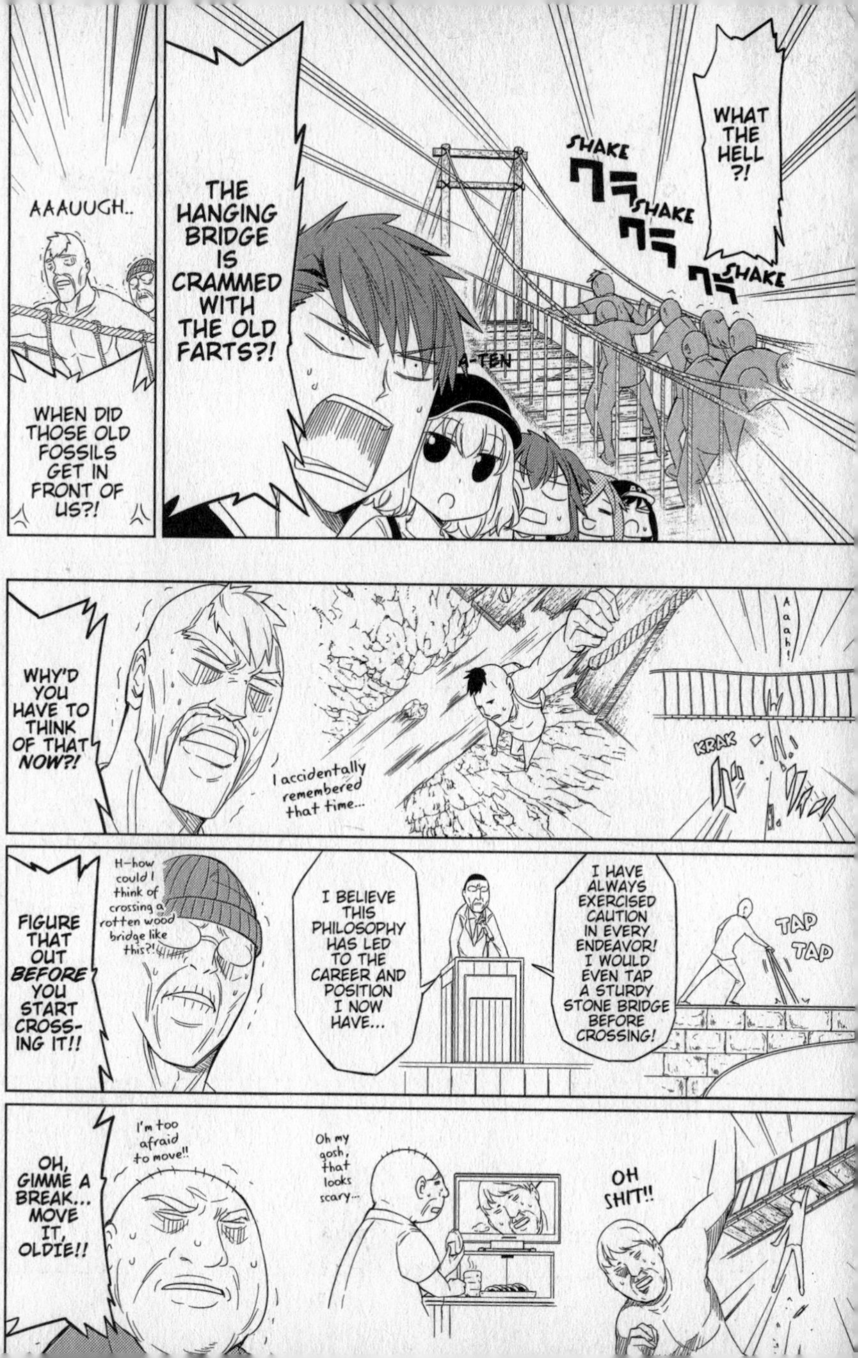
WHAT THE HELL?!
SHAKE
SHAKE
SHAKE
THE HANGING BRIDGE IS CRAMMED WITH THE OLD FARTS?!
A-TEN
AAAUUGH..
WHEN DID THOSE OLD FOSSILS GET IN FRONT OF US?!
Aaah!
KRAK
I accidentally remembered that time...
WHY'D YOU HAVE TO THINK OF THAT NOW?!
TAP TAP
I HAVE ALWAYS EXERCISED CAUTION IN EVERY ENDEAVOR! I WOULD EVEN TAP A STURDY STONE BRIDGE BEFORE CROSSING!
I BELIEVE THIS PHILOSOPHY HAS LED TO THE CAREER AND POSITION I NOW HAVE...
H-how could I think of crossing a rotten wood bridge like this?!
FIGURE THAT OUT BEFORE YOU START CROSSING IT!!
OH SHIT!!
Oh my gosh, that looks scary...
I'm too afraid to move!!
OH, GIMME A BREAK... MOVE IT, OLDIE!!

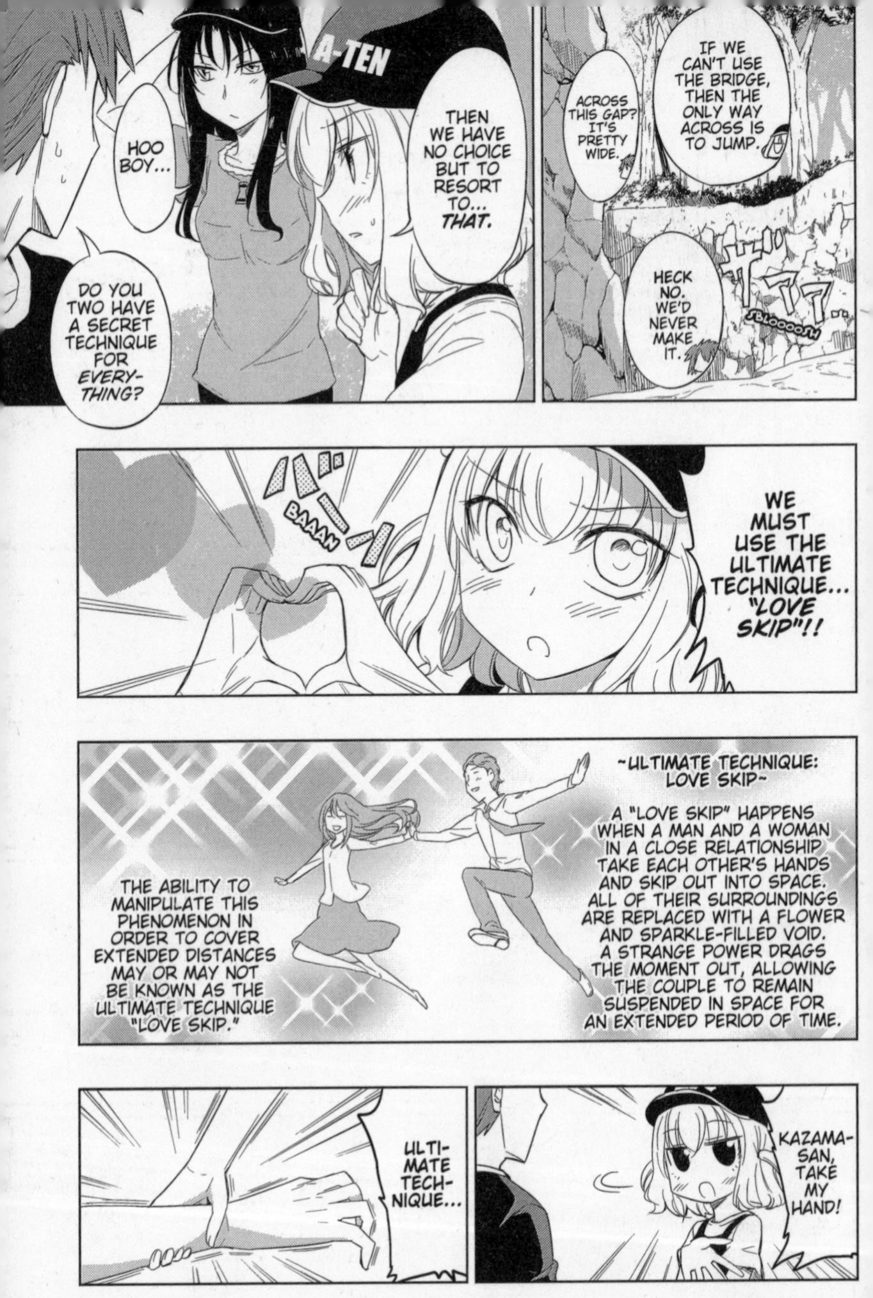
IF WE CAN'T USE THE BRIDGE, THEN THE ONLY WAY ACROSS IS TO JUMP.
ACROSS THIS GAP? IT'S PRETTY WIDE.
HECK NO. WE'D NEVER MAKE IT.
SBLOOOOSH
THEN WE HAVE NO CHOICE BUT TO RESORT TO... *THAT.*
HOO BOY...
DO YOU TWO HAVE A SECRET TECHNIQUE FOR *EVERY-THING?*
BAAAN
WE MUST USE THE ULTIMATE TECHNIQUE... *"LOVE SKIP"*!!
~ULTIMATE TECHNIQUE: LOVE SKIP~
A "LOVE SKIP" HAPPENS WHEN A MAN AND A WOMAN IN A CLOSE RELATIONSHIP TAKE EACH OTHER'S HANDS AND SKIP OUT INTO SPACE. ALL OF THEIR SURROUNDINGS ARE REPLACED WITH A FLOWER AND SPARKLE-FILLED VOID. A STRANGE POWER DRAGS THE MOMENT OUT, ALLOWING THE COUPLE TO REMAIN SUSPENDED IN SPACE FOR AN EXTENDED PERIOD OF TIME.
THE ABILITY TO MANIPULATE THIS PHENOMENON IN ORDER TO COVER EXTENDED DISTANCES MAY OR MAY NOT BE KNOWN AS THE ULTIMATE TECHNIQUE "LOVE SKIP."
KAZAMA-SAN, TAKE MY HAND!
ULTI-MATE TECH-NIQUE...

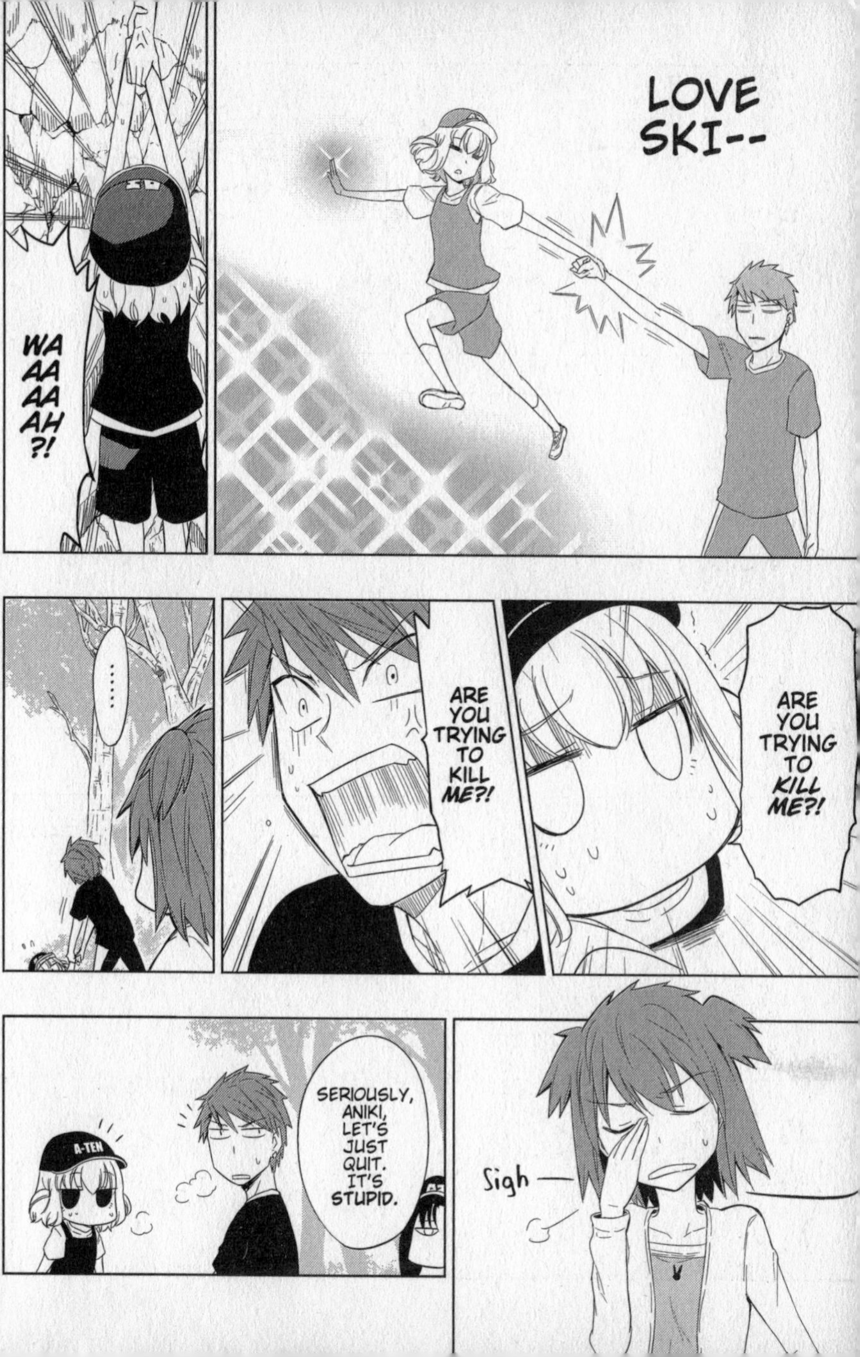
LOVE SKI--
WAAAAAAAH?!
ARE YOU TRYING TO KILL ME?!
ARE YOU TRYING TO KILL ME?!
......
Sigh —
SERIOUSLY, ANIKI, LET'S JUST QUIT. IT'S STUPID.

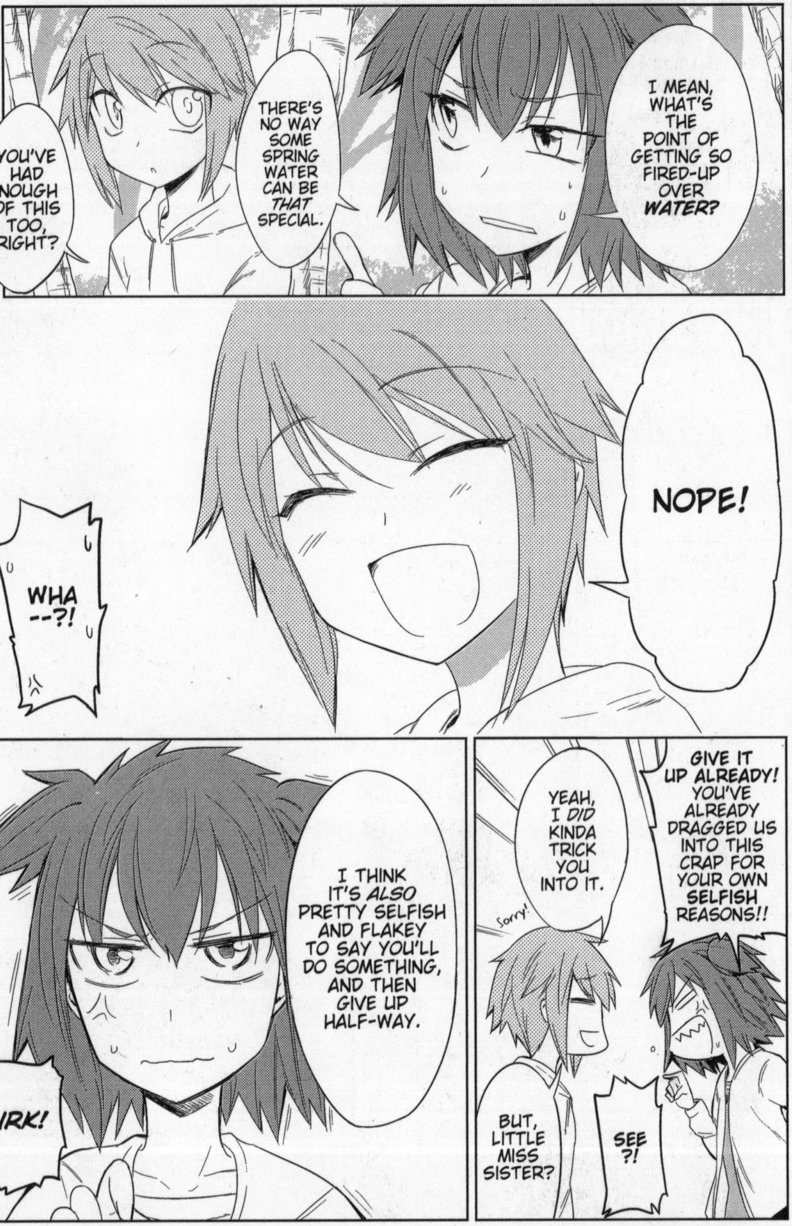
I MEAN, WHAT'S THE POINT OF GETTING SO FIRED-UP OVER *WATER?*
THERE'S NO WAY SOME SPRING WATER CAN BE *THAT* SPECIAL.
YOU'VE HAD ENOUGH OF THIS TOO, RIGHT?
NOPE!
WHA--?!
GIVE IT UP ALREADY! YOU'VE ALREADY DRAGGED US INTO THIS CRAP FOR YOUR OWN SELFISH REASONS!!
YEAH, I *DID* KINDA TRICK YOU INTO IT.
Sorry!
SEE?!
BUT, LITTLE MISS SISTER?
I THINK IT'S *ALSO* PRETTY SELFISH AND FLAKEY TO SAY YOU'LL DO SOMETHING, AND THEN GIVE UP HALF-WAY.
URK!

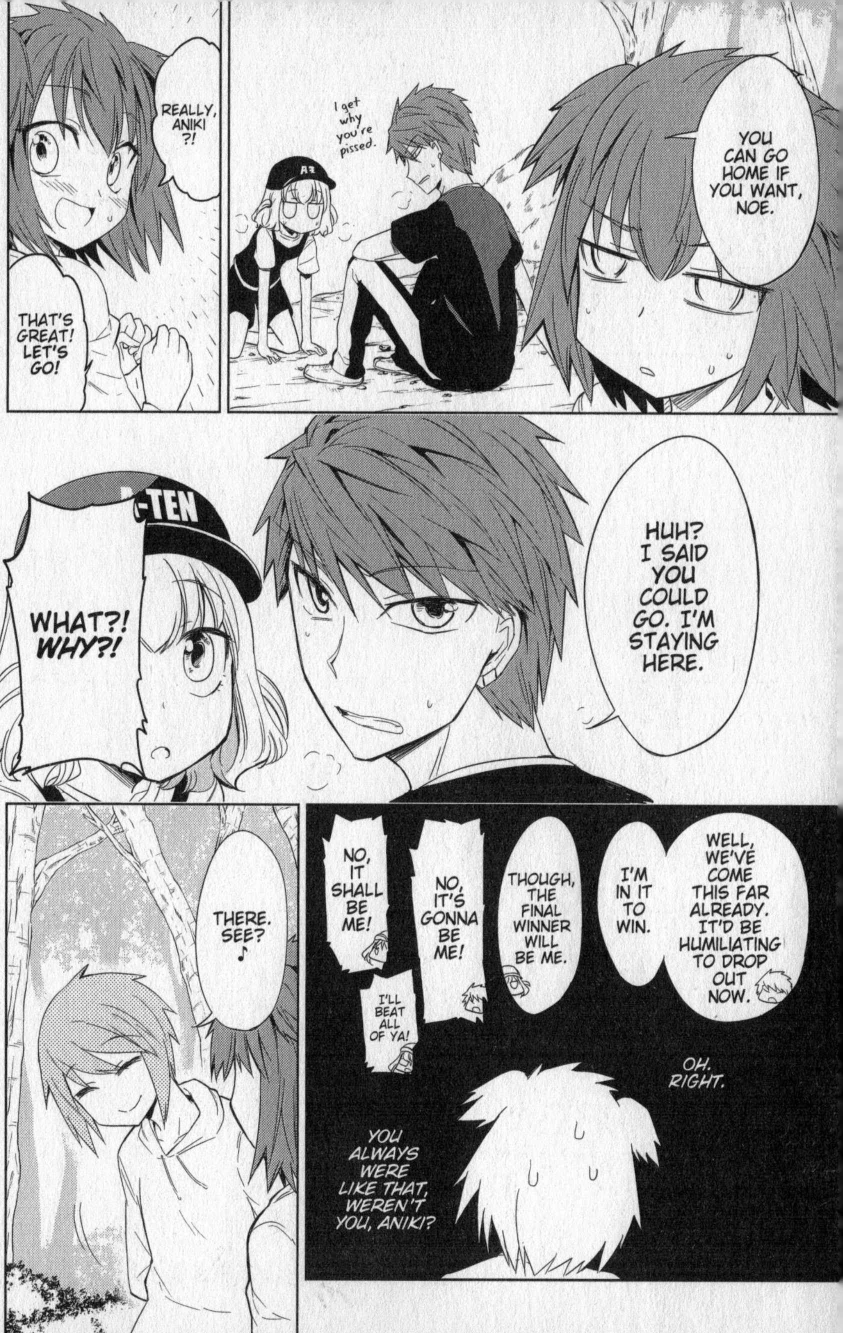
YOU CAN GO HOME IF YOU WANT, NOE.
I get why you're pissed.
REALLY, ANIKI?!
THAT'S GREAT! LET'S GO!
HUH? I SAID YOU COULD GO. I'M STAYING HERE.
WHAT?! *WHY?!*
WELL, WE'VE COME THIS FAR ALREADY. IT'D BE HUMILIATING TO DROP OUT NOW.
I'M IN IT TO WIN.
THOUGH, THE FINAL WINNER WILL BE ME.
NO, IT'S GONNA BE ME!
I'LL BEAT ALL OF YA!
NO, IT SHALL BE ME!
OH. RIGHT.
YOU ALWAYS WERE LIKE THAT, WEREN'T YOU, ANIKI?
THERE. SEE? ♪

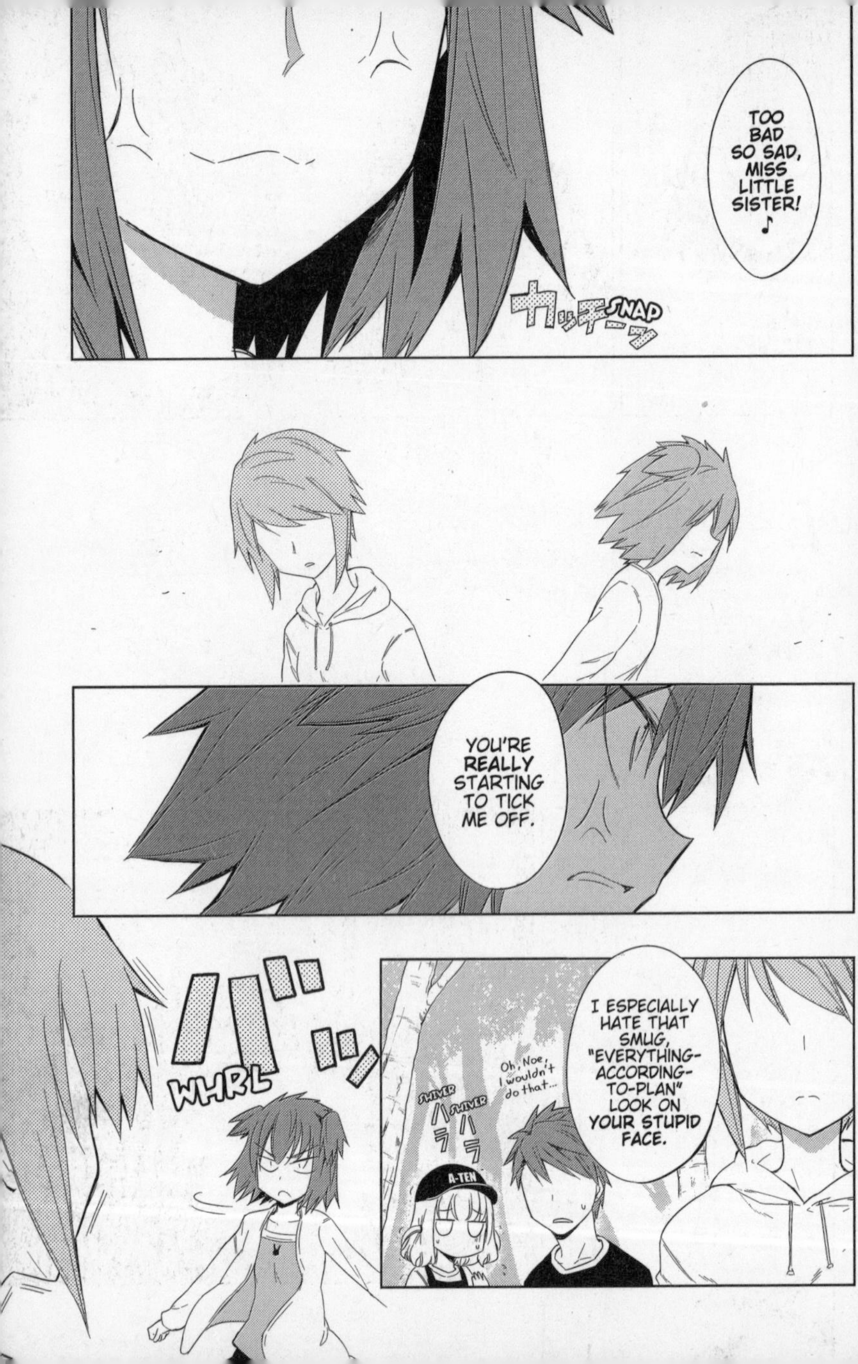
TOO BAD SO SAD, MISS LITTLE SISTER! ♪
カッチーン
SNAP
YOU'RE REALLY STARTING TO TICK ME OFF.
I ESPECIALLY HATE THAT SMUG, "EVERYTHING-ACCORDING-TO-PLAN" LOOK ON YOUR STUPID FACE.
Oh, Noe, I wouldn't do that...
ハラハラ
SHIVER SHIVER
バッ
WHRL

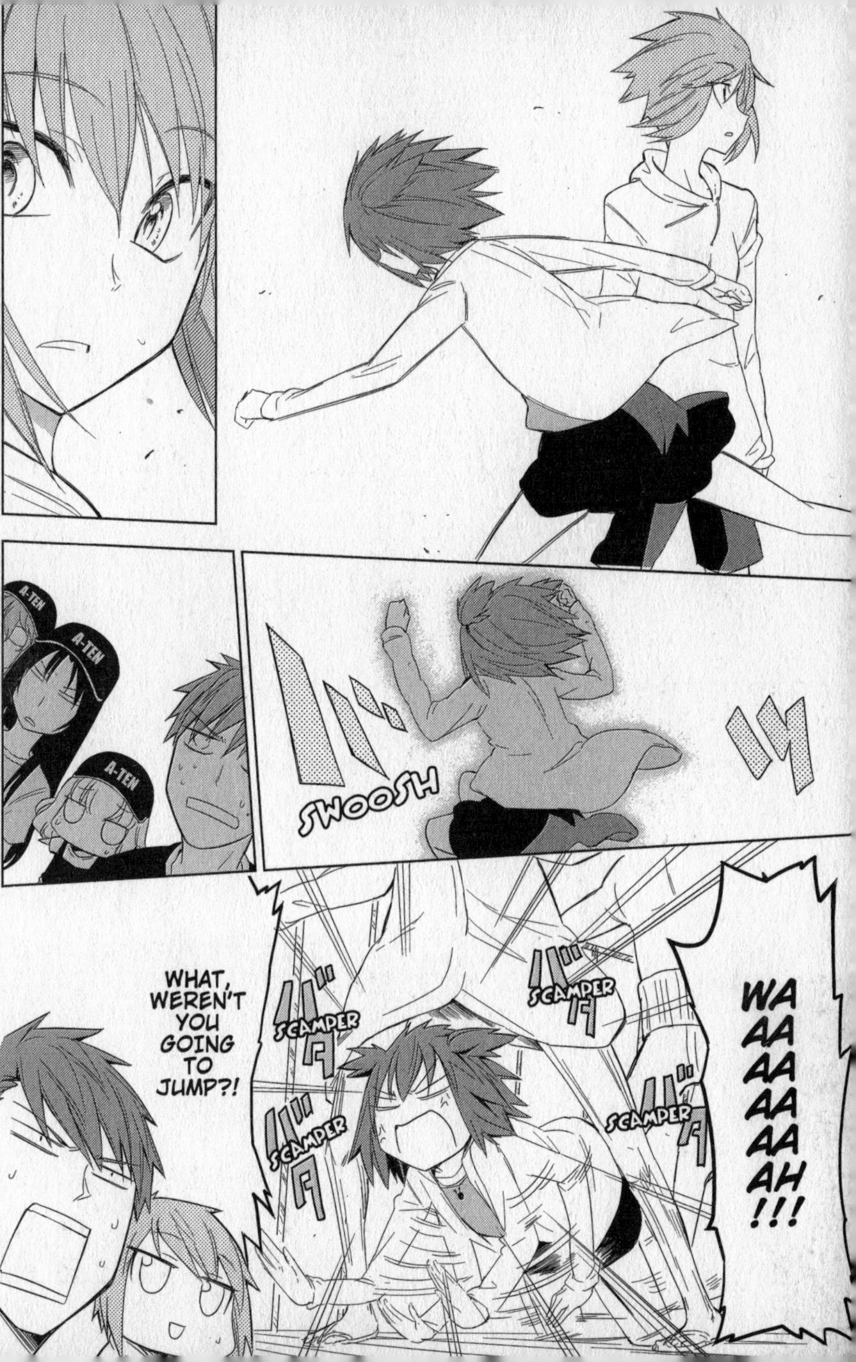
SWOOSH
WAAAAAAAAAAH!!!
SCAMPER
SCAMPER
SCAMPER
SCAMPER
WHAT, WEREN'T YOU GOING TO JUMP?!

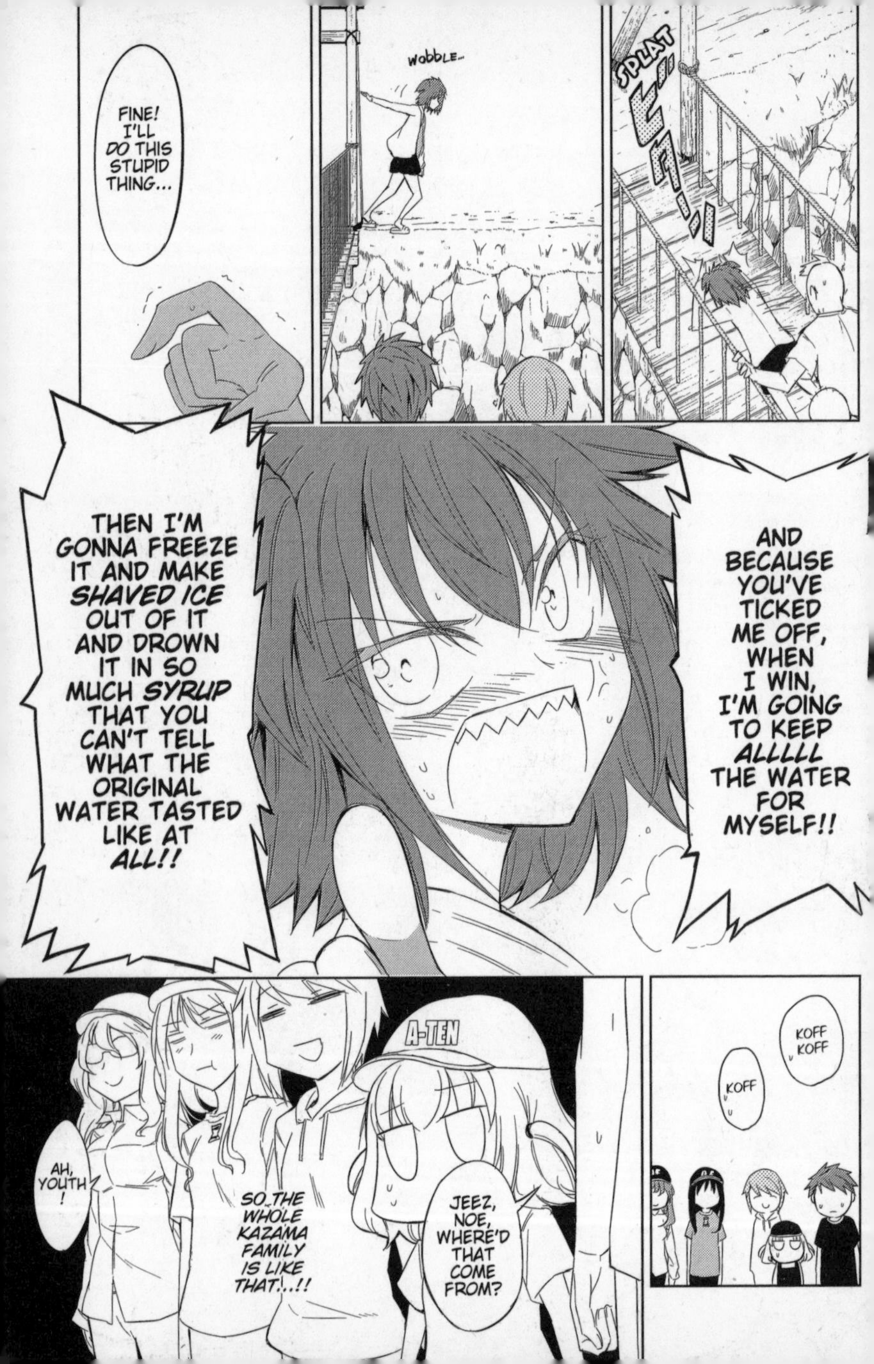
SPLAT
WOBBLE...
FINE! I'LL DO THIS STUPID THING...
AND BECAUSE YOU'VE TICKED ME OFF, WHEN I WIN, I'M GOING TO KEEP ALLLLL THE WATER FOR MYSELF!!
THEN I'M GONNA FREEZE IT AND MAKE SHAVED ICE OUT OF IT AND DROWN IT IN SO MUCH SYRUP THAT YOU CAN'T TELL WHAT THE ORIGINAL WATER TASTED LIKE AT ALL!!
KOFF KOFF
KOFF
A-TEN
JEEZ, NOE, WHERE'D THAT COME FROM?
SO THE WHOLE KAZAMA FAMILY IS LIKE THAT...!!
AH, YOUTH!

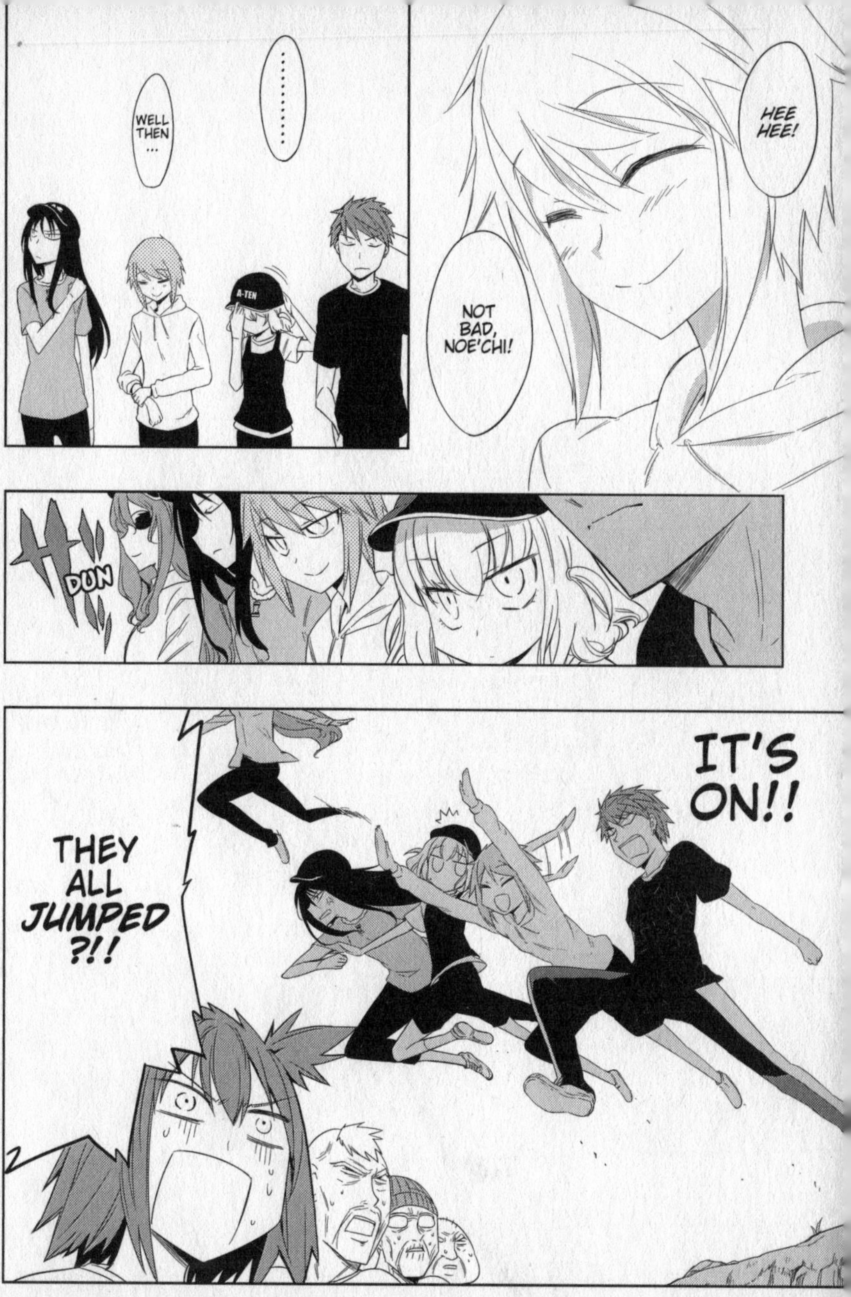
HEE HEE!
NOT BAD, NOE'CHI!
......
WELL THEN...
DUN
IT'S ON!!
THEY ALL JUMPED?!!

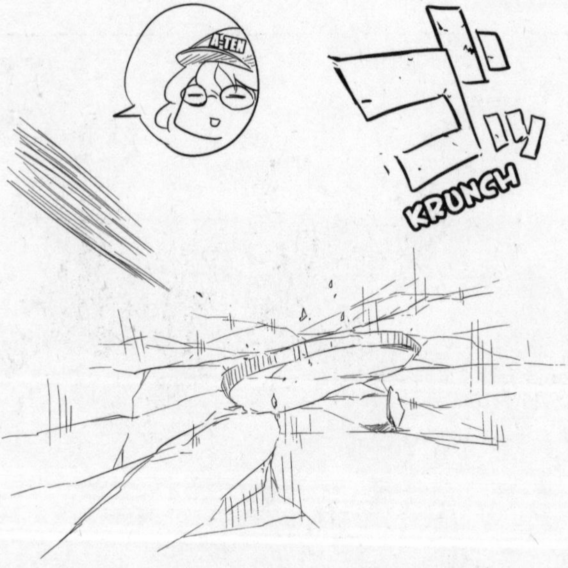
KRUNCH
A-TEN

D-FRAGMENTS
ディーふらぐ！

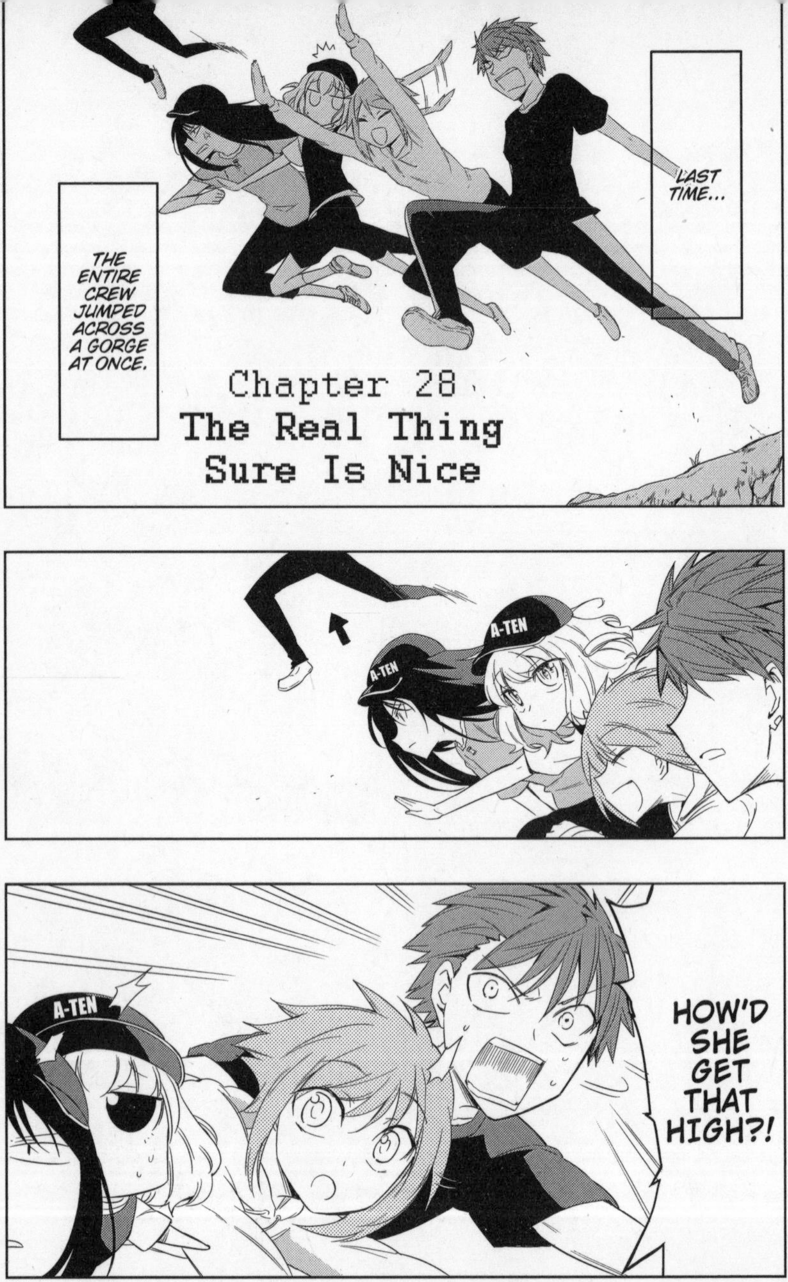
LAST TIME...
THE ENTIRE CREW JUMPED ACROSS A GORGE AT ONCE.
Chapter 28
The Real Thing Sure Is Nice
A-TEN
A-TEN
A-TEN
HOW'D SHE GET THAT HIGH?!

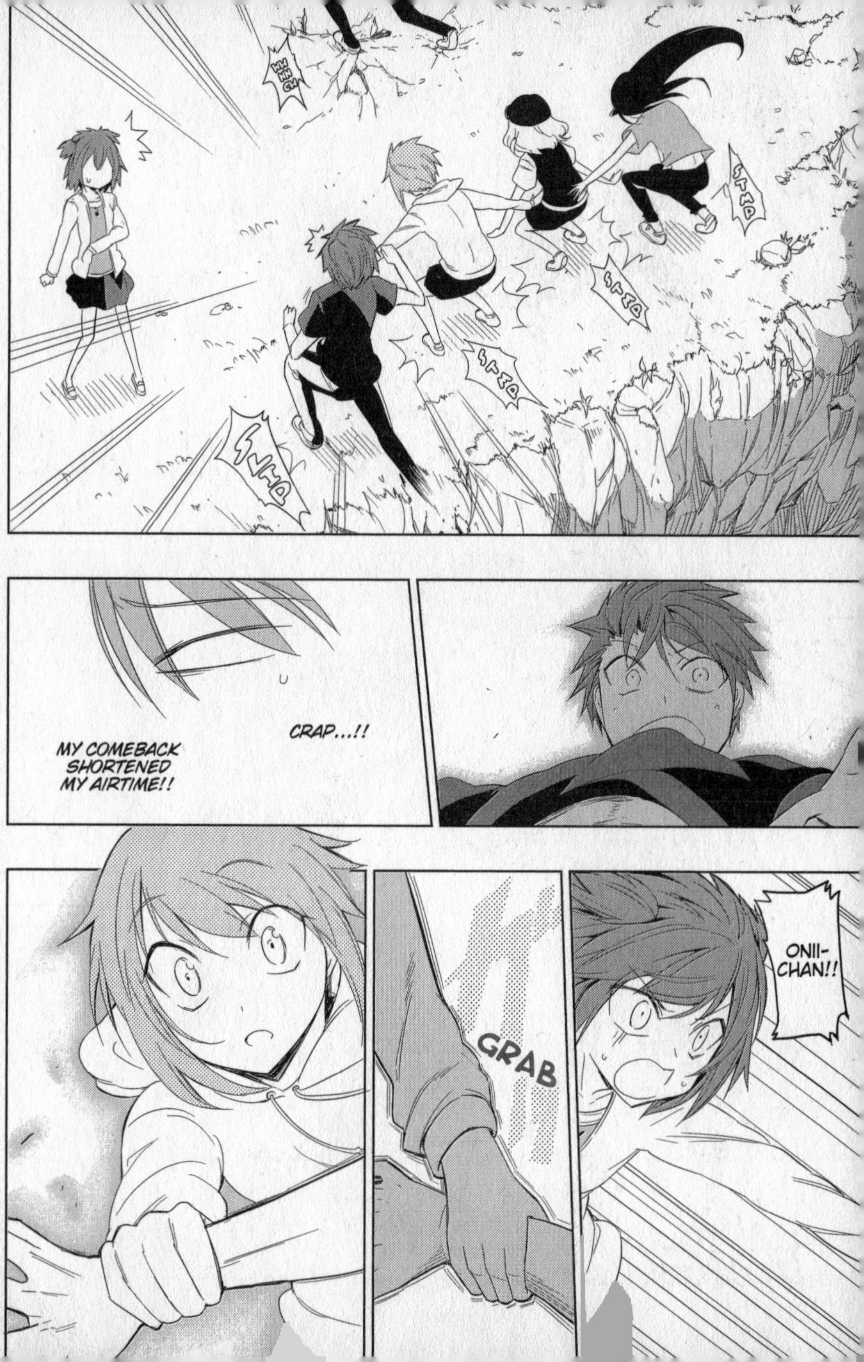
STMP
STEP
STEP
WHNCH
CRAP...!!
MY COMEBACK SHORTENED MY AIRTIME!!
ONII-CHAN!!
GRAB

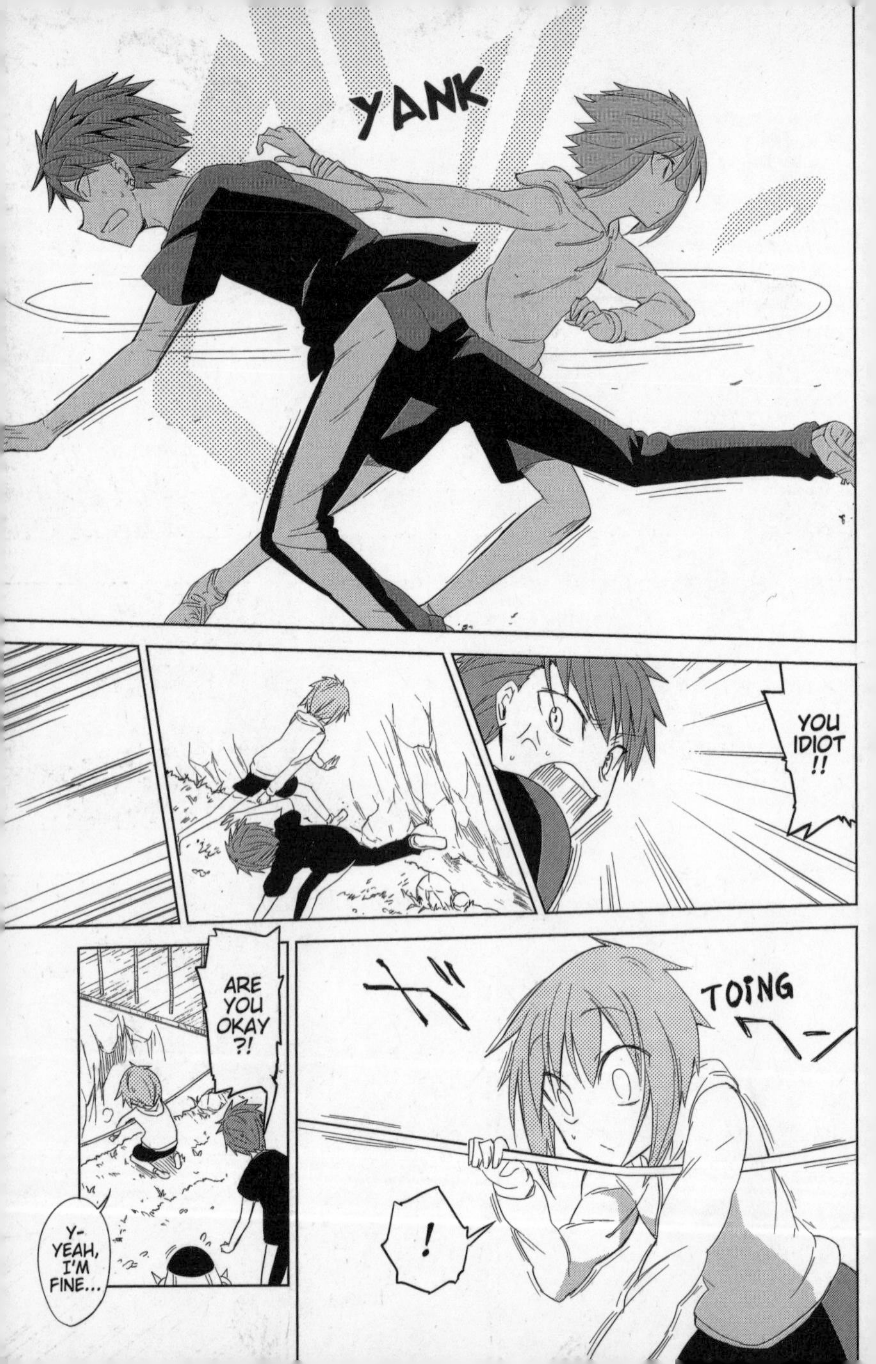
YANK
YOU IDIOT !!
TOING
!
ARE YOU OKAY ?!
Y- YEAH, I'M FINE...

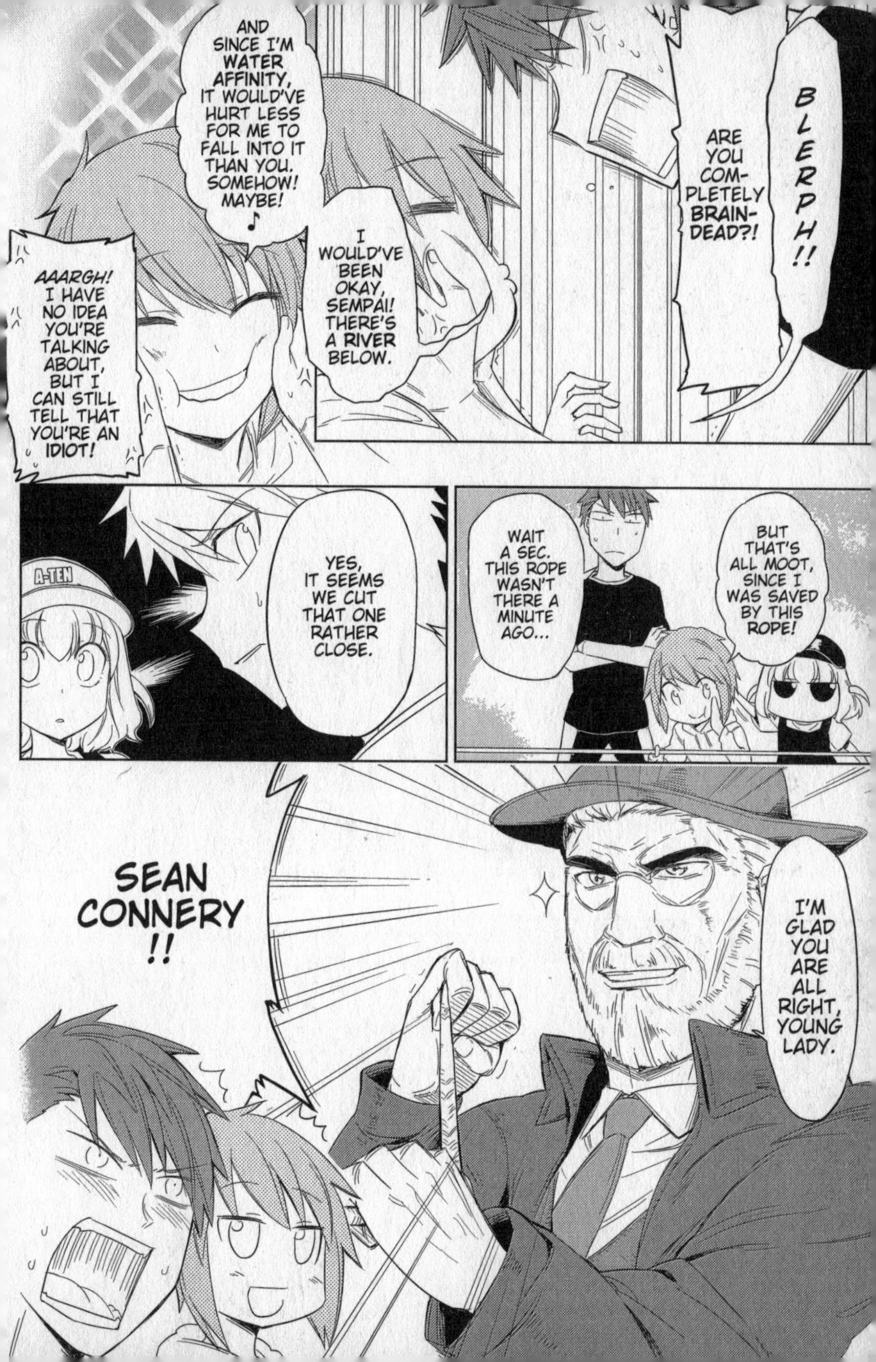
BLERPH!!
ARE YOU COMPLETELY BRAIN-DEAD?!
I WOULD'VE BEEN OKAY, SEMPAI! THERE'S A RIVER BELOW.
AND SINCE I'M WATER AFFINITY, IT WOULD'VE HURT LESS FOR ME TO FALL INTO IT THAN YOU. SOMEHOW! MAYBE! ♪
AAARGH! I HAVE NO IDEA YOU'RE TALKING ABOUT, BUT I CAN STILL TELL THAT YOU'RE AN IDIOT!
BUT THAT'S ALL MOOT, SINCE I WAS SAVED BY THIS ROPE!
WAIT A SEC. THIS ROPE WASN'T THERE A MINUTE AGO...
YES, IT SEEMS WE CUT THAT ONE RATHER CLOSE.
A-TEN
I'M GLAD YOU ARE ALL RIGHT, YOUNG LADY.
SEAN CONNERY !!

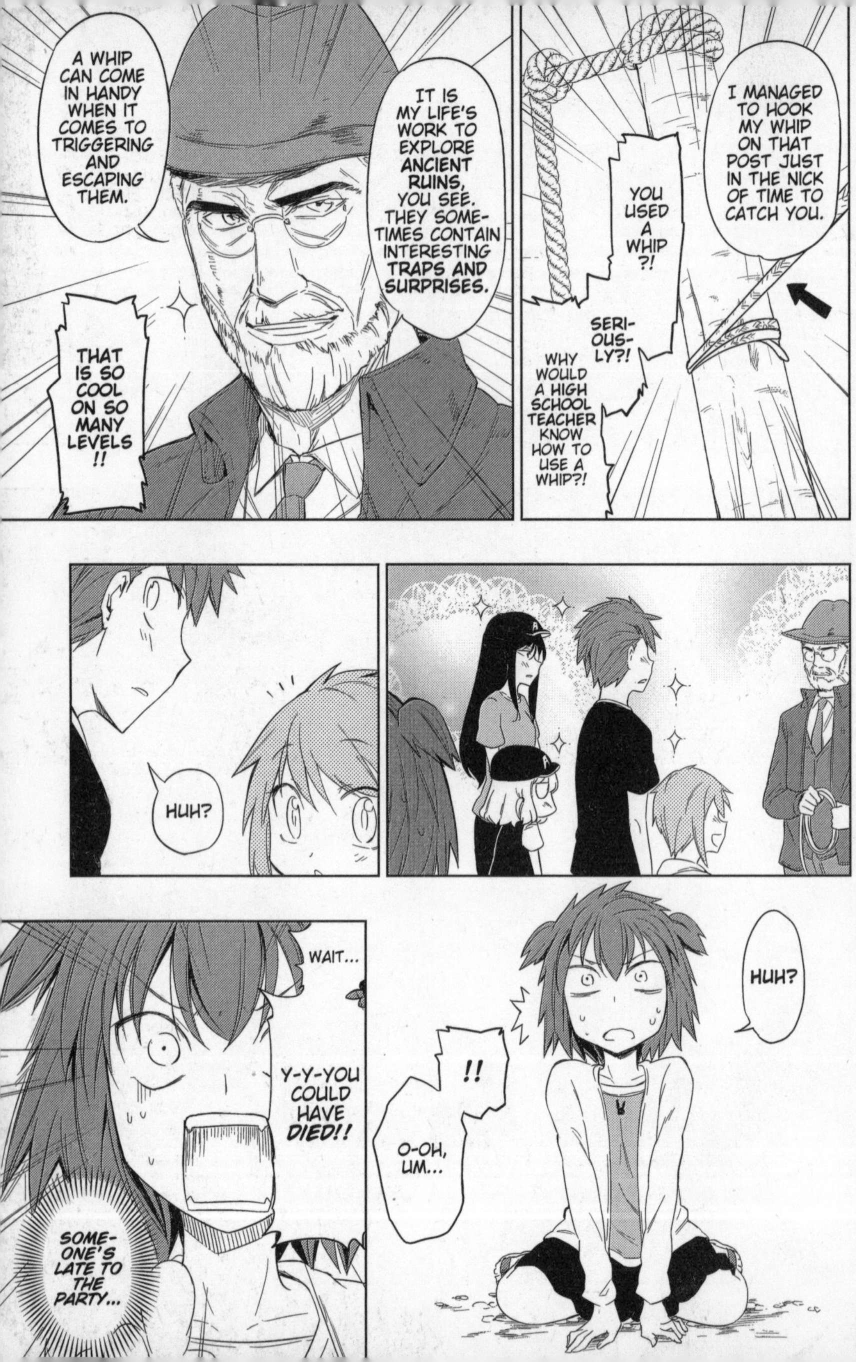
I MANAGED TO HOOK MY WHIP ON THAT POST JUST IN THE NICK OF TIME TO CATCH YOU.
YOU USED A WHIP?!
SERI-OUS-LY?!
WHY WOULD A HIGH SCHOOL TEACHER KNOW HOW TO USE A WHIP?!
IT IS MY LIFE'S WORK TO EXPLORE ANCIENT RUINS, YOU SEE. THEY SOME-TIMES CONTAIN INTERESTING TRAPS AND SURPRISES.
A WHIP CAN COME IN HANDY WHEN IT COMES TO TRIGGERING AND ESCAPING THEM.
THAT IS SO COOL ON SO MANY LEVELS!!
HUH?
HUH?
!!
O-OH, UM...
WAIT...
Y-Y-YOU COULD HAVE DIED!!
SOME-ONE'S LATE TO THE PARTY...

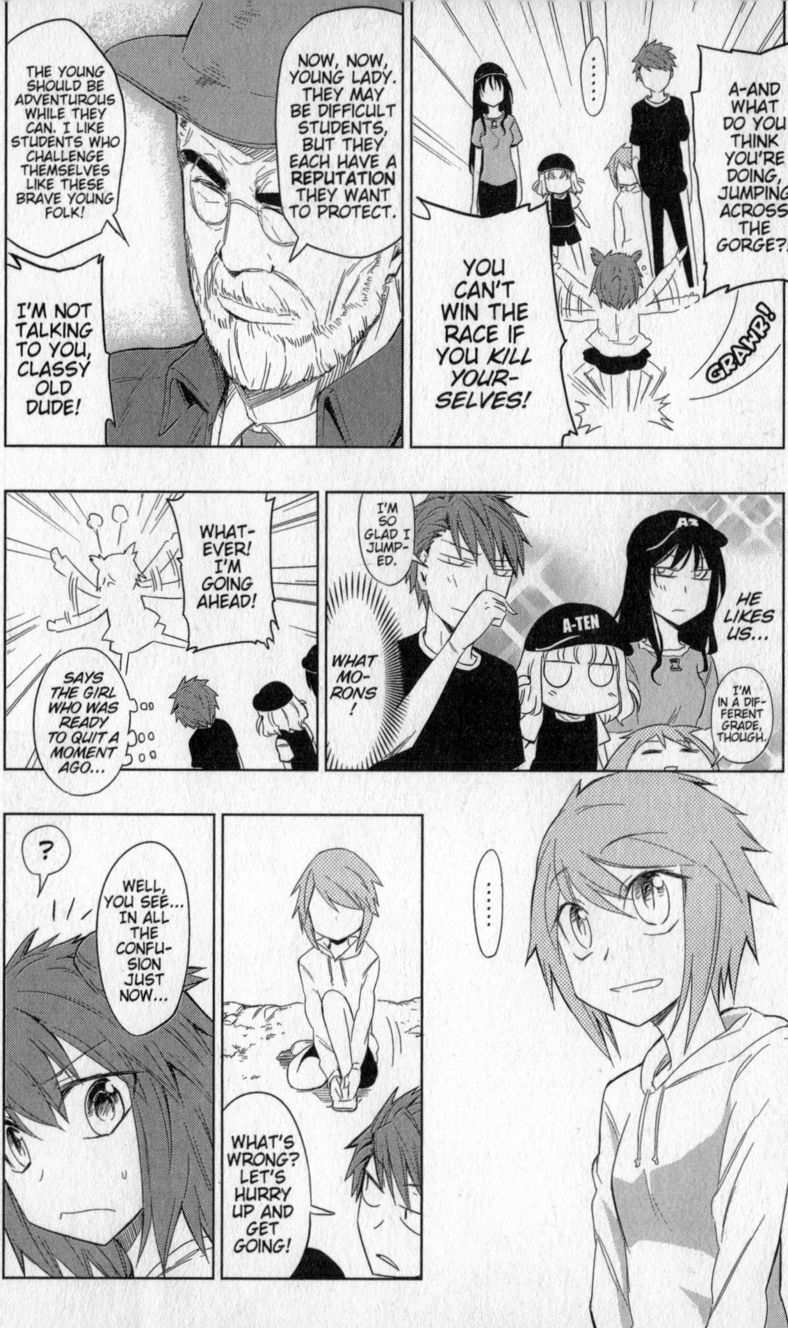
......
A-AND WHAT DO YOU THINK YOU'RE DOING, JUMPING ACROSS THE GORGE?!
YOU CAN'T WIN THE RACE IF YOU *KILL* YOURSELVES!
GRAWB!
NOW, NOW, YOUNG LADY. THEY MAY BE DIFFICULT STUDENTS, BUT THEY EACH HAVE A REPUTATION THEY WANT TO PROTECT.
THE YOUNG SHOULD BE ADVENTUROUS WHILE THEY CAN. I LIKE STUDENTS WHO CHALLENGE THEMSELVES LIKE THESE BRAVE YOUNG FOLK!
I'M NOT TALKING TO YOU, CLASSY OLD DUDE!
I'M SO GLAD I JUMPED.
HE LIKES US...
WHAT MORONS!
I'M IN A DIFFERENT GRADE, THOUGH.
A-TEN
WHATEVER! I'M GOING AHEAD!
SAYS THE GIRL WHO WAS READY TO QUIT A MOMENT AGO...
......
WHAT'S WRONG? LET'S HURRY UP AND GET GOING!
?
WELL, YOU SEE... IN ALL THE CONFUSION JUST NOW...

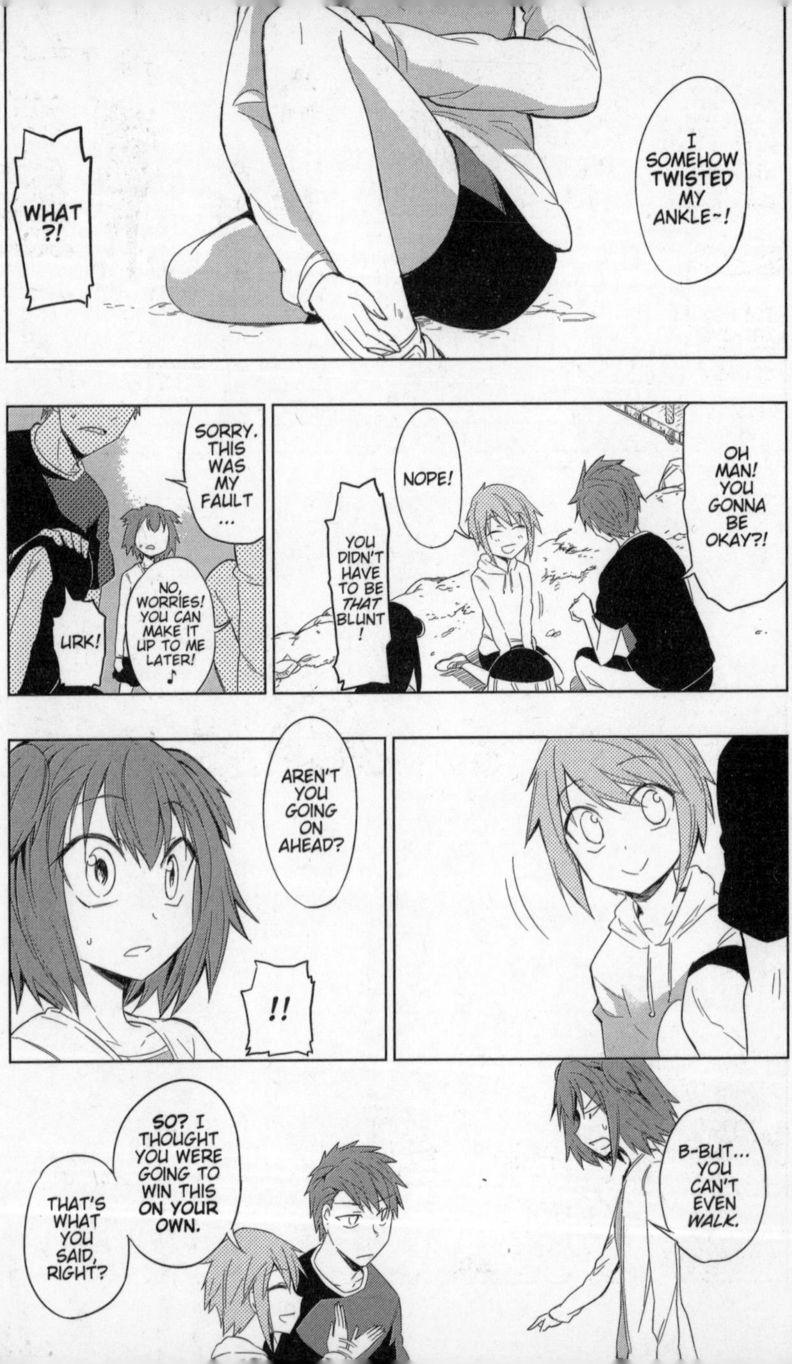
I SOMEHOW TWISTED MY ANKLE~!
WHAT?!
OH MAN! YOU GONNA BE OKAY?!
NOPE!
YOU DIDN'T HAVE TO BE *THAT* BLUNT!
SORRY. THIS WAS MY FAULT...
NO, WORRIES! YOU CAN MAKE IT UP TO ME LATER! ♪
URK!
AREN'T YOU GOING ON AHEAD?
!!
B-BUT... YOU CAN'T EVEN *WALK.*
SO? I THOUGHT YOU WERE GOING TO WIN THIS ON YOUR OWN.
THAT'S WHAT YOU SAID, RIGHT?

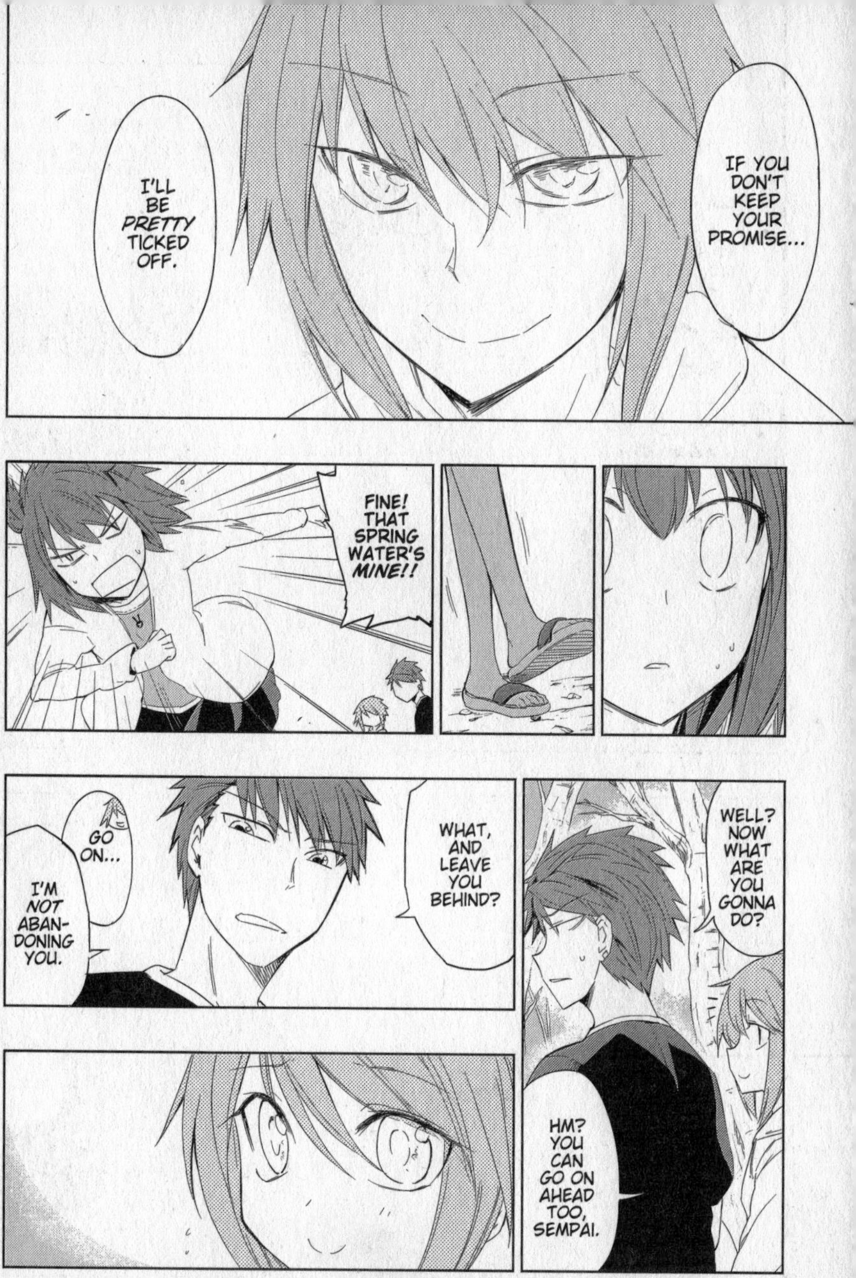
IF YOU DON'T KEEP YOUR PROMISE...
I'LL BE *PRETTY* TICKED OFF.
FINE! THAT SPRING WATER'S *MINE!!*
WELL? NOW WHAT ARE YOU GONNA DO?
HM? YOU CAN GO ON AHEAD TOO, SEMPAI.
WHAT, AND LEAVE YOU BEHIND?
GO ON...
I'M *NOT* ABAN-DONING YOU.

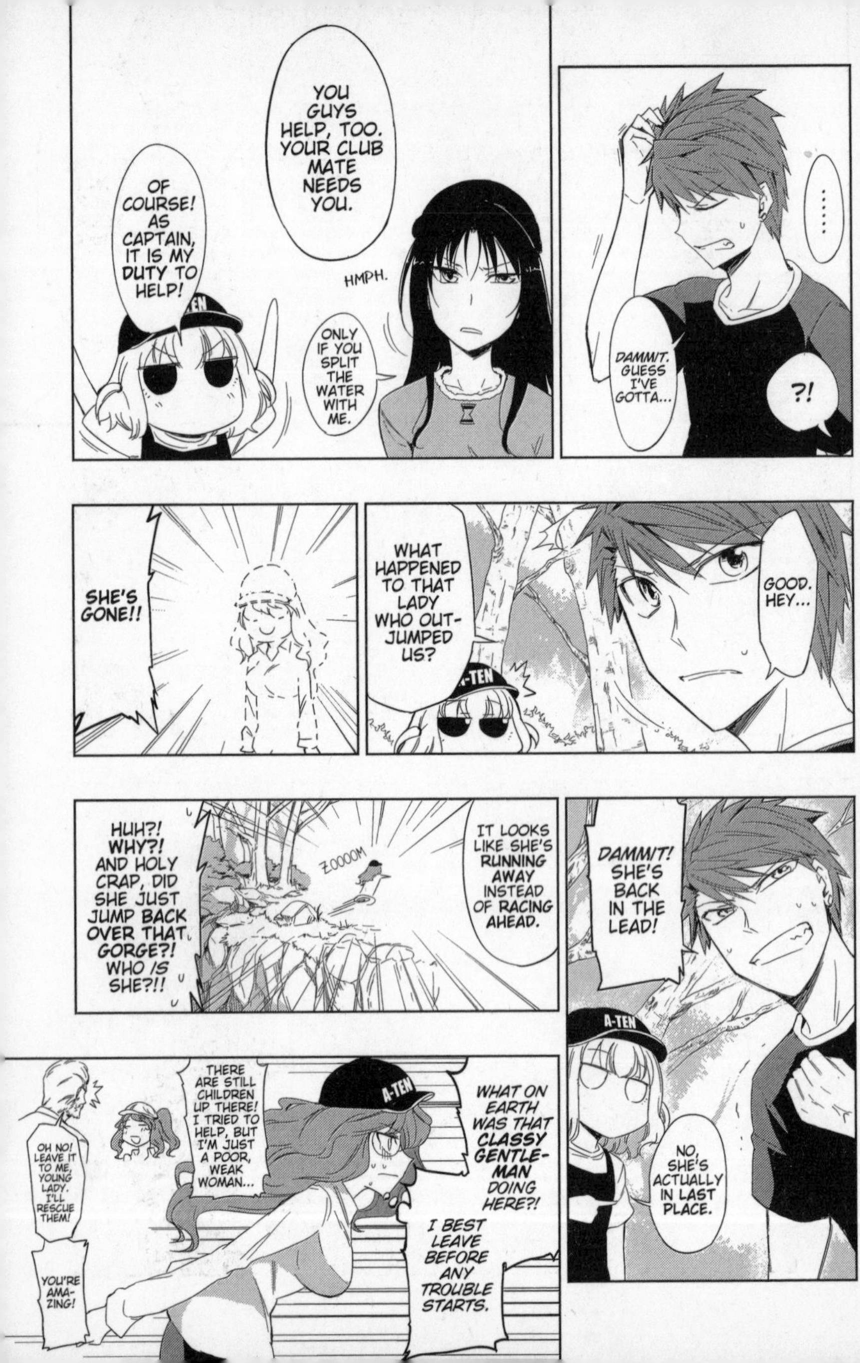
......
DAMMIT. GUESS I'VE GOTTA...
?!
YOU GUYS HELP, TOO. YOUR CLUB MATE NEEDS YOU.
HMPH.
ONLY IF YOU SPLIT THE WATER WITH ME.
OF COURSE! AS CAPTAIN, IT IS MY DUTY TO HELP!
A-TEN
GOOD. HEY...
WHAT HAPPENED TO THAT LADY WHO OUT-JUMPED US?
A-TEN
SHE'S GONE!!
DAMMIT! SHE'S BACK IN THE LEAD!
NO, SHE'S ACTUALLY IN LAST PLACE.
A-TEN
IT LOOKS LIKE SHE'S RUNNING AWAY INSTEAD OF RACING AHEAD.
ZOOOOM
HUH?! WHY?! AND HOLY CRAP, DID SHE JUST JUMP BACK OVER THAT GORGE?! WHO *IS* SHE?!!
WHAT ON EARTH WAS THAT CLASSY GENTLEMAN DOING HERE?!
I BEST LEAVE BEFORE ANY TROUBLE STARTS.
A-TEN
THERE ARE STILL CHILDREN UP THERE! I TRIED TO HELP, BUT I'M JUST A POOR, WEAK WOMAN...
OH NO! LEAVE IT TO ME, YOUNG LADY. I'LL RESCUE THEM!
YOU'RE AMA-ZING!

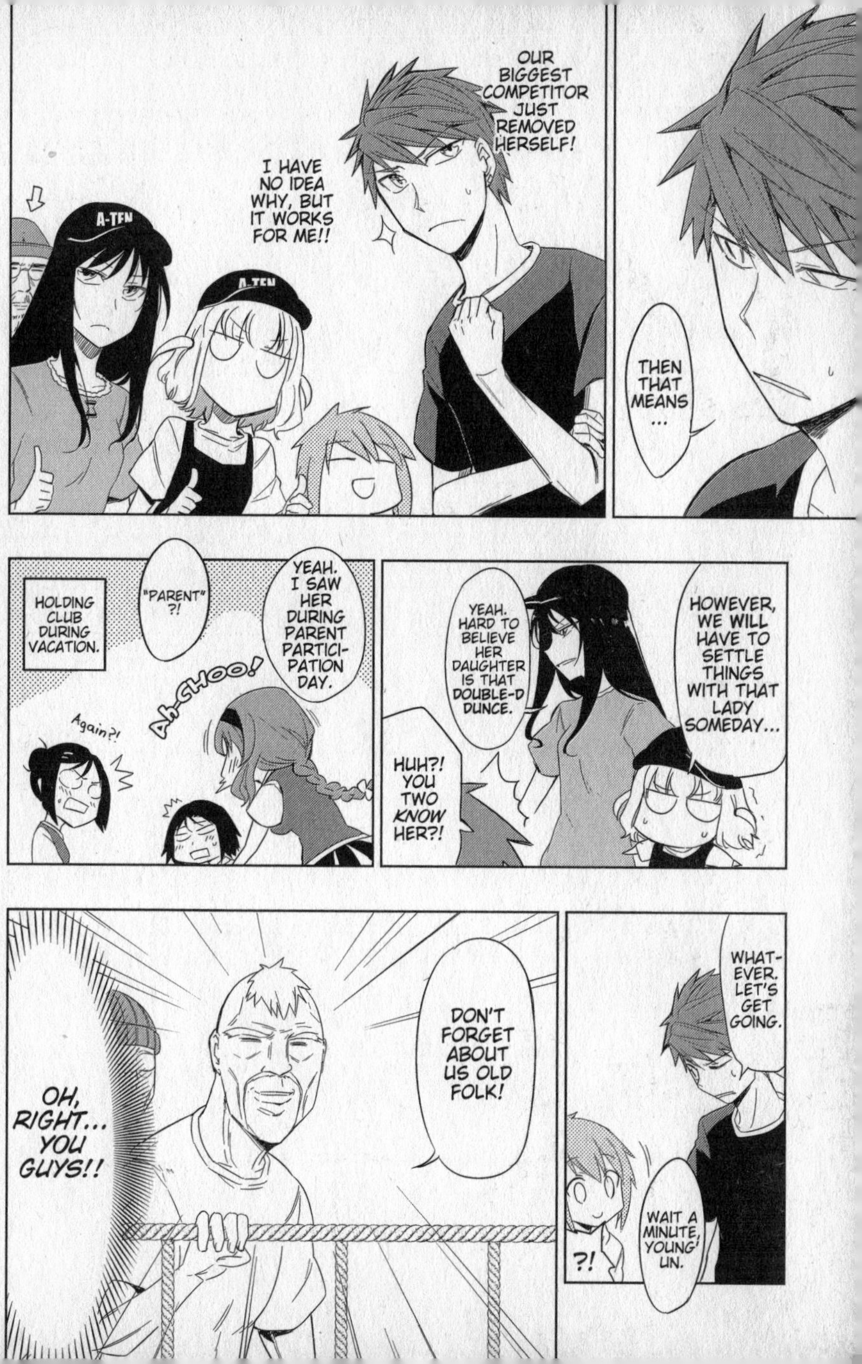
THEN THAT MEANS ...
OUR BIGGEST COMPETITOR JUST REMOVED HERSELF!
I HAVE NO IDEA WHY, BUT IT WORKS FOR ME!!
HOWEVER, WE WILL HAVE TO SETTLE THINGS WITH THAT LADY SOMEDAY...
YEAH. HARD TO BELIEVE HER DAUGHTER IS THAT DOUBLE-D DUNCE.
HUH?! YOU TWO KNOW HER?!
YEAH. I SAW HER DURING PARENT PARTICIPATION DAY.
"PARENT"?!
HOLDING CLUB DURING VACATION.
Ah-CHOO!
Again?!
WHATEVER. LET'S GET GOING.
WAIT A MINUTE, YOUNG' UN.
?!
DON'T FORGET ABOUT US OLD FOLK!
OH, RIGHT... YOU GUYS!!

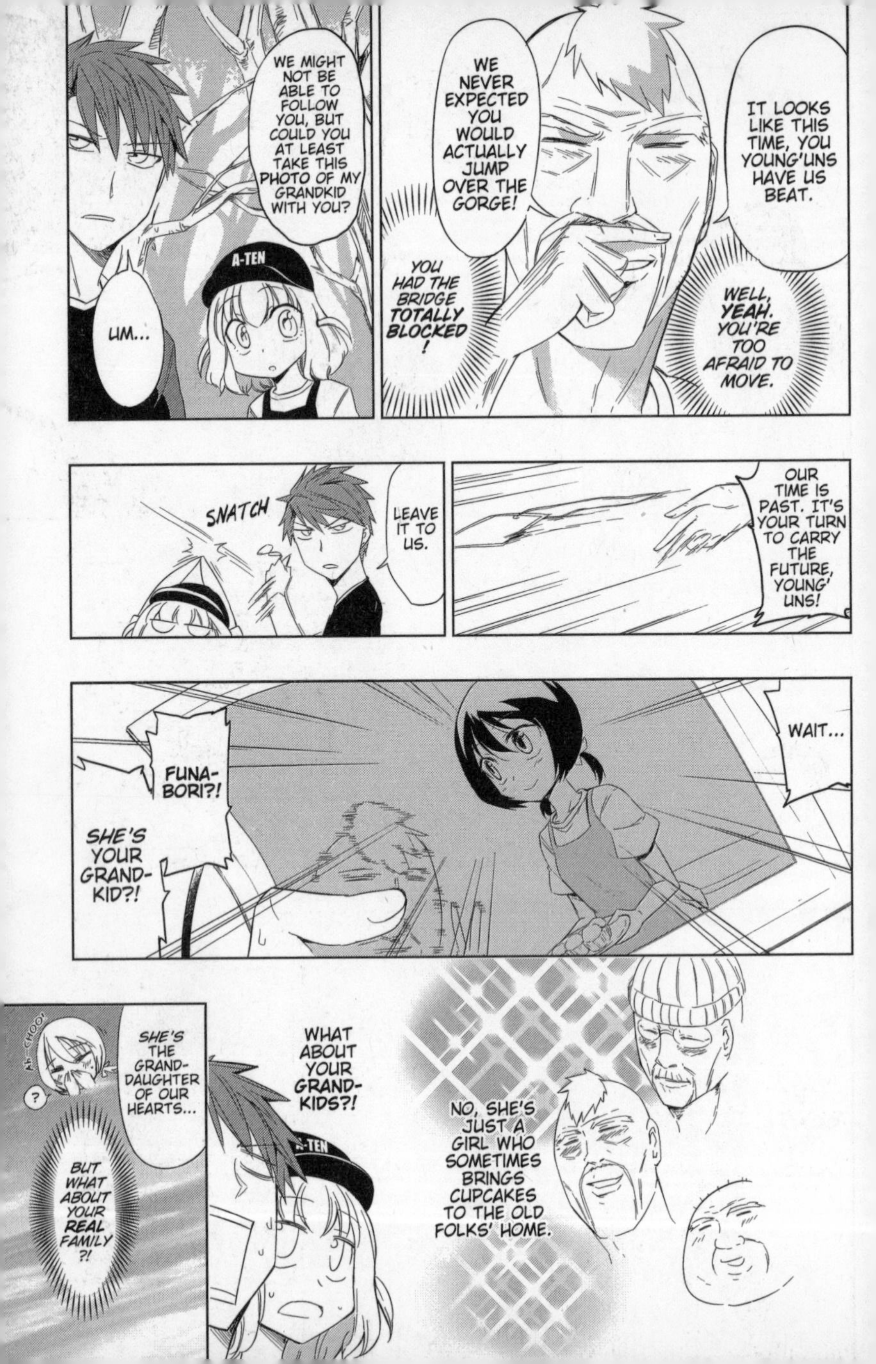
IT LOOKS LIKE THIS TIME, YOU YOUNG'UNS HAVE US BEAT.
WELL, YEAH. YOU'RE TOO AFRAID TO MOVE.
WE NEVER EXPECTED YOU WOULD ACTUALLY JUMP OVER THE GORGE!
YOU HAD THE BRIDGE TOTALLY BLOCKED!
WE MIGHT NOT BE ABLE TO FOLLOW YOU, BUT COULD YOU AT LEAST TAKE THIS PHOTO OF MY GRANDKID WITH YOU?
A-TEN
UM...
OUR TIME IS PAST. IT'S YOUR TURN TO CARRY THE FUTURE, YOUNG' UNS!
LEAVE IT TO US.
SNATCH
WAIT...
FUNA-BORI?!
SHE'S YOUR GRAND-KID?!
NO, SHE'S JUST A GIRL WHO SOMETIMES BRINGS CUPCAKES TO THE OLD FOLKS' HOME.
WHAT ABOUT YOUR GRAND-KIDS?!
A-TEN
SHE'S THE GRAND-DAUGHTER OF OUR HEARTS...
BUT WHAT ABOUT YOUR REAL FAMILY?!
Ah-CHOO!
?

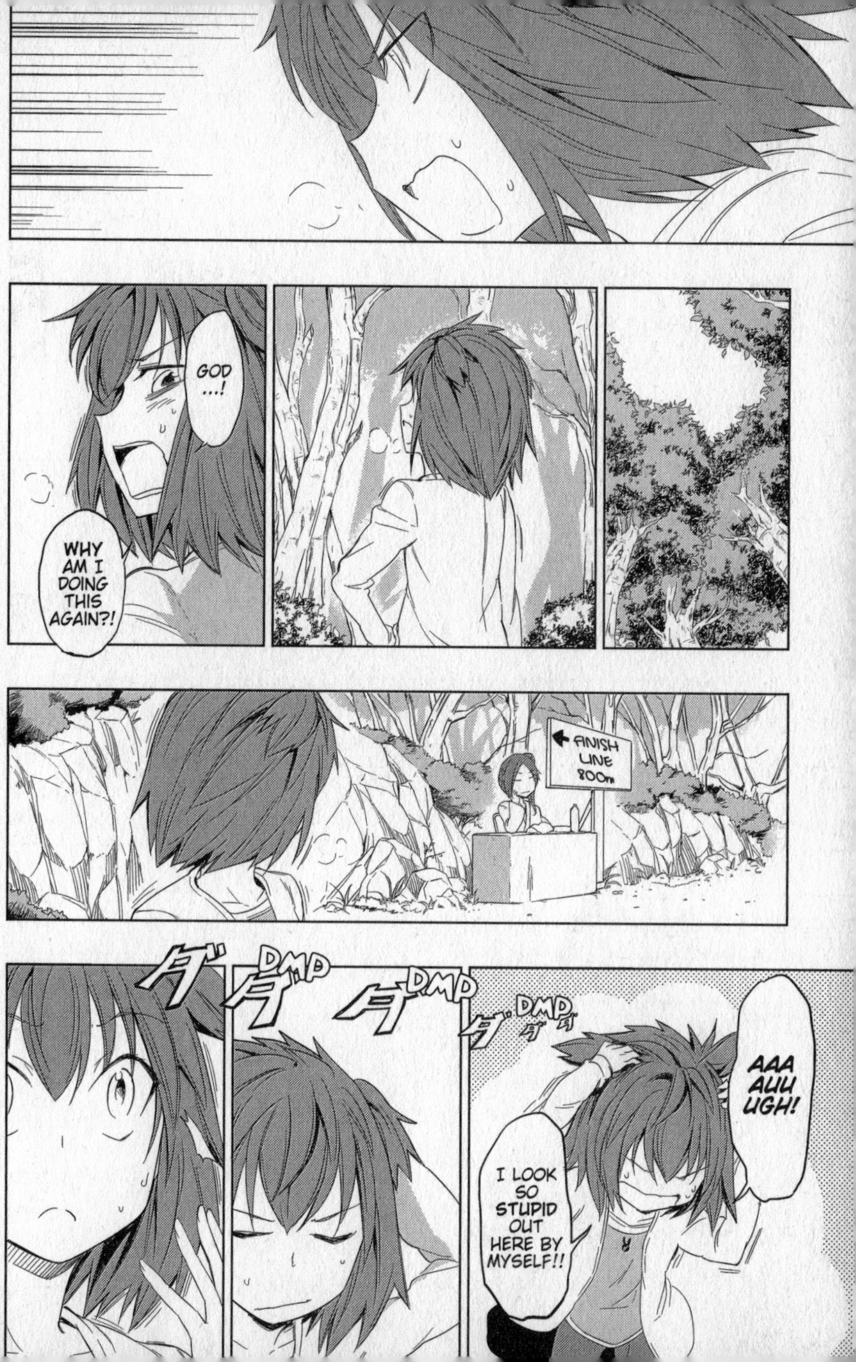
GOD ...!
WHY AM I DOING THIS AGAIN?!
FINISH LINE 800m
DMP
AAA AUU UGH!
I LOOK SO STUPID OUT HERE BY MYSELF!!
DMP
DMP

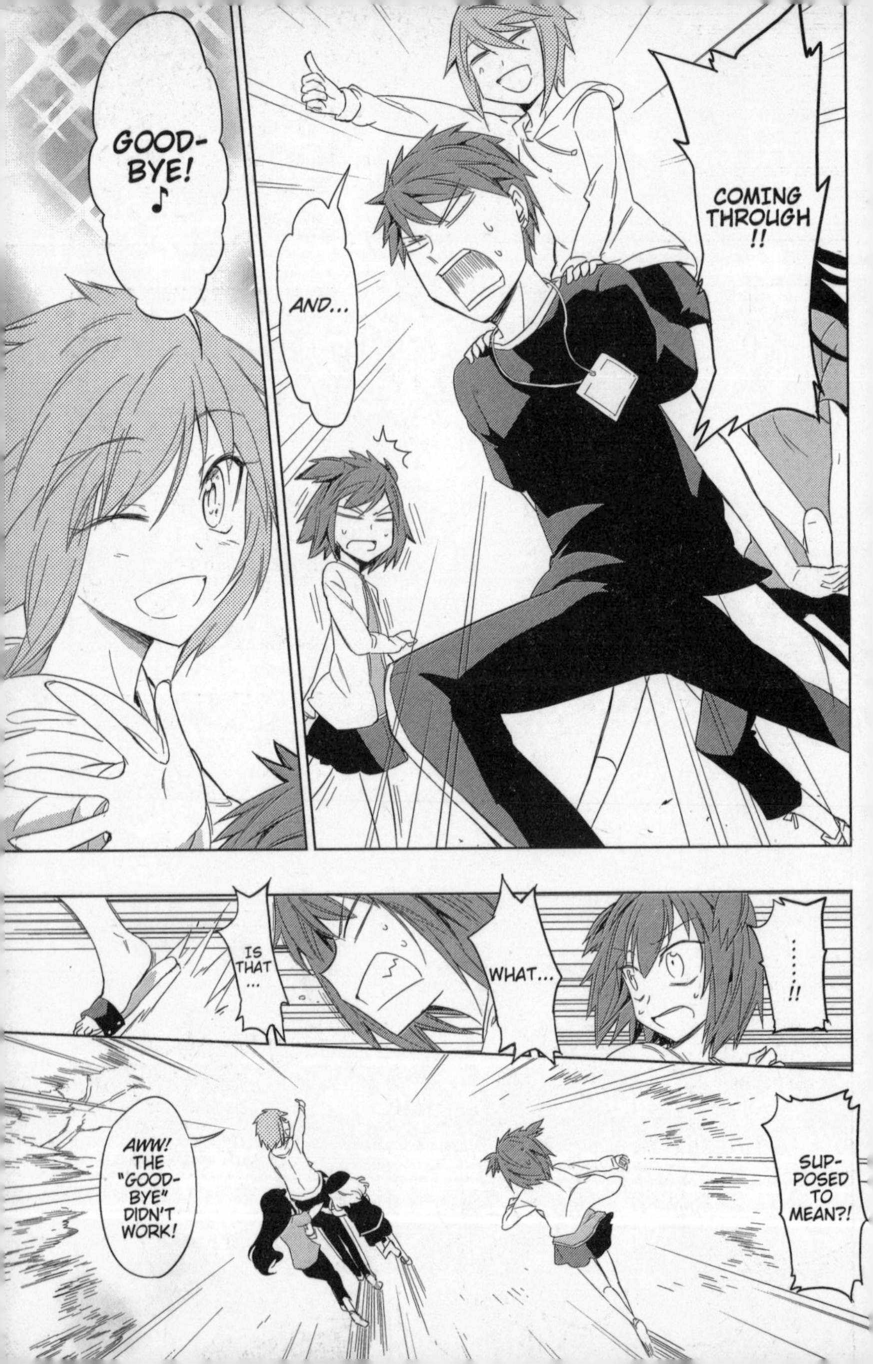
COMING THROUGH!!
AND...
GOOD-BYE! ♪
......!!
WHAT...
IS THAT ...
SUP-POSED TO MEAN?!
AWW! THE "GOOD-BYE" DIDN'T WORK!

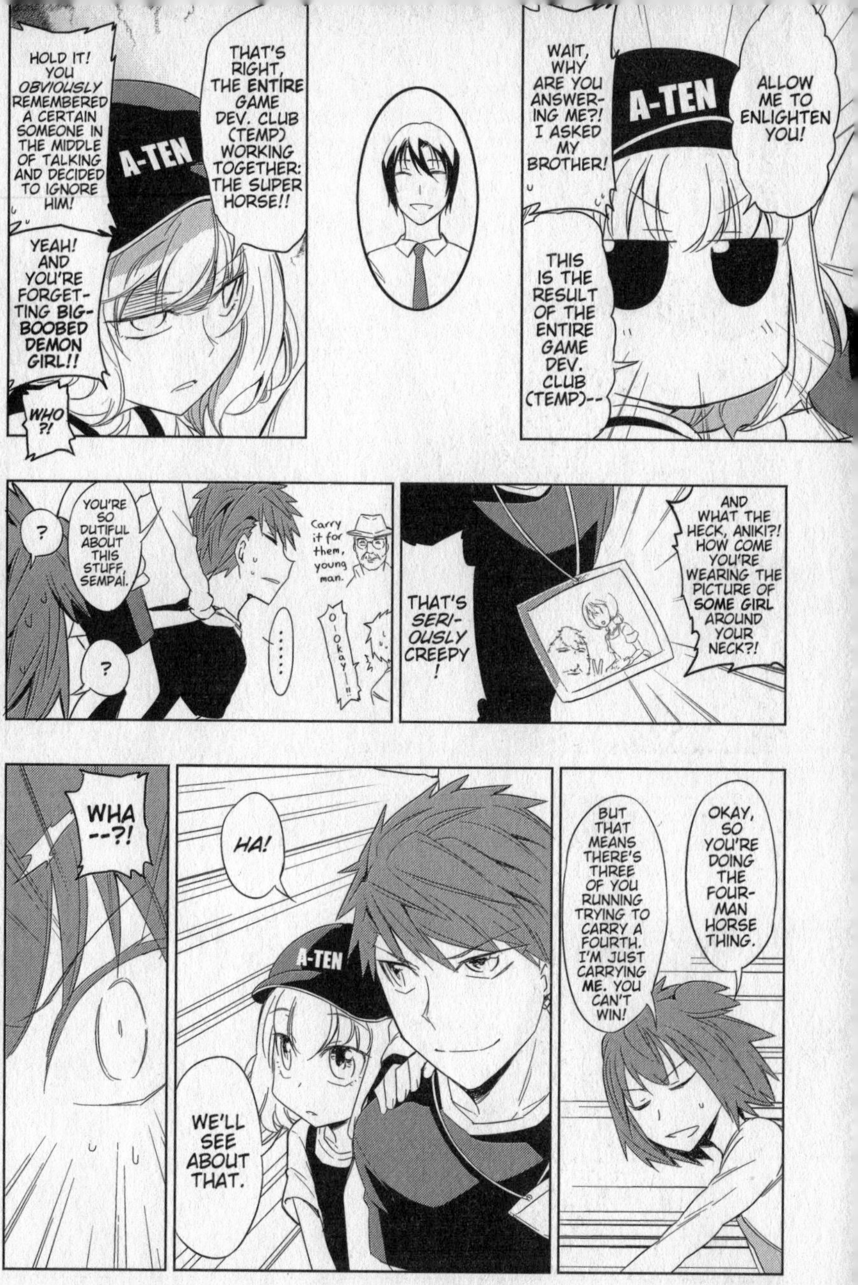
ALLOW ME TO ENLIGHTEN YOU!
WAIT, WHY ARE YOU ANSWERING ME?! I ASKED MY BROTHER!
A-TEN
THIS IS THE RESULT OF THE ENTIRE GAME DEV. CLUB (TEMP)--
THAT'S RIGHT, THE ENTIRE GAME DEV. CLUB (TEMP) WORKING TOGETHER: THE SUPER HORSE!!
HOLD IT! YOU *OBVIOUSLY* REMEMBERED A CERTAIN SOMEONE IN THE MIDDLE OF TALKING AND DECIDED TO IGNORE HIM!
A-TEN
YEAH! AND YOU'RE FORGETTING BIG-BOOBED DEMON GIRL!!
WHO?!
AND WHAT THE HECK, ANIKI?! HOW COME YOU'RE WEARING THE PICTURE OF SOME GIRL AROUND YOUR NECK?!
THAT'S *SERIOUSLY* CREEPY!
YOU'RE SO DUTIFUL ABOUT THIS STUFF, SEMPAI.
?
?
Carry it for them, young man.
O-Okay!!
......
OKAY, SO YOU'RE DOING THE FOUR-MAN HORSE THING.
BUT THAT MEANS THERE'S THREE OF YOU RUNNING TRYING TO CARRY A FOURTH. I'M JUST CARRYING ME. YOU CAN'T WIN!
HA!
A-TEN
WE'LL SEE ABOUT THAT.
WHA--?!

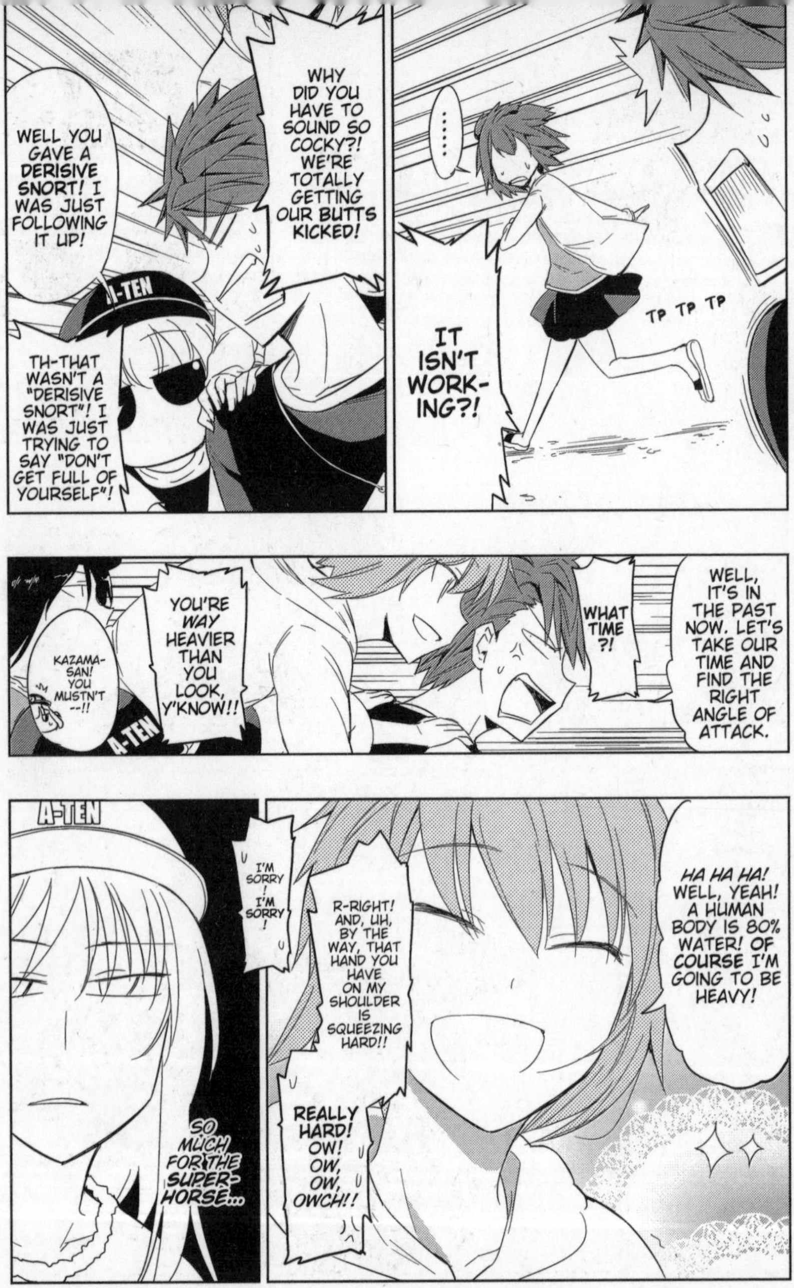
......
TP TP TP
IT ISN'T WORK-ING?!
WHY DID YOU HAVE TO SOUND SO COCKY?! WE'RE TOTALLY GETTING OUR BUTTS KICKED!
WELL YOU GAVE A DERISIVE SNORT! I WAS JUST FOLLOWING IT UP!
A-TEN
TH-THAT WASN'T A "DERISIVE SNORT"! I WAS JUST TRYING TO SAY "DON'T GET FULL OF YOURSELF"!
WELL, IT'S IN THE PAST NOW. LET'S TAKE OUR TIME AND FIND THE RIGHT ANGLE OF ATTACK.
WHAT TIME?!
YOU'RE WAY HEAVIER THAN YOU LOOK, Y'KNOW!!
KAZAMA-SAN! YOU MUSTN'T--!!
A-TEN
HA HA HA! WELL, YEAH! A HUMAN BODY IS 80% WATER! OF COURSE I'M GOING TO BE HEAVY!
R-RIGHT! AND, UH, BY THE WAY, THAT HAND YOU HAVE ON MY SHOULDER IS SQUEEZING HARD!!
I'M SORRY! I'M SORRY!
REALLY HARD! OW! OW, OW, OWCH!!
A-TEN
SO MUCH FOR THE SUPER-HORSE...

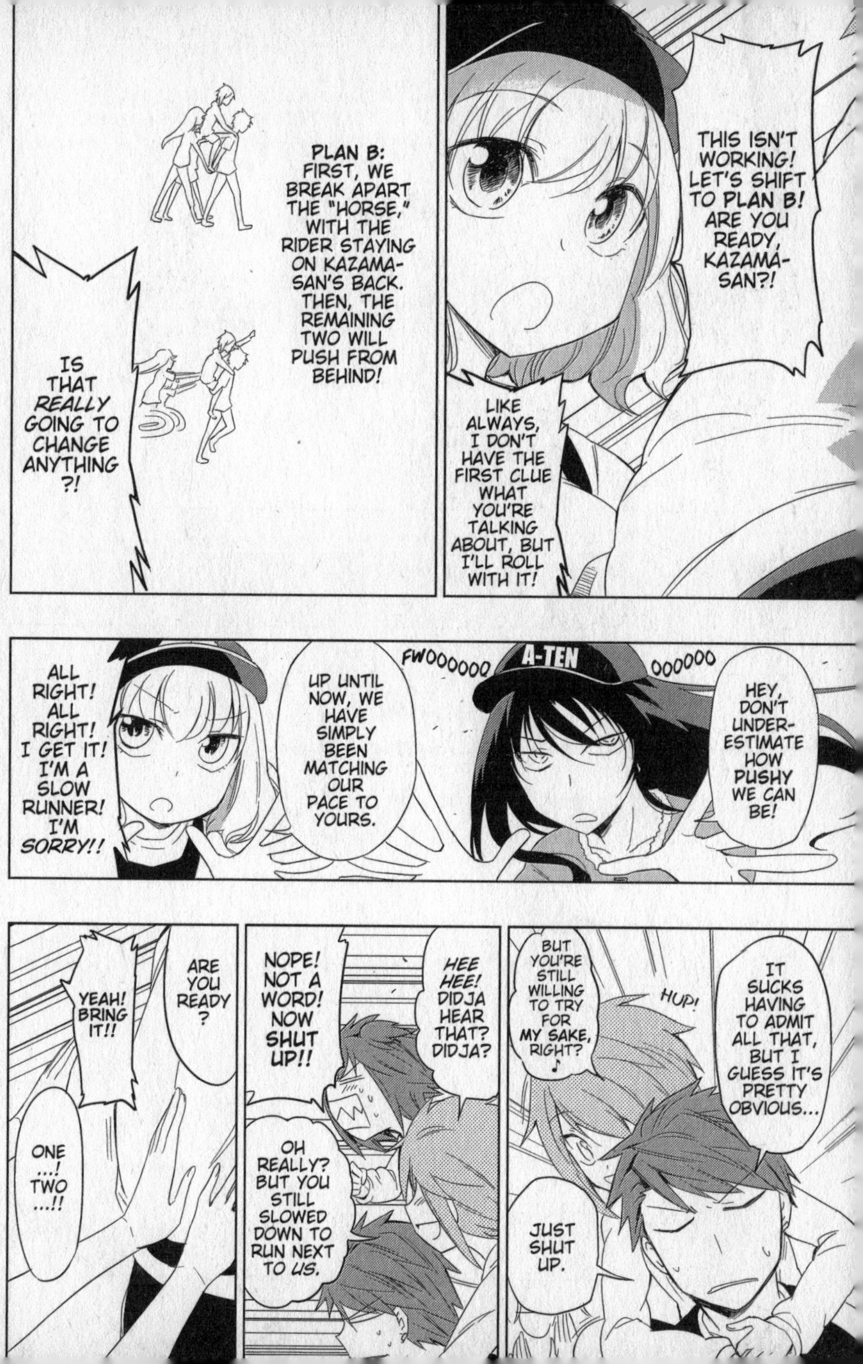
THIS ISN'T WORKING! LET'S SHIFT TO PLAN B! ARE YOU READY, KAZAMA-SAN?!
LIKE ALWAYS, I DON'T HAVE THE FIRST CLUE WHAT YOU'RE TALKING ABOUT, BUT I'LL ROLL WITH IT!
PLAN B: FIRST, WE BREAK APART THE "HORSE," WITH THE RIDER STAYING ON KAZAMA-SAN'S BACK. THEN, THE REMAINING TWO WILL PUSH FROM BEHIND!
IS THAT *REALLY* GOING TO CHANGE ANYTHING?!
HEY, DON'T UNDER-ESTIMATE HOW PUSHY WE CAN BE!
FWOOOOOO OOOOOO
A-TEN
UP UNTIL NOW, WE HAVE SIMPLY BEEN MATCHING OUR PACE TO YOURS.
ALL RIGHT! ALL RIGHT! I GET IT! I'M A SLOW RUNNER! I'M *SORRY!!*
IT SUCKS HAVING TO ADMIT ALL THAT, BUT I GUESS IT'S PRETTY OBVIOUS...
HUP!
BUT YOU'RE STILL WILLING TO TRY FOR MY SAKE, RIGHT? ♪
JUST SHUT UP.
HEE HEE! DIDJA HEAR THAT? DIDJA?
NOPE! NOT A WORD! NOW **SHUT UP!!**
OH REALLY? BUT YOU STILL SLOWED DOWN TO RUN NEXT TO *US.*
ARE YOU READY?
YEAH! BRING IT!!
ONE...! TWO...!!

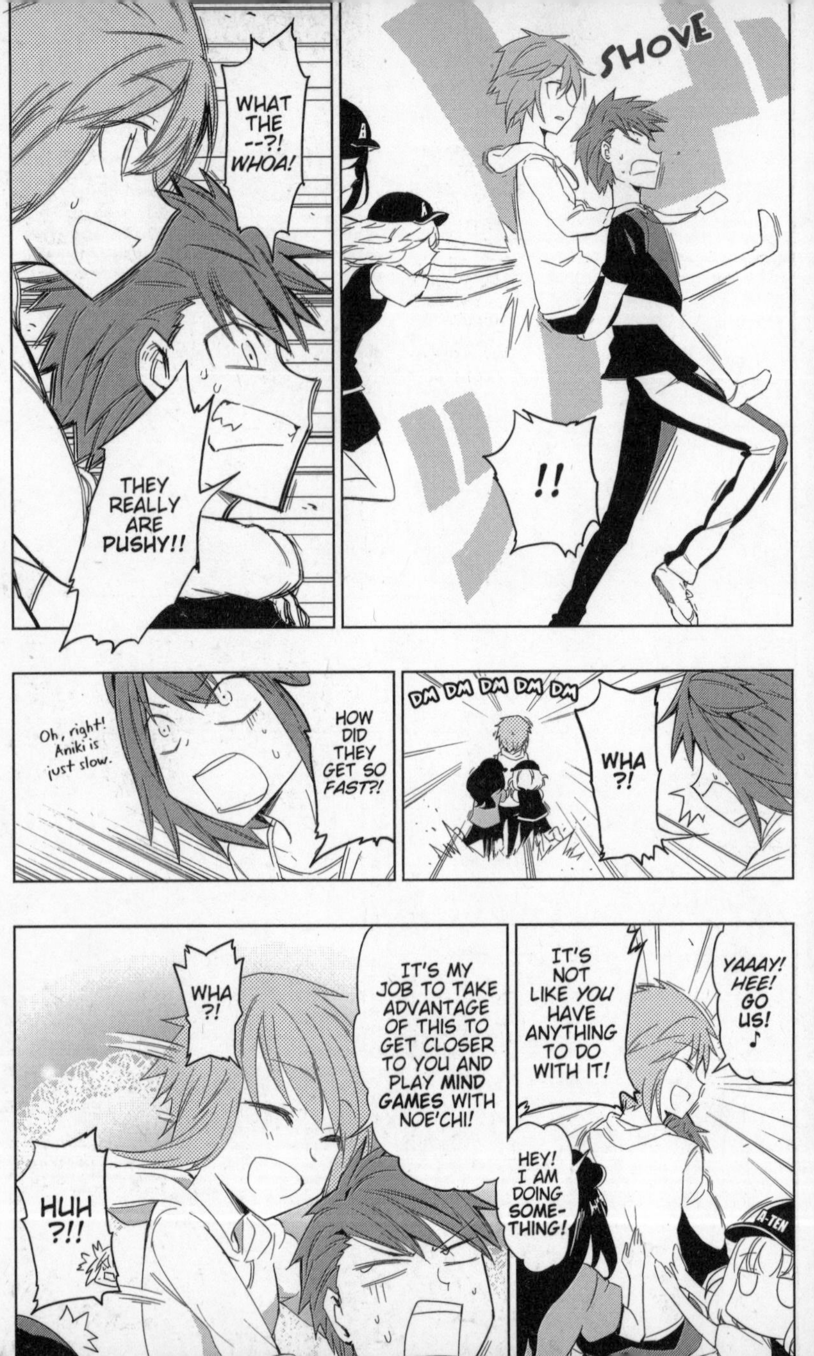
SHOVE
!!
WHAT THE --?! WHOA!
THEY REALLY ARE PUSHY!!
DM DM DM DM DM
WHA ?!
HOW DID THEY GET SO FAST?!
Oh, right! Aniki is just slow.
YAAAY! HEE! GO US! ♪
IT'S NOT LIKE YOU HAVE ANYTHING TO DO WITH IT!
HEY! I AM DOING SOME-THING!
IT'S MY JOB TO TAKE ADVANTAGE OF THIS TO GET CLOSER TO YOU AND PLAY MIND GAMES WITH NOE'CHI!
WHA ?!
HUH ?!!

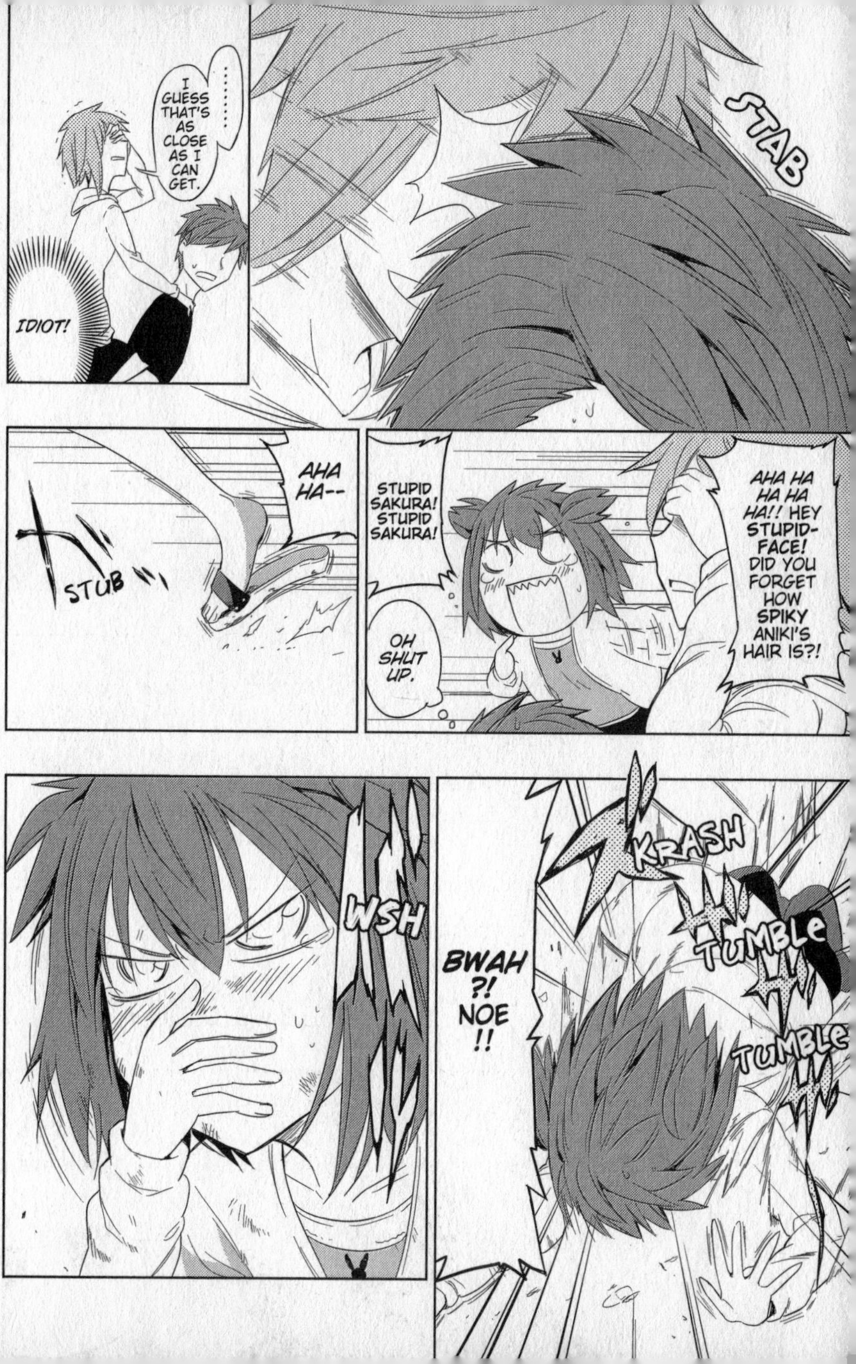
STAB
......
I GUESS THAT'S AS CLOSE AS I CAN GET.
IDIOT!
AHA HA HA HA HA!! HEY STUPID-FACE! DID YOU FORGET HOW SPIKY ANIKI'S HAIR IS?!
STUPID SAKURA! STUPID SAKURA!
OH SHUT UP.
AHA HA--
STUB
KRASH
TUMBLE
TUMBLE
BWAH?! NOE!!
WSH

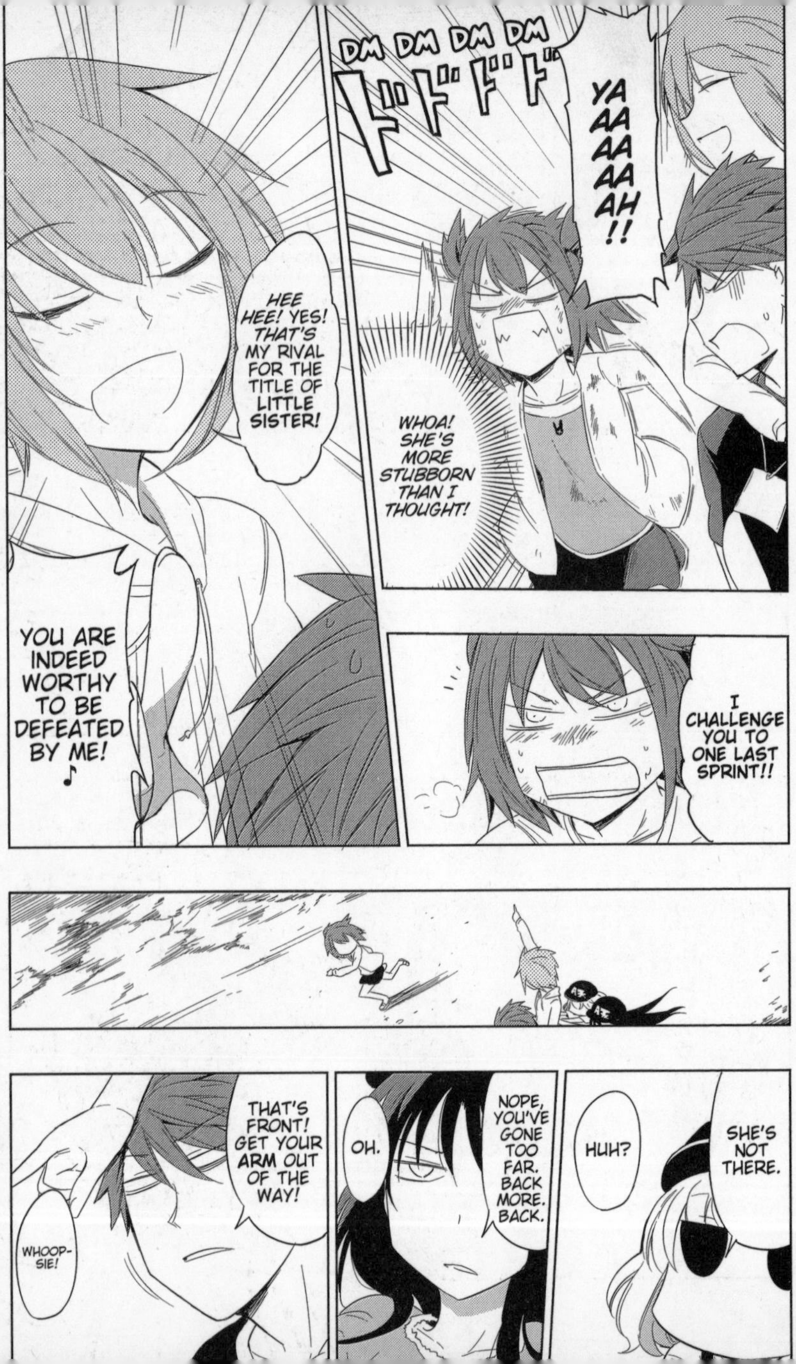
YAAAAAAAAH!!
DM DM DM DM
ドドドド
WHOA! SHE'S MORE STUBBORN THAN I THOUGHT!
I CHALLENGE YOU TO ONE LAST SPRINT!!
HEE HEE! YES! THAT'S MY RIVAL FOR THE TITLE OF LITTLE SISTER!
YOU ARE INDEED WORTHY TO BE DEFEATED BY ME! ♪
SHE'S NOT THERE.
HUH?
NOPE, YOU'VE GONE TOO FAR. BACK MORE. BACK.
OH.
THAT'S FRONT! GET YOUR ARM OUT OF THE WAY!
WHOOP-SIE!

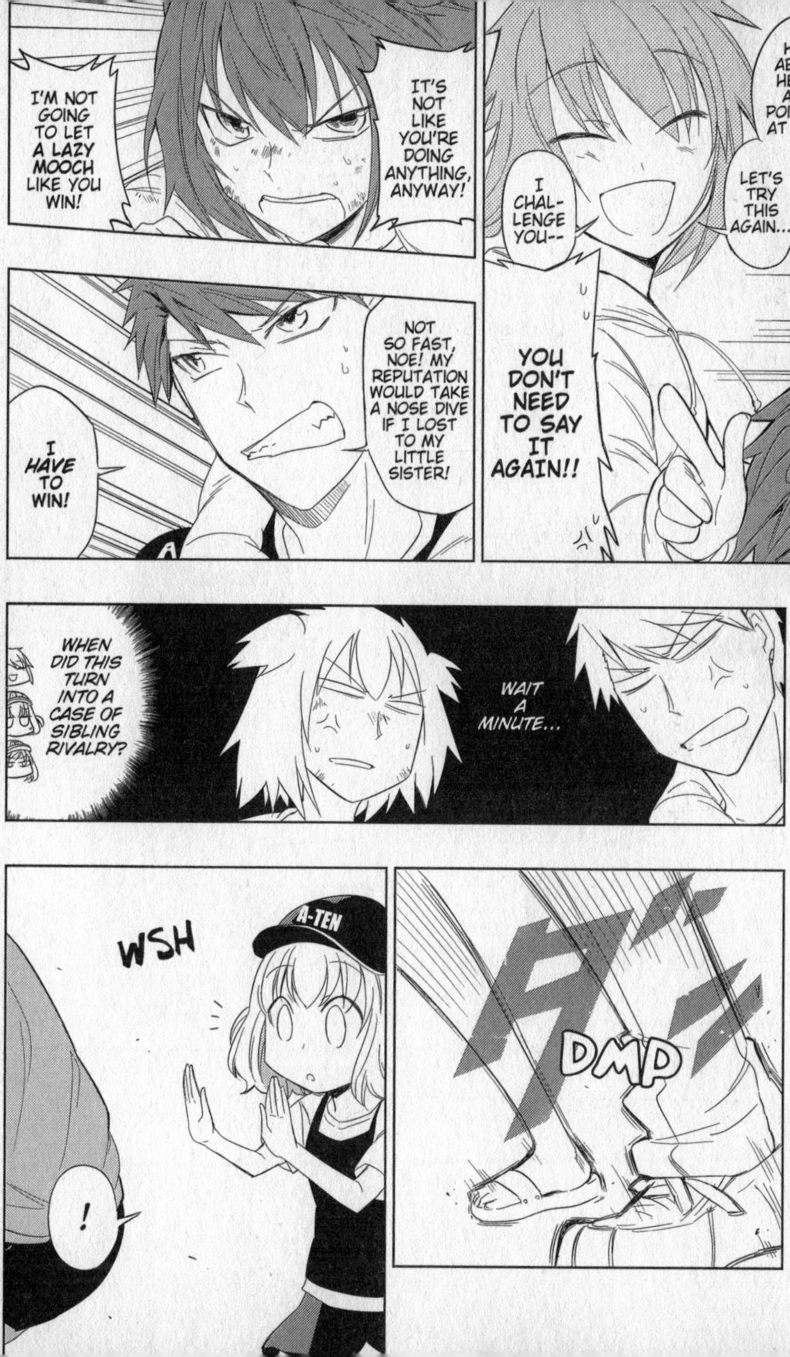
HOW ABOUT HERE? AM I POINTING AT HER?
LET'S TRY THIS AGAIN...
I CHAL-LENGE YOU--
YOU DON'T NEED TO SAY IT AGAIN!!
IT'S NOT LIKE YOU'RE DOING ANYTHING, ANYWAY!
I'M NOT GOING TO LET A LAZY MOOCH LIKE YOU WIN!
NOT SO FAST, NOE! MY REPUTATION WOULD TAKE A NOSE DIVE IF I LOST TO MY LITTLE SISTER!
I *HAVE* TO WIN!
WAIT A MINUTE...
WHEN DID THIS TURN INTO A CASE OF SIBLING RIVALRY?
DMP
WSH
A-TEN
!

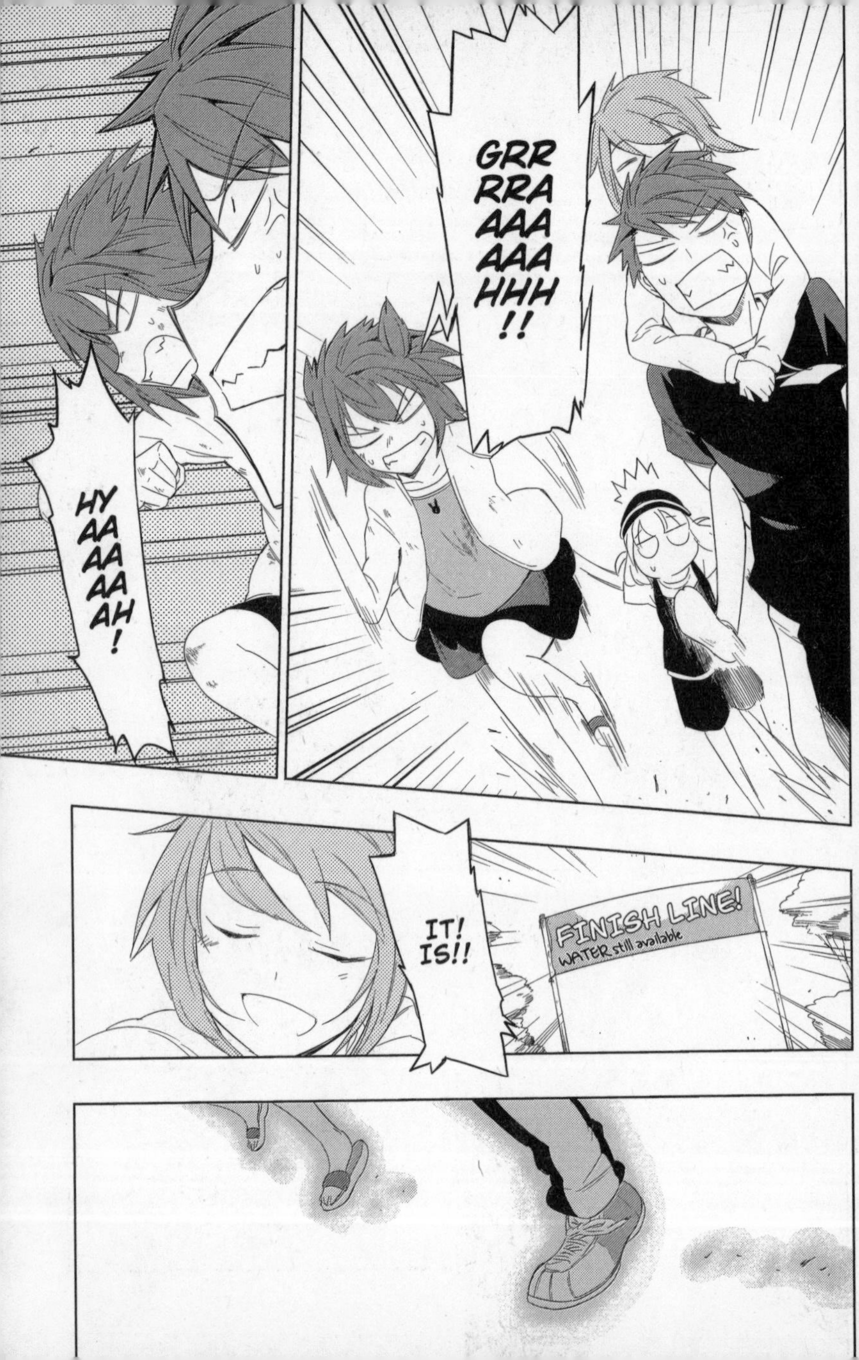
GRR RRA AAA AAA HHH !!
HY AA AA AA AH!
IT! IS!!
FINISH LINE!
WATER still available

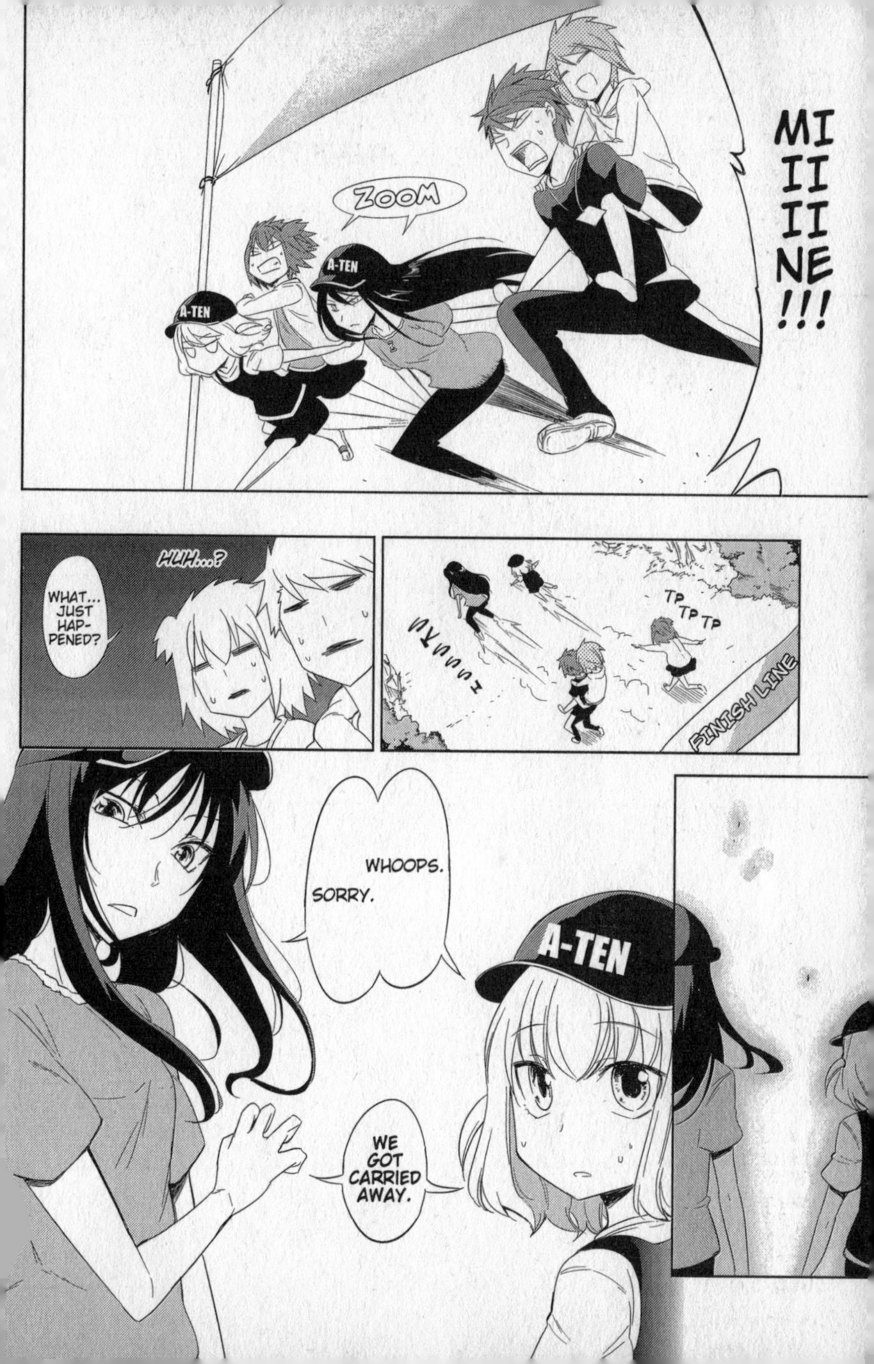
MIIIINE!!!
ZOOM
TP TP TP
FINISH LINE
HUH...?
WHAT... JUST HAP-PENED?
WHOOPS. SORRY.
WE GOT CARRIED AWAY.

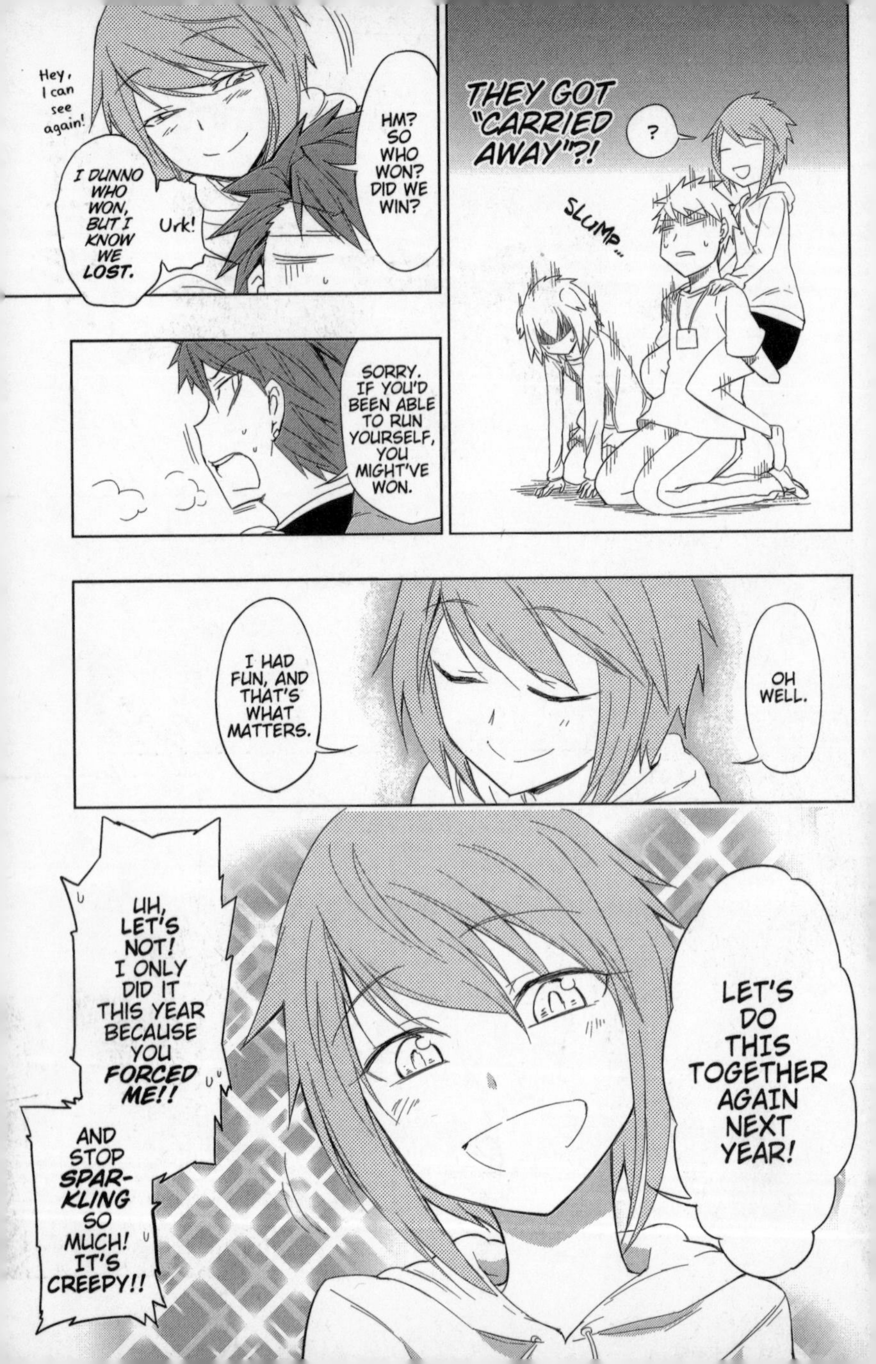
THEY GOT "CARRIED AWAY"?!
?
SLUMP...
HM? SO WHO WON? DID WE WIN?
Hey, I can see again!
I DUNNO WHO WON, BUT I KNOW WE **LOST.**
Urk!
SORRY. IF YOU'D BEEN ABLE TO RUN YOURSELF, YOU MIGHT'VE WON.
OH WELL.
I HAD FUN, AND THAT'S WHAT MATTERS.
LET'S DO THIS TOGETHER AGAIN NEXT YEAR!
UH, LET'S NOT! I ONLY DID IT THIS YEAR BECAUSE YOU ***FORCED ME!!***
AND STOP ***SPAR-KLING*** SO MUCH! IT'S CREEPY!!

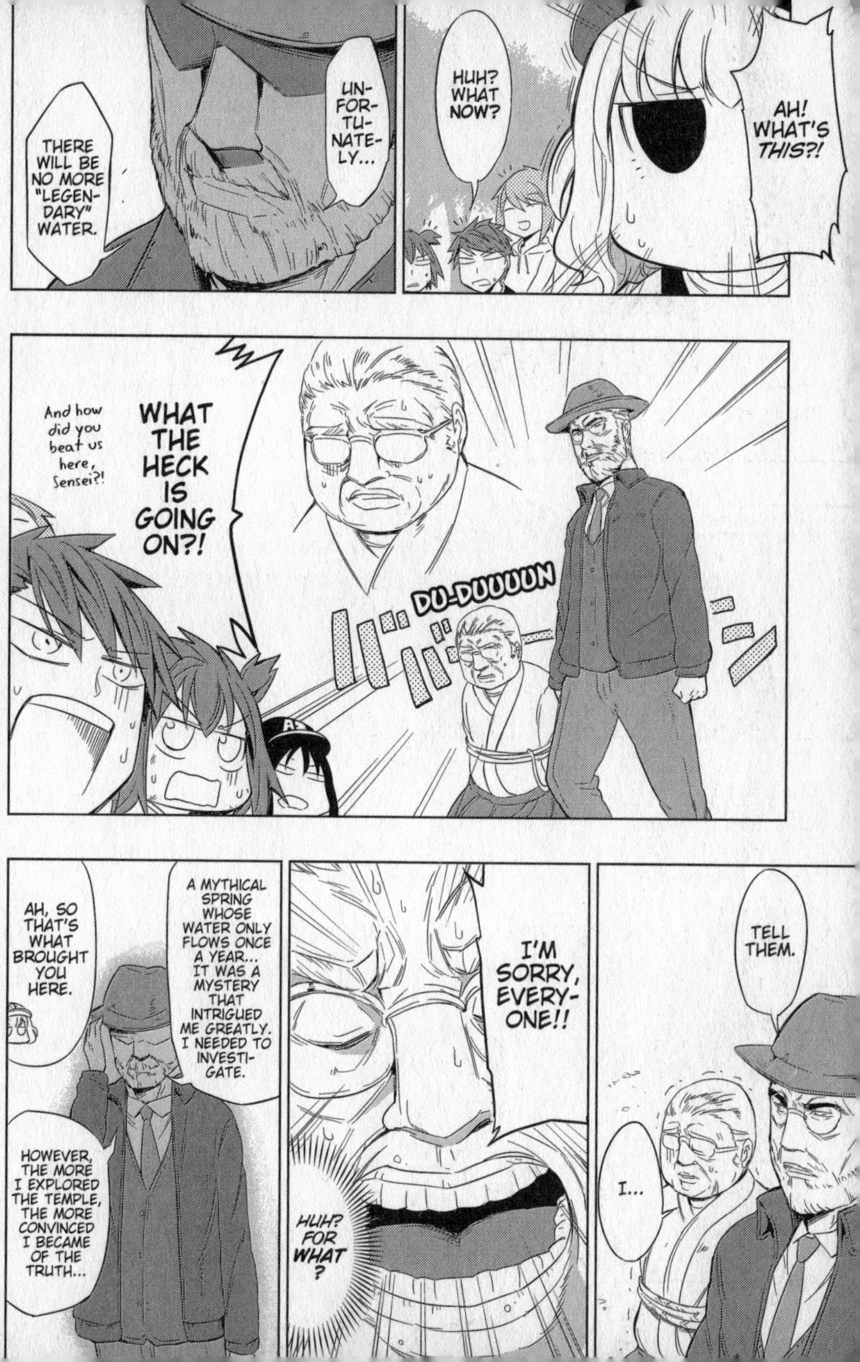
AH! WHAT'S THIS?!
HUH? WHAT NOW?
UNFORTUNATELY...
THERE WILL BE NO MORE "LEGENDARY" WATER.
WHAT THE HECK IS GOING ON?!
And how did you beat us here, Sensei?!
DU-DUUUUN
TELL THEM.
I...
I'M SORRY, EVERYONE!!
HUH? FOR WHAT?
A MYTHICAL SPRING WHOSE WATER ONLY FLOWS ONCE A YEAR... IT WAS A MYSTERY THAT INTRIGUED ME GREATLY. I NEEDED TO INVESTIGATE.
AH, SO THAT'S WHAT BROUGHT YOU HERE.
HOWEVER, THE MORE I EXPLORED THE TEMPLE, THE MORE CONVINCED I BECAME OF THE TRUTH...

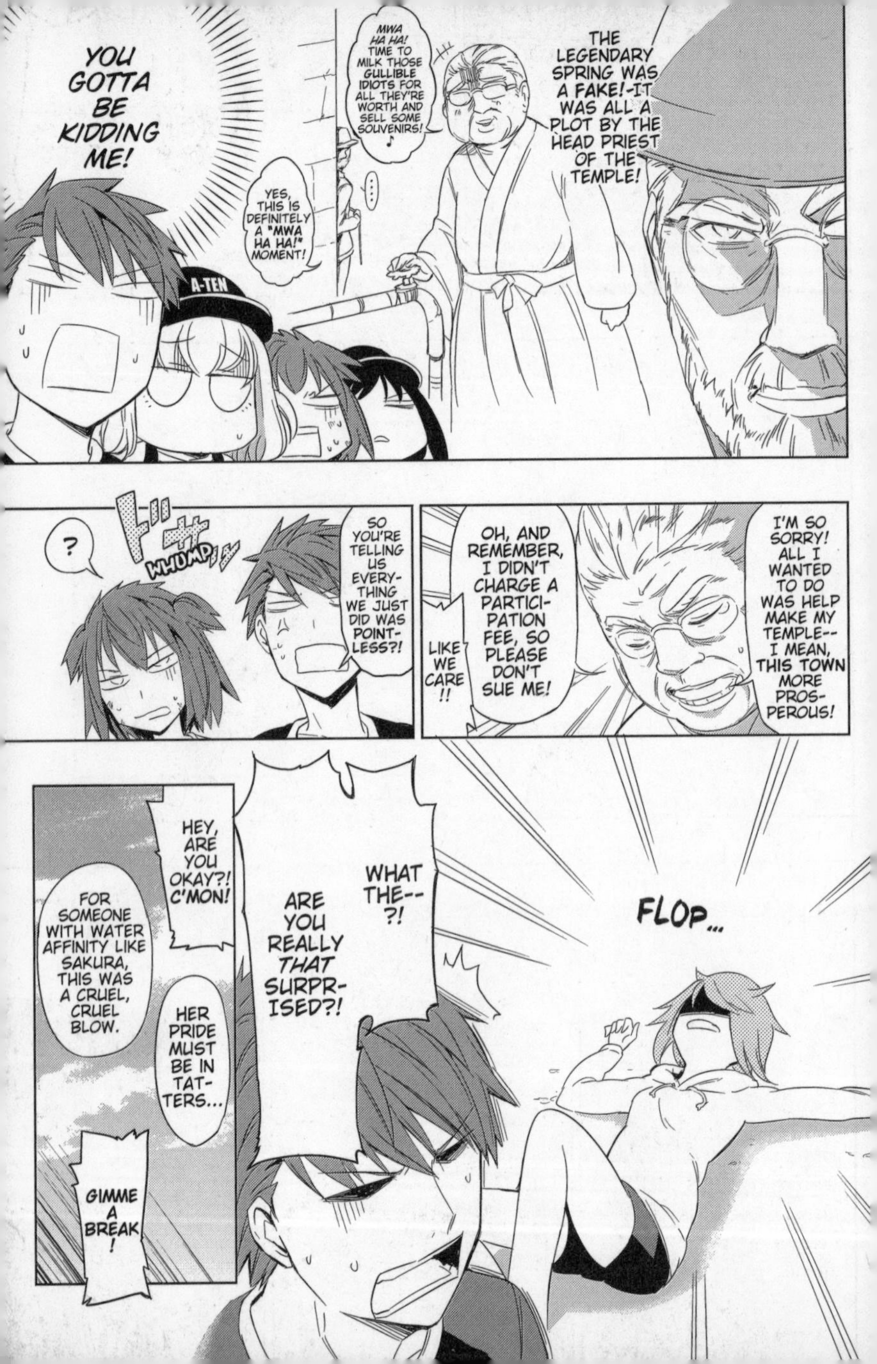
THE LEGENDARY SPRING WAS A FAKE!-IT WAS ALL A PLOT BY THE HEAD PRIEST OF THE TEMPLE!
MWA HA HA! TIME TO MILK THOSE GULLIBLE IDIOTS FOR ALL THEY'RE WORTH AND SELL SOME SOUVENIRS! ♪
...
YES, THIS IS DEFINITELY A "MWA HA HA!" MOMENT!
YOU GOTTA BE KIDDING ME!
I'M SO SORRY! ALL I WANTED TO DO WAS HELP MAKE MY TEMPLE-- I MEAN, THIS TOWN MORE PROS-PEROUS!
OH, AND REMEMBER, I DIDN'T CHARGE A PARTICI-PATION FEE, SO PLEASE DON'T SUE ME!
LIKE WE CARE!!
SO YOU'RE TELLING US EVERY-THING WE JUST DID WAS POINT-LESS?!
WHUMP
?
FLOP...
WHAT THE--?!
ARE YOU REALLY *THAT* SURPR-ISED?!
HEY, ARE YOU OKAY?! C'MON!
FOR SOMEONE WITH WATER AFFINITY LIKE SAKURA, THIS WAS A CRUEL, CRUEL BLOW.
HER PRIDE MUST BE IN TAT-TERS...
GIMME A BREAK!

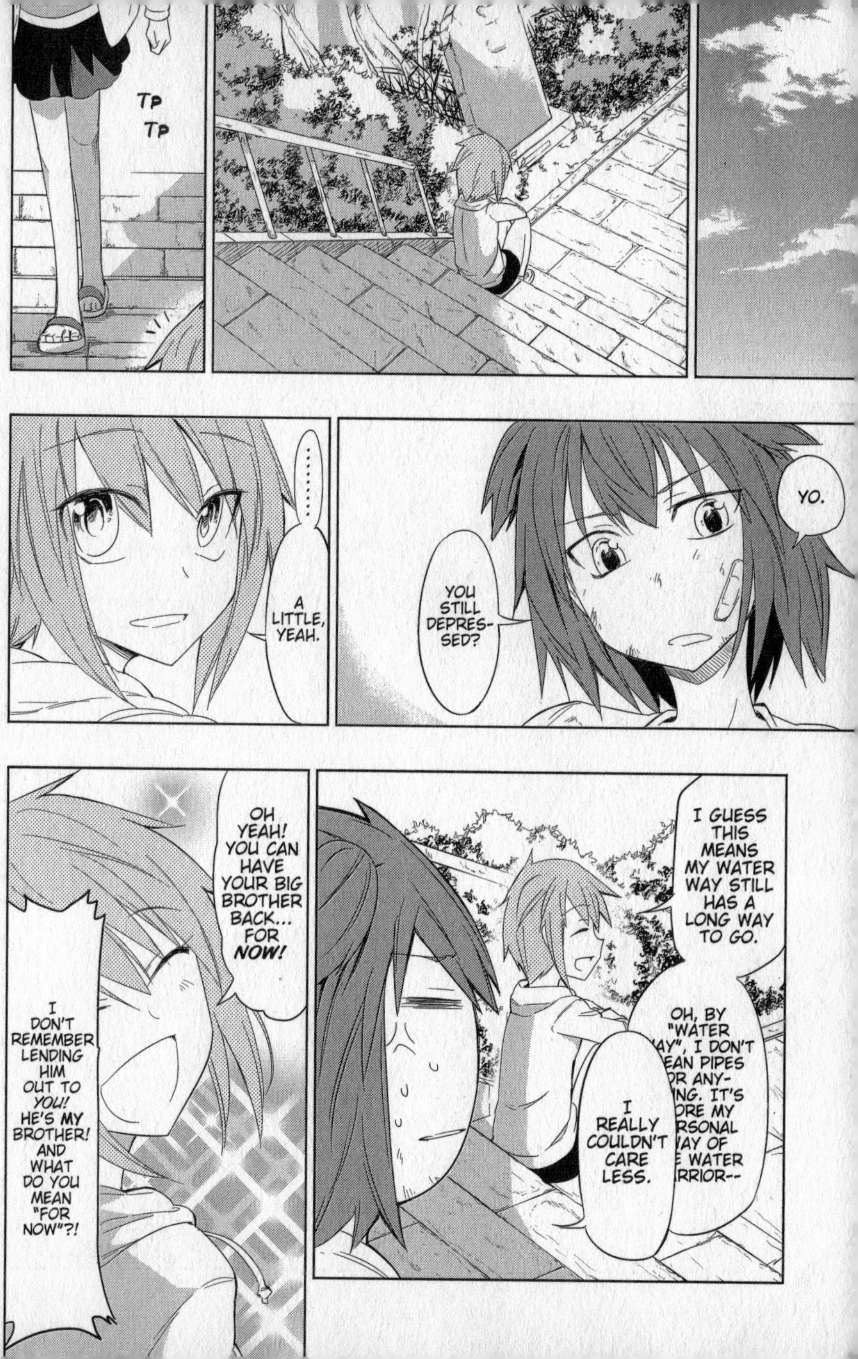
TP TP
YO.
YOU STILL DEPRESSED?
......
A LITTLE, YEAH.
I GUESS THIS MEANS MY WATER WAY STILL HAS A LONG WAY TO GO.
OH, BY "WATER AY", I DON'T EAN PIPES OR ANY- NG. IT'S ORE MY RSONAL AY OF E WATER RRIOR--
I REALLY COULDN'T CARE LESS.
OH YEAH! YOU CAN HAVE YOUR BIG BROTHER BACK... FOR *NOW!*
I DON'T REMEMBER LENDING HIM OUT TO *YOU!* HE'S MY BROTHER! AND WHAT DO YOU MEAN "FOR NOW"?!

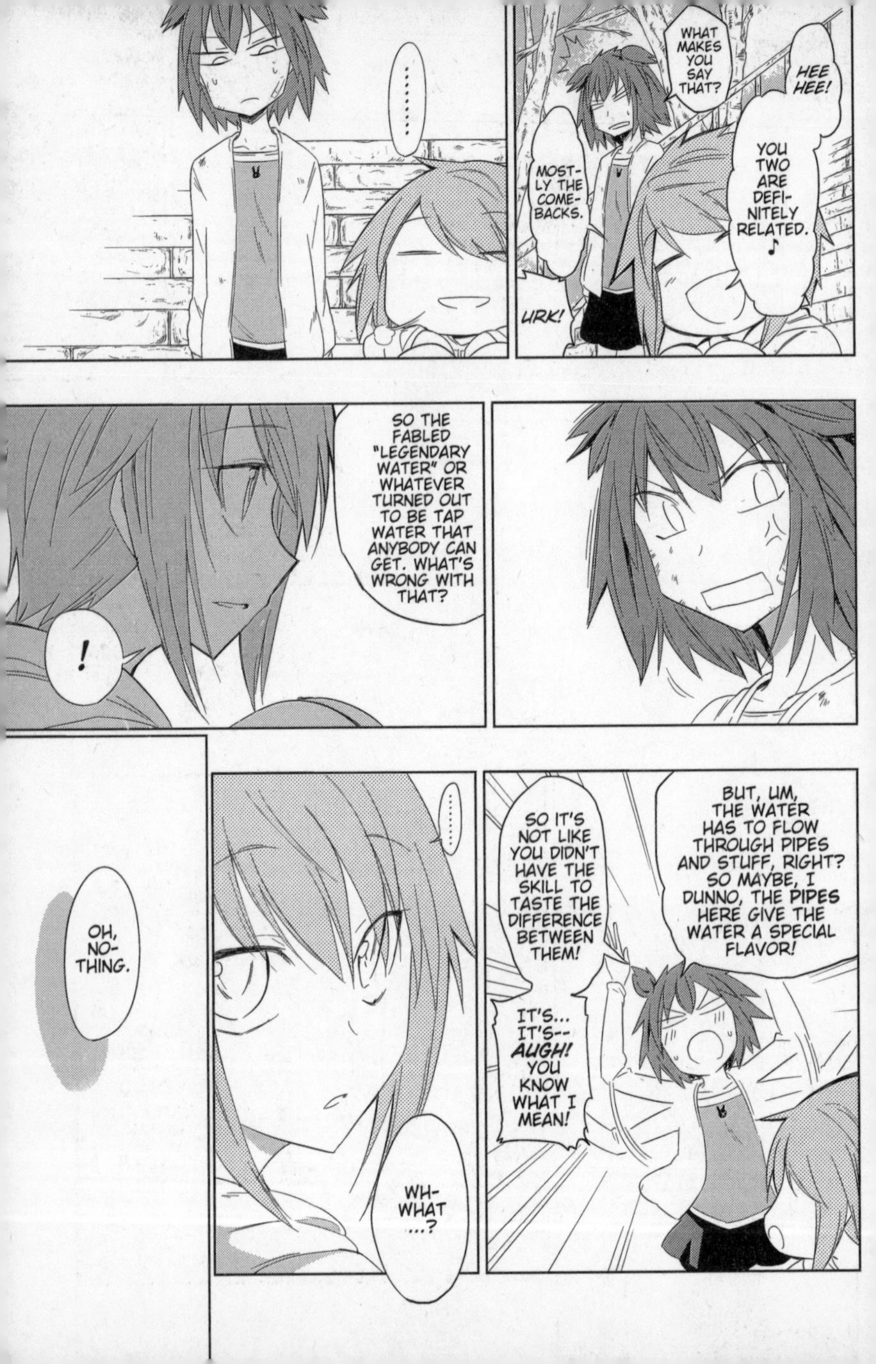
HEE HEE!
YOU TWO ARE DEFINITELY RELATED. ♪
WHAT MAKES YOU SAY THAT?
MOSTLY THE COMEBACKS.
URK!
......
SO THE FABLED "LEGENDARY WATER" OR WHATEVER TURNED OUT TO BE TAP WATER THAT ANYBODY CAN GET. WHAT'S WRONG WITH THAT?
!
BUT, UM, THE WATER HAS TO FLOW THROUGH PIPES AND STUFF, RIGHT? SO MAYBE, I DUNNO, THE PIPES HERE GIVE THE WATER A SPECIAL FLAVOR!
SO IT'S NOT LIKE YOU DIDN'T HAVE THE SKILL TO TASTE THE DIFFERENCE BETWEEN THEM!
IT'S... IT'S-- AUGH! YOU KNOW WHAT I MEAN!
......
WH-WHAT...?
OH, NOTHING.

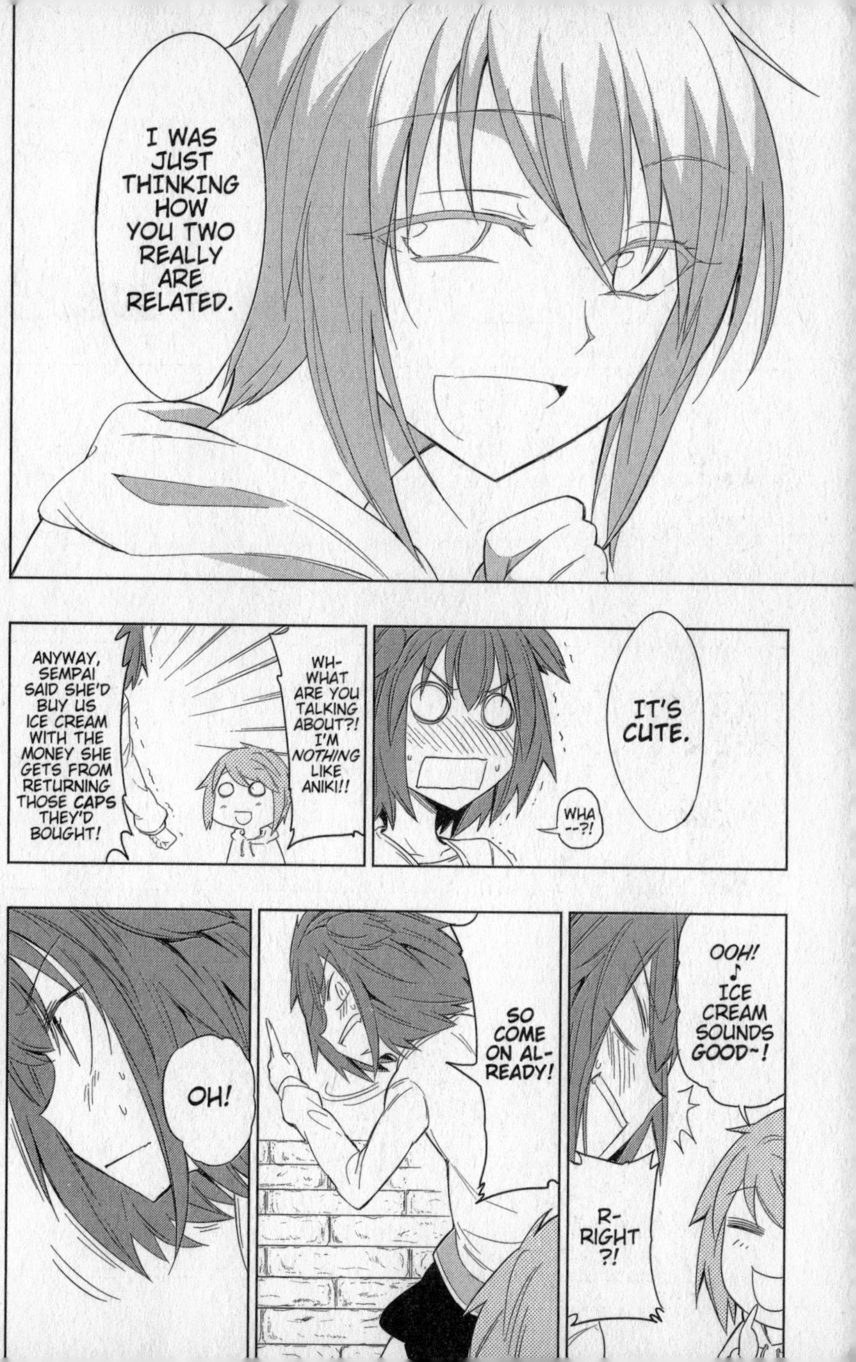
I WAS JUST THINKING HOW YOU TWO REALLY ARE RELATED.
IT'S CUTE.
WHA--?!
WH-WHAT ARE YOU TALKING ABOUT?! I'M *NOTHING* LIKE ANIKI!!
ANYWAY, SEMPAI SAID SHE'D BUY US ICE CREAM WITH THE MONEY SHE GETS FROM RETURNING THOSE CAPS THEY'D BOUGHT!
OOH! ♪ ICE CREAM SOUNDS GOOD~!
R-RIGHT?!
SO COME ON AL-READY!
OH!

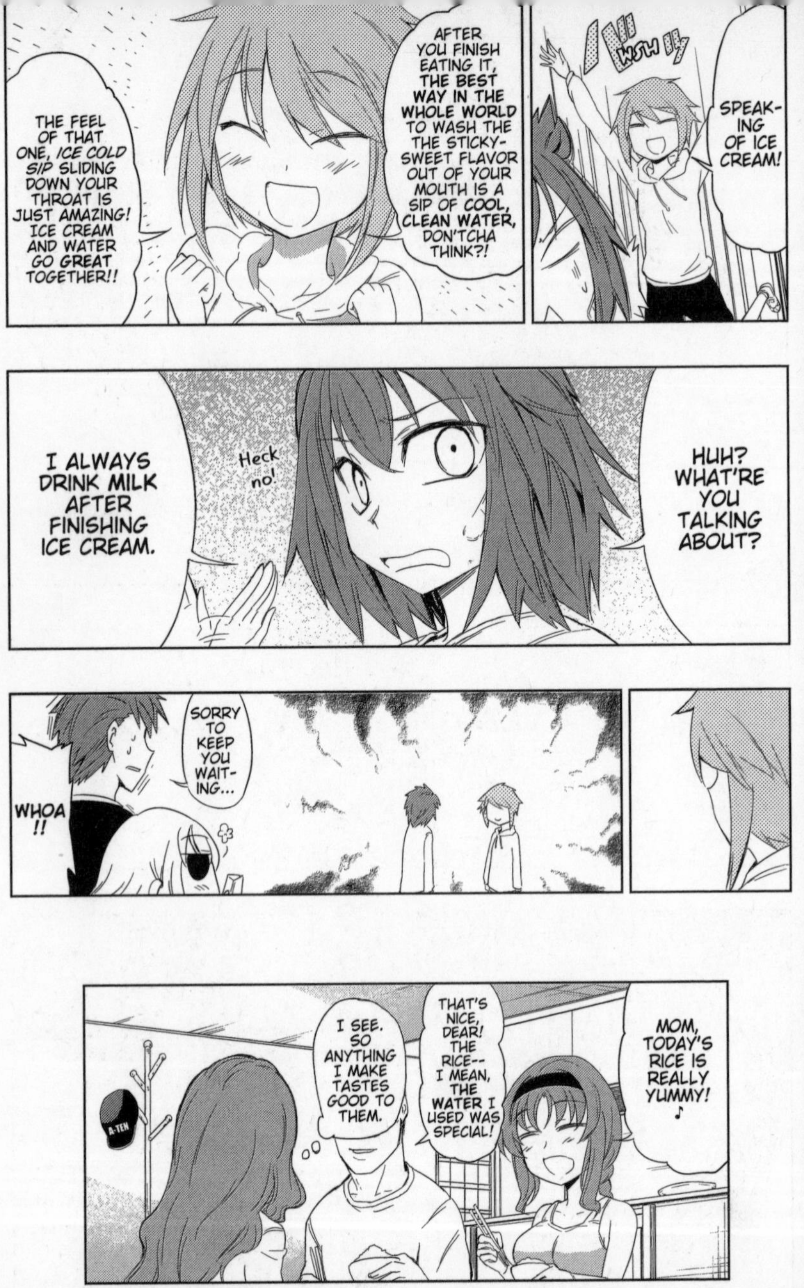
SPEAK-ING OF ICE CREAM!
WSH
AFTER YOU FINISH EATING IT, THE BEST WAY IN THE WHOLE WORLD TO WASH THE THE STICKY-SWEET FLAVOR OUT OF YOUR MOUTH IS A SIP OF COOL, CLEAN WATER, DON'TCHA THINK?!
THE FEEL OF THAT ONE, *ICE COLD SIP* SLIDING DOWN YOUR THROAT IS JUST AMAZING! ICE CREAM AND WATER GO GREAT TOGETHER!!
HUH? WHAT'RE YOU TALKING ABOUT?
Heck no!
I ALWAYS DRINK MILK AFTER FINISHING ICE CREAM.
SORRY TO KEEP YOU WAIT-ING...
WHOA !!
MOM, TODAY'S RICE IS REALLY YUMMY! ♪
THAT'S NICE, DEAR! THE RICE-- I MEAN, THE WATER I USED WAS SPECIAL!
I SEE. SO ANYTHING I MAKE TASTES GOOD TO THEM.
A-TEN

NEXT: Vol.05...

D-FRAGMENTS

ディーふらぐ!

Bonus Manga #1

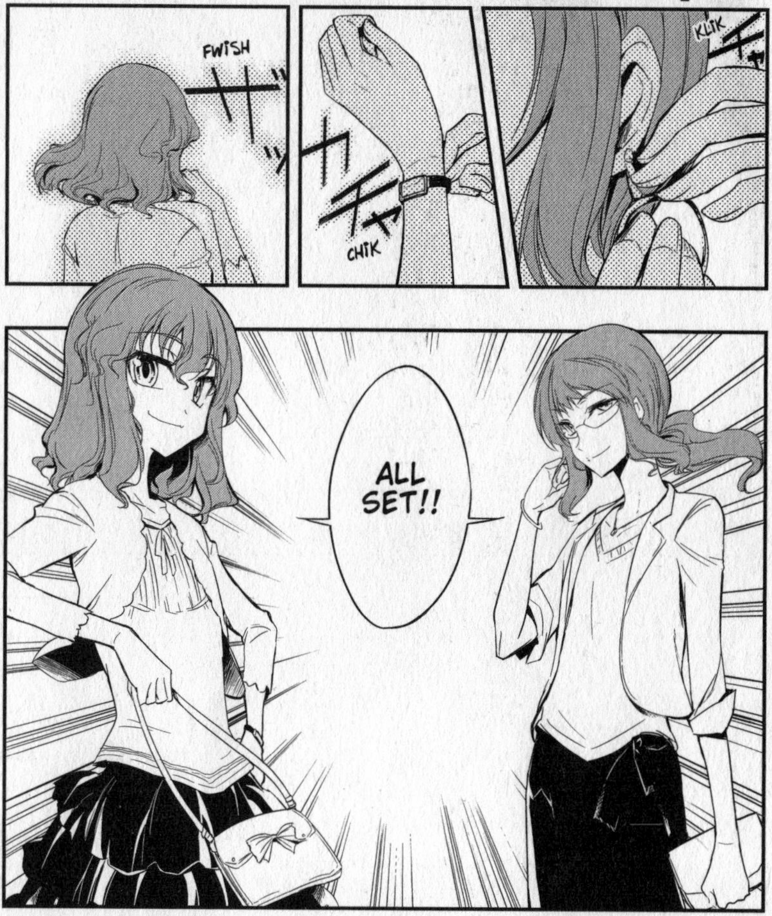
KLIK
CHIK
FWISH
ALL SET!!
HEH HEH HEH! PERFECT! I CAN ALREADY TELL THAT TODAY'S BLIND DATE...
IS GOING TO BE A MAM-MOTH-MAN SUCCESS!
MOTH-MAN
UH, RIGHT.
IF SHE CAN KEEP HER FASCINATION WITH CRYPTIDS UNDER HER HAT, THEN MAYBE...
MY, MY! DON'T THE TWO OF YOU LOOK VERY FANCY TODAY!

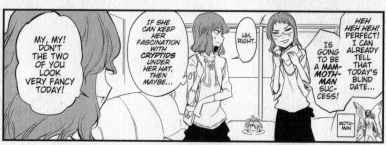

Mothman: A UMA (Unidentified Mysterious Animal), also known as a cryptid, that was reportedly sighted multiple times in West Virginia between 1966 and 1967. There is a stainless steel statue of Mothman in Point Pleasant, West Virginia.

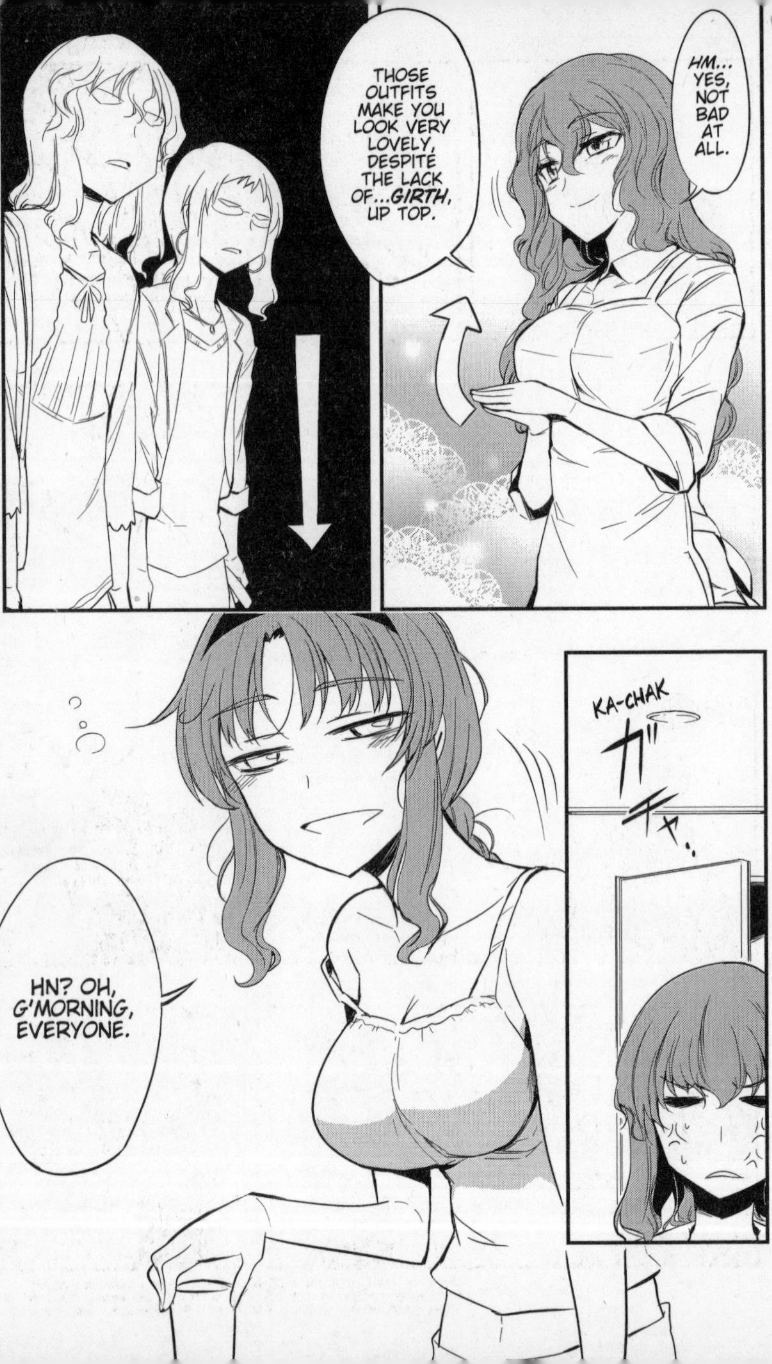
HM... YES, NOT BAD AT ALL.
THOSE OUTFITS MAKE YOU LOOK VERY LOVELY, DESPITE THE LACK OF...GIRTH, UP TOP.
KA-CHAK
ガチャ
HN? OH, G'MORNING, EVERYONE.

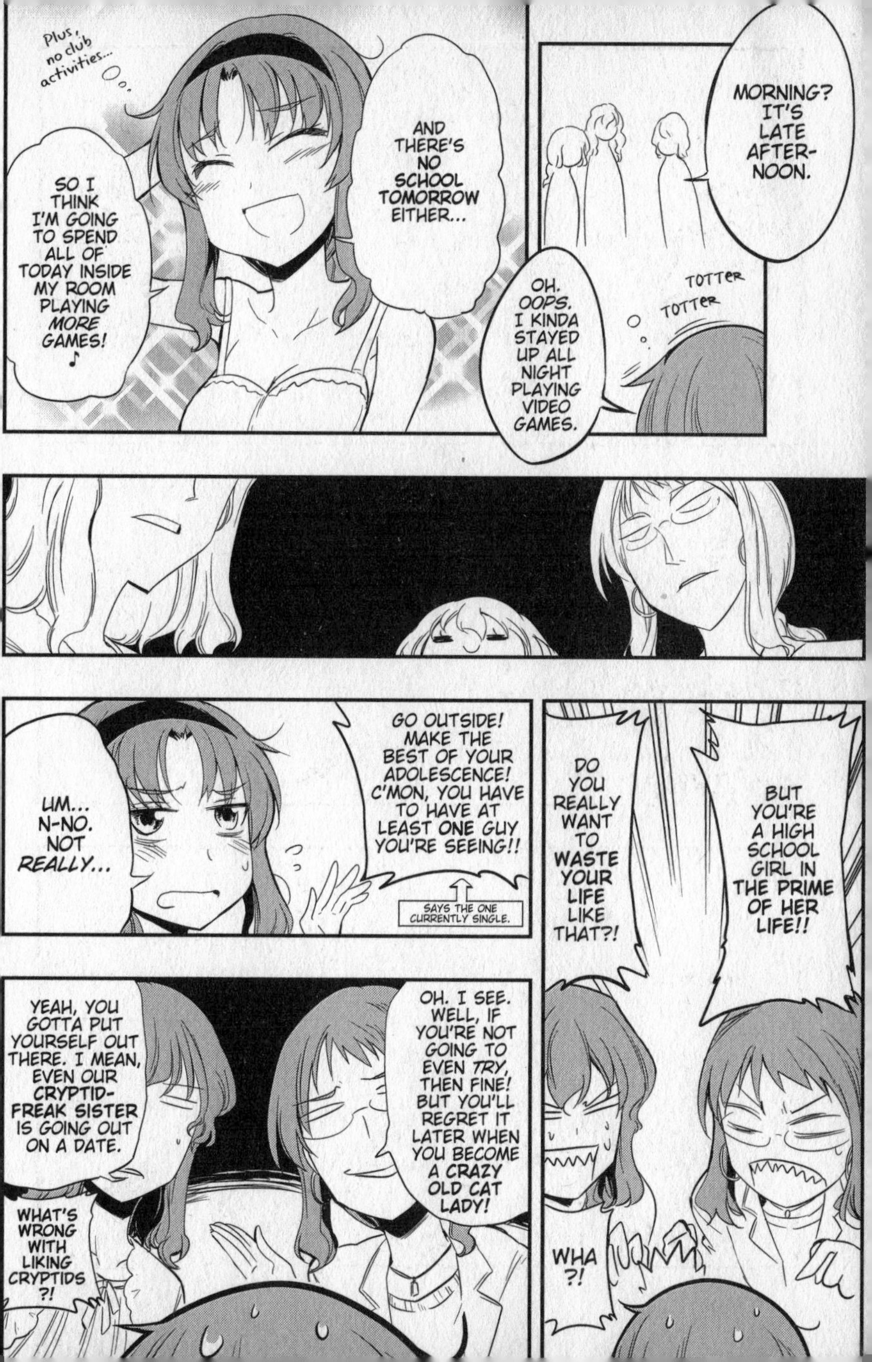
MORNING? IT'S LATE AFTER-NOON.
TOTTER TOTTER
OH. *OOPS.* I KINDA STAYED UP ALL NIGHT PLAYING VIDEO GAMES.
AND THERE'S NO SCHOOL TOMORROW EITHER...
Plus, no club activities...
SO I THINK I'M GOING TO SPEND ALL OF TODAY INSIDE MY ROOM PLAYING *MORE* GAMES! ♪
BUT YOU'RE A HIGH SCHOOL GIRL IN THE PRIME OF HER LIFE!!
DO YOU REALLY WANT TO WASTE YOUR LIFE LIKE THAT?!
WHA ?!
GO OUTSIDE! MAKE THE BEST OF YOUR ADOLESCENCE! C'MON, YOU HAVE TO HAVE AT LEAST *ONE* GUY YOU'RE SEEING!!
SAYS THE ONE CURRENTLY SINGLE.
UM... N-NO. NOT *REALLY*...
OH. I SEE. WELL, IF YOU'RE NOT GOING TO EVEN *TRY*, THEN FINE! BUT YOU'LL REGRET IT LATER WHEN YOU BECOME A CRAZY OLD CAT LADY!
YEAH, YOU GOTTA PUT YOURSELF OUT THERE. I MEAN, EVEN OUR CRYPTID-FREAK SISTER IS GOING OUT ON A DATE.
WHAT'S WRONG WITH LIKING CRYPTIDS ?!

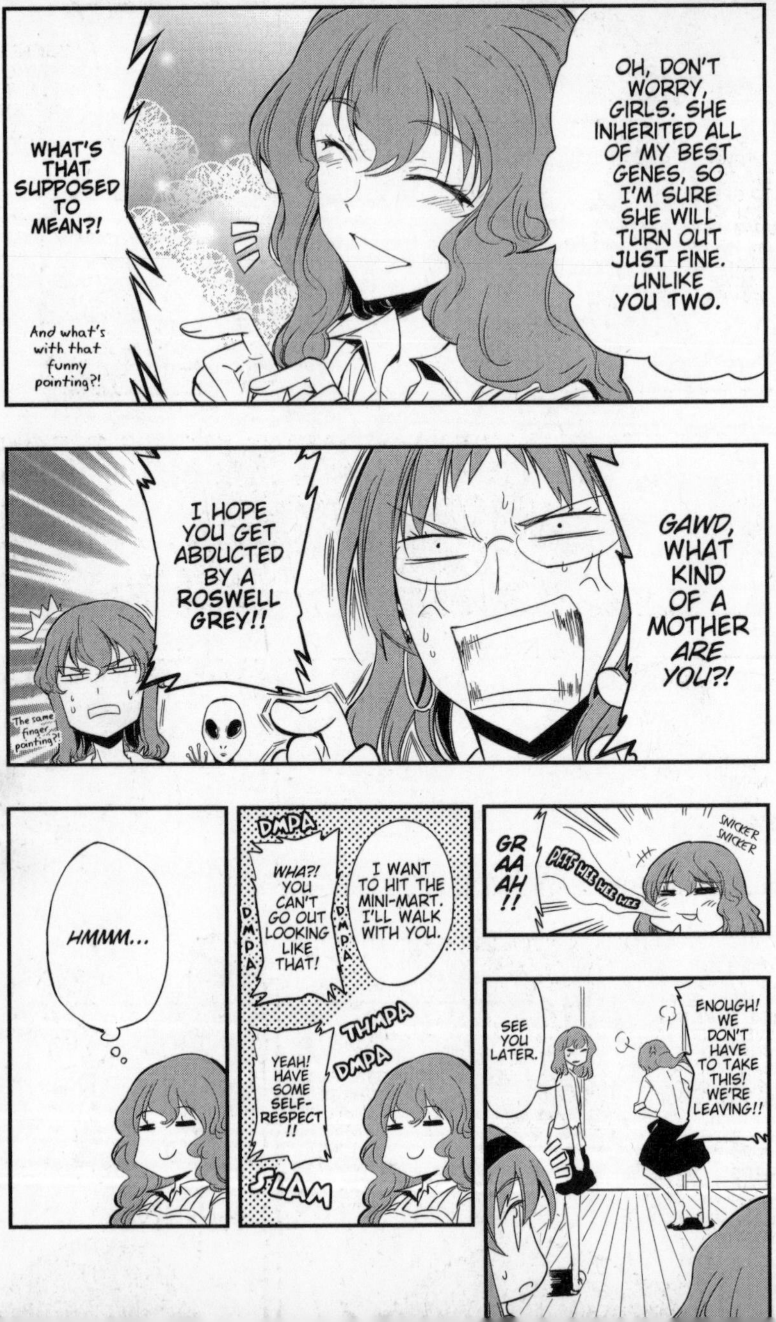
OH, DON'T WORRY, GIRLS. SHE INHERITED ALL OF MY BEST GENES, SO I'M SURE SHE WILL TURN OUT JUST FINE. UNLIKE YOU TWO.
WHAT'S THAT SUPPOSED TO MEAN?!
And what's with that funny pointing?!
GAWD, WHAT KIND OF A MOTHER ARE YOU?!
I HOPE YOU GET ABDUCTED BY A ROSWELL GREY!!
The same finger pointing?!
SNICKER SNICKER
PFFF HEE HEE HEE
GRAAAH!!
ENOUGH! WE DON'T HAVE TO TAKE THIS! WE'RE LEAVING!!
SEE YOU LATER.
DMPA
I WANT TO HIT THE MINI-MART. I'LL WALK WITH YOU.
DMPA
WHA?! YOU CAN'T GO OUT LOOKING LIKE THAT!
DMPA
THMPA
DMPA
YEAH! HAVE SOME SELF-RESPECT!!
SLAM
HMMM...

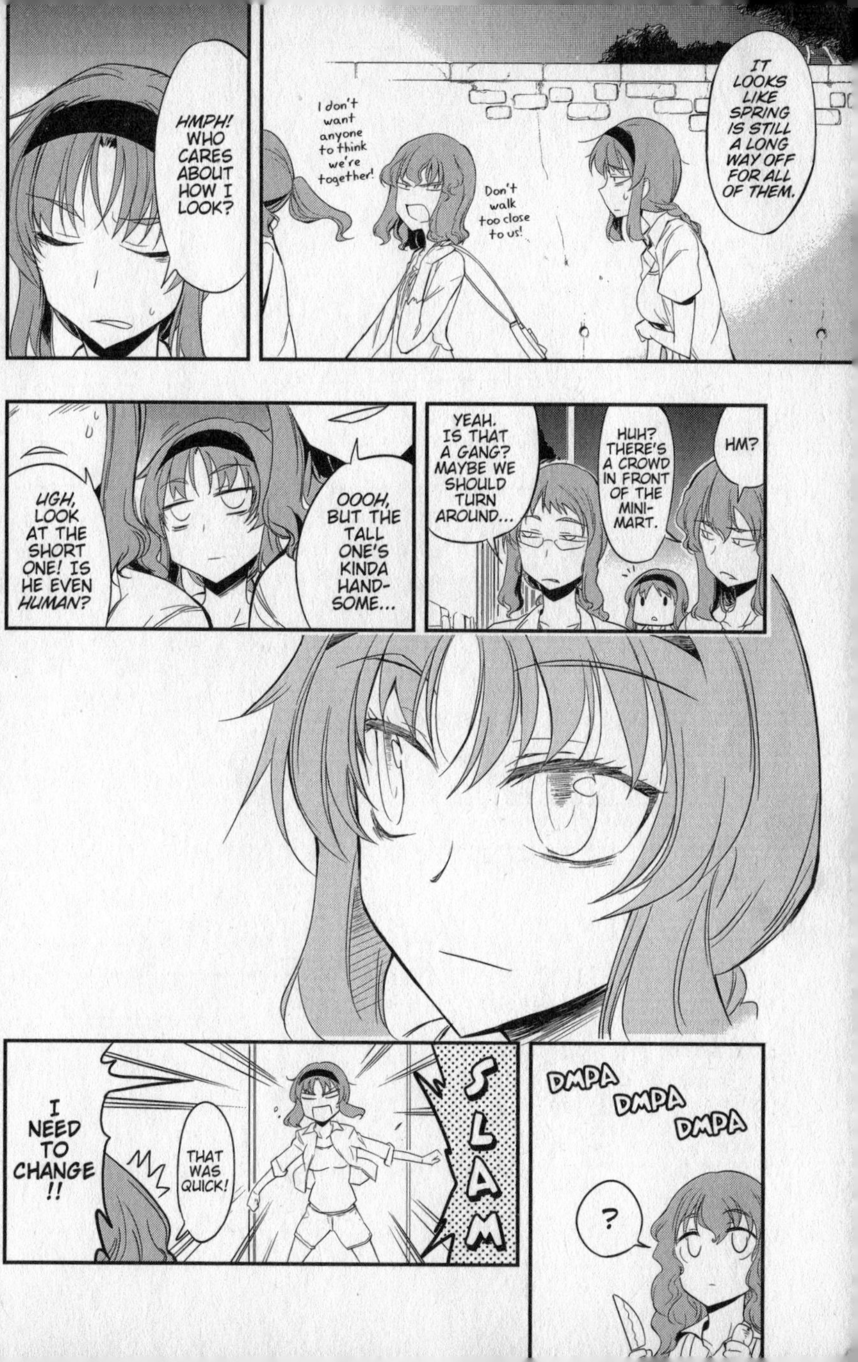
IT LOOKS LIKE SPRING IS STILL A LONG WAY OFF FOR ALL OF THEM.
Don't walk too close to us!
I don't want anyone to think we're together!
HMPH! WHO CARES ABOUT HOW I LOOK?
HM?
HUH? THERE'S A CROWD IN FRONT OF THE MINI-MART.
YEAH. IS THAT A GANG? MAYBE WE SHOULD TURN AROUND...
OOOH, BUT THE TALL ONE'S KINDA HANDSOME...
UGH, LOOK AT THE SHORT ONE! IS HE EVEN HUMAN?
DMPA
DMPA
DMPA
?
SLAM
THAT WAS QUICK!
I NEED TO CHANGE!!

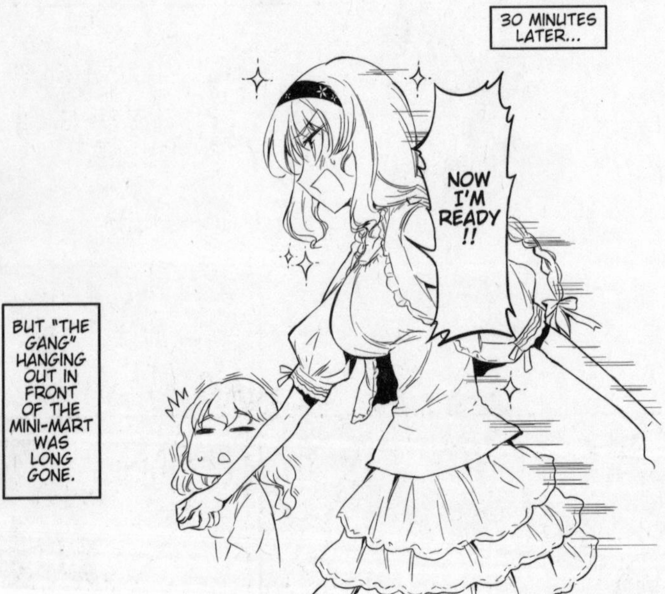
30 MINUTES LATER...
NOW I'M READY !!
BUT "THE GANG" HANGING OUT IN FRONT OF THE MINI-MART WAS LONG GONE.

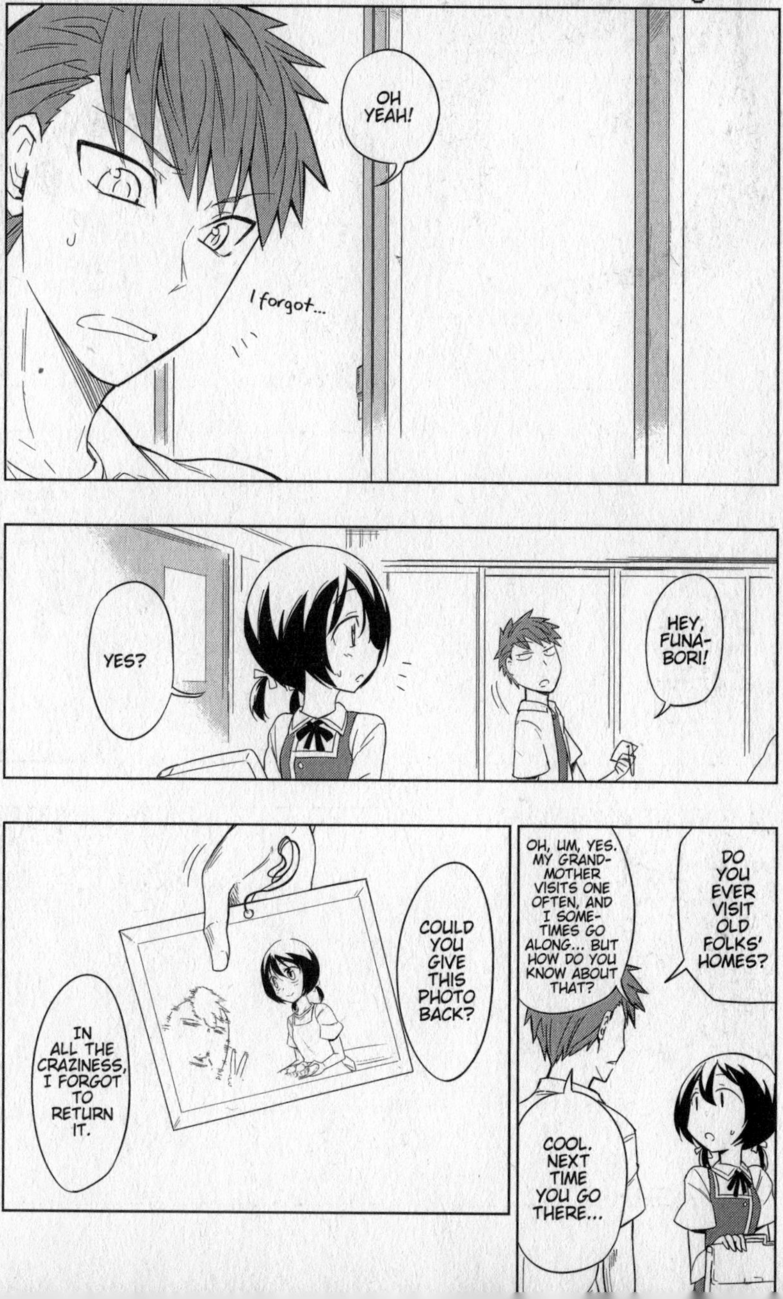
OH YEAH!
I forgot...
HEY, FUNA-BORI!
YES?
DO YOU EVER VISIT OLD FOLKS' HOMES?
OH, UM, YES. MY GRAND-MOTHER VISITS ONE OFTEN, AND I SOME-TIMES GO ALONG... BUT HOW DO YOU KNOW ABOUT THAT?
COOL. NEXT TIME YOU GO THERE...
COULD YOU GIVE THIS PHOTO BACK?
IN ALL THE CRAZINESS, I FORGOT TO RETURN IT.

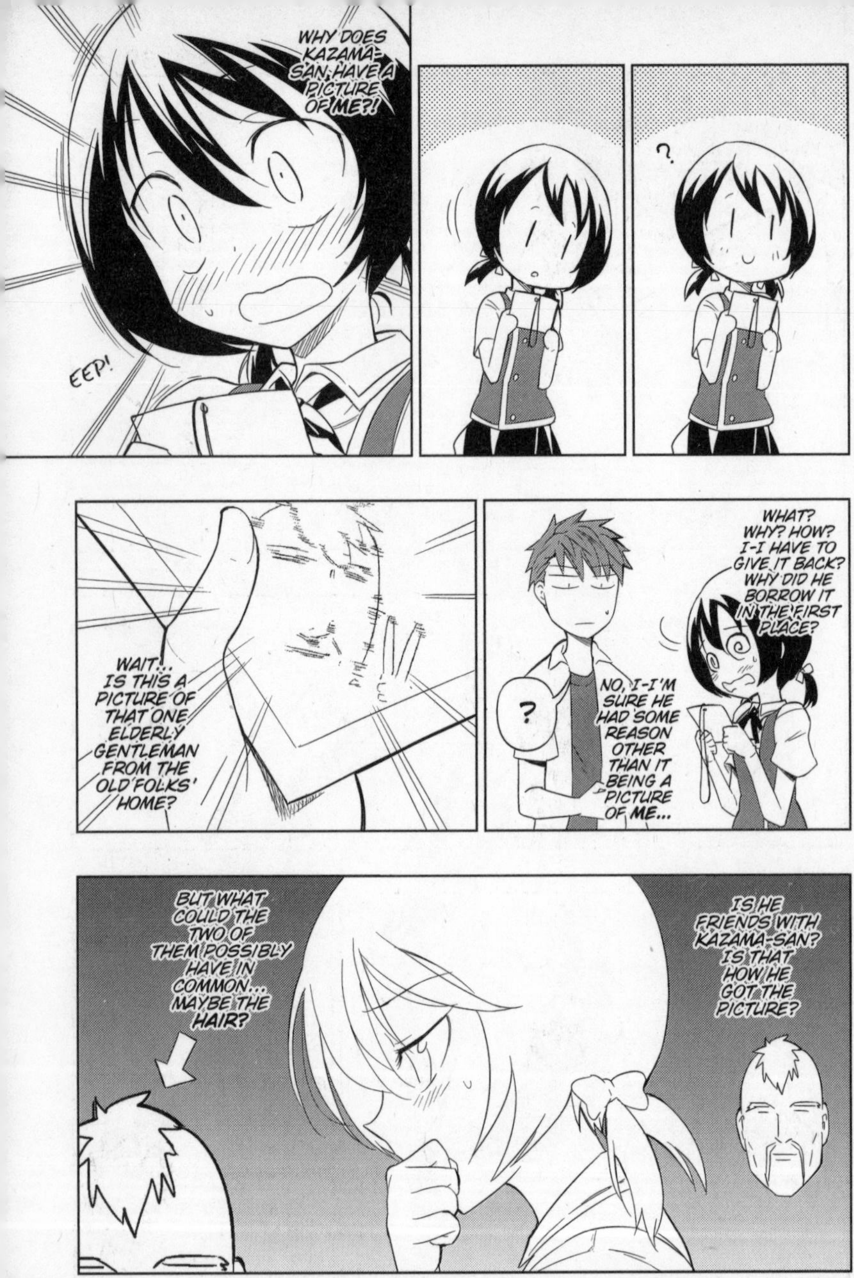
?
WHY DOES KAZAMA-SAN HAVE A PICTURE OF ME?!
EEP!
WHAT? WHY? HOW? I-I HAVE TO GIVE IT BACK? WHY DID HE BORROW IT IN THE FIRST PLACE?
NO, I-I'M SURE HE HAD SOME REASON OTHER THAN IT BEING A PICTURE OF ME...
?
WAIT... IS THIS A PICTURE OF THAT ONE ELDERLY GENTLEMAN FROM THE OLD FOLKS' HOME?
IS HE FRIENDS WITH KAZAMA-SAN? IS THAT HOW HE GOT THE PICTURE?
BUT WHAT COULD THE TWO OF THEM POSSIBLY HAVE IN COMMON... MAYBE THE HAIR?

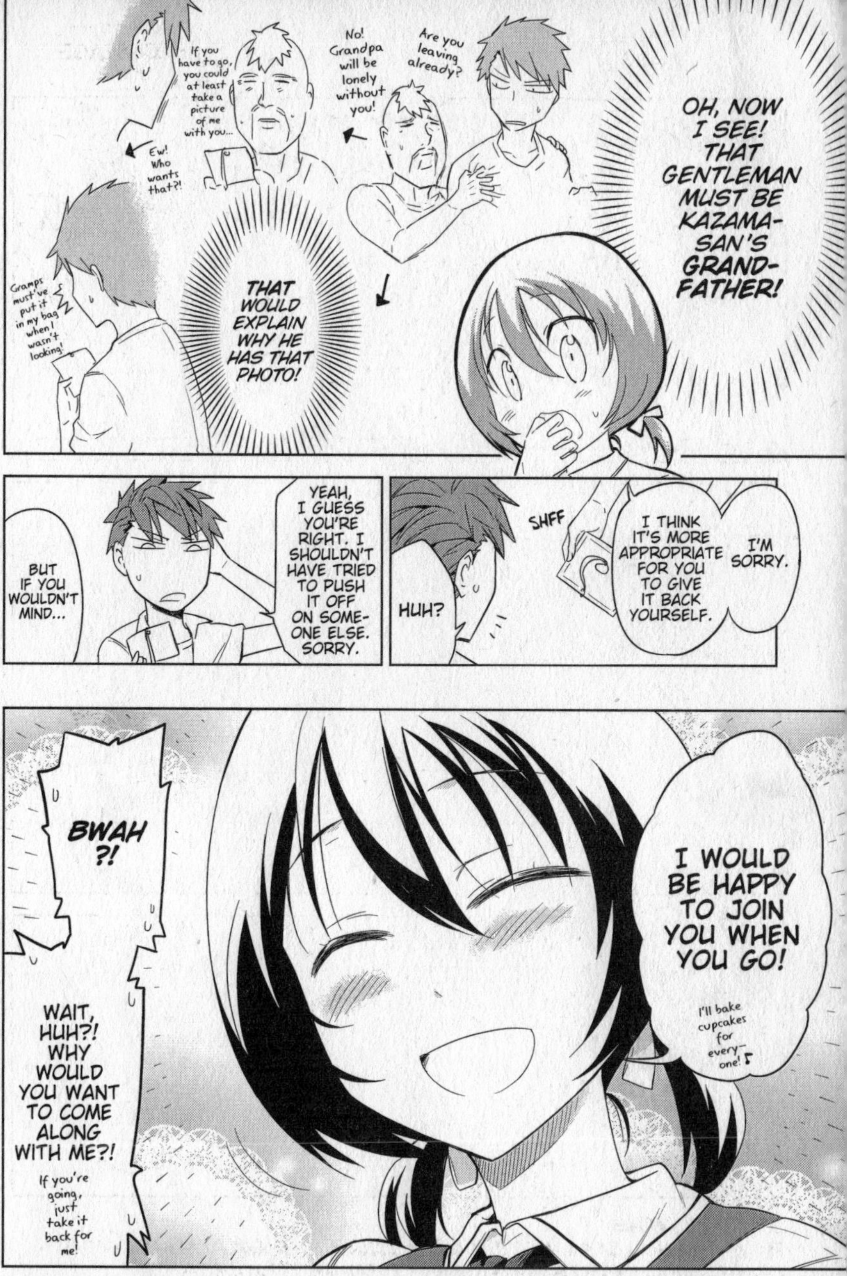
OH, NOW I SEE! THAT GENTLEMAN MUST BE KAZAMA-SAN'S GRAND-FATHER!
Are you leaving already?
No! Grandpa will be lonely without you!
If you have to go, you could at least take a picture of me with you...
Ew! Who wants that?!
THAT WOULD EXPLAIN WHY HE HAS THAT PHOTO!
Gramps must've put it in my bag when I wasn't looking!
I'M SORRY.
I THINK IT'S MORE APPROPRIATE FOR YOU TO GIVE IT BACK YOURSELF.
SHFF
HUH?
YEAH, I GUESS YOU'RE RIGHT. I SHOULDN'T HAVE TRIED TO PUSH IT OFF ON SOME-ONE ELSE. SORRY.
BUT IF YOU WOULDN'T MIND...
I WOULD BE HAPPY TO JOIN YOU WHEN YOU GO!
I'll bake cupcakes for every— one! ♪
BWAH ?!
WAIT, HUH?! WHY WOULD YOU WANT TO COME ALONG WITH ME?!
If you're going, just take it back for me!

END!

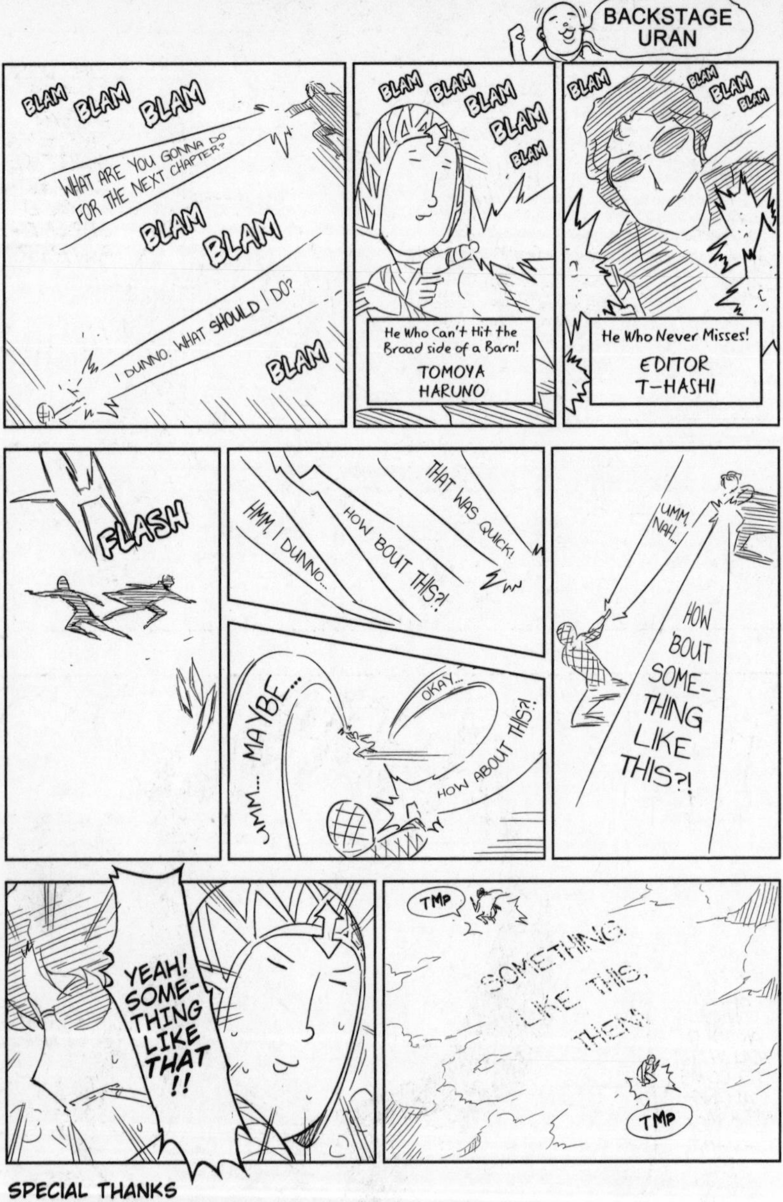
BACKSTAGE URAN
BLAM
BLAM BLAM BLAM
He Who Never Misses!
EDITOR T-HASHI
BLAM BLAM BLAM BLAM BLAM
He Who Can't Hit the Broad side of a Barn!
TOMOYA HARUNO
BLAM BLAM BLAM
WHAT ARE YOU GONNA DO FOR THE NEXT CHAPTER?
BLAM BLAM
I DUNNO. WHAT SHOULD I DO?
BLAM
UMM, NAH...
HOW 'BOUT SOMETHING LIKE THIS?!
THAT WAS QUICK!
HOW 'BOUT THIS?!
HMM, I DUNNO...
OKAY...
HOW ABOUT THIS?!
UMM... MAYBE...
FLASH
TMP
SOMETHING LIKE THIS, THEN.
TMP
YEAH! SOMETHING LIKE THAT!!

SPECIAL THANKS
RAI AKASE-SAN, BAKU MIKAGE-SAN, TSUZURU TOYA-SAN, YUKINOJOU-SAN
OBI: SATOSHI MIZUKAMI-SENSEI DESIGN: LIGHTNING-SAN
AND MY WONDERFUL READERS!!

AFTERWARDS AT TENJIN TEMPLE...

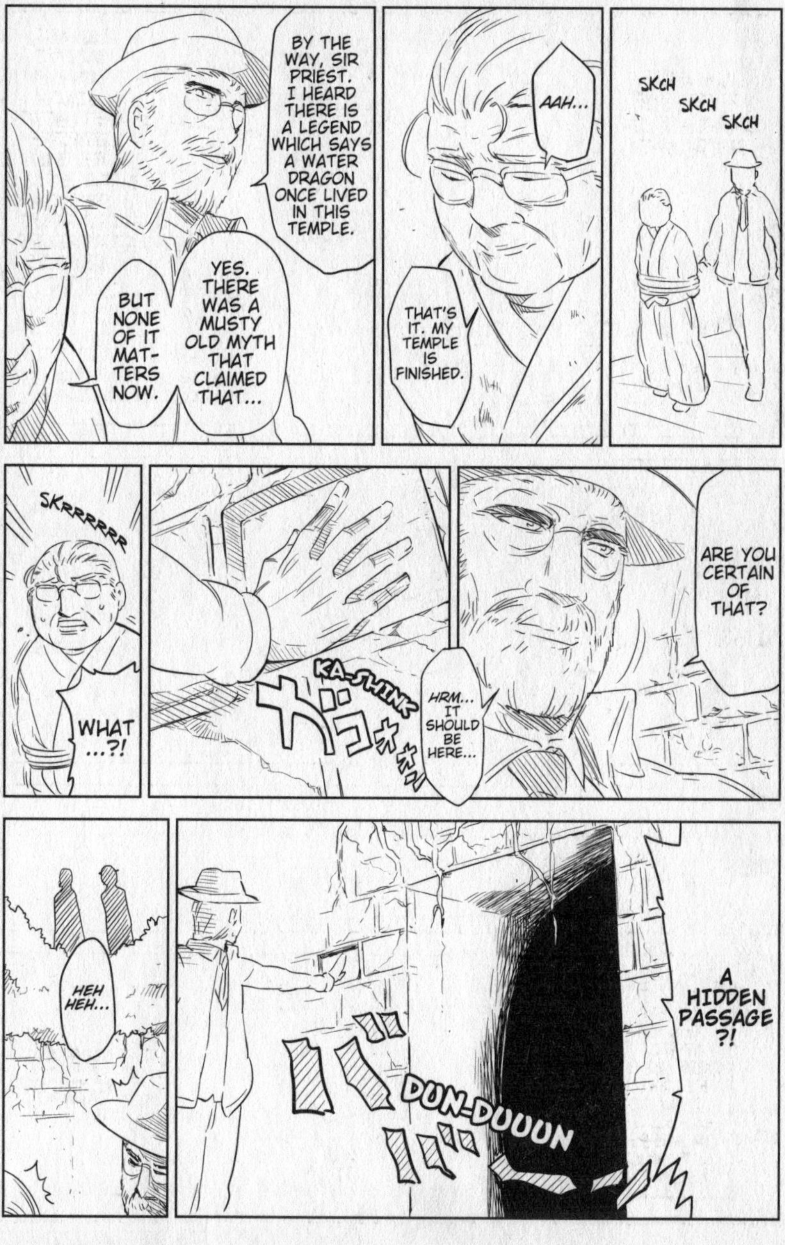
SKCH SKCH SKCH
AAH...
THAT'S IT. MY TEMPLE IS FINISHED.
BY THE WAY, SIR PRIEST. I HEARD THERE IS A LEGEND WHICH SAYS A WATER DRAGON ONCE LIVED IN THIS TEMPLE.
YES. THERE WAS A MUSTY OLD MYTH THAT CLAIMED THAT...
BUT NONE OF IT MAT-TERS NOW.
ARE YOU CERTAIN OF THAT?
HRM... IT SHOULD BE HERE...
KA-SHINK
SKRRRRRR
WHAT ...?!
A HIDDEN PASSAGE ?!
DUN-DUUUN
HEH HEH...

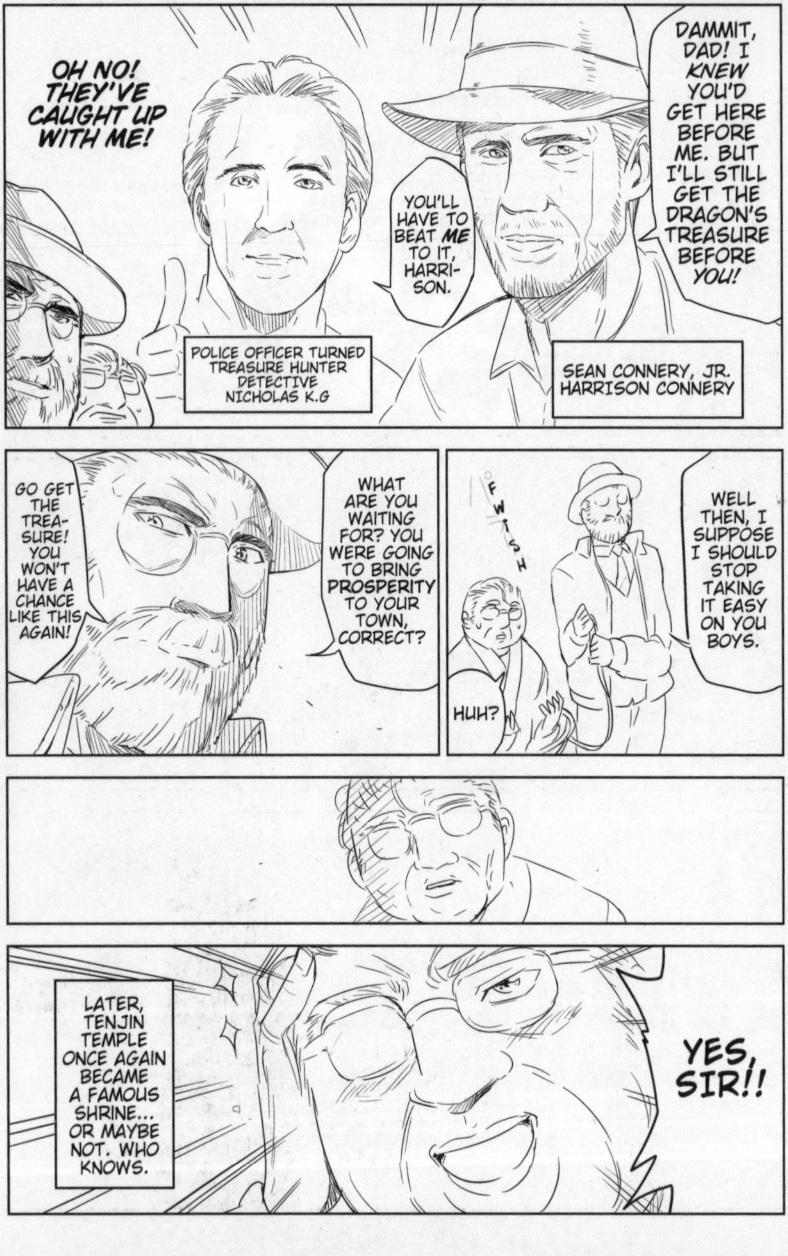
DAMMIT, DAD! I KNEW YOU'D GET HERE BEFORE ME. BUT I'LL STILL GET THE DRAGON'S TREASURE BEFORE YOU!
YOU'LL HAVE TO BEAT ME TO IT, HARRISON.
SEAN CONNERY, JR. HARRISON CONNERY
POLICE OFFICER TURNED TREASURE HUNTER DETECTIVE NICHOLAS K.G
OH NO! THEY'VE CAUGHT UP WITH ME!
WELL THEN, I SUPPOSE I SHOULD STOP TAKING IT EASY ON YOU BOYS.
FWISH
HUH?
WHAT ARE YOU WAITING FOR? YOU WERE GOING TO BRING PROSPERITY TO YOUR TOWN, CORRECT?
GO GET THE TREASURE! YOU WON'T HAVE A CHANCE LIKE THIS AGAIN!
YES, SIR!!
LATER, TENJIN TEMPLE ONCE AGAIN BECAME A FAMOUS SHRINE... OR MAYBE NOT. WHO KNOWS.

YOU'VE READ THE MANGA, NOW WATCH THE GAME DEVELOPMENT CLUB'S WILD ANTICS COME TO LIFE IN THE ANIME!

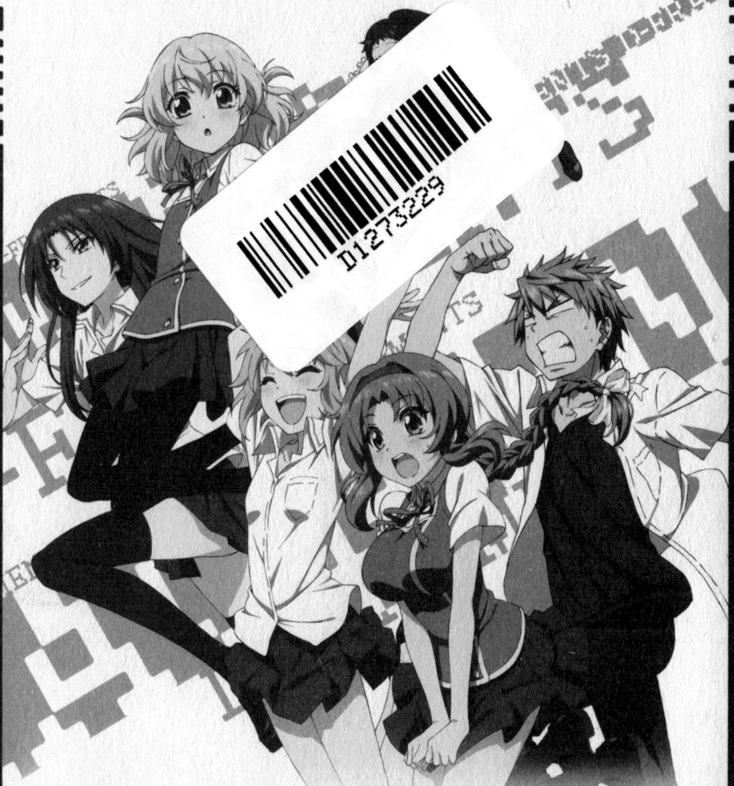

D-FRAG!

Watch the complete series streaming ad-free in HD for subscribers on funimation.com!

You should be watching funimation.com/d-frag

KADOKAWA FUNIMATION